# MY LIFE AND EXPERIENCES AMONG OUR HOSTILE INDIANS

O. O. Howard
Major-General U.S. Army

# MY LIFE AND EXPERIENCES AMONG OUR HOSTILE INDIANS

*A Record of Personal Observations, Adventures, and Campaigns Among the Indians of the Great West*

*With Some Account of Their Life, Habits, Traits, Religion, Ceremonies, Dress, Savage Instincts, and Customs in Peace and War*

By Oliver O. Howard

New Introduction by Robert M. Utley

DA CAPO PRESS · NEW YORK · 1972

Library of Congress Cataloging in Publication Data

Howard, Oliver Otis, 1830-1909.
My life and experiences among our hostile Indians.

Reprint of the 1907 ed.
Bibliography: p.
1. Indians of North America. 2. Indians of North America—Wars—1866-1895. I. Title.
E83.866.H84 1972 970.1 76-87436
ISBN 0-306-71506-6

First published, 1907, by A. T. Worthington & Co., Hartford, Connecticut; republished, 1972, with a new introduction and with the color plates reproduced in black and white.

Da Capo Press, Inc.
A Subsidiary of Plenum Publishing Corporation
227 West 17th Street, New York, New York 10011


Manufactured in the United States of America

# INTRODUCTION

Oliver Otis Howard is known to students of the Indian Wars as the one-armed "praying general" who in 1872 persuaded the implacable Apache chieftain Cochise to abandon the warpath, and who, five years later, pursued Chief Joseph and the Nez Perces across Idaho and Montana almost to Canada. He is known, too, for his autobiography of fourteen years on the Indian frontier, *My Life and Experiences Among Our Hostile Indians.* General Howard was an important figure in the frontier army; his view of his career as Indian fighter and Indian diplomatist, and his observations about the tribes with which he came in contact, make his recollections an essential entry in any well-rounded bibliography of the American West.

As a frontier commander, Howard was overshadowed by such contemporaries as Crook, Miles, Mackenzie, and Custer. Any estimate of the man, however, must take account of the diversity of careers in which he attained prominence. Besides his Indian service, he was corps and army commander in the Civil War, head of the Freedmen's Bureau during Reconstruction, educator, humanitarian, churchman, author, and lecturer. He lived a long and richly productive life, one that posterity has ample cause to recall and record.

The outbreak of the Civil War found Howard a thirty-year-old ordnance lieutenant, veteran of seven years in the Regular Army. A staff billet in the little prewar Army offered few opportunities for distinction, and his career to that point had not been notable. He had been married for six years and had fathered three children. He had also found Christ, and increasingly the ministry beckoned. But the bombardment of Fort Sumter intervened, fixing his destiny permanently, if not unwaveringly, in military pathways.

Two important assets favored Howard's subsequent rapid rise. He was well educated—Bowdoin College as well as the United States Military Academy; and he was well connected with the political luminaries of his home state of Maine—Governor Israel Washburn, U.S. Representative Anson P. Morrill, and the Speaker of the Maine House of Representatives, James G. Blaine. The last, destined to become the Republican "Plumed Knight" of the 1870's and 1880's, became Howard's personal friend and provided official support for more than three decades. Nevertheless, in a time when military officers assiduously courted political help in securing promotion, Howard seems not to have deliberately sought the favor he enjoyed. Rather, creditable battlefield performance won the support of state leaders eager to nourish and be nourished by such military talent as Maine boasted.

As colonel of the Third Maine Volunteers, Howard fought at First Manassas. Elevation to brigadier general followed at once. At Seven Pines, on June 1, 1862, two balls shattered his right arm. A surgeon amputated it at the elbow, and for the rest of his life, the empty sleeve hooked to a button, together with the Bible, fixed Howard's image in the public mind. Quickly back in the saddle, he fought at Antietam, Fredericksburg, Chancellorsville, and Gettysburg. Promotion to major general came in November, 1862.

At Chancellorsville Howard's corps formed General Joseph Hooker's right flank. Stonewall Jackson smashed it, routed the corps, and won the battle. Howard never admitted culpability—and there were mitigating circumstances—but he never again allowed himself to be surprised. His role at Gettysburg is also controversial. On the first day his corps was again thrown back, but he rallied the retreating troops on Cemetery Hill, and Congress later formally thanked him for selecting the position that proved so crucial to victory. There were others, however, who thought the distinction theirs, or at least not so exclusively Howard's, and the honor caused resentment for years afterward.

Chancellorsville and Gettysburg burdened Howard with disabilities in the Army of the Potomac that would have been difficult to overcome. Fortunately, transfer to the western armies in the autumn of 1863 afforded opportunity for a fresh start. He made the most of it.

One of Howard's strengths was a capacity to learn from experience, to avoid repeating mistakes. In the actions that broke the Confederate hold on Chattanooga, and in the succession of battles that carried General William T. Sherman's armies to Atlanta, Howard handled his corps, part of General George H. Thomas' Army of the Cumberland, with quiet competence and without any error or reverse of importance. His leadership qualities, tactical skill, and ability to act in concert with associates gained for him the confidence and respect of both Thomas and Sherman.

In the savage fighting on the outskirts of Atlanta, a ball felled General James B. McPherson, Sherman's striking arm, and Sherman named Howard to succeed him as commander of the Army of the Tennessee. This assignment bypassed the heir apparent, the able and popular Illinois political general John A. Logan, and gave Howard, Sherman, and the postwar Regular Army a bitter and unrelenting foe. Actually, Sherman picked Howard because Thomas said he could not work with the unpredictable, publicity-hungry Logan, but the latter believed he had been deprived of his rightful command by the West Point fraternity. After the war Logan founded the politically powerful Grand Army of the Republic and served in the Senate, on occasion chairing the Committee on Military Affairs. Devoting the rest of his career to exalting the militia tradition and assailing military professionals and professionalism, he was the cause of two decades of acute discomfort for the tiny Regular Army and its leaders.

For Howard, Sherman's subsequent operations did not afford a test of generalship comparable to the Atlanta campaign, for the Confederate armies that had contested the advance on the Georgia capital were in disarray. Nonetheless, in the celebrated "March to the Sea" and in the Carolina campaign that followed, Howard led the Army of the Tennessee with a competence that fully met Sherman's expectations. For both, the war ended on May 24, 1865, when the western armies paraded down Pennsylvania Avenue in Washington, D.C. The two generals rode side by side, for Howard, bowing to his chief's request, had yielded his place at the head of the Army of the Tennessee to the disgruntled Logan.

By the close of the war, Howard's distinguishing traits of character had become fixed and widely-known. The most conspicuous one, at times even ostentatious, was an all-pervading religion outlook. This gave him courage, compassion, strong resolve, and fixed purpose; but displayed like a conquering banner, it also occasionally irritated more worldly associates. Sherman is quoted as declaring on one occasion: "Well, that Christian-soldier business is all right in its place, but he needn't put on airs when we are among ourselves."[1] Generals Joseph Hooker and George Crook made far less charitable remarks, and a fellow corps commander under Sherman, General Jefferson C. Davis, whose vocabulary was a marvel of the western armies, countered Howard's piety with spectacular exhibitions of profanity. But those who penetrated Howard's reserve discovered that his religion was not excessively prudish or moralistic and that a keen sense of humor lurked within. Few, however, perceived as acutely as he did himself the constant inner struggle between the humility decreed by his religion and the hunger for public approval born in his youth and encouraged by the military milieu.

A second notable characteristic, doubtless spawned by the first, was a well-developed social consciousness which led Howard into a lifelong crusade for the elevation of disadvantaged and minority groups. He welcomed the assignment to head the Bureau of Refugees, Freedmen, and Abandoned Lands—the instrument fashioned by Congress to care for the recently freed slaves. This work in turn prompted him in 1867 to help establish Howard University in Washington, D.C. He served as its president from 1869 to 1874, while managing the Freedmen's Bureau at the same time. During his frontier service, Howard sought to assume a similar humanitarian stance toward the Indian, but in this he enjoyed less success. The gulf separating his Christianity from the Indian's spiritual beliefs inhibited genuine communication. Years later, near the end of his life, he labored in behalf of Lincoln Memorial University, an enterprise dedicated

[1] Lloyd Lewis, *Sherman, Fighting Prophet* (New York: Harcourt, Brace & Co., 1932), pp. 349–50.

to providing educational opportunities for Tennessee's mountain whites.

General Sherman, head of the postwar Regular Army, in which Howard had received the rank of brigadier general, frowned on his lieutenant's social work. He believed that the few soldiers permitted the Army should stick to soldiering and leave "education, charity and religion" to civilian philanthropists.[2] He forecast the grief that the Freedmen's Bureau would bring to Howard once the politicians got after him. In fact, Howard's loose administration and innocent trust in unworthy subordinates hastened the reckoning. He emerged only slightly tarnished, but happy enough at last to heed Sherman's advice and, in 1874, to accept command of a military department.

Howard took with him to his first frontier command, the Department of the Columbia, a reputation as an Indian diplomatist. In 1872 President Grant had sent him on a special peace mission to war-wracked Arizona. His dealings there with the Apaches form a significant chapter in southwestern history.

Howard made two trips to Arizona in 1872. The first is well documented in official reports and in this book. Its chief result was the founding of San Carlos Indian Reservation, which was to become the focus of so much strife in the next fifteen years. The trip was notable, too, for an agonizing controversy over disposition of Indian children taken captive by the Tucson citizens who had perpetrated the notorious Camp Grant Massacre.

Howard's arrival in Arizona followed an unfortunate tour of the Territory by another peace emissary, Vincent Colyer. Arizona's citizens and General George Crook

---

[2] Sherman to Howard, Nov. 29, 1873, Sherman Papers, Library of Congress, vol. 90, pp. 301–02.

and his officers had not yet recovered from their frustration over the misguided attempts of "Vincent the Good" to "mesmerize the Apaches into peace."[3] Neither Howard's official report nor his account in this book discloses the full magnitude of the annoyance with which his visit was greeted by citizens, officials, and military authorities, all of whom thought the time had come to quit temporizing and to fight. Furthermore, Howard's version of his relations with General Crook stands in striking contrast to Crook's version as set forth in his own autobiography. Howard minimizes disagreement and depicts a basic harmony of thought and action. Crook's account reeks of contempt for Howard and all he stood for.

Howard's second trip proved vastly more consequential than his first, but it is not as well documented. His official report was brief. His detailed account in this book is, accordingly, history's main source for his dramatic journey with frontiersman Tom Jeffords into the heart of Cochise's stronghold. Howard made peace with Cochise and his Chiricahua Apaches, and ended a decade of bloody warfare against white settlers and travelers. Without minimizing this truly significant achievement, it may be suspected that history, drawing almost solely on Howard's own account, has cloaked the episode in a romanticism that is not entirely warranted. Cochise had been signaling a desire to make peace for more than a year, and, in fact, he had spent the winter of 1871–1872 on the Tularosa Reservation in New Mexico. Against this background, Howard's daring in going all but unescorted into Cochise's stronghold assumes less importance than the negotiations—and concessions—that led to peace.

3 *Army and Navy Journal,* Aug. 5, 1871, p. 816.

The agreement between Howard and Cochise seems not to have been committed to writing. Apparently it was simply that the Chiricahuas could have a reservation in the familiar haunts of the Chiricahua Mountains, with Tom Jeffords as their agent. This arrangement did not satisfy the citizenry, the Army, or the Indian Bureau. Crook was certain that there had been a tacit understanding that the Chiricahuas could continue to raid in Mexico if they left Arizona alone; and this, in fact, is what they did. The reservation lasted three years, until after Cochise's death. Then the Chiricahuas were moved to San Carlos. As imperfect and transitory as the peace settlement proved, however, the fact remains that Howard ended the Cochise wars. For this feat alone his name must be entered large in the annals of the Southwest.

The other outstanding episode of Howard's frontier career was the Nez Perce War of 1877. Besides the six chapters devoted to it in this book, he had earlier written a full volume, *Nez Perce Joseph.* Both accounts have been used extensively by historians of that tragic conflict. Unlike the peace mission to Cochise, however, the Nez Perce War produced voluminous first-hand documentation, and Howard's version is subject to verification.

The tortured sequence of moves by which the non-treaty Nez Perces were deprived of their lands in the Pacific Northwest and driven to armed resistance forms a dismal chapter in American history. Howard played a commanding role throughout, one so basically incompatible with his humanity and sense of justice that he must have suffered great anguish. His writings are labored efforts to justify his course of action. Alvin Josephy has noted that as history they are not wholly reliable, but that "as evidence of Howard's personal distress they are more interesting; they reveal points of view whose hollowness Howard himself could not have failed to recognize."[4]

Howard's writings about the Nez Perce War exalt Chief Joseph into a master strategist and tactician, practitioner of "civilized warfare," and chief of all the nontreaty Nez Perces. Joseph was certainly a man of stature and influence among his people and an appealing figure to the whites; but he was neither the chief of all the nontreaty bands nor a military genius—in fact, he was not even a war chief. Until recent years, however, most histories of the Nez Perce War, drawing on Howard, have perpetuated the legend, in the process helping to rationalize the spectacle of eight-hundred Indian people leading a U.S. Army general a merry chase across a thousand miles of mountains and plains.

Much has been written of the heroic flight of the Nez Perces over the Bitterroot Mountains and across Montana, and of the equally heroic efforts of Howard and his troops to overtake them before they could reach sanctuary in Canada. Howard endured merciless press criticism at the time and has not fared too well from history since. In retrospect, it seems that he delayed too long in starting the pursuit and that at times his resolution wavered. But in spite of enormous logistical obstacles, sheer bad luck, and repeated discouragements, he stayed on the trail to the very end. Colonel Nelson A. Miles' troops intercepted Joseph's people just short of their Canadian destination and gained most of the credit for ending the Nez Perce War. But as General Sherman pointed out, the "long, toilsome pursuit" by Howard and his column "made that success possible." Miles' selfish

[4] Alvin M. Josephy, Jr., *The Nez Perce Indians and the Opening of the Northwest* (New Haven: Yale University Press, 1965), p. 475n.

attempt to exclude Howard from the honors brought rejoinders from Howard and led to a controversy that at length had to be stopped by Sherman himself.

A perceptive evaluation of Howard's performance was written on July 31, 1877, at the height of the pursuit, by General Irvin McDowell, Howard's immediate superior, in a confidential letter to General Sherman. "I have a deep sympathy for Howard," he wrote,

> who whilst doing his best was hounded by the press and had all manner of abuse heaped on him. But his orders seem addressed to another audience as well as to his troops, and he cannot quite confine himself rigidly to his mere soldier work. I think it is to this, in dealing with Joseph's case in the beginning, that largely caused the attack on him in the papers when the effort to put Joseph on the reservation failed! Both your orders and mine required this work to be left absolutely to the Indian Dept., he merely aiding with his military force in case of need. But he could not keep in the background and hence received the stings of the press when the effort failed.[5]

That Howard regarded himself as especially gifted to deal with Indians is evident throughout his book. In truth, his humanity did endow him with a genuine interest in and sympathy for his adversaries. Ascribing virtually all conflicts to white provocation, he looked upon them as tragically victimized by the dominant race. He saw himself as a true friend of the Indians, and he convinced himself that they saw him in the same light.

---

[5] McDowell to Sherman (confidential), July 31, 1877, Sherman Papers, Library of Congress, vol. 46.

At the same time, however, like most of his contemporaries, Howard was dedicated to the goal of lifting the Indians from "savagery" to the grace of Christianity and "civilization." While abhorring racial extermination, he advocated cultural extermination. His powerful brand of religion, moreover, imbued him with an ethnocentrism so inimical to insight that the religious motivation of the Indians, as strong and pervasive as his own, almost entirely eluded him. *My Life and Experiences Among Our Hostile Indians* is a classic revelation of how Indians and whites so frequently and so completely failed to understand each other.

Howard commanded the Department of the Columbia, with headquarters in Portland, Oregon, from 1874 to 1880. Besides his part in the Nez Perce War, he led his troops in the field during the Bannock outbreak of 1878 and conferred often with leaders of all the tribes within his jurisdiction. In Portland as in Washington, he was active in church affairs and YMCA work.

In 1880 President Rutherford B. Hayes summoned Howard to the capital and appointed him Superintendent of the United States Military Academy, then rocked by scandal involving a black cadet. Sherman, who had not been consulted, bluntly told Howard that his assignment was motivated by the race question. "I believe the army and the country construe you to be extreme on this question," he wrote, and therefore he favored another officer for the post.[6]

After a quiet two years at West Point, Howard returned west to command the Department of the Platte, with headquarters in Omaha. Promoted to major general in 1886, he moved to San Francisco and assumed com-

6 Sherman to Howard, Dec. 7, 1880, Sherman Papers, Library of Congress, vol. 91, pp. 545–46.

mand of the Military Division of the Pacific. He arrived just as General Miles was ending the Geronimo outbreak in Arizona, but he exerted almost no influence on the conduct of operations. Two years later, in 1888, Howard took command of the Military Division of the Atlantic and settled his family on Governors Island in New York Harbor. In November, 1894, retirement ended his forty-four years of active service in the Army.

Settling in Burlington, Vermont, Howard continued to live an energetic and productive life. He wrote extensively, publishing magazine articles and books—juveniles, biography, history, reminiscence. He lectured widely on the Civil War and on religious topics. And he campaigned vigorously for the Republican Party in the national elections of 1896 and 1900. Church, YMCA, and educational work occupied him to the end. Death came on October 26, 1909, two weeks before his seventy-ninth birthday.

If General Crook can be credited, Howard believed himself divinely commissioned to uplift the Indian. "I was very amused at the General's opinion of himself," Crook wrote of Howard's visit to Arizona in 1872. "He told me that he thought the Creator had placed him on earth to be the Moses of the Negro. Having accomplished that mission, he felt satisfied his next mission was with the Indian."[7] Howard did not lead the Indian to the promised land. Indeed, his ethnocentrism gave him a vision of the promised land quite at variance with the Indian's. But in him the Indians found a kindly, sympathetic man who usually treated them decently and who labored for their best interests as he conceived them. It is for this, rather than for his failure to develop insights

[7] Martin F. Schmitt, ed., *General George Crook: His Autobiography* (Norman, Oklahoma: University of Oklahoma Press, 1946), p. 169.

that were also beyond most of his contemporaries, that he should be judged. He was truly one of the frontier army's "humanitarian generals."

*Washington, D.C.*
*April 1970*

Robert M. Utley

## SUGGESTED READING


Beal, Merrill D. *"I Will Fight No More Forever": Chief Joseph and the Nez Perce War.* Seattle: University of Washington Press, 1963.

Brimlow, George F. *The Bannock Indian War of 1878.* Caldwell, Idaho: The Caxton Printers, 1938.

Brown, Mark H. *The Flight of the Nez Perce: A History of the Nez Perce War.* New York: G. P. Putnam's Sons, 1967.

Carpenter, John A. *Sword and Olive Branch: Oliver Otis Howard.* Pittsburgh: University of Pittsburgh Press, 1964.

Howard, Oliver Otis. *Autobiography.* 2 vols. New York: Baker & Taylor Company, 1907.

———. *Famous Indian Chiefs I Have Known.* New York: The Century Company, 1907–1908.

———. *Nez Perce Joseph.* Boston: Lee and Shepard, 1881.

———. "The True Story of the Wallowa Campaign." *North American Review* 129 (1879) :1-7.

Josephy, Alvin M., Jr. *The Nez Perce Indians and the Opening of the Northwest.* New Haven: Yale University Press, 1965.

McFeely, William S. *Yankee Stepfather: General O.O. Howard and the Freedmen.* New Haven: Yale University Press, 1968.

United States. Department of the Interior. *Report of the Commissioner of Indian Affairs for 1872.* Washington, D.C., 1872, pp. 148–178 [Howard's official report of the Arizona mission of 1872].

United States. Department of War. *Report of the Secretary of War for 1877.* Washington, D.C., 1877, pp. 114–133, 585–660 [official reports and correspondence of the Nez Perce operations].

TO

CAPTAIN JOSEPH A. SLADEN, UNITED STATES ARMY

(*Now Clerk of the United States Circuit Court.*)

PORTLAND, OREGON,

MY LOYAL AND FAITHFUL AIDE-DE-CAMP AND SINCERE AND DEVOTED FRIEND, WHO FOR TWENTY-THREE YEARS WAS BY MY SIDE THROUGH CAMPAIGNS AND BATTLES, RISING FROM A PRIVATE SOLDIER TO HIS PRESENT RANK, WHOSE RETIREMENT FROM ACTIVE MILITARY DUTY WAS THE RESULT OF LOSING HIS LEG WHILE IN SERVICE UNDER MY COMMAND,

**This Volume is Affectionately Dedicated**

BY

THE AUTHOR.

# PREFACE.

AFTER passing the meridian of life, and especially when old age is silently creeping upon us with an advance that cannot be checked, our minds are wont to revert to the experiences of our youthful days and the years when, in manhood's prime, no task was too formidable to be undertaken, no obstacle too great to be overcome, and health and strength gave keen zest to the work in hand. In this volume I have endeavored to tell the story of my life and personal experiences among the Indian tribes with which the fortunes of war brought me in contact, sometimes in efforts to bring about peace, at other times in deadly strife with a foe as brave, resourceful, and relentless as any savage race of which we have knowledge.

In whatever I have hitherto written of myself I have been accustomed to present my experiences in autobiographical form, for it seems natural and easy for me to do so, and I have adhered to that plan in the following narrative. I have endeavored to show how my grandfather's stories of the wild Indians with whom he had to do, affected my childhood; how these tales became almost like a nightmare to me and continued to haunt me even when I was a cadet at West Point. The thrilling experiences of old Indian fighters entered into the lives of, and were never-ending topics of discussion among the young army officers who were my companions. Like Sherman and Thomas, early in my career as a lieutenant, my first Indian experiences were with the Seminoles in Florida. It was there after graduating from the Military Academy that I first saw actual field service. Later, some of my best beloved fellow officers were taken from my side during the great Civil War and were hurried off to the West and Northwest to meet the oft recurring outbreaks of cruel and stealthy Indians, who massacred white settlers by hundreds and left a trail of blood and ashes behind them. The campaigns and battles of these officers against such a crafty and elusive foe intensely interested me.

While I was Commissioner of freedmen, working from Washington as a center, and deeply engaged in that work for the negroes, as one might well be, an aged Quaker friend, a noncombatant, interviewed the officials who were mainly responsible for the Indian conditions that existed at that time, and entreated that I should be sent to the far Southwest as a representative of the extreme peacemakers of the country. This friend was an influential member of the Indian Commission, and the result of his appeal was that I was detailed by President Grant to go to Arizona and New Mexico, not as a commander of troops or of the Department, but as a "Peace Commissioner" with instructions to assuage difficulties and settle troubles that had arisen between various savage Indian tribes, and between them and white settlers. Some of the tribes and bands involved were the Yumas, the Maricopas, and the Pimas, who were just then being introduced to civilized ways; the Papagos, who wanted more land and better schools; the Arivipa Apaches, who had been murderously dealt with by so-called white men of the territory; the White Mountain Apaches, then at peace, but suffering from disease and always seemingly on the verge of war; and the roaming bands of wild Apaches who made their living principally by stealing ungathered corn from Mexican inhabitants of the river valleys of New Mexico. In carrying out my instructions I was brought into close contact with the Navajos, seven thousand strong, who had always quarreled more or less with their Indian neighbors, and who had been bitterly complained of by all American frontiersmen and settlers in their vicinity; and also with the Chiricahuas, who were then actively engaged in war, led by the notorious and bloodthirsty Cochise, under whom Apaches kept up a constant and irritating border warfare. Cochise's captains led their wild bands through Arizona and New Mexico, and even through parts of Old Mexico, stealing horses, cattle, sheep, and whatever they could lay their hands on, and waging a war of extermination against the whites.

They never spared a stagecoach nor its passengers. It was even said that only one white man among the many captives they had taken from over-land stagecoaches and wagon trains was known to have escaped death at their hands, and his ascendency over Cochise was not easily explained.

But President Grant wanted peace, and he firmly established and developed his well known " Peace Policy." It took from early in March until December to accomplish the task set for me by the President and the Indian Department. In doing this I had not only the inertia and indifference of some Indians, and the active hostilities of others to contend with, but many hindrances from some of my old comrades of the army, and the unanimous combined opposition of the American and Mexican settlers who were neighbors to the Indian reservations. I tried in every way to settle these troubles without bloodshed.

I had hardly finished my work in the East as Commissioner of Freedmen and Refugees, when I was hastened off to the extreme Northwest, where my first duty was to take care of Modoc prisoners. Next I visited the tribes of Alaska and the Pacific Coast; then came remarkable experiences with the Columbia River Indians and their allied bands, followed by the notable and no less arduous Nez Percé campaign. In peace the non-treaty Nez Percés were restless and fretful; in war none fought with greater bravery; nor do I believe that any other body of Indians was ever more ably led than they under Chief Joseph, who displayed consummate generalship in his conduct of that campaign. As a consequence of this campaign, the Bannocks and Pi-Utes subsequently waged a bloody war of depredation and murder that tested the endurance of our troops in long forced marches and swift racings through almost endless wastes and forests. These bloody wars involved directly and indirectly many other Indian tribes, such as the Flat-heads, the Shoshones, the Snakes, the Crows, and others.

To me, the most satisfactory operation in the Northwest was inaugurated by a very small band of savage Indians near the head waters of the Salmon river. In this campaign I did not take the field, but my trusted subordinates subdued the Indians, captured the whole tribe, and brought them down the Columbia river to my headquarters, which were then near

Vancouver Barracks. Here we had the opportunity of applying the processes of civilization, namely, systematic work and persistent instruction to Indian children and youth. These Indians were well fitted to abandon their tepees and blankets, dress as white men, and join the civilized Warm Spring Indians who dwelt just beyond the Dalles of the Columbia. In this work of preparation, or I may say of probation, the young Indian princess, Sarah Winnemucca, — of whom I shall have something to say in this volume, — was my interpreter, and bore a prominent and efficient part.

It is often said that the Indian child, even after receiving the best education that we can give, will return to barbarism at the first good opportunity. It is a fact that some Indian children and youth *do* go back to the blanket and their wild life. How can they help it? I think if I should dwell a year or two with any savage tribe I should live as they live; I should dress as they dress; I should reside as they do in tepees or lodges, and not in houses; and I should probably eat out of the common pot, and be, to all intents and purposes, an Indian. Those who have been the most successful in civilizing Indians, brought about a gradual separation from savage ways of living and introduced various peaceful industries among them. It was a necessity. There is no virtue that I have not seen exemplified in some of the different Indian tribes with which I had to do. As a rule, they kept their promises to me with wonderful fidelity, often putting themselves to extraordinary exertion and peril.

The writing of this book has brought to the surface a flood of recollections of those exciting days, and again thrown into strong light many incidents which at the time intensely interested me. Indian life, as I observed it then, always afforded me enjoyment. Yet, when I glance backward over the field of my dealings with hostile Indians, I reckon my experiences as President Grant's Peace Commissioner, as the most trying; but thanks to Divine help, which I love to recognize and acknowledge, the strenuous efforts then put forth resulted in great success. President Grant's peace policy was made to prevail. At the close of that year I believe that all our Indian tribes were at peace, though they did not long remain so, as will be seen from the stirring events set forth in the following pages.

Some of the seed of the outbreaks that followed were already germinating, and subsequently sprang into vigorous life in spite of every effort of the administration to suppress them.

It has been my aim to give to the world a connected and comprehensive narrative of varied experiences with these Indians, with some account of life as I observed it among them in peace and war, together with as much history of some of them as my personal knowledge would justify. We must always, when we glance at the low, the vile, and the bad, get our eyes as quickly as possible away and fix them upon the high, the beautiful, and the good, and remember that, by God's help in Christ, we can elevate men to the noblest.

O. O. Howard
Major-General U. S. Army

From special photographs supplied by the United States Bureau of Ethnology and from other sources, reproduced in facsimile expressly for this book.

26 BURIAL OF INDIANS KILLED IN THE BATTLE OF WOUNDED KNEE . . . . . . . *To face* 484

27 FACSIMILE OF AN INDIAN DRAWING BY RED HORSE, A SIOUX, SHOWING GENERAL CUSTER'S TROOPS CHARGING AN INDIAN CAMP IN THE BATTLE OF THE LITTLE BIG HORN . . . . . . *To face* 496

28 FACSIMILE OF AN INDIAN DRAWING BY RED HORSE, A SIOUX, SHOWING THE SIOUX FIGHTING CUSTER'S BATTALION IN THE BATTLE OF THE LITTLE BIG HORN . . . . . . . . . . *To face* 500

Red Horse was present at the battle. In his drawing he shows dead soldiers in the foreground with limbs and heads cut off, and the bodies otherwise mutilated. Bugles, hats, and flags are scattered around, some of the wounded cavalrymen are shown falling from their horses. Wounds are generally indicated by spots from which blood is flowing. One cavalryman is shot in the mouth with an arrow. The drawing will repay careful study.

29 (1) THE KNOLL ON THE BATTLEFIELD OF THE LITTLE BIG HORN WHERE GENERAL CUSTER AND HIS MEN FELL AND WERE BURIED . .

The cross marks the spot where General Custer fell. Gravestones mark the places where some of his soldiers fell around him. General Custer's monument is at the top of the knoll. One hundred and ninety-two soldiers killed in this battle are buried on this spot.

(2) SOLDIERS' CEMETERY ON CUSTER'S BATTLE-FIELD . . . . . . . . . . .

The remains of one hundred and six soldiers massacred by Indians at Fort Phil. Kearney were removed to Custer's battlefield and buried on this spot. The white spots in the distance mark places where some of Custer's men fell at the battle of the Little Big Horn.

*To face* 506

30 NOTED CHEYENNE INDIANS IN THEIR WILD STATE *To face* 516

PLENTY HORSES — LITTLE CHIEF — STARVING ELK

31 COMMUNICATION BY SIGNS . . . . . *To face* 534

(1) FRIEND OR FOE? — "STANDING OFF" INDIANS

(2) A POWWOW WITH THE CHEYENNES IN THE SIGN LANGUAGE

# LIST

OF

# CHROMO-LITHOGRAPH PLATES

WITH

## Descriptions and Explanations

[*For a description of how these plates were made see the Publisher's Preface.*]

## PLATE I.

*To face page* 46

### BOY'S BUCKSKIN SHIRT; GIRL'S BUCKSKIN BEADED LEGGINGS; BELT, POUCHES, ETC.

1. IROQUOIS MOCCASINS.
   Made of cloth, bound with silk, and handsomely ornamented with beads.
2. KIOWA BOY'S BUCKSKIN SHIRT.
   An exceedingly handsome specimen. Made of buckskin tanned as soft as velvet. The erect flap at the top was worn turned down over the back of the wearer.
3. KIOWA GIRL'S LEATHER BELT.
   Ornamented with silver disks. To the belt is attached toilet and umbilical pouches.
4. CHEYENNE GIRL'S BUCKSKIN LEGGINGS.
   Handsomely ornamented with beads.
5. KIOWA GIRL'S BUCKSKIN LEGGINGS WITH MOCCASINS ATTACHED.
   Handsomely ornamented with beads and metal disks. These leggings are of a different pattern from those shown in No. 4.
6. APACHE POUCH.
   Decorated with original designs.
7. APACHE POUCH.
   Beautifully ornamented with quills.

## PLATE II.

*To face page* 78

### DOLLS, MALE AND FEMALE, OF VARIOUS TRIBES, DOLL WARRIORS, TOYS, ETC.

1. INDIAN DOLL WITH WOODEN HEAD.

   Dressed in buckskin, and ornamented with beads. Tribe unknown.

2. KIOWA DOLL WARRIOR MOUNTED ON A DOLL HORSE.

   The doll is dressed in fringed buckskin; the horse is made of soft buckskin, and is stuffed with horsehair.

3. SIOUX DOLL WARRIOR.

   Dressed in buckskin and pieces of flannel; equipped with a miniature bow-case and quiver; scalp lock carefully braided.

4. PUEBLO FEMALE DOLL.

   Made of clay, with hideously painted face; dressed in pieces of flannel; head ornamented with tufts of horsehair.

5. CHEYENNE MALE DOLL.

   Dressed in buckskin, calico, and flannel; scalp lock attached.

6. PRAIRIE INDIAN FEMALE DOLL.

   Dressed in soft buckskin; profusely ornamented with beads.

7. CHEYENNE DOLL.

   Dressed in buckskin and calico.

## PLATE III.

*To face page* 158

### WAR AND CEREMONIAL TOMAHAWKS, CLUBS, SLING SHOTS, WAR WEAPONS, ETC.

1. WAR CLUB WITH BLADE INSERTED AT THE HEAD.

   Ornamented with scalp locks at the top, and fur and beaded flannel at the bottom; handle studded with brass nails.

2. APACHE SLING SHOT.

   The head is made of a round stone encased in rawhide; the handle is ornamented with part of a horse's tail.

3. CHEYENNE WAR TOMAHAWK.

   To the handle is attached a piece of flannel ornamented with feathers. This is a real war weapon, and differs from the tomahawk pipe which has a bowl at the head for tobacco, and a perforated handle through which to draw the smoke.

4. GENUINE WAR TOMAHAWK. Tribe unknown.

5. PIEGAN TOMAHAWK PIPE.

   Has a hollow head for holding tobacco; the handle is perforated so that smoke can be drawn through; to the handle is attached a fringed piece of leather elaborately beaded.

6. GENUINE WAR TOMAHAWK. Tribe unknown.

7. STONE WAR CLUB.

   The head is of stone, shaped by the Indians, and bound with rawhide to the handle; bottom of handle is ornamented with scalp locks, horsehir, and feathers.

8. Genuine War Tomahawk. Tribe unknown.
9. War Knife taken from the Rogue River Indians.
10. Genuine War Tomahawk. Tribe unknown.
11. Stone War Club.
    Ornamented with braided scalp locks.
12. War Club with Spiked Wooden Head.
13. War Club with Spiked Wooden Head.
14. Spokane Indian Club.
15. Arapahoe Tomahawk Pipe.
16. War Club with Barbed Spikes.

## Plate IV.

*To face page* 200

### RED CLOUD'S BUCKSKIN WAR SHIRT, ORNAMENTED WITH HUMAN SCALPS AND BEADS; BEADED LEGGINGS AND MOCCASINS.

1. War Shirt of Red Cloud, the Famous Sioux Chief.
   This is one of the finest specimens of an Indian war shirt in existence. It is made of soft buckskin, beautifully tanned and dyed, and is elaborately ornamented with beads. It is decorated with an extraordinary number of human scalps.
2. Nez Perces Beaded Moccasins.
   Made of buckskin and ornamented with beads.
3. Kiowa-Apache Buckskin Beaded Leggings.
   These leggings are remarkably fine specimens, and are very profusely and handsomely decorated with beads.
4. Kiowa Boy's Beaded Moccasins.
   Beautifully ornamented with beads and rich in color.

## Plate V.

*To face page* 260

### WAR AND SACRED SHIELDS; BEADED BLANKET BAND; WOMAN'S BELT; WARRIOR'S DISK STRAP; HEADDRESS, ETC.

1. Fancy Beaded Blanket Band.
2. Arapahoe War Shield.
   Ornamented with eagle feathers and panther claws. Indian drawings and symbols are shown on the face of the shield.
3. Kiowa Warrior's Disk Strap.
   Made of leather, to which are attached silver disks. These ornamented straps were usually fastened to the scalp lock and left hanging down the back. They were frequently worn in battle.

4. WOMAN'S BEADED LEATHER BELT WITH HANGING STRAP, ORNAMENTED WITH SILVER DISKS.

   To the belt is attached a toilet pouch, awl and needle-case.

5. KIOWA CEREMONIAL HEADDRESS.

   Made of bristles of turkey beard and hair of the elk dyed red; ornamented with ribbons and eagle feathers.

6. KIOWA SACRED SHIELD.

   A perfect facsimile of the most sacred shield of the Kiowas, dedicated to the "Taime" spirit or Sun God, and painted with symbolical figures of the sun and moon; ornamented with the carcass of a crow and claws of a panther. This shield was formerly owned by the Kiowa Medicine Chief, Thunder, and was with great difficulty procured by Mr. James Mooney and by him presented to the government.

## PLATE VI.

*To face page* 346

## GIRL'S BUCKSKIN BEADED CLOTHES BAG; GARTERS; TOILET AND TOBACCO POUCHES; MOCCASINS, NEEDLE CASE, FIRE BAG, ETC.

1. KIOWA MOCCASINS.

   Made of soft buckskin, beautifully colored and ornamented with beads and fringe.

2. KIOWA BEADED FIRE BAG.

   Used for carrying flint, steel, and tinder.

3. CHEYENNE TOILET POUCH.

   Made of the skin of a calf's head.

4. SANTEE-SIOUX BEADED GARTERS.

   These garters were obtained from a wounded survivor of the battle of Wounded Knee. They are beautiful specimens of fine bead work.

5. BEADED BUCKSKIN CLOTHES BAG.

   A very unique and handsome specimen. It is made of soft buckskin, and is elaborately ornamented with beads. Used by Indian girls as a receptacle for their clothes and personal belongings.

6. ORNAMENTED TOBACCO POUCH.

   A handsome specimen from the Plains Indians. Tribe unknown.

7. BEADED BAG.

   Supposed to be a tobacco pouch. Made of soft buckskin, and handsomely ornamented with beads. Tribe unknown.

8. KIOWA MOCCASINS.

   Richly colored and profusely ornamented with beads and fringe.

9. CROW BEADED TOBACCO POUCH.

   Made of soft buckskin, handsomely ornamented with beads.

10. SIOUX TOBACCO POUCH.

    A fine specimen, decorated with beads and porcupine quills.

11. KIOWA GIRL'S PERFUME POUCH.

    Also frequently used to carry simple toilet articles.

## PLATE VII. *To face page* 366

### WAR BONNET OF RED FLANNEL ORNAMENTED WITH SCALP LOCKS, EAGLE FEATHERS, AND BUFFALO HORNS; PIPES, FLUTES, ETC.

1. DANCE STAFF.

   Commonly carried in the hands while dancing.

2. SUPERB WAR BONNET.

   Ornamented with buffalo horns and eagle feathers attached to red flannel.

3. COMMON TOMAHAWK PIPE.
4. COMMON RED CLAY PIPE.
5. ELABORATE PEACE PIPE.
6. KIOWA FLUTE.

   Made of two pieces of hollow wood fastened together with thongs.

7. CADDO FLUTE.
8. INDIAN WHISTLE.

   Made of the wing bone of an eagle. These whistles are frequently carried in the Sun Dance, and blown incessantly by the dancers.

9. RED CLAY PIPE.

## PLATE VIII. *To face page* 468

### FACSIMILE OF AN ORIGINAL INDIAN DRAWING OF A CEREMONIAL DANCE.

Drawn with colored crayons and pencils by Big Back, a Cheyenne. It shows facial decoration in various designs and colors intended to make the face as hideous as possible.

## PLATE IX. *To face page* 544

### 1. NECKLACE OF HUMAN FINGERS, ARROW HEADS AND TEETH, ATTACHED TO BEADED BUCKSKIN COLLAR.

Made of human fingers attached to a beaded buckskin collar, ornamented with medicine arrows, medicine bags, and human teeth. To the collar are attached eight left-hand middle fingers of Indians of hostile tribes, killed by High Wolfe, a Cheyenne. This last ghastly trophy of his prowess was worn by him as evidence of the number of the enemy he had killed. It was captured by Capt. John G. Bourke, U. S. A., an experienced Indian fighter, who loaned it to the publishers for reproduction in this book. Capt. Bourke died while this volume was in press. A full account of the necklace and its capture is given in Chapter XXVIII in Capt. Bourke's own words.

### 2. NECKLACE MADE OF THE FIRST JOINTS OF HUMAN FINGERS ATTACHED TO A LEATHER COLLAR.

The history of this necklace is unknown. It is supposed that each one of the nineteen finger joints represents a human life. To whom the necklace belonged, or from what tribe it was taken, and by whom, is unknown.

## PLATE X.

*To face page* 556

### INDIAN AND WHITE SCALPS, SCALPING KNIVES, SHEATHS, BOW, BOW CASE AND QUIVER, ARROWS, ETC.

1. MEDICINE ARROW.
   To it are attached two closely braided scalp locks, fastened to beaded disks.
2. SCALPING KNIFE SHEATH.
   Handsomely ornamented with beads. Northern Plains Indians.
3. SCALP OF A BLACKFOOT INDIAN.
   A study of the scalp will show how the Indians divided a single scalp into many scalp locks, which were used in ornamenting war shirts, war bonnets, and for other purposes. A single scalp was frequently divided into a dozen or more scalp locks. Each lock does not, as is popularly supposed, represent one dead person, but might be only one of many locks of the same scalp.
4. SIOUX BUCKSKIN QUIVER AND BOW-CASE.
   A handsome specimen, richly ornamented with quills, and filled with arrows.
5. SCALPING KNIFE SHEATH.
   Sioux. Handsomely ornamented with beads.
6. CHEYENNE SCALP.
   This scalp is stretched within a small hoop and shows how scalps were prepared for the scalp dance. After being stretched in this manner, they were carried aloft on poles during the dance, usually by women.
7. SIOUX BOW.
   This bow belongs to outfit No. 4.
8. SCALPING KNIFE.
9. WHITE MAN'S SCALP WITH COMB ATTACHED.
   This scalp was taken from the Sioux and is stretched on a wooden frame ornamented with fur. The comb attached was probably taken from the body of the victim. The scalp is shown just as prepared for the scalp dance.
10. AN INDIAN CAP OR HEADDRESS.
11. SCALPING KNIFE.
12. SCALPING KNIFE.
13. SCALPING KNIFE SHEATH.
    From the Plains Indians. Handsomely ornamented with beads.
14. CARTRIDGE BELT, SCALPING KNIFE AND SHEATH.
    Taken from the Kiowas. This outfit has evidently seen much service, and was probably captured by them from a white trapper or plainsman. The sheath is studded with brass nails.
15. SCALPING KNIFE SHEATH.
    Taken from the Sioux.
16. WAR AND HUNTING ARROWS.
    These are specimens from the quiver No. 4.
17. RAWHIDE WHIP OR QUIRT.
    A severe instrument in the hands of Indians, who belabored their animals unmercifully with it. Also used in many of their ceremonies.
18. SCALPING KNIFE SHEATH.

## CHAPTER I.

### MY BOYHOOD AND EARLY HOME — SCHOOL AND COLLEGE DAYS — APPOINTED AS A CADET TO WEST POINT MILITARY ACADEMY.



## CHAPTER II.

### CHASING INDIANS THROUGH THE EVERGLADES OF FLORIDA — INDIAN FIGHTERS WHO AFTERWARDS BECAME GREAT MILITARY LEADERS IN THE CIVIL WAR.

## CHAPTER III.

GRADUATING FROM WEST POINT — MY MARRIAGE — FIRST CALL TO ACTIVE DUTY — BREAKING UP OUR HOUSEHOLD.



## CHAPTER IV.

CAMPAIGNING AGAINST THE SEMINOLES — INCIDENTS AND EXPERIENCES OF MY ARMY LIFE IN FLORIDA.



## CHAPTER V.

SKETCH OF MY MILITARY CAREER DURING THE CIVIL WAR — ATTITUDE OF OUR WILD INDIANS DURING THAT PERIOD.

## CHAPTER VI.

GREAT UPRISING OF HOSTILE INDIANS IN THE NORTHWEST — THE TERRIBLE SIOUX MASSACRE IN MINNESOTA.



## CHAPTER VII.

ASSIGNED TO DUTY AMONG THE BLOODTHIRSTY APACHES — MY ARRIVAL IN ARIZONA.



## CHAPTER VIII.

CAMPAIGNING IN ARIZONA — JOURNEYING ACROSS THE "ALKALI DESERT" — LIFE AMONG THE PIMAS AND MARICOPAS.

## CHAPTER IX.



## CHAPTER X.



## CHAPTER XI.

## CHAPTER XII.

### I SET OUT TO FIND THE NOTORIOUS CHIEF, COCHISE.



## CHAPTER XIII.

### SCOUTING FOR THE APACHE CHIEF, COCHISE — ENTERING HIS MOUNTAIN STRONGHOLD — FIRST NIGHT IN A WILD CAMP.



## CHAPTER XIV.

### MY EXPERIENCES IN A WILD APACHE CAMP — FAREWELL TO COCHISE.

## CHAPTER XV.

### ASSIGNED TO THE DEPARTMENT OF THE COLUMBIA, EMBRACING ALL THE NORTHWEST — THE MODOCS AND THE MODOC WAR.



## CHAPTER XVI.

### THREATENED HOSTILITIES — A TRIBE THAT CAUSED TERROR TO THE WHITE PEOPLE OF THE NORTHWEST.



## CHAPTER XVII.

### MY ARRIVAL AT FORT LAPWAI — GROWING DISCONTENT AND INSOLENCE OF THE INDIANS — FEARS OF AN OUTBREAK.

## CHAPTER XVIII.

AMONG THE COLUMBIA RIVER INDIANS — INCIDENTS AND PERSONAL EXPERIENCES — "CUT-MOUTH JOHN."



## CHAPTER XIX.

BIDDING ADIEU TO MY FAMILY FOR WHAT PROVES TO BE A LONG ABSENCE — ON THE VERGE OF A BLOODY INDIAN WAR.



## CHAPTER XX.

OPENING OF HOSTILITIES — BATTLES OF WHITE BIRD CANYON AND THE CLEAR WATER.

## CHAPTER XXI.

PURSUIT AND DEFEAT OF THE INDIANS — SURRENDER OF CHIEF JOSEPH.



## CHAPTER XXII.

STARTING FOR ALASKA — EXPERIENCES WITH ALASKAN CHIEFS AND TRIBES.



## CHAPTER XXIII.

OUR JOURNEY TO ALASKA CONTINUED—A VISIT TO THE CHILCATS, THE SUMDUMS, AND OTHER PACIFIC COAST TRIBES.

## CHAPTER XXIV.

THE STORY OF MARCUS WHITMAN — THRILLING ACCOUNT OF HIS PERILOUS OVERLAND JOURNEY.



## CHAPTER XXV.

A FRONTIER TRAGEDY — THE COLD-BLOODED MASSACRE OF MARCUS WHITMAN AND HIS FAMILY.



## CHAPTER XXVI.

CAMPAIGNING ON THE UPPER COLUMBIA — EXPERIENCES WITH MOSES, WAR-CHIEF OF THE SPOKANES — HIS OWN NARRATIVE.

## CHAPTER XXVII.

### ADVENTURES AMONG THE BANNOCKS — A MIDNIGHT WAR DANCE AND ITS SEQUENCE.



## CHAPTER XXVIII.

### PREPARATIONS FOR ANOTHER CAMPAIGN — OPENING OF THE PI-UTE AND BANNOCK WAR.



## CHAPTER XXIX.

### IN ACTIVE FIELD SERVICE AGAIN — SARAH WINNEMUCCA'S REMARKABLE RIDE — NEARING THE INDIAN STRONGHOLD.

## CHAPTER XXX.

INCIDENTS AND HARDSHIPS OF AN INDIAN CAMPAIGN — THE BATTLE OF BIRCH CREEK — FLIGHT OF THE INDIANS.



## CHAPTER XXXI.

A LONG AND EXCITING CHASE — THE ENGAGEMENTS THAT FOLLOWED — THRILLING INCIDENTS OF THE CAMPAIGN.



## CHAPTER XXXII.

AMONG THE SHEEP-EATERS — CAMPAIGNING IN "THE LAND OF THE SEVEN DEVILS."

## CHAPTER XXXIII.

AMONG THE SPOKANES — I AM WELCOMED BY CHIEF LOT — INSTANCES OF INDIAN GRATITUDE.



## CHAPTER XXXIV.

PERSONAL EXPERIENCES AMONG THE CROWS — SECRET HELPERS OF OUR FOES.



## CHAPTER XXXV.

LIFE AMONG THE FLATHEADS — THEIR PECULIARITIES AND CUSTOMS — OUR INDIAN RESERVATION METHODS.

## CHAPTER XXXVI.

### LIFE AND EXPERIENCES AMONG THE WARLIKE SIOUX — SOME DANGEROUS CHARACTERS.



## CHAPTER XXXVII.

### THE MESSIAH CRAZE AMONG THE SIOUX — INDIAN DREAMERS AND THE GHOST DANCE — FRONTIER TRAGEDIES.



## CHAPTER XXXVIII.

### IN THE COUNTRY OF THE CHEYENNES — MASSACRE OF CUSTER AND HIS COMMAND — A FRONTIER TRAGEDY.

## CHAPTER XXXIX.

### GENERAL MACKENZIE'S FIGHT WITH THE NORTHERN CHEYENNES — A NIGHT ATTACK ON AN INDIAN CAMP — A STORY OF TERRIBLE SUFFERING.



## CHAPTER XL.

### SQUAW MEN — HOME LIFE OF WHITE MEN WHO HAVE MARRIED INDIAN WOMEN — INCIDENTS.



## CHAPTER XLI.

### CHARACTERISTICS OF AMERICAN INDIANS — THE SIGN LANGUAGE — CEREMONIAL DANCES — A NECKLACE OF HUMAN FINGERS.

## CHAPTER XLII.

### CHARACTERISTICS OF AMERICAN INDIANS, CONTINUED—THEIR STOLIDITY, SECRETIVENESS, AND HUMOR—INDIAN SPIES—CURIOUS STORY TOLD BY A KIOWA.



## CHAPTER XLIII.

### CHARACTERISTICS OF AMERICAN INDIANS, CONTINUED—ORATORS AND ORATORY—EXPERT HORSEMANSHIP—SURPRISES AND AMBUSCADES—FUTURE OF OUR INDIANS.

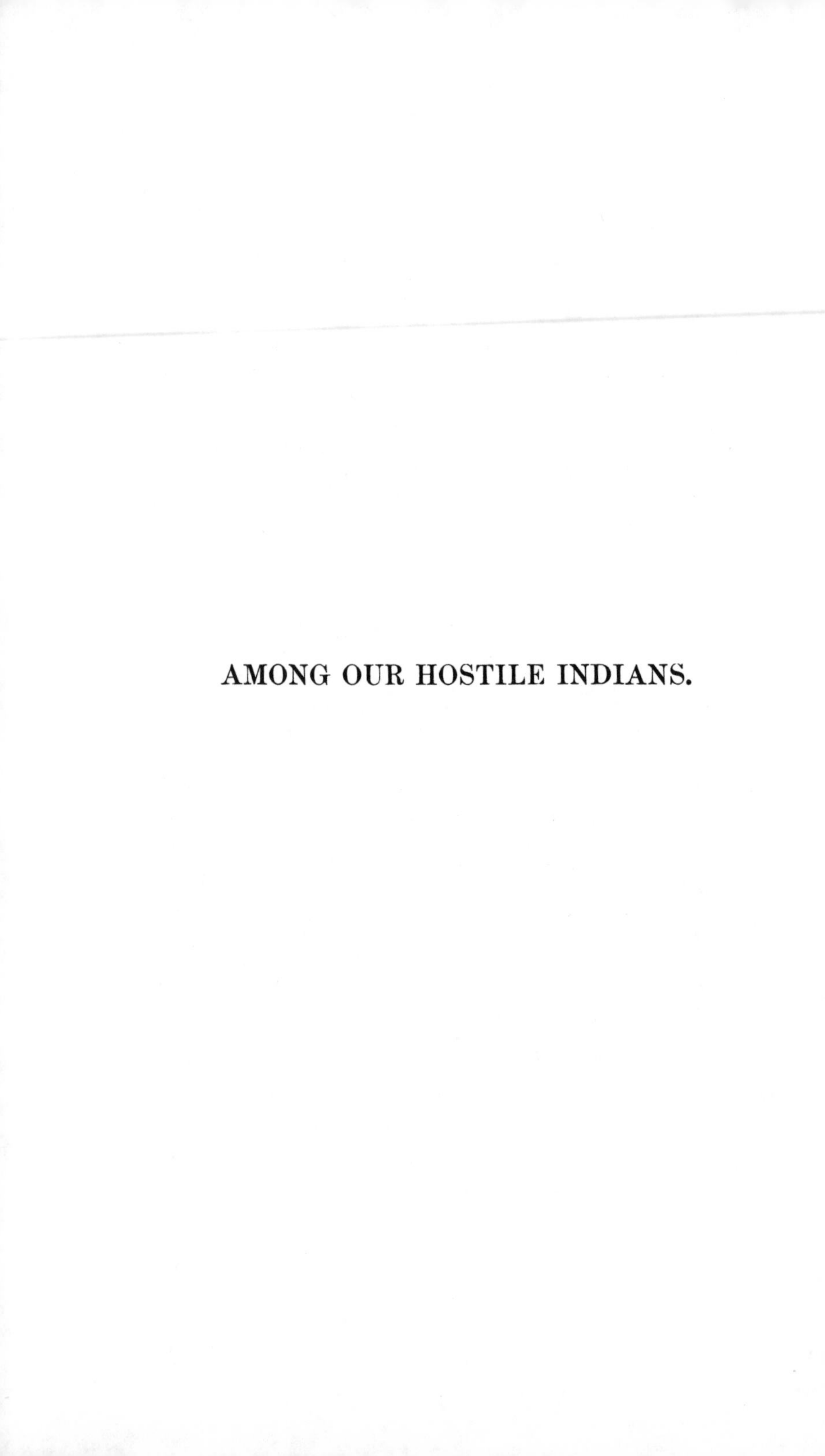

# AMONG OUR HOSTILE INDIANS.

# MY LIFE AND PERSONAL EXPERIENCES AMONG OUR HOSTILE INDIANS.

## CHAPTER I.

### MY BOYHOOD AND EARLY HOME — SCHOOL AND COLLEGE DAYS — APPOINTED AS A CADET TO WEST POINT MILITARY ACADEMY.

Looking Backward — Recollections of my Parents — Grandfather's Chimney Corner — The Old Home in Maine — Listening to Grandfather's Indian Tales — My Father's Death — Working as Man-of-all-Work for my Board — Attending the Village School — Entering Bowdoin College — Appointed as a Cadet to West Point — A Momentous Step — Going Forth into the World — Arrival at West Point — Warned to Dispense with my Silk Hat and Cane — "Stand Straight, Sir!" — Reminiscences of West Point.

AFTER passing the seventieth milestone men usually and naturally look back to early days. Certainly the writer of these pages is doing so now and often dwelling upon different epochs of his boyhood. There are periods that stand forth like pictures on the wall; they may or may not have connection with other periods. When you meet such pictures in larger galleries you gladly renew their acquaintance and are gratified if you find them of intrinsic worth; so with remembered portions of your young life, they find their way into larger galleries and have a relative value not dreamed of at first.

Our household at Leeds, Maine, at the dawn of my childish memory, surely belongs to the first period of thoughtful observation. It consisted of my mother, father, and grandfather, and Sam Finnemore, our hired man. My young mother's appearance at that time is dim to my vision. She seems to have been going here and there about the family room or about the house, with a healthy, happy look, though at times very grave, and habitually talking pleasantly to my grandfather. He was a tall, spare man, erect of figure, although already past seventy, and with that genial expression of countenance that attracts a child. Because of some infirmity of age my grandfather usually remained indoors. I see him now as he sat in the chimney corner and smoked his pipe of dusky hue, turning often to help me and my small dog in our plays, to tie or loose a knot, or yield laughing obedience to the changing whimsies of his grandchild. Again I behold him seated in his kitchen chair near the east window that looked out toward the old orchard, reading the paper, sometimes aloud; while mother was at the spinning wheel, moving steadily back and forth, creating as she did so a peculiar music by thread and spindle, like an orchestral accompaniment to a song, for, besides his reading, she and grandfather held an intermittent conversation distinct enough above the buzzing sounds. When tired of play the little dog stretched himself before the open fire, and the child crept into grandpa's lap, daring to pull off his spectacles and stop his reading.

Three times a day our goodly dining table was set. When the proper hour came, there was my father at the end farthest from the kitchen door; he was always a little careworn, had heavy eyebrows, sandy side whiskers, and high forehead with dark hair slightly lifted up at the middle front. Mother sat opposite him. My chair, the seat raised by a covered bench, was at her right; grandfather, always in his kitchen chair, at the side next to me; while the sturdy Sam, with English face and light, thin, closely curled hair, sat in silence opposite me. No need to draw the picture further. That was a frugal board, but it was a New England home-table; and ours was a frugal, self-reliant family which never dreamed of great riches nor extreme want.

The house was built by my grandfather about thirty years before, when my father was a lad of eleven years. It was of timber, except the cellar walls and the entire foundation of stone, two stories above ground, foursquare, with a central front door, and hall running through, and a number of back buildings connecting the kitchen to a sizable barn. Erected high up on the north slope of the great hill of Leeds, it could be seen from Turner and Livermore westward across the Androscoggin, and from Wayne eastward across the lake. Painted white, adorned with green blinds, and protected by a few large elms, well away from the common roads, Seth Howard's house afforded to farmers and travelers far and near a notable landmark.

Our home farm, embracing open fields, garden, groves, and woodland, all together did not exceed eighty acres. Father was at this time, as I afterward knew, working too diligently and persistently for his strength. But he had an unselfish object in view. By the products of his farm work, also by taking small droves of horses to Massachusetts for the Boston market, by buying patent threshers at a bargain and selling them, going sometimes as far as New York state, and by other helpful operations, he had succeeded in paying off an oppressive mortgage on grandfather's farm. He had also purchased the sandy "Day place" at South Leeds for a sheep pasture. None of these things were ever much talked of at home; still there was to me, in time, an educational significance in the hard work and self-denial ever practiced by my father and mother.

"Sam," the hired man, was kind to me in his way. He made rough sleds, snow-shoes, small wagons, and other playthings for me, but found my sensitive spots and liked to touch them. His teasings brought some tears, and first awakened in the confiding child the doubt and distrust that, soon or late, must come to us all. But father and mother, never trifling with a child, were always in earnest with me. They both were fond of music; mother sang in church, and usually when about her work and not in conversation was humming some good old hymn, while at evening my father often played the flute.

Grandfather had a native humor in his kind heart, and was always bubbling over to lighten and sweeten his manners. He was my favorite companion during my boyhood. It was when sitting in his lap that I began my knowledge of the Howard family history. He told me much of the great journey from Bridgewater, Mass., to Maine, with my grandmother and their six children. Later, their family increased to nine. He praised my father's feats of horsemanship when ten years old, — telling me how he rode a fine horse all the way, more than three hundred miles, from the old home to Leeds; how Uncle Stillman had cut a willow riding whip on the way, which, after arriving, he had stuck into the ground by the roadside about a mile south of us, from which grew a huge willow tree that I had often seen.

He also related tales of the "Red Coats" which prejudiced me fearfully against them; some of the stories included "the Tories," who burned houses and killed people with little mercy or discrimination. Old comrades of the Revolution occasionally came to see him, one a wounded lieutenant, who seemed to me uncommonly kind and affectionate. I did not then understand half of their war stories; but I listened to them with keen interest, and well remember their hearty fellowship.

The name of Jesse Howard, my great-grandfather, is found recorded in the Massachusetts archives as "a lieutenant in Captain Ames' Company" at the beginning of the Revolution. But my grandfather said that his father Jesse was a captain in the Army of the Revolution, and often actively engaged during the long war. Recently I have been able to verify this statement. My grandfather, Seth Howard, being young at the time of the Revolution, had remained at home to take care of his good mother; but subsequently he was permitted to enlist and go with his father during one of the later years of the struggle, serving as a private soldier.

What interested me most after I was old enough to understand grandfather, and to remember what he said to me, concerned the Indians. It appears that when he was on duty during that year of the war, between 1777 and 1779, he was a mere boy of seventeen; but after that service, being of a military turn, he, during his young manhood, accepted from the Commonwealth the captaincy of a militia company. This company was several times called out to meet outbreaks of one kind and another. These included the riots of white men, like those of "Shay's rebellion," 1786-87; also the combined offensive action of Tories and Indians, insurrections which were not wholly quelled till some years after the Yorktown surrender.

In the "Life of Joseph Brant" (whose Indian name was Thayen-da-negea) a few words indicate the state of affairs in the region on both sides of the line where Massachusetts and Vermont border upon New York. These disturbances, reaching far into the New England states, were frequent as late as 1872. The writer says: "Their chastisement by Major Ross [one of Washington's commanders who had surprised and defeated the hostile Indians in eastern New York], equally severe and unexpected, had discouraged the enemy from making any further attempt in that quarter. Not, however, that the Indians were entirely quiet. On the contrary, they hung around the borders of the settlements in small parties, sometimes causing serious alarm and at others great trouble and fatigue, and likewise inflicting considerable injury."

How clearly in my childhood grandfather described to me those wild red men, some of whom were still in his youth inhabitants of New England. He talked of their war-paint; of their dress made of skins of animals; of their queer tents, wigwams, and lodges; of their straight and heavy jet-black hair; of the eagle feathers and ornaments for their chiefs and their women; of their weapons, their bows and arrows of different sorts, and their cruel tomahawks and scalping-knives. I had at that time never seen an Indian, nor do I remember to have looked at pictures of them till about two years later, when father brought home, on his return from Troy, New York, my first geography and atlas. These contained pictures of the aborigines. Better than prints my grandfather's clear and pleasant voice had set the reality before my mind, just how they looked and lived and fought. My heart for years was steeled against such wild, unmerciful savages, who, worse than Tories, spared nobody, not even women and children. It took the broadening influence of years, and the stories of William Penn, and of Pocahontas, besides the persuasive charm of James Fenimore Cooper's novels, to allay my strong prejudice and show me the equal or greater sinfulness of the Anglo-Saxon.

I was greatly interested in grandfather's description of the way he and his men were called out to guard a village, and how they picketed a grove or forest. The watchmen on the outer lines, like our pickets, were placed within hearing of each other. They habitually lay upon the ground and concealed themselves behind logs, stumps, and trees. Their blunderbusses had at first a match-lock and later the flint and priming powder. In complete readiness the men would lie for hours perfectly silent.

An Indian spy would creep up so quietly that his approach could with difficulty be detected. On one occasion, after an alarm my grandfather's men were distributed as explained, and he was with them helping to keep watch. About midnight an Indian succeeded in getting within a few paces of one of the watchmen without detection; suddenly he heard a sound and fell upon his face, remaining for some time motionless; at last, thinking that he was mistaken with regard to the proximity of a white man, the Indian raised his head just a little to look around, when the watchman, catching a glimpse, fired, hitting the Indian in the throat; he gave a gurgling sound and fell dead. The death of that spy caused his comrades to flee and grandfather scored a victory for his company.

His work in the Revolution and in the local disturbances of his state, such as I have referred to, appeared to be very much in his mind and was often the subject of his conversation with me and with others in my presence. He was never wholly free from the startling impressions of those younger days; they troubled his dreams and disturbed his sleep. He fought over again, as I well remember, in his night visions, sometimes with actual demonstration, his never-forgotten battles.

At the time of my father's death, which oc-

BOY'S BUCKSKIN SHIRT; GIRL'S BUCKSKIN BEADED LEGGINGS; BELT, POUCHES, ETC.

*For Description see page 13*

PHOTOGRAPHED AND PAINTED FROM THE ORIGINAL OBJECTS EXPRESSLY FOR THIS WORK.

curred when I was nine years of age, in April, 1840, I had two brothers, one four years and the other eight years younger than myself. One Sunday morning, six months before this event, my father had called me from a distant field in order that I might accompany him and my mother to the church at Leeds Centre. The wind was blowing in his face and made it difficult for me to catch the sound of his voice. I came at once, but for some reason was excused from going with them. The strain of the morning had been too much for the lungs of my good father, and he was seized with a hemorrhage while he was sitting in his pew during the church service. I was much startled and affected by the return of my father and mother earlier than usual, and by his illness, which was accompanied with constant bleeding that seemed impossible to control.

When he died, the grief of my mother, the gloom of the household, and all the circumstances of the funeral, the first which I had ever witnessed, gave a new coloring to my thoughts and cast a shadow upon my young life. I began to feel the responsibility of being the eldest child in the little family, and my mother began to advise with me as with a friend. This epoch — my father's death — soon separated me from my grandfather. He went to live with his son Stillman Howard, some three miles distant from the old homestead, and I saw him only occasionally from that time till his death. This occurred while I was away at North Yarmouth Academy attending a school preparatory to college. Could I have anticipated the consequences of such a separation, I think I should have forestalled them and spent four years more with my grandfather. From ten to fourteen what might I not have gained in veritable historic knowledge of the Revolutionary War, and of the Indian tribes of the east and north which were round about him in his early life?

With a view to make the sketch of these early days more complete, prior to my special acquaintanceship and extensive experience with various Indian tribes, I may say that after a little more than a year my widowed mother married Colonel John Gilmore, and moved to South Leeds, where, on his larger estate, the Gilmore and Howard families were united, and lived on very happily with a degree of prosperity which mother's boys were ever pleased to recall.

It was soon after this that I was sent away from home in order that I might enjoy greater educational advantages than the school in our neighborhood afforded. The year before I was twelve it was arranged that I should go to Hallowell, situated just below Augusta on the Kennebec River. Here I lived with my mother's brother, the Honorable John Otis, performing the tasks of a man-of-all-work for my board, and going to the village high school, kept by Mr. Jonas Burnham, who had been a classmate of my uncle in Bowdoin College. At this school, where I stayed for nearly two years, I entered with a class upon a college preparation, making considerable progress not only in English studies, but in both Latin and Greek.

In the same village lived another relative who

exerted a great influence upon my life, my mother's father, Oliver Otis. As I was born the day he was sixty-two years old, my mother gave me his name. He was a man of mark, careful and conscientious in everything that he did, especially so in the making, keeping, and expending of money. Just before he died he called me to him and talked with me faithfully concerning my future. One expression which I did not quite understand when he uttered it has always remained in my mind: "Otis, be sure always to treat your employees with kindness." The prospect of my ever having the privilege of employing anybody was not then very clear; but how many thousands have since come under my command as an officer, or have been otherwise employed for useful service.

During the summer vacation I used to ride with my uncle to his farm a few miles outside the village, and do what a strong, healthy boy of my age could accomplish in the farm work by helping others. In these two years, with varied experiences, I gained my uncle's good will and confidence. A little later he became the member of Congress from his district and was in position, as we shall see, to do his favorite nephew a good turn.

In the spring of 1845, after being well fitted out with home-made clothing, I was taken, together with my luggage, in a sleigh, which we called a "pung," from Leeds to North Yarmouth. There I undertook to put a two years' course of study into one. Being behind the class which was to enter college in June, 1846, I determined to catch up with the others and to enter upon the college course with them at that time. We had an example before us of a young man, Spencer Wells, who had done so. Following his example I had a standing desk and sometimes actually worked at my books from sixteen to twenty hours out of the twenty-four. This course enabled me to enter college a year before the Hallowell class, but I believe now that it was a positive detriment to my scholarship, because my preparation was not as thorough as it ought to have been, and the reaction upon my physical strength weakened my subsequent efforts the first year in college. Poor Spencer Wells lost his health after a few years, later his mind failed, and he died a complete wreck in an asylum. Certainly overstraining in anything, especially in study, is not the part of wisdom.

In college I stood fairly well in my studies for one so young; but I think the greatest gain to me came from my intimate connection with college mates, and with the members of the faculty, every one of whom has left a good record of character and of instruction that no student of the college will ever forget. Among my classmates were young men whose names have become of national repute, such as Hon. William P. Frye, Rev. Dr. John S. Sewall, and Prof. Carroll S. Everett of Harvard University..

As I was finishing my course of four years at Bowdoin, my uncle, of whom I have spoken, gave me a nomination as a cadet to the Military Academy at West Point. My decision as to whether I should accept the appointment that ensued, or not, was held under consideration for a few days. Our different studies had been finished and the examinations properly passed, and a Commencement part was assigned to me. At that time, in 1846, from the final examinations to the Commencement proper, a period of nearly two months was allowed the students to prepare for the Commencement exercises. Much was made of the graduating day and every senior looked forward to it with intense interest, as it was indeed the crowning epoch of college life. Meanwhile, I returned to my home at Leeds and showed my mother, with whom I counseled at every important step, my cadet nomination and appointment. She shook her head; she did not quite like to have me become a soldier, but when she looked into my eyes she said at once: "I must leave this matter to you; I see you have already made up your mind."

I accepted the appointment after being excused from our Commencement, and, furnished with such articles of wearing apparel as the West Point circular prescribed, set out from Leeds for the Military Academy. My kind step-father, Colonel Gilmore, took me and my small trunk in his wagon as far as Lewiston, the factory town near the falls of the Androscoggin, twelve miles below us. I bade him farewell, with difficulty repressing my emotions as he spoke his last words of affection and good will. From Lewiston I went by the new "Atlantic & St. Lawrence Railroad" to Portland; a night on the steamer brought me to Boston; by the Old Colony route I went on to New York, spending another night upon one of those Long Island Sound steamers, then considered palatial.

It took four days in all to complete the journey. Twenty-four hours will now take one from Leeds Centre to the city of New York.

How immense the metropolis of fifty years ago appeared to my inexperienced vision! and yet the changes since are so numerous that it is difficult to recognize the city of those days in the present New York. It covers five times more ground than it did then. Its principal business buildings, at that time never more than three stories in height, now run from ten to twenty or more; and the population going in and out marches in processions larger than brigades and divisions of a great army. The Astor House was then the first-class hotel, and the Washington House, near the foot of Broadway, furnished me my first entertainment.

In the morning I entered a car of the Hudson River Railroad at Chambers Street, and ascended the river to have my first view of the changing and variegated scenery all the way from the city to the Highlands; surely there is none more attractive, none grander in any country on the globe. In two hours time we reached Cold Spring, three miles north of West Point. After a few inquiries, I managed to find my way to the dock with my small trunk, and arranged with the boatmen to be taken over to the Academy. Among other passengers was a tall, rather slenderly built, genteel-looking man, wearing spectacles. His familiarity with everything attracted my attention, and shortly after we had started he gave me his name as Captain E. Kirby Smith. The pleasant manner in which he drew me into conversation had a peculiar charm in it. He gave me many useful lessons while we were together, and must have been amusingly entertained over my questions and answers, which doubtless recalled his own similar experiences.

Of course I was in haste to report immediately on my arrival, as the written instructions required, but Captain Smith advised me to go first to the West Point hotel and stay there that night, because neither the superintendent's nor adjutant's office would be open to me till the orderly hour, nine o'clock the next morning. He further suggested that I go to the evening parade and to guard-mounting early on the morrow, and look on so as to get a little used to my surroundings before undertaking anything else. This kind officer, early in the Civil War, joined the Confederacy. In the first battle of Bull Run, on the right of McDowell's line, I met him in battle. He was wounded in the action, but we were defeated.

By Captain Smith's courtesy and timely information given me on the ferryboat I escaped much of the annoyance to which every new cadet, even in those good old days, was exposed. There was, however, no serious hazing to trouble me, a little fun in the line of compliments coming from certain yearlings at my expense, a few orders to bring buckets of fresh water for my tent-mates,—this is all that I remember. Hazing of the freshmen in college had been much worse.

The genuine set-up drill which we September cadets (usually called "Septs") had to go through with three times a day was the greater trial. Having been a teacher of winter schools, a principal of a fall high school, and a graduate of Bowdoin, I believe I had acquired at that time a self-reliance and a pride of bearing that I never again realized. Shortly after my appointment as a cadet I was warned by a West Point graduate to dispense with my silk hat and cane. I did this with some reluctance, for the passing so soon from the college senior's dignity to the lowly position of a "plebe" at West Point had a peculiar bitterness in it that no philosophy could wholly alleviate.

Two cadet corporals were put over our two squads, having five or six "Septs" in each. These corporals, to my relief, now and then exchanged work; one was a martinet, curt and severe in manner, while the other was dignified and always courteous in giving his orders and in all he said to us. "Stand straight, sir! Put your heels together; draw in your chin and your stomach; steady there! Head straight back; raise the shoulders slightly; keep the little fingers on the seams of your trousers!" One corporal after a command would say to me: "What are you about, Howard? Try to behave like a man and not like a monkey!" The other, Corporal Boggs, bless his heart! always omitted the offensive addenda.

In a few weeks the "Septs" obtained their cadet suits of uniform, were incorporated in the battalion, and lost forever, to their comfort, that unenviable distinction which they had experienced while their squad drill continued. At the end of August the summer encampment broke up just after the furlough class had returned, and all moved together into barracks.

I will not attempt here to detail my West Point experiences and associations. From them was derived much of my knowledge of the principal actors in our country's later history. Their public work ranges from 1850 till today.*

My classmate John T. Grebble was the first to fall in battle at Big Bethel, Va. His rank, by the prompt action of the War Department on receiving the news of his death, became that of a Colonel. O'Connor, Smead, Davis, and others were early killed in action, each having risen to the Colonel's grade. In fact, many of my choicest friends and associates did not rise above the rank of field officers.

Thomas, Sheridan, Gregg, Forsythe, Henry, Crook, Bliss, Carr, Miller, and McCook, of my Military Academy friends, had extensive experience in dealing with Indians, both in war and in peace. Their service on the plains was important both before and after our civil war; so that in bringing together in this work my varied experi-

* There I met and had personal acquaintance with Abbott, Alexander, Ames, Baird, Bayard, Bingham, Bliss, Breck, Boggs, Crook, Craighill, Casey, Comstock, Carroll, Carr, Deshler, Delafield, Evans, Forsythe, Field, Fry, Gilbert, Gilmore, Gillespie, Greene, Gracie, Garrard, Gregg, Hardee, Holabird, Hawkins, Henry, Haskell, Hascall, Harker, Jones (Roger), Jones (Samuel), Kearney, Kilpatrick, Lee (R. E.), Lee (G. W. Custis), Lee (Stephen D.), Lee (Fitzhugh), McClellan, McPherson, McKeever, Michie, McCook, Miller, Morgan, Merritt, Perry, Pender, Pennington, Porter (Fitz John), Ruggles, Reynolds (J. J.), Reynolds (John F.), Ruger, Sheridan, Stuart, Schofield, Sawtelle, Smith (G. W.), Smith (E. Kirby), Stanley, Smith (W. S.), Slocum, Saxton, Thomas (Geo. H.), Thomas (Lorenzo), Townsend, Villepigue, Vincent, Williams (Seth), Williams (Robert), Wright (Moses), Weitzel, Walker, Wheeler (Junius), Wheeler (Joseph), Whipple, Wilcox, Wilson (J. M.), Wilson (J. Harry), Warren, Weed, all of whom reached the grade of general officers either in the line or staff.

ences among the Indians, and events with which I was directly or indirectly connected, I naturally begin at West Point.

Just after I entered the academy, on my first half holiday in barracks, I sauntered out to examine the surroundings, with my roommate Thomas J. Treadwell, who had come to West Point from Dartmouth College and was a genial companion. As we passed down the pathway near the Hudson River the first noticeable object we came upon was the monument erected to the memory of Major F. L. Dade and his detachment of over a hundred officers and men. Its simple structure and the history engraven upon it greatly impressed me. As it was altogether a new chapter in my knowledge of Indian matters, I will here introduce, with some detail, the story of the brave major and his fellow soldiers who bedewed with their blood the soil of Florida, which the Seminole Indians claimed as their own, and for which they were so fiercely fighting.

# CHAPTER II.

## CHASING INDIANS THROUGH THE EVERGLADES OF FLORIDA — INDIAN FIGHTERS WHO AFTERWARDS BECAME GREAT MILITARY LEADERS IN THE CIVIL WAR.

The Story of Major Dade — Indian Campaigns in Florida — General Sherman's Early Indian Experiences — In the Heart of the Everglades — A Sudden and Unexpected Attack — Massacre of Major Dade and His Command — Viewing the Slain and Mutilated Bodies of Our Troops — Defeat and Flight of the Indians — My First Meeting with General George H. Thomas — Some of His Early Indian Experiences — His Own Account of a "Scout" Against the Apaches — Pulling Arrows out of His Own Flesh — His Unwavering Loyalty to the Union.

FROM the simple inscription on the monument to Major Dade and his comrades in arms we did not gather all the facts set forth in this chapter. That it was a massacre, however, was evident enough. Upon myself, in spite of my sanguine temperament and hopeful disposition, I confess that the monument alone had a sufficiently depressing effect, which was not relieved when a little later I studied the details of the situation in the library of the academy. I felt as I did when I once stood beside a target riddled with bullets and my companion asked: "How would you like to face that, Howard?" I answered resolutely: "What of that?" but in my heart I long remembered the warning.

Francis L. Dade, who, like Admiral Dewey, had his one opportunity, entered the United States service in the 12th Infantry, the 29th of March,

1813. He was promoted step by step through different grades to a captaincy, and in 1826 became a major by brevet, "for ten years' faithful service in one grade." The record in the old register gives these words at the close of his career: "Massacred by Indians in Florida the 28th of December, 1835."

The bands of Indians with which he had to do, and which caused the United States so much in treasure and in precious blood, occupied the peninsula of Florida, and were well known as the Seminoles. Their mode of life, dress, wigwams, and weapons for war and for the chase differed little from those of kindred neighboring tribes, such as the Creeks and Choctaws, with whom they traded and intermarried.

In studying the early career of General W. T. Sherman years ago I wrote: "It indicates the rapid changes of army life to find Lieutenant Sherman, in the October after his graduation, in charge of a company *en route* for Florida." Soon after his arrival at St. Augustine Sherman ascended the Indian River. He noticed and remembered everything, the bar, the surf, the incoming tide, the shape of the inlet, the Mangrove Islands, the roosting pelicans, the gulls without number tilting their white wings in the air, and other birds poising and sailing and screaming over his head, the water swarming with fish, the phosphoric effect in the wake of the boat, but particularly the exciting stories of exploits in the Indian wars, which the pilot depicted in a vivid and spirited style.

A few sketches from Sherman's pen indicate

the nature of the country and the character of the officers' work. They chased the Indians through the everglades, occasionally capturing men, women and children; they surprised a Seminole camp, killing some warriors and capturing others. Lieutenant Van Vliet, Sherman's lifelong friend, shot at warriors while he was riding at full speed among the trees; Sergeant Broderick gained a victory over three dusky Seminoles, which triumph he thought fit to celebrate by a spree, and so on.

In retrospect years afterward Sherman said: "Florida was the Indian's paradise." Here it was that he came into close relationship with General Ord and General George H. Thomas. They were acquainted at West Point, it is true, but never became as intimate as when serving together in such a unique, isolated region as was then found amid the islands, the numerous lakes, and the curious everglades of Florida.

Such was the situation in Florida during the first war between our troops and the Seminoles. Of course this war was not confined to the parties named, but, as usual after an uprising, the savages moved against the settlements, burning the houses, killing men, women, and children, and carrying off the stock. It is difficult to say what were the causes of the Indian outbreaks in 1835 which led up to the massacres. The alleged difficulties began upon complaints of the settlers that the Indians ran off their stock and harbored their escaping slaves. The Indians, on their side, insisted that the entire peninsula, particularly the interior, including rivers, lakes, and everglades, belonged to them by absolute title, and that the whites had no right to settle there.

Several councils took place from time to time after Florida came into our possession. At a celebrated council held May 9, 1832, the "Treaty of Payne's Landing" was concluded, and it was ratified in April, 1834. This treaty was to the effect that the Seminoles should relinquish to the United States all their claim to the land they occupied in Florida, should emigrate to the Creeks beyond the Mississippi, and become a part of the Creek Nation. This treaty was signed by James Gadsden, Commissioner of the United States, and purported to be signed on the part of the Indians by fifteen chiefs of the Seminoles. Each chief was the leader of a tribe. In reality only eight out of the fifteen assented to the treaty. The case was the same as with the Nez Percés with whom I had to do in after years. The minority of the non-treaty Indians was indeed too large to be ignored.

Long before Payne's Treaty was enacted a great half-breed leader, Osceola, who properly belonged with the Creeks, had come into Florida and been accepted as the principal war chief of the Seminoles. The mother of Osceola belonged to the Red Stick tribe of the Creek Nation. She was the wife of a British trader by the name of Powell, so that Osceola had English blood. Some trouble arose in the family, which aroused her anger to such an extent that she took her son away and returned to her own people. Soon after this, in 1808, Powell moved to the West, taking both of his daughters with him, leaving Osceola and his mother with the Indians in the southern part of Georgia.

When, in 1817, General Jackson was pushing the Indians southward, Osceola, already an acknowledged leader, retreated before him and finally settled near Fort King, Florida, uniting his fortunes with a branch of the Seminoles. At the time that Payne's Treaty was signed he declared that he would not sign it and that he would kill any of his followers who did so. Osceola's bad temper was shown as early as 1834, when a United States Survey Corps was camping at Fort King. Captain Ming, the commander of the corps, received a visit from Osceola, who declined every friendly invitation and refused to break bread with the white men. In council, showing a menacing manner and seizing the surveyor's chain, he said: "If you cross my land I will break this chain in as many pieces as there are links in it, and then throw the pins so far you can never get them again!"

On another occasion General Wiley Thompson, the Indian agent, ordered Osceola to come up and sign the emigration list. He replied, "I will not!" Thompson told him of President Jackson, the big chief in Washington, who would teach him better. Osceola answered: "I care no more for Jackson than for you!" Then going to the treaty he stuck his knife through the parchment.

For a short time Osceola was imprisoned on account of his contumacy, but somehow he managed to secure his release and then immediately began to prepare his warriors for battle. They were secretly ordered to have their knives in readiness, their rifles on hand, and plenty of powder. He went from place to place, hardly stopping for food or rest until he had collected a strong Indian force. The first actual bloodshed came from the side of the whites. They publicly whipped five Indians whom they caught in the act of stealing. Then an Indian was killed and three whites were wounded. Next, a dispatch rider, Aug. 11, 1835, carrying the mails between Fort Brooke and Fort King, was murdered. Hostilities quickly followed, beginning with the slaying of Charlie Emathla, one of the chiefs, who was friendly to the whites and who advocated the emigration.

Soon after this Osceola selected ten of his boldest warriors who hovered around the fort with a view of killing his special enemy, the Indian agent, General Thompson. It was the afternoon of December 28, 1836. The general and Lieutenant Smith, who had dined with him that day, were quietly walking towards the sutler's store which was quite a distance outside of the military post. Osceola and his band saw their opportunity. They cut them off from all help and slew them both. General Thompson was perforated with fourteen bullets and Smith with five. At the sutler's store they killed the trader and four others, robbed the store, and set fire to the building. The smoke from the burning building gave the first alarm to the garrison at Fort King.

Osceola, who had long hated General Thompson, had ordered his larger force, numbering nearly eight hundred Indians, to push on without him down the military road for forty miles, and to waylay a body of soldiers which he had learned from his scouts was coming from Fort Brooke, on Tampa Bay, to reinforce Fort King. The wild and excited warriors had reached and passed the Wahoo Swamp and found an excellent place for an ambuscade five miles beyond. Hoithlee Matee (in English, "Jumper"), a fierce and persistent enemy of white men, was chosen by Osceola as first in command, to be supported by Chief Micanopy, an equally pronounced malcontent.

Near the road in advance of his force, like a sentinel of a picket-post, Micanopy concealed himself behind a tree to await, with Indian patience, the approach of the Fort Brooke detachment. His men, with loaded rifles, and knives in their belts, about a third of the eight hundred, lay among the small palmettos and in the tall grass, wholly hidden, but within easy range. Jumper, farther from the road, arranged the remainder of his force so as to cut off every chance of escape after the first attack. There was not a settlement, and scarcely a ranch, on the route from Tampa Bay to Fort King. The distance was a hundred and eighty miles.

There were several swamps along the route, some quite extensive. They were dotted with what were called hammocks, small fertile islands covered with luxuriant vegetation. Here the trees and underbrush and vines were so dense that hundreds of men could be concealed, and their presence not even be suspected by soldiers who were skirmishing through the thickets till they were within a few yards of the hiding place. So great was Jumper's confidence in the bravery and number of his Indians, that he chose for a battlefield a thinly wooded tract from which he could see the soldiers approaching when several hundred yards away, and he used only the low palmetto growth and the tall and thick grass for shelter. Such was the ambuscade, well planned and well arranged.

Major Dade's command was composed of eight officers and one hundred and two enlisted men. He took with him a wagon hauled by oxen to carry the extra baggage, and a six-pounder field-piece with all its equipment. They could not easily make more than twenty miles a day; for the sand was heavy, and they had been several days on the march when the battle occurred. The order of march appears to have been an advance guard which Major Dade himself usually accompanied, then the first company, with Captain Fraser at its head, then the field-piece followed by the wagon, and last, acting as a rear guard, the second company, commanded by Captain Gardiner. Both companies belonged to the Third Artillery. In those days the artillery soldiers were armed and used as infantry. The major belonged to the Fourth Infantry, — the regiment to which Lieutenant U. S. Grant was attached after his graduation. Other officers were distributed along the column.

After a little experience such companies swing along with an easy pace at route-step, and starting at sunrise could make a twenty-mile march, even in Florida, by one or two o'clock without much fatigue. The oxen, however, when they were used, would regulate the gait and probably prolong the march until much later in the day. Thus, after their encampment on the night of the 27th, without any knowledge whatever of the near proximity of Indians, Dade and his men were marching along in their usual formation, chatting with each other. Captain Fraser appears to have quickened his pace and come up near to Major Dade, probably that they might talk together more easily and while away the time. They were within some five miles of the Wahoo Swamp when, like a bolt of lightning from a clear sky, Micanopy's gun rang out and Major Dade fell. Quicker than it can be told his Indians fired and killed or wounded the entire advance guard, including Captain Fraser. Then followed a running fire which cut off everything in advance of the companies proper.

Captain Gardiner seems to have met the situation with promptness, coolness, and dispatch. While some of his men were thrown out to skirmish, the remainder used their axes and shovels with desperate haste to throw up a triangular breastwork of old logs and such trees as could be easily cut down and thrown together. Naturally this breastwork was not very well laid out, and before it could be finished a second attack came from the whole body of Indians, and the little force were very soon shot down. All Dade's command perished except four who succeeded in making their escape. They ran toward Tampa, avoiding the roads and paths, taking themselves as quickly as possible to the swamps. It is marvelous that they escaped the watchful eyes of the fierce warriors. One of them, however, was trailed and slain by some Indians the next day, while three succeeded in reaching Tampa Bay in a few days and gave a confused report of what had taken place.

Captain E. A. Hitchcock of the First Infantry, acting Inspector General, gave a very graphic report of the visit of General Gaines to the battlefield February 22, 1836. One or two extracts will show something of the situation. "We saw first some broken and scattered boxes, then a cart, the two oxen of which were lying dead, as if they had fallen asleep, their yokes on them; a little to the right one or two horses were seen."

He further speaks of the temporary breastwork: "Within the triangle, along the north and west faces of it, were about thirty bodies, mostly mere skeletons, although much of the clothing was left upon them, . . . lying in precisely the position they must have occupied during the fight, their heads next to the logs over which they had delivered their fire, and their bodies stretched with striking regularity parallel to each other. They had evidently been shot dead at their post, and the Indians had not disturbed them except by taking the scalps of most of them." General Gaines and Captain Hitchcock found the bodies of eight officers and ninety-eight enlisted men. All, after being identified, were carefully buried. The cannon was recovered from a neighboring swamp and placed in an upright position near the grave of the officers, and long remained there as a monument to mark the spot where these brave men fought and fell.

In the very next battle, where General Clinch

was in command, Osceola himself was present. He had increased his eight hundred Indians to over a thousand; but this time he had considerably more than one thousand regulars to face. They were marching southward and met the hostiles at the crossing of the Withlacoochee River. The Indians followed the example of their fierce leader and fought with desperation as long as their ammunition held out, intermingling with their riflemen those who used only bows and arrows.

Osceola brought his warriors into action in groups well arranged to resist every practicable crossing, and he set an example of bravery and effectiveness never exceeded by any savage leader. He took a conspicuous place at the front, but cautiously fought behind tree after tree as he advanced or retired, and, according to the Indian accounts, killed and wounded more than forty white soldiers. Notwithstanding the terrible fighting of the Indians, General Clinch would neither give up nor retire; he continued the conflict till he had worn out his foe, and at last, though with heavy loss, he succeeded in forcing the passage of the river and in defeating and putting to flight Osceola's entire force.

While I was a cadet I came in contact, as I have intimated, with many army officers who were serving on the frontier, which in the '50s extended beyond the Mississippi from the English possessions on the north to Texas and New Mexico on the south. Among them was Major Geo. H. Thomas, who had been bronzed by much service, and who had already received three brevet commissions for gallant conduct in fighting the Indians and the Mexicans. While in Florida Major Thomas was much with Sherman and Ord, who had been his mates at West Point, and he participated in the last work of the army there under General Worth, who was always a favorite leader whether warring against Indians or white men.

Through the pathless forests and swamps the Indians would creep and shoot into a moving column, or into a camp at midnight, appearing and disappearing with incredible swiftness. It took the best of health, temperate habits, devotion to duty, and great firmness of character to spend a year in southern Florida and not become to some degree demoralized. George H. Thomas met his first trials there admirably and came out not only unscathed but with added honors. In 1841 he participated in an Indian expedition and did such royal service that Worth, joining with his captain, warmly recommended him for the first brevet.

To cadets then at West Point, myself included, Major Thomas of Virginia, who had been in bloody battles and had been three times brevetted for gallantry, was not a figure to pass without notice. Even now I remember his strong, mandatory voice while he drilled us in artillery amid the rattle of the gun-carriages and the clamor of section officers. His soldierly appearance and solid seat on a good-sized horse when he led a cavalry charge in our cavalry school, or jumped the hurdles, caught every eye. It was especially in the section-room that he was a favorite. His kind manner and the good marks he awarded us for average recitations made our boyish hearts glad. After he left us he served in Texas and had considerable active work among the roving bands of Apaches.

A few words concerning one of Thomas' "scouts," from his own pen, will give an idea of the perils of an expedition in 1856: "As we were overhauling them (the Indians) one fellow more persevering than the rest, who still kept his position in rear of the loose animals, suddenly dismounted and prepared to fight; and our men in their eagerness to dispatch him hurried upon him so quickly that several arrows took effect, wounding myself in the chin and chest, also Private William Murphy of Company D in the left shoulder, and Privates John Tile and Cooper Sidle of the band each in the leg, before he, the Indian, fell by twenty or more shots." This scout of Thomas' was against a very wild and troublesome band of Apaches that roamed near the headwaters of the Concho and the Colorado Rivers of Texas. His wound was a very painful one. While he was alone he had drawn out the arrows from his own flesh with great difficulty; they made such deep and serious cuts that a noticeable scar was left upon his chin and an uglier one upon his breast.

After I first knew Thomas I became interested in him and always followed his career with eager attention and expectancy. While returning from Texas, on a leave of absence after he had become a major in the Second Cavalry, he met with a serious railroad accident, being rolled with his car down a steep embankment. This injured his spine so that for a time he despaired of ever being well enough again for field service. During the first few months of his disability, he sought in his own state for some military school where he could reside permanently and teach young men. It is this which gave rise to the suspicion that Thomas was willing to go South and join the forces of secession. It is now well known that he never veered in his loyalty to his government. Soon after the outbreak of the Civil War, he was promoted from a majority to the colonelcy of the Second Cavalry, from which Lee, Johnston, and Hardee had gone when they tendered their resignations and joined the Confederacy.

General Thomas' early experiences among hostile Indians for two periods in Florida, and one upon the frontier of Texas against the Apaches and Comanches, largely helped him to acquire coolness and self-command in fierce battles, and prepared him in great measure for his grand and patriotic service in the Civil War.

# CHAPTER III.

## GRADUATING FROM WEST POINT—MY MARRIAGE—FIRST CALL TO ACTIVE DUTY—BREAKING UP OUR HOUSEHOLD.

My Graduation from West Point—A Memorable Year—My Marriage—Settling our Home—First Sudden Call to Duty—The Consternation it Occasioned—Scattering of the Family—Ordered to Florida—A Renowned Indian Fighter—The Seminoles—Hiding in the Great Cypress Swamps—"Billy Bowlegs," the Chosen Seminole Leader—Raiding the Settlements—An Amusing Interpreter—Meeting Young Officers Who Were Afterwards Generals in the Civil War—Recollections of Them—A Crazy Soldier and an Unpleasant Episode—An Undignified Escape from Indians.

HAVING been graduated from the Military Academy sufficiently high in general standing in a class reduced to thirty-six members, I was entitled to a place in the topographical engineers; but I chose for the service, as I had a right to do, the Ordnance Department. After a pleasant furlough spent in Maine, I went to my first station, Watervliet Arsenal, in the fall of 1854. In 1855, quite early in the season, I was surprised with a separate command, that of Kennebec Arsenal. That same year was furthermore a memorable one to me, as my marriage occurred on the 14th of February to Miss Elizabeth Ann Waite, the daughter of Alexander B. Waite, Esq., of Portland, Me.; the 16th of the following December our eldest son, Guy, was born.

After being nearly a year on duty at Kennebec, I returned with my little family to Watervliet.

We had excellent quarters which were made very comfortable, being as well furnished as our limited means would afford. We had the use of a good garden and plenty of stable room. I had bought a Canadian pony, and a carriage and harness, which when I was off duty afforded us fine opportunities for driving about the country. My brother and my wife's mother had come from Maine to live with us. He was attending the famous law school at Albany, and it was very convenient for him to come and go from our home. Taking it all in all, our comforts and enjoyments were very complete when suddenly in December, 1856, I was ordered by the Washington authorities to proceed to Tampa, Florida, and report to General W. S. Harney, then commanding that department. This was the beginning of my Indian campaigning.

Quite a remnant of the Seminoles had been left hidden in the Everglades and the big cypress swamps when the great body of that nation, at the end of the war which I have before mentioned, were transported to the Indian Territory. In ten years their numbers had greatly increased. Many of the boys had grown to manhood and become warriors. Their chosen leader was a singular character, very plausible in his deportment and very deceptive in his dealings with white men. The name given him by the settlers was "Billy Bowlegs." This chieftain and his followers had of late had the usual conflicts with the white settlers, on account of their gradual encroachments upon the hunting and fishing grounds still stoutly claimed by these Indians. No reasoning would convince them that the treaty which had been signed by the heads of tribes who had long since emigrated was binding upon them.

They raided the settlements, ran off cattle and horses, waylaid wagon trains and robbed them. Stage lines became unsafe. Now and then a settler was shot; a terrible retribution upon the Indians would soon follow, and the middle and southern part of Florida speedily became a land of terror and trouble. The Indian raids were, of course, exaggerated, but the fear of them was widespread. Undoubtedly, greedy land owners and many unscrupulous village traders took advantage of the situation to magnify rumors and to call for troops, with a view principally of furnishing abundant supplies. They insisted upon raising volunteers, which, after being mustered in, had to be furnished with arms, ammunition, and food. There were, of course, not very many Indians, probably not to exceed five hundred all told, yet enough to keep up a continuous panic and constant calls upon the government at Washington for aid.

This was the state of things when I was directed to leave my home and report to General Harney, the most renowned Indian fighter that we had at that time in the field.

My family, before many years, became accustomed to such sudden calls to duty; but this was the first one, and it would be hard to exaggerate the surprise — almost consternation — which it produced. Our garden and house had to be given up; the pony, carriage, and harness were sold. My household was divided, the other members returning to Maine, while I proceeded through Washington to Savannah, Pilatka, and Tampa. It was my first journey through the South, and from a thousand incidents it became memorable. Passing from the extreme cold of Watervliet to the sunny shores of Tampa Bay, no young man was ever more delightfully entertained with the contrasts of scenery and climate, with the people, and the newness of his surroundings.

Not finding General Harney at Tampa, I went on board the old steamer *Fashion* which afterwards, during the Civil War, became a Confederate cruiser. It was a beautiful moonlight night, and at about ten o'clock I reached the steamer at anchor. The weather was warm and the bay quiet, without a ripple upon its surface. I seemed to be already in another world, and in spite of the separation from my family I was charmed with the new experience. As soon as the tides would permit we hoisted anchor and steamed out into the gulf and down to the mouth of the Caloosahatchee River. The *Fashion* was anchored at this point (Punta Rassa) and put in charge of some watchmen. The crew of the steamer, with the captain in command, lowered their ship's boat, and taking all the passengers on board, myself included, rowed us up the river twenty miles to Fort Meyers, the first sizable post along the river. The forests extended all the way on both banks, with very few openings.

It was night when we reached the post, — a beautiful summer night it seemed to me. The post was well laid out and the quarters for the officers proved very comfortable. I hastened to find General Harney. He had been described to me as a tall, handsome man, often very severe in his style and hard to approach. He was sitting by his table in a sort of basement office reading a paper. He looked up as I entered the door of his room, rose and gave me a hearty welcome. So cordial was his manner that I felt I had been misinformed.

"Why, Mr. Howard," he said, "I have long wanted an ordnance officer, and I am glad you have come! Take a seat and make yourself at home." I did so and found him companionable, remarkably so considering the difference in rank between a brigadier-general and a lieutenant. But in a few minutes a sack of mail-matter was brought in and emptied on his large table. He put on his glasses and began to examine the mail. Something in a letter from Washington displeased him; he at once became excited and angry, and his rough language corresponded to the heat of his passion. I was glad to make some excuse and retire from his presence. I saw then that Harney in quiet social life was one person, but quite another when official matters ruffled his temper. Harney was as handsome as Joe Hooker and as tall as General Scott; genial as a friend in ordinary intercourse, but terrible as an enemy and often unreasonable as a commander.

Here at Fort Meyers on my first visit I found a camp, or rather a bivouac, of Seminoles who had been captured. At this season of the year, January, the climate was exceedingly mild, except when a "Norther" swept in upon the fort. During my stay there was a strong cold wind, sometimes accompanied by rain, which affected our soldiers quite as much as a sudden snowstorm would in Ohio or Illinois. They made great fires near their posts when permitted, and stood shivering around them with their blankets over their shoulders much after the Indian fashion. The Indians, however, though excited by the storm and very noisy when they could get anything stronger than water to drink, appeared less disturbed than our people by the sudden changes of climate.

They had for an interpreter a half-breed usually called "Natto," or "Natto Joe." One peculiarity of Natto was that in his talk he made no distinction whatever of sex. When speaking of a woman he always said "he" and "him," and he was very brief in his English utterance. For example, be it of man or woman, he would say: "He lib Eberglade, big lake!" meaning that he or she lived in the Everglades near the big lake. One day he ran down to the office of the commander of the fort and cried, in plaintive tones: "He scream! He all over drunk! He scratch and bite! Natto Joe 'fraid!" The interpretation is that one of the women was intoxicated, and she was screaming, scratching, and biting so that Natto Joe was afraid of her. Somehow this woman had gotten into her possession a bottle of commissary whisky and was making a great ado, so that the surrounding woods resounded with her wild complaints. Nothing ever appeared so dreadful to me or half so plaintive as the cries of a drunken Indian, and of course the woman's savage shrieks in a high key were even more wild and piercing.

DOLLS, MALE AND FEMALE, OF VARIOUS TRIBES; DOLL WARRIORS, TOYS, ETC.

*For Description see page 14*

PHOTOGRAPHED AND PAINTED FROM THE ORIGINAL OBJECTS EXPRESSLY FOR THIS WORK.

Fort Meyers was indeed nothing but a military post, with roughly-constructed quarters for men and officers, and a few log buildings for storehouses. By much practice the soldiers had learned to make these rough structures very presentable and comfortable. With axe and saw they cut out the material from the neighboring forests, brought it together and made their shanties, often beginning and completing a post in a single week. This post as I looked at it the day after my arrival was very pleasant; it was carefully arranged and had an abundance of ornamental trees and shrubs. The oleanders were especially beautiful. They were sizable trees, and later, on my second visit, were in full bloom.

I met here for the first time several officers who later became very prominent in our nation's history. For example, Captain Winfield Scott Hancock was the depot quartermaster; Captain W. W. Burns, who as brigadier-general commanded Baker's Brigade after the terrible battle of Ball's Bluff, was the post commissary; and Captain Alfred Pleasanton, who at Gettysburg commanded our cavalry, was then acting as Harney's assistant adjutant-general. Here, too, was Captain R. B. Marcy of the Fifth Infantry, who became a major-general, and was General George B. McClellan's father-in-law. He was very fond of the ordnance department and often invited me to his quarters to talk about the different arms of the service. Just then he was ambitious to become paymaster with the rank of major.

I remember, too, Captain Stevenson of the Fifth

Infantry, a man always very attentive to the interests of his company, working out his discipline through the boasted efficiency of his first sergeant. The real governor of a company in those days was the orderly sergeant. Matters came by appeal from him to the captain, and the captain usually sustained the rough discipline of his sergeant. Captain Dolph de Russy of the Fourth Artillery commanded a company of that arm, that is, nominally artillery, but really what the soldiers then called "Red-legged Infantry."

Quite early in the morning, the day after I had reported, I was notified that General Harney was going up to Tampa Bay, and that, with other officers designated, I was to accompany him. I have a very distinct recollection of the party after it assembled on board a large rowboat at the river wharf. Harney sat in the stern and proposed to steer the boat. By his side on the left was Dr. McFarland, an army surgeon, already nearly old enough for retirement, and a great personal friend of the general. To his right, at arm's length from him, sat Captain Pleasanton, who had a very handsome face, but was demure and reserved; he seldom spoke to anybody, having at the time an unhappy look upon his face as if he were discontented with his situation. I was shown a seat opposite Pleasanton. Two clerks went along to take care of all papers and accounts at headquarters. They, with the oarsmen, completed the little company.

There were three oarsmen on a side. The boat had a mast and rigging for a sail to be used should the weather favor us. When we were ready to start the soldiers acting as sailors fixed their oars in the locks and began to row. The boat shot out from the dock and was moving smoothly down the river, when suddenly one of the oarsmen locked his oar with another. Harney ordered him to be careful, but his oar caught a second time and a third, causing the boat to whirl around in spite of the rudder. General Harney then became white with anger, stood up, seized a boat-hook near at hand, and struck at the soldier. The man avoided the blow and sought protection behind the mast. He put his face round one side of the mast and jeered at the general, saying: "Oh, no, you wouldn't! No, you wouldn't!" laughing wildly as he did so.

All except Harney saw at once that the soldier was delirious and did not realize what he was doing. The general's anger waxed hotter and hotter as he tried in vain to strike the delinquent oarsman. At last the doctor seized his hand and begged him to sit down, telling him that the soldier was insane. Instantly the general's anger turned upon the quartermaster. It was fortunate for Hancock that he was not present. "A fine quartermaster!" exclaimed Harney with some harder expressions, "to send me such a boatman!"

Another oarsman was substituted for the crazy soldier and the boat moved with speed quietly down the river. As General Harney's face recovered its usual expression, he said: "I wouldn't hurt the lad; the crazy fellow probably thought I wanted to kill him." Very soon after that, as we were gliding along with forests on the right and on the left, we saw an opening like a glade near the right bank of the river. "It was in that neighborhood," said Harney, "that I got caught by those harum-scarum Indians and had to escape in my night clothes." The whole story, well told by Harney, interested me deeply. The facts are given substantially in an official report by Lieutenant Griffin as follows:

"It becomes my painful duty to inform you of the assassination of the greater part of Lieutenant-Colonel Harney's detachment by the Indians on the morning of the 23d (about 1840), on the Caloosahatchee River, where they had gone in accordance with the treaty at Fort King to establish a trading-house. The party consisted of about twenty-eight men armed with rifles; they were encamped on the river, but unprotected by defense of any kind, and, it is said, without sentinels. The Indians in large force made the attack before the dawn of day and before reveille, and it is supposed that thirteen of the men were killed, among whom were Major Dalham and Mr. Morgan, sutlers. The remainder, with Colonel Harney, escaped, several of them severely wounded. It was a complete surprise."

In this encounter the Indians killed ten men belonging to the military service, and eight more citizens employed by the sutlers. Colonel Harney and fourteen others succeeded in making their escape, though the colonel, as he said, made off in his night clothing without waiting for coat or trousers.

In that encounter the Indians obtained fourteen rifles, six carbines, some three or four kegs of powder, and about three thousand dollars' worth of goods. Lieutenant Hanson, commanding at the time, on receipt of the order quickly captured some thirty Indians while visiting his camp, and sent them immediately to Charleston, South Carolina. From Charleston they were carried off to the far West to join the other Seminoles and Creeks upon their reservation beyond the Mississippi.

This incident occurred in a previous Indian war when Osceola was in his prime. Harney was then only a lieutenant-colonel. He had, since the Mexican War, become a brigadier-general and a department commander. He owned in his story that the Indians had surprised him, but stoutly averred that they never did it again and never could.

## CHAPTER IV.

### CAMPAIGNING AGAINST THE SEMINOLES—INCIDENTS AND EXPERIENCES OF MY ARMY LIFE IN FLORIDA.

Breakfasting with General Harney — "Mr. Howard, you will be my Chief of Ordnance" — Becoming Accustomed to my Surroundings — A Pleasant Resort — Mustering Volunteers into Service — General Harney Relieved from Command — "We Haven't Lost any Indians" — Dislike of the Regulars for Indian Service — Chasing Indians from Place to Place — Seeking Peace — Ordered to Find "Billy Bowlegs" — A Journey into the Interior — New and Fresh Experiences — A Nap Better than a Toddy — Great Stature of the Seminoles — Their Physical Superiority over other Indians — Seminole Women — Making a "Good Peace."

LATE in the afternoon of the same day we found the steamer *Fashion* at anchor near the mouth of the river, and we were soon on board and made comfortable for the night. During the evening not much was said concerning the military situation, or of an official character. Harney and the doctor played at draughts while the remainder of the party looked on, much interested in the game. The moon was shining and the evening was delightful, for all that night the bay was as smooth as a mill-pond, and the temperature so moderate that I was reluctant to leave the deck for my berth.

The next morning General Harney had us all at breakfast with him, and told us many stories of the Florida Indians, especially of battles I have alluded to, besides those he knew of, fought by Worth and Taylor. He informed me that for the present campaign he was to have some ten companies of volunteers, all mounted. They were to come from Georgia and Alabama and from different parts of Florida. Turning suddenly to me he said: "Mr. Howard, it is well you are here. You will be my chief of ordnance. You must get muskets for the volunteers, their equipments and ammunition, and make the issues. The regulars stationed all about are already fairly well supplied." I assured the general that I was glad to be of use and would attend as well as I could to the duties of my department.

As soon as we had worked our way up to the landing near Fort Brooke all went ashore. Fort Brooke was then the headquarters of the Department of Florida. The buildings, though roughly constructed, were very presentable. Live oaks, with their widespreading branches, covered much of the ground, and the officers' quarters, stretched along by the shore of the bay, were nicely fenced. The buildings, thoroughly whitewashed, were relieved by the verdure of tropical plants and shrubbery. There were numerous shell walks, one of which ran the whole length of the reservation.

About a quarter of a mile from the rest of the garrison, in the southeast corner of the reservation, was a large frame building made of rough boards, at that time without paint or whitewash. It was propped up some six or eight feet from the ground on piles. This was the arsenal, and near it was a small building for an office. An ordnance sergeant, who had already seen considerable service on the plains, was in charge, and appeared pleased enough to have me assume command, and glad to become my factotum. I soon became accustomed to my surroundings and in time made my corner a pleasant resort for officers of the garrison and citizens of the village.

The volunteers were soon mustered into service and I issued to them their supplies. It was not long before the dissatisfaction which existed between General Harney and the Secretary of War culminated in his being relieved from command of the department. He had laid out his work well, occupied forts on both coasts, and some important points like Fort Myers and Fort Kissimmee in the interior, and was preparing to give on the one hand a fair protection to white settlements, and on the other to make aggressive movements against the Indians who were raiding the country and doing mischief; but for some unexplained reason he was not in favor in the War Office. The senior colonel, L. L. Loomis, of the Fifth Infantry, was placed in charge. It was a delightful change to me, as he took much interest in his young ordnance officer, and used me in many another capacity on his personal staff.

During my year with him I do not recall an important engagement between the Indians and the regular troops. The regulars disliked the Indian service, and the officers would often say, "We haven't lost any Indians." But the volunteers were very active. They had good captains and lieutenants, but the rank and file were made up for the most part from the roughest white population of the South. Sometimes orders did not restrain them; they chased the Indians from place to place and shot them down mercilessly, men, women, and children — taking very few prisoners.

At last Colonel Loomis, much grieved at the severity of this active campaigning, made up his mind to seek peace with the Indians without waiting for them to sue for it. So one day in June he sent for me and said he wanted me to go as a "peace commissioner" to the Indians in the Everglades, or in any other place where I could find them, and explain to them how easy and advantageous it would be for them to submit to the government and end the war. If possible, I was to find Chief Billy Bowlegs and use all the influence I could with him to induce him to take his tribe and join the remainder of his people in the West.

I undertook the mission, first going to Fort Myers and getting the interpreter, Natto Joe, and the woman with her child, who was still detained at that post. This I did as quickly as possible. The woman in her miserable condition, poorly clad, wrapped in an army blanket, looked as if she were beyond middle age, but her little child, who was perhaps five years old, with a comfortable gown and two or three necklaces of blue beads, had a healthy look and was really pretty. She would, however, shake her hair over her face and act as shy and wild as a young bronco. When white men were about she generally clung to her mother's skirt, endeavoring to hide herself in its folds.

With some difficulty Natto and I took this pair with us to Fort Deynaud far up the Caloosahatchee. There we found Captain Brown with two companies of the Second Artillery. Lieutenant S. D. Lee, a classmate of mine at West Point, who in the Civil War became a lieutenant-general in the Confederate Army, was in command of one of the companies. Captain Brown, leaving but a small guard behind, took with him his two companies, and wagons with supplies for a ten days' trip, and escorted me and my charge into the interior. We took the direction of Lake Okeechobee.

Lieutenant Lee and I were close friends and we had an enjoyable expedition. The forests through which we made our way, often being obliged to change paths into passable roadways, the sweet open glades near which we encamped for the night, and the easy marches of every day, I have never forgotten. All this experience was new and fresh to me, and everything in tropical nature filled me with an enthusiasm which much amused my companion. At any brief halt while *en route* I found a nap of twenty or thirty minutes better than any other refreshment; and here was begun my habit of taking short sleeps in the midst of active campaigning. Lee once said: "Howard thinks a nap better than a toddy," and so indeed in time it proved to be.

On arriving at Lake Okeechobee a wonderful transformation took place in our Seminole woman. She bathed herself and her child; she managed to repair her clothing, and combed the tangles out of her matted hair. Digging some roots that had a saponaceous juice she powdered them and soaked them in water, washing her hair with the lathery substance till it was smooth and glossy. She found different ways to beautify her child, and, indeed, one would not take the mother, after her toilet had been completed, to be more than twenty-five. From a haggard old squaw she had been transformed into a good-looking young Indian woman. She promised us so faithfully that she would bring us into communication with her people that with some reluctance I gave her instructions and let her go.

Natto was afraid to accompany her. He had been too long and too evidently a friend of the white man. He said: "He, Indian kill me. I no go!" I hoped almost against hope that Mattie, as we called the Indian woman, would prove true and bring about a meeting with the nearest tribe, but I was to be disappointed. I could not get an interview with any chief. My mission was, to all appearances, a failure. Still, it is probable that the news the woman carried brought about before many months the peace which was secured by Colonel Loomis and his men soon after I left his department — a peace which has lasted without interruption from that time until today.

On our return, not far from Lake Okeechobee, while we were crossing a long stretch of meadow land which the daily showers had refreshed and brightened, I witnessed for the first time a wonderful mirage. Lee and I were riding some distance from the command. Suddenly we saw what appeared to be the whole command — soldiers, ambulances, and army wagons, lifted high in air and moving along with regularity amid the clouds in the sky. Such a mirage was more familiar to officers and soldiers who had served on the plains, but it was a startling sight to my vision. It was a complete illusion. My companion and I rode on toward the point where we supposed Captain Brown and his men were marching and had apparently come quite near them before the vision disappeared.

My impressions of the characteristics of the Seminoles are that they differ in many respects from all other Indian tribes with which I am acquainted. Generally the men averaged from five feet ten to six feet in height. Even Natto Joe, a half-breed, was five feet and eleven in his stockings. The Indians of one of the bands, called by some writers "the Tiger clan," were larger than any other, and were, as a rule, very dark. They had small hands and feet, but were nevertheless strong and muscular in their limbs. Their foreheads were as broad and high as those of the white men, and their heads generally as large. I never saw a Seminole who had eyes so full and open as the Sioux or Apaches; they were intensely black, and, like windows under a cornice, had their own peculiar appearance and outlook. Their teeth were very even, faces square-cut, and their other features hardly differed from the European type.

In common with all Indians the Seminoles possessed great physical endurance, which was never wanting, except in infancy and extreme age. Clay MacCauley gives an instance of this. He says: "Even among the children this physical superiority is seen. One morning Ko-i-hat-co's son, a tall, slender boy not quite twelve years old, shouldered a heavy Kentucky rifle, left our camp and followed in his father's long footsteps for a day's hunt.

After tramping all day, at sunset he reappeared in camp, carrying slung across his shoulder, in addition to rifle and accoutrements, a deer weighing perhaps fifty pounds, a weight he had borne for miles. The same boy in one day went with some older friends to his permanent home twenty miles away and returned."

The Seminole women that I met were, as a rule, taller than the Apache women, but seemed comparatively short on account of the prevailing height of the men. I do not know that any Indian women were finer-looking or more shapely in their figures than these unless it were the Nez Percés. By strangers, especially white men, these women, with their wild and fierce look, were often thought repulsive; but all the repulsiveness disappeared when they met those who neither feared nor hated them.

Usually the Seminole warrior managed to have on something approximating the dress of his tribe, — leggings of flannel, a single shirt, the usual breech-clout, and a peculiar headgear like a low-crowned hat, indeed, a turban three or four inches wide made by winding a comforter or thin shawl several times around the head. The first time I saw Natto Joe, the half-breed, I noticed that he had one or two red handkerchiefs so tied about his neck as to make a hammock-shaped pocket. Every male Indian had one or more of these handkerchiefs, and sometimes several, always in gay colors. They were intended as choice ornaments of distinction, and were used by them for pockets. Of course, like every Indian, the Seminole wore a belt about his waist into which he thrust his implements for the chase and war.

The men had a strange style of wearing their hair. A strip extended over the head and ended in a braid or two behind the neck, and another narrow border of hair was left just above the forehead — all the rest being cut close.

There was nothing very remarkable in the women's attire. They always had one long skirt fastened around the waist, and an upper garment to meet it, covering the breast and shoulders. The material was light and cheap, usually of *manta* (bleached or unbleached cotton). The wearing of beads — many strings of them — gave distinction. They wore no shoes or moccasins. The smaller children had no clothing; and, like Mattie's child, the larger ones would have a single garment like a shirt cut low in the neck.

At my rough arsenal I soon had all the arms, equipments, and ammunition necessary for the troops, both volunteers and regulars. Major Page, the permanent adjutant-general of the department, came and mustered in man by man, with his horse, saddle, bridle, and blanket, and I issued the remainder of his outfit for field service, holding each volunteer captain responsible for his company. Colonel Loomis kept his command constantly in motion, and, as far as he could, had his men capture rather than kill the Indians, for whom he had great pity. The prisoners were placed in camps and guarded.

I have always considered the Seminoles intellectually superior to most Indians, and I understand that in the Indian Territory they proved capable of attaining to a high order of civilization.

After my return to West Point in the fall of 1857 I learned with much satisfaction that Colonel Loomis had succeeded in bringing in Chief Billy Bowlegs to Fort Meyers, had also made a "good peace," and that all but a small fragment of the Seminole tribe had been sent to their friends west of the Mississippi.

# CHAPTER V.

## SKETCH OF MY MILITARY CAREER DURING THE CIVIL WAR — ATTITUDE OF OUR WILD INDIANS DURING THAT PERIOD.

**On Duty at West Point as Instructor in Mathematics — A Congenial Position — Thoughts of Entering the Gospel Ministry — Fall of Fort Sumter — Opening of the Civil War — Solving Some Personal Problems — I Become Colonel of a Maine Regiment — Rapid Promotion — Active Military Service — Restless and Troublesome Indians — Condition of Affairs in the Indian Territory — Recruiting Indians for the Confederate Army — An Important Treaty — Effect of the Civil War on the Indian Question.**

AFTER my brief Indian campaign in Florida I was on duty at the Military Academy as instructor in mathematics until the spring of 1861. Having then a position suited to my taste, that of assistant professor, with the pay of a captain in the army, and more comfortable quarters than my rank had previously enabled me to enjoy, every consideration of personal interest for myself and my growing family would have induced me to remain at West Point. There was still another consideration favoring my continuance there. It was an expectation on my part soon to leave the service and enter the Gospel ministry. But just after the fall of Fort Sumter a dispatch was received from Augusta, Maine, proposing to me, if elected, to take command of a regiment, — the first from the state, for three years or for the war. Then immediately I faced and solved both problems and decided that it was my duty favorably to answer the call from Maine.

Having become the colonel of that regiment, I commanded it and three others, as a brigade, in the first battle of Bull Run. Soon after, in September, 1861, I became a brigadier-general of volunteers, and, with the exception of two months and twenty-two days absence occasioned by my wounds, commanded a brigade under General Sumner in all McClellan's operations until the battle of Antietam. There on the field I took General Sedgwick's place after he was wounded, and held his division through the subsequent battles till the end of the year 1862.

In April, 1863, the President assigned me, now a major-general of volunteers, to command the Eleventh Army Corps. This command I held through the battles of Chancellorsville and Gettysburg, and then, transferred to the West, in Lookout Valley, Lookout Mountain, Missionary Ridge, and the march to Knoxville. My first experiences in the West were under General U. S. Grant, who then conducted all the affairs of a large military division. When General Grant was ordered to Washington, in the spring of 1864, General Sherman took his place in the military division, and I was sent to Loudon, east Tennessee, to take command of the Fourth Army Corps, then a part of the Army of the Cumberland, under General George H. Thomas. This corps was at that time twenty thousand strong. This command was mine during General Sherman's campaign from Chattanooga to Atlanta; a campaign which comprised, while I was with the Fourth Corps, thirteen battles, ending with what has recently been named "The Battle of Atlanta," in which, on the 22d of July, 1864, the young and well-beloved McPherson was slain.

On the 26th of that month President Lincoln assigned me to McPherson's place to command the Army and Department of the Tennessee. I had a portion of it, the Fifteenth, Sixteenth, and Seventeenth Corps, in round numbers about thirty-three thousand, on the active line from that day forward. It constituted General Sherman's right wing in the March to the Sea and through the Carolinas, ending with the battle of Bentonville, North Carolina, March 19 and 20, 1865.

We made a rapid march, averaging about twenty-five miles a day, from Raleigh to Richmond, Virginia, — a march that was begun just after the announcement of the assassination of Abraham Lincoln. On arriving at Richmond I received a dispatch from General Grant, then in Washington, instructing me to let my army march overland in charge of my staff officers, while I should come by water as quickly as possible and report in person to the Secretary of War. This I did; and on the 12th of May I was assigned to the new duty of Commissioner of Freedmen and Refugees, — a new bureau in the War Department.

This brief sketch is a skeleton of my military career during the four years of the Civil War, and indicates why I was not more directly cognizant of Indian affairs during that stirring period.

The Indians, however, all this time were very

restless and made constant trouble, and several officers left my side to participate in operations necessary to hold them in check. Some of the Indians were on reservations and some were not, and they represented every phase of civilization. "Some in naked savage bands, adorned with paint and feathers, armed with the tomahawk and scalping knife, roamed the wilderness. Others, differing from the planter or farmer only in their complexion, possessed cultivated lands, flocks, and herds."

The Seminoles, Cherokees, Chickasaws, and Choctaws dwelt in what was called the Indian Territory proper, a country west of Arkansas and north of Texas. At the opening of the Civil War it was, as a rule, under the supervision of officials who sympathized with secession. This was unfortunate for the United States government, for with little inducement these officials and agents broke up connection with the United States and offered allegiance to the southern Confederacy. Of course, when Mr. Lincoln came in, the superintendent and agents who had not kept faith with us were removed from office and other men were put in their places, but the new appointees were unable to reach their posts of duty, so that great confusion prevailed.

To aggravate matters still further, the old Indian superintendent and many of the agents, joining interests with the southern army, stirred up the Indians till they began to commit acts of hostility. These men justified themselves by claiming that they were acting under authority of the government of the Confederate States. About this time a treaty with the Choctaws was ratified by the Confederate Congress, under which delegates from that nation had the right to sit in Congress. Two full regiments of Indians were organized and attached to the Confederate army, and a third was made ready during the first year of the war. This constituted an Indian Confederate brigade.

It is only just to the Indians to say that they could not hear from President Lincoln's administration. They witnessed the surrender of United States army posts in their neighborhood and the departure of government troops, and were uncertain as to what their allegiance ought to be under these new and trying circumstances. The celebrated John Ross, chief of the Cherokees, resisted the hostile action of his people as long as he could and issued a proclamation. The instrument ended thus:

"For these reasons I earnestly urge on the Cherokee people the importance of non-interference with the people of the states, and the observance of unswerving neutrality between them; trusting that God will not only keep from our own borders the desolation of war, but that He will in His infinite mercy and honor stay its ravages among the brotherhood of states."

Ross was overborne. It is said that his wife was more staunch than her husband and held out till the last. When an attempt was made to raise a Confederate flag over the Indian council house her opposition was so spirited that it prevented the completion of the design. However, the Indians that I have mentioned fell into line and gave their sympathy and positive help to the cause of the Confederacy.

When the war was over the Choctaws and other tribes within the Indian Territory, who had gone against the United States, made special effort to regain their position. Having been forced from their homes and their lands by the operation of war, or by the action of government agents, they now desired to return. They had taken up arms and thereby forfeited all rights and privileges which had been theirs under their treaties before the war; but the administration decided to act with clemency toward them, feeling confident that this clemency would not be misunderstood but would result in future good conduct on the part of the Indians.

During President Johnson's administration an important commission was appointed, upon which was the Commissioner of Indian Affairs, the superintendent of Indians for the southwest, General Ely Parker, a full-blooded Indian who had served on General Grant's staff. With him were Generals Herron and Harney of the United States Army. They met at Forth Smith, Arkansas, in September, 1865, and made a treaty with the Cherokees, Creeks, Choctaws, Chickasaws, Osages, Seminoles, Senecas, Shawnees, and Quapaws. Some extracts from this treaty are of special interest to the lovers of our Union. For example:

"Whereas the aforesaid nations and tribes, or bands of Indians, or portions thereof, were induced by the machinations of the emissaries of the so-called Confederate States to throw off their allegiance to the Government of the United States and to enter into treaty stipulations with said so-called Confederate States, whereby they had made themselves liable to a forfeiture of all rights of every kind, character, and description which had been promised and guaranteed to them by the United States; and whereas, the Government of the United States has maintained its supremacy and authority within its limits; and whereas, it is the desire of the Government to act with magnanimity with all parties, deserving its clemency, and to re-establish order and legitimate authority among the Indian tribes; and whereas, the undersigned representatives or parties connected with said nations and tribes of Indians have become satisfied that it is for the general good of the people to reunite with and be restored to the relations which formerly existed; . . . The Undersigned do hereby acknowledge themselves to be under the protection of the United States of America, and covenant and agree that hereafter they will in all things recognize the Government of the United States as exercising exclusive jurisdiction over them, and will not enter into any allegiance or conventional agreement with any State, Nation, power or sovereignty whatsoever; and that any treaty or allegiance for the cession of lands, or any act heretofore done by them or any of their people, by which they renounced their allegiance to the United States, is hereby revoked and repudiated."

The government promised to afford ample protection to all persons and property of the nations and tribes within the Indian Territory. It also declared its willingness to enter into treaties to arrange and settle all vexatious questions that might arise in consequence of their part in the rebellion.

Besides this treaty another was signed by the commissioners and the Choctaws and Chickasaws, which provided for something more than peace and friendship. The Indians promised therein to exert all their influence to compel the Indians of the Plains to maintain peaceful relations with each other, with the Indians of the Territory, and with the United States. They agreed further that slavery should be abolished forever, that the freedmen should be suitably provided for, that lands should be issued to the Indians of Kansas and elsewhere, that the right of way should be granted to railroads, and that a consolidation of Indian tribes with a territorial form of government should be recommended by them to their respective councils.

In view of this treaty, which has been more or less faithfully kept, it would seem that the Civil War resulted in the United States gaining a better control over the Indians, and the Territorial tribes were saved from outside annoyance by the Indians of the Plains.

In 1862 it will be remembered General Pope came to the East, and for a while commanded an independent force sent out directly from the District of Columbia and vicinity to meet and hold in check General Lee's Confederate army while McClellan changed his base from the James River to Washington, bringing up from the peninsula the Army of the Potomac as a support to Pope's forces. Pope's last engagement was the second battle of Bull Run, which ended in his defeat.

After an enforced vacation on account of my wounds my first active engagement was near the close of this battle. I was in command of a brigade, and was required to make a reconnaissance from Centreville to ascertain if Lee's forces were still present, or if they had withdrawn from our front.

The night after this movement we began a retreat in different columns. General Sully, with myself, commanded the rear guard of one of those columns, and we had a bloody experience. I found Sully in action an admirable commander; cool, clear-headed, and full of expedients. This retreat had hardly been completed when General Pope and, somewhat later, General Sully also, was hurried off to the Northwest to meet and withstand a fearful onslaught of Indians, which was reported to have taken place on the western borders of Minnesota.

# CHAPTER VI.

## GREAT UPRISING OF HOSTILE INDIANS IN THE NORTHWEST — THE TERRIBLE SIOUX MASSACRE IN MINNESOTA.

Trouble with the Indians on the Border — Uneasy Savages of the Northwest — Threatened Outbreak of the Sioux — Red Iron's Eloquent Speech — The Great Uprising — The Crafty and Notorious Chief Little Crow — A Reign of Terror, Murder, Rapine, and Pillage — Indiscriminate Slaughter of White Men, Women, and Children — Settlers Banding Together for Defense — A Resolute White Leader — A Fearful Onslaught — Bloody Campaign Against the Sioux — Defeat of Little Crow — Trial of Five Hundred Hostile Indians — Execution of Thirty-eight of them upon One Scaffold — Where and How They Were Buried — Death of Little Crow — Indians as Soldiers in the Union Army.

THE great uprising of the Sioux in 1862 is now almost forgotten, and this is doubtless due to the fact that it occurred at a time when the North and South were engaged in deadly strife. The trouble with the Indians on the border, particularly in Minnesota, culminated about the time of the second battle of Bull Run, in August, 1862. About this time several large tracts of land were purchased from the Indians. The agents and traders took advantage of this, and large quantities of goods were sold at enormous prices to the irritated Indians, who speedily showed their dissatisfaction. Councils were held, at one of which Red Iron, an influential old chief, said:

*"Council, we will receive our next annuity,

* From the *New York Sun*, March 17, 1901, and copied by it from the *Chicago Record*.

but we will sign no papers for anything else. The snow is on the ground, and we have been waiting a long time to get our money. We are poor; white Father has plenty. His fires are warm; his tepees keep out the cold. We have nothing to eat. We have been waiting a long time for our money. Our hunting season is past. A great many of our people are sick for being hungry. We may die because you will not pay us; we may die, but if we do we will leave our bones on the ground where our great Father may see where his Dakota children died. We are very poor. We have sold our hunting grounds and the graves of our fathers. We have sold our own graves. We have no place to bury our dead, and you will not pay us the money for our lands."

For making this eloquent and pathetic speech Red Iron was locked up in the guardhouse for twenty-four hours. The Indians, led by Lion Bear, departed sullenly from the council. Lion Bear was a large, sinewy, resolute man and of great influence with his people. When Red Iron was imprisoned Lion Bear made the following speech:

"Dakotas, the big men are here; they have got Red Iron in a pen like a wolf. They mean to kill him for saying the big men cheat us out of our lands and the money the great Father has sent us. Dakotas, must we starve like buffaloes in the snow? Shall we let our blood freeze like the little stream? Or shall we make the snow red with the blood of the white braves? Dakotas, the blood of your fathers talks to you from the graves where we stand. Their spirits come up into your arms and

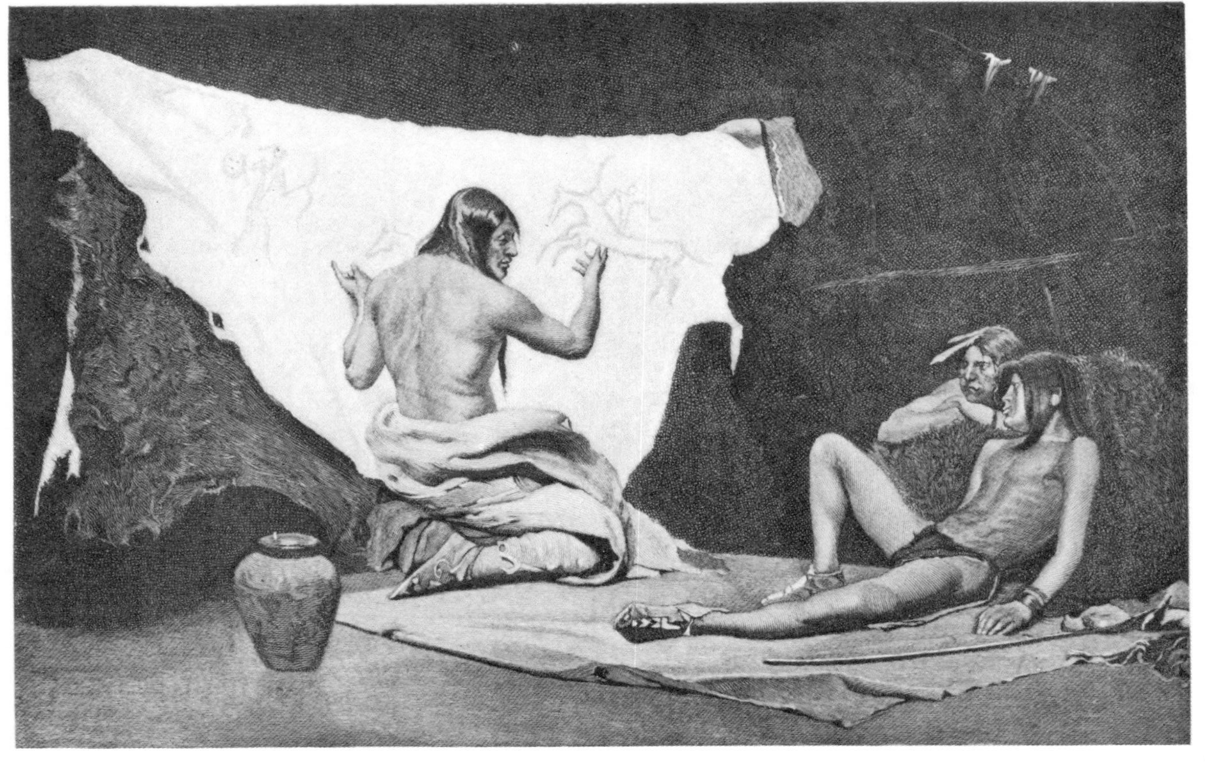

AN INDIAN ARTIST AT WORK IN HIS LODGE PAINTING A BUFFALO ROBE.

make them strong. Tonight the blood of the white man shall run like water in the rain, and Red Iron shall be with his people. Dakotas, when the moon goes down behind the hills be ready, and I will lead you against the long knives and the big men who have come to cheat us and take away our lands and put us in a pen for not helping to rob our women and children."

But Red Iron was released, and the outbreak for a time was prevented. The trouble with the Indians continued, however, and their sufferings during the winter and spring were intense. Some 1,500 of the old men, women, and children died of exposure, and those who survived were obliged to eat their horses and dogs. The dissatisfaction thus engendered was fearfully augmented by the failure of the government to make the annual payment which had before taken place in June, and by the traders refusing any more credit.

In the South the Union army had met with reverses, and rumors of disastrous battles reached the Indians. Their faith in the great Father was shaken. Exaggerated stories were told by the half-breeds and others interested in stirring up strife. The enlistment of all the young men on the frontier, of all the government employees not absolutely necessary, and of half-breeds, strengthened the Indians' belief that the great Father was in desperate straits.

The head chief of the band of Sioux located there was Little Crow. He had been in Washington, was an Indian of unusual intelligence and highly skilled in the art of savage warfare.

The outbreak came on August 15, 1862, when four young braves left Little Crow's village, near Redwood, Minnesota, to go hunting. They became intoxicated on whisky sold them by a white man, and then, as drunken men do, they had a dispute with each other as to which was the bravest. At last they determined to put the matter beyond controversy by killing white men. Once started on their murderous errand they killed whole families and plundered their homes. The excitement and terror among the white people was intense; the Indians were pursued and fled back to their village, where they swarmed about Little Crow's tepee.

Previously to this, Little Crow, seeing how much our garrisons had been weakened to supply the wants of the Civil War, had carefully planned a hostile rising on the part of his Indians with a view to pillage and the driving back of new settlements. He was waiting for further preparation and for promised allies from other Sioux bands, but seeing the storm already setting in, and expecting immediate retaliation for the murders committed, he determined to make an immediate move. In answer to his excited braves he said: "Trouble with the whites must come; it is here. It may as well take place now as later. I am with you. Let us go to the agency, kill the traders and take their goods."

With a force of about three hundred he pushed on to what was known as the Yellow Medicine Agency, situated in southwestern Minnesota not far from the border. Here was begun at once a terrible slaughter of men, women, and children. The agent himself, Mr. Galbraith, was away on a short leave of absence, but his family perished with the others in the outbreak.

As has been done so often, the commanding officer of Fort Ridgely, the nearest garrison, dispatched an inadequate force, only forty-five soldiers, and, as one would have expected, half of them were killed. The Indians, excited more and more by their great success, widened their sphere of operations, committed murders, killed unarmed and helpless citizens right and left, and dealt out to them the brutal treatment of savages. They swept away the settlers on their isolated farms, and robbed and outraged their women and children. The tales of suffering and woe are too bloody and sickening to be repeated. One writer says: "They practiced every species of atrocity which their fiendish natures prompted."

They did not reach the village of New Ulm until the 21st of August. It was the capital of Brown County, settled principally by Germans. Outside of the village they had plenty of victims, but their main attack upon New Ulm itself did not take place until the 23d of August, 1862. Judge Flandrau, a resolute man, highly honored on the frontier, had organized and armed a body of citizens. He succeeded in repulsing the attack, but the hostiles still hung around, closely besieging him and preparing to repeat the assault, when a detachment of regulars sent by General Sibley brought relief to the citizen garrison and scattered the assailants. Some two thousand women and children, who had escaped in great alarm from the settlements round about, had taken refuge at New Ulm, so that it was a place hard to defend for any length of time against an increase of the assailants. Fort Ridgely itself had been hemmed in for many days and had hard work to hold its own against repeated attacks of the Sioux. General Sibley therefore caused New Ulm to be abandoned. The women and children were sent to a place of safety, and the troops, as many as he could spare, were ordered to proceed under Lieutenant-Colonel McPhail to reinforce the garrison and the fort.

The cunning hostiles, perceiving that General Sibley was on their trail, instantly changed direction, going northward, killing and robbing as they went. They, in part, crossed the Minnesota border and began a siege against Fort Abercromby in Dakota. The 3d of September a hundred and fifty others suddenly showed themselves as far north as Cedar City in the center of Minnesota, and actually attacked the company of volunteers there. So furious was their onslaught that they drove them back as far as Hutchinson, while another band of hostiles rushed upon Forest City, but found the citizens armed and organized and ready to meet them. This attack was quickly met and successfully resisted. A similar result occurred when the savages came upon Hutchinson. The citizens, now fully alive to their peril, drove them back from that village. The headquarters of the department at St. Paul was aroused. The able general, John Pope, assumed command, gathered all the troops of volunteers and regulars available in his vicinity, and sent them to the villages named and to every point of danger.

The hostile Indians soon discovered that they were met by superior numbers of soldiers who had been sent to take summary vengeance upon them, and they began to lose heart. Their enthusiasm for war, outrage, and pillage never did last very long. When their enemy was weak they were strong; but when they began to feel that his strength and ability for war was far greater than theirs, they ran to cover.

The hostile besieging force at Fort Abercromby made two severe attacks. The garrison repulsed both, the second with great loss to the Indians. Now the Indians from all directions were fleeing from Minnesota and soon crossed the western border. When our troops had once taken up the pursuit they did not stop for borders of states or for rivers. At Wood Lake, however, the 22d of September, the hostile bands, now pretty well concentrated, with their women and children, the whole under the command of Little Crow, were forced to a battle that they would gladly have avoided. It was sharp and decisive. The women and children and some of the men, with the chief himself, fled for shelter to the Yankton Sioux of Dakota. Five hundred Indians were taken prisoners.

During this outbreak blood flowed freely on the northwest frontier, and on every hand could be seen by day the smoke from the settlers' cabins, and at night the flames lit up the horizon. About 700 persons were massacred.

It is said that the military authorities tried by court-martial five hundred Indians who had participated in this massacre. Three hundred and three of them were sentenced to death. But President Lincoln, always lenient and hating the death penalty, allowed but thirty-eight to be executed.

These thirty-eight were hanged upon one scaffold at Mankato, Minn., February 26, 1863. The few days preceding the execution were spent in singing death songs and parting with relatives. On Wednesday each of the condemned was permitted to send for two or three relatives or friends. The Indians were fastened in pairs and chained to the floor. Their ages ranged from 16 to 70 years, although the majority were young men. All but three half-breeds were dressed in breech-clout, leggings, and blankets.

Early on Friday morning the irons were knocked off the condemned and their arms tied behind with cords at the elbows and at the wrists. At ten o'clock began the march to the scaffold. As they ascended the steps the death song was started, and when they had got upon the platform the noise of their deep, swelling voices was truly hideous. The ropes were adjusted about their necks, the white caps pulled down, and at a signal followed three slow but distinct taps on a drum. The rope holding the scaffold was cut by a man named Duly, whose family had been murdered.

The lifeless bodies were cut down, placed in four army wagons, and taken to a trench prepared for their reception. They were all deposited in one grave, thirty feet in length by twelve in width, and four feet deep. They were laid in the bottom, in two rows, with their feet together and their heads to the outside. They were simply covered with blankets and the earth thrown over them. There they lie to this day.

The others of the condemned, but not executed, were taken down the Mississippi to an island near Davenport, Iowa, where they were closely confined for a year. They were then taken to a reservation, and it is probable that not one of them lives today.

As soon as the excitement had died down and an investigation could be made, it was ascertained that the Minnesota Sioux engaged in this business did not exceed a thousand. Many of the Indians in Minnesota took no part in the conflict. The prompt defeat of the Indians at war, and the subsequent execution of thirty-eight of them, had a decided effect in restraining other bands of Sioux who were ready to help Little Crow clear out the troublesome and ever-increasing settlements of white men in their neighborhood. These operations postponed further danger to the citizens of Minnesota for another year.

In 1863 the Minnesota frontier was well guarded with a force of never less than two thousand. Little Crow was not so badly beaten that he did not make some experiments to regain what he had lost the year before, particularly the Indian hunting-grounds which had been abandoned to the returning settlers. While we were absorbed in watching the advance of Lee's army into Maryland and Pennsylvania and fighting the battle of Gettysburg, where the heaviest responsibility of my life came upon me, Little Crow's Indians in small bands were creeping within our far-off lines and succeeded in reaching the country about St. Paul. They would murder a settler's family and glide on, serpent-like, to strike another. At least thirty white persons had been killed and several friendly Indians massacred.

This remarkable raid of the savages throughout the State of Minnesota kept all the people in constant alarm. One can hardly imagine, in time of profound peace, the extraordinary ferment and general terror that then existed. Of course our military authorities were widely denounced in the newspapers of the northwest for inefficiency. General Sibley, however, knew what was going on, but could not well divide his forces against a handful of guerillas appearing here and there all over the state in such insignificant numbers. He was, however, waiting his opportunity to strike an effective blow.

Little Crow had visited other bands beside his own, and had gone twice to the British territory to secure allies. He did not have much success, and none beyond our borders. At last he gathered near Miniwakan, a salt lake five hundred miles northwest of St. Paul, a band of about five thousand Indians, this number including their women and children. He had the Minnesota tribes, and a thousand from the Yankton Sioux, and others. In June, General Sibley was already approaching the lake with three thousand soldiers. At the same time General Sully, who had spent half his military life in watching and fighting wild Indians, was making his way from Sioux City up the Missouri River, with a view to cut off the retreat should Sibley drive Little Crow and his band southward from their selected fighting ground near the lake.

While these expeditions were making their fatiguing marches and hoping for a decisive engagement Little Crow himself, taking one of his sons with him, had ventured across the lines, coming in almost as far as Hutchinson. One day he was seen by a settler by the name of Lamson, who managed to use the rifle in his hand so quickly that even the wily Indian could not anticipate the shot. Lamson knew that he had killed an Indian, but did not know for some weeks that it was the crafty and ruthless Little Crow.

One of Little Crow's sons immediately succeeded him in command of his accumulated band of warriors. The young man at first retreated rapidly before Sibley, who continued the pursuit. The 24th of July, however, the general came upon the Indians in force. This battle began, like many others, with an act of what we denominate treachery. An army surgeon approached the hostiles to meet a flag of truce which they had displayed. They instantly killed this officer and a sharp battle quickly followed. The Indians soon ran and were pursued for ten miles, experiencing a heavy loss in men and stores.

Again on the 26th of July, at Dead Buffalo Lake, the hostiles made a quick and unexpected effort to capture the horses and mules of the command, as they afterward did with me in the battle of Camas Meadow, Montana. Still, as Sibley's troops were ready, the Indians were successfully and promptly resisted, and many of them were slain.

On the 28th of July they were at Stony Lake and skirmished with our forces, experiencing again loss and defeat. Nevertheless, the young Indian commander showed great generalship in working his way across the Missouri River and putting a stop to further pursuit by Sibley's men.

On the 3d of September General Sully struck a large force of Indians, including Young Crow's, at White Stone Hill, a hundred and thirty miles above the mouth of the Little Cheyenne, and thirty below where they had crossed in front of Sibley. One of Sully's battles instantly occurred. It was a bloody one to both sides. Sully lost twenty soldiers killed and thirty-eight wounded; the Indians lost vastly more in numbers, leaving a hundred and fifty prisoners in Sully's hands. This battle, with the operations of 1863, delivered Minnesota from the great burden of Indian occupation and fear of further massacres.

The events narrated in this chapter indicate the serious trouble that the United States experienced during the trying period of the Civil War from the hostility of many Indian tribes along the border.

Referring again to the hostiles of the Indian Territory I may note that Indians were used on both sides in the Civil War. The loyal Indians of the Cherokee, Creek, and Seminole nations were organized into three regiments and put under the command of Colonel William A. Phillips of Kansas. "In all the operations in which they participated they acquitted themselves creditably and to the satisfaction of the Union commander in the Indian Territory." *

The three Confederate Indian regiments previously mentioned were commanded by General Albert Pike. They did not exceed three thousand five hundred men. They were engaged in the battle of Chusto Talasah, where Colonel Cooper, the Confederate leader, reported that about five hundred loyal Indians were killed and wounded. Their own loss, not given in the records, was considerable. These same Indians participated in the battle of Pea Ridge in March, 1862. They were accused of scalping our prisoners. General Pike was indignant on hearing the report, and after search found but one Union man scalped. To his credit be it said he issued an order condemning the barbarous practice in the strongest possible terms. Wiley Britton says: "They fought very well when they had an opportunity to take shelter behind trees and logs (in Indian fashion), but could not easily be brought to face artillery, and a single shell thrown at them was generally sufficient to demoralize them and put them to flight."

At a later day the Indians became used to artillery, and were as able to guard themselves against its ravages and to withstand a battery as other fighting men, that is, as soon as they understood the range and effectiveness of the guns.

---

* See Wiley Britton's "Battles & Leaders."

# CHAPTER VII.

## ASSIGNED TO DUTY AMONG THE BLOODTHIRSTY APACHES—MY ARRIVAL IN ARIZONA.

A New Field of Labor—"Grant's Peace Policy"—The Fierce and Murderous Apaches—A Roaming and Warlike Tribe—Cochise, the Notorious Apache Chief—An Elusive and Dangerous Foe—Their Sudden Descents on Scattered Settlements—Slaying Every White Man Far and Near—My Arrival at Fort Yuma—No Rain for Three Years—A Six-mule Ambulance—"Dismal Jeems"—An Extraordinary Driver—Comical Dignity of an Indian Chief—Vanished Pomp and Pride—Appearance of the Yumas—Arizona Sand Storms.

IN compliance with a request of President Lincoln, made a few days before his assassination and left with Hon. Edwin M. Stanton, the Secretary of War, I was detailed as Commissioner of the Bureau of Freedmen and Refugees. After my arrival in Washington I attended to the duties of this bureau from early in May until the spring of 1874. But in 1872 there was an interval of nearly a year in which General Eliphalet Whittlesey discharged the duties of the bureau for me and in my name, while I was away, by President Grant's order, in another field of labor.

My work concerned what was called "General Grant's Policy with the Indians," and came about in this way: Before this time the Indian management, in its dealings with the Indians all through the country even to its remote corners, had acquired a reputation not at all to be desired. Extravagance, deception, extortion, cruelty, and all

Iron Mountain's Camp.

Hand Shaker's Camp.

TYPICAL WILD INDIAN CAMPS.—COMANCHE.

sorts of crimes were here and there imputed, and charged up by the public press and by writers of books against Indian agents and employees.

Such was the case when General U. S. Grant became President. He placed at the head of the bureau a full-blooded Indian, General Ely Parker, who had been during the Civil War an intelligent and efficient member of his staff. He next asked the representative societies of all the churches of the land to correspond with the bureau and recommend new agents and other employees. A distribution of the agencies was then made among these several societies. Many were reserved to the Roman Catholics, some assigned to the Methodists, some to the Episcopalians, some to the Presbyterians, some to the Baptists, Lutherans, and other denominations. This arrangement was called "Grant's Indian Policy." A little later it was termed "Grant's Peace Policy." It was not long before a peace, nominal at least, was effected with nearly all the Indians throughout the country.

Omitting some little difficulties between the whites and Indians in New Mexico and Arizona, we may say that the "Peace Policy" had been accepted by all the tribes except one, and that one belonged to the large Apache division of the southwest. A celebrated and very able chief, Cochise by name, had successfully fought our troops and continued his robberies and murders for many years. The grievances of this tribe had long before been very great, and for ten years previous to General Grant's announcement of his peace policy these, the Chiricahua Apaches, under Cochise, had carried on a system of aggression and spoliation in Arizona, New Mexico, and across the borders of Old Mexico, which gave the government and the people of that region unheard-of trouble. These Apaches would roam over the country in small bands, destroy the stages with their passengers, rob supply trains, slay every white man far and near, and break up every party sent out to prospect for mines or establish surveys.

After General Parker became Commissioner of the Indian Bureau, and the Hon. Columbus Delano Secretary of the Interior, a strong effort was made to reach this tribe by a special commissioner. A member of the Society of Friends, Vincent Colyer of New York, was selected for this office and dispatched to Arizona. Mr. Colyer was a well-known philanthropist, who during the Civil War had freely rendered the most devoted personal service to the soldiers, especially in the work of the Christian Commission. In 1868 President Grant appointed him a member of the board of Indian commissioners. He was afterward elected secretary, remaining in charge as chief executive officer for three years.

General Crook, then commanding the Department of Arizona, gave Mr. Colyer a fine escort of cavalry and facilitated his expedition in every way possible, but he could never find the redoubtable chieftain; he could not, in fact, get beyond Cochise's scouts who were on the *qui vive* a hundred miles away from his stronghold. After many futile efforts to communicate with the Indians, Mr. Colyer gave up the quest and returned home.

Then it was, the last of February, 1872, that a member of the board of Indian commissions, a "Friend" from Maine, usually called "Father Lang," went to Mr. Delano and said to him: "Why not try General Howard as a special commissioner to Arizona and New Mexico to settle the troubles down there, and especially to make peace with the Chiricahua Apaches under old Cochise?" One object in choosing me was that I was known as a friend of the Indians, and another that I had sufficient rank as a major-general to command everybody in the military service in the department and districts of the southwest.

After a little thought Mr. Delano said: "I will write to General Howard and see if he is willing to go, and I will also speak to the President and ascertain what he thinks about it." I answered Mr. Delano that I was willing to go, if he and the President thought well of it, and would then do what I could to secure the desired peace. General Grant paid me a high compliment when Mr. Delano spoke to him, and one which I am proud to have a matter of record. It was to the effect that no man was better adapted to the purpose; but he couldn't see how even General Howard could accomplish what they desired. They resolved, however, that I should undertake the expedition, so that very speedily the necessary preparations were made.

I was ordered to report to the Secretary of the Interior for instructions and the necessary outfit. These instructions revealed a host of complaints and grievances on the part of various tribes; for example, by the Yumas, the Pimas, the Maricopas, the Arivipas, the Mojaves, the Tontos, and the White Mountain Apaches. There were also lively disturbances in the Warm Spring tribe, recently moved to Tulurosa, a disagreeable region in the western part of New Mexico; and feuds of all sorts existed between the Navajos and their neighbors. There were Indians at Fort Stanton who were breaking out from their reservation and depredating upon the scattered settlements. All these surrounding tribes were to be quieted by my expedition, but the main thing was to make peace with the warlike Chiricahuas under Cochise.

I made up my party as far as I could from Washington, taking an aide-de-camp, Captain M. C. Wilkinson, an interpreter who spoke Spanish, and a celebrated Indian agent from the White Earth Reservation, E. P. Smith, who afterward became Commissioner of Indian Affairs at Washington. Mr. Smith had shown marked ability in dealing with Indians in the northwest, and in Christian work during the war, and afterwards in school work among the freedmen. He had been my friend and coadjutor for years.

With these acceptable assistants I set out the 7th of March and made my way to California. General John M. Scofield in San Francisco was commanding the Pacific Division, which included General George Crook's command of Arizona and New Mexico. General Grant had given me special letters, written in his own hand, to both Schofield and Crook. From the former on my arrival I received every necessary help, orders for transportation and supply, and for an escort should I need it.

The journey down the coast on a comparatively smooth sea, upon the old steamer *Newbern,* had few incidents worth recording. Mrs. Crook, the wife of the general, formed part of our company and added life and pleasure to our voyage. She, with her brother, was on her way to join her husband at his headquarters in Prescott, Arizona. Books, singing, and simple games made the days pass quickly. Mrs. Crook and Captain Wilkinson were good singers, so part of the way we had an abundance of songs and hymns to entertain and refresh us.

At the mouth of the Colorado River we exchanged from the *Newbern* to a river steamboat. I remember little of this part of our journey, except that the cooking was about as bad as it could be, and that garlic appeared to enter into every dish that came upon the table. It was a great trial to Captain Wilkinson, for, though he was well again after sundry attacks of seasickness, he seemed, after our transfer, unequal to the rough fare of that steamboat.

Fifty miles below Arizona City Indian runners from Yuma began to come in. I was greatly interested in them. They were lightly clad, usually with an undershirt, a breech-clout, moccasins, and a Spanish hat, either a light sombrero or a broad-brimmed straw. They brought us letters and dispatches, and took our communications back to be mailed at Arizona City. So much swifter were they than the steamboat, which, of course, had to pursue a crooked route, that our letters carried by the runners were mailed two days before we arrived.

Arizona City was only a village. The Yuma chief had a small tract of country and a bivouac of his people, which he presided over with great dignity, not far from the city, and on the opposite side of the Colorado River. This region, as a rule, was very dry. For miles around there had been, when we were there, no rain for a period of nearly three years. People often became deaf from the exceeding dryness of the air and the prolonged and intense heat. Water for all purposes had to come from the Colorado River. Above Fort Yuma there were irrigating ditches. Near the city were curiously made pumps run by windmills, but most of the people — Indians, citizens, and soldiers — brought water from the river in pails, or hauled it in barrels and tubs.

What was called the fort, only an army post, a mile or more above the city, was a portion of ground perhaps a mile square, fenced in, and with a sufficient number of buildings for two companies of infantry and the quartermaster's stores. The irrigating ditches, drawing water from the river above it, had enabled the officers to cover the reservation fairly well with shrubbery and cotton trees. It was delightful to see the green leaves within the enclosure, and it gave us all a keen sense of comfort to escape from the intolerable dust and heat outside into the spacious quarters of Major J. G. C. Lee, who was in charge of the quartermaster's depot, and who, with his wife, welcomed us most cordially and entertained us with generous hospitality.

My first duty was with the Yumas. Major Lee gave us our choice, — horses to ride, or a spring wagon with a good driver. For short journeys we chose the horses, and for long ones across the sand desert we had the spring wagon, large enough to carry our whole party inside, with the driver up high on a seat arranged like those of the stages of the country. Such a wagon is usually called an ambulance, and was always drawn by six mules. Lee gave us an extraordinary driver whom we named "Dismal Jeems." The reason for giving him this name will appear as my narrative proceeds.

After a rest of a single night I attended a council of the Yumas, at which the Yuma chief, Pascual, was present. It had been already arranged for by a local agent, who for a small compensation had been doing the slight work of an Indian agent in addition to his ordinary business.

The Yumas appeared very glad to see me. The chief, whom the whites called by the Spanish name "Pascual," was an old man, I suspect more than eighty. He was dressed very much as the messengers whom I have described. He was very tall and thin. His shirt was open at the front, exposing the bones of his chest, and his limbs, without leggings, were long and bony. The moccasins upon his feet guarded him against the prickly-pear and other thorny cacti that abounded. He had all the dignity of an ancestral king when he rose to greet me as the alleged representative of the President of the United States; but his dignity seemed to disappear after he squatted upon a low bench and began to recite his wants and his troubles with the plaintive voice of an old man.

The Yumas were very poor. The men about us were dressed in rags — yet little clothing was required — and all those approaching age were ill-looking and squalid. The younger portion, for the most part, showed signs of scrofula, or of some sort of loathsome disease, introduced by the dissolute men that had followed our merchant trains, or those of our army. Many of the younger women, however, were well clad. Some had ornaments about their necks, such as beads, strings of silver pieces, or kerchiefs. They wore calico gowns or skirts, with here and there an upper garment. From every quarter I heard that these poor Indians, hanging about the village of Arizona City, had been demoralized through their dealings with the whites.

Some eight or ten of the men that I saw had much the advantage of the rest of their tribe in personal appearance. They were tall and broad-shouldered. Their hair was cut square just above the neck, and they were in good flesh. I was told that they obtained their living by cutting wood for the river steamers and by working about the wharves of the village. Every one of these wore, like the Mexicans and half-breeds, trousers which were fastened closely about their middle, secured by a waist-belt in which was the usual sheath-knife.

When a Yuma ran away from the tribe and got his living by hunting with wilder tribes he was called an "Apache-Yuma," and I began to see from the use of the word that Apache meant simply wild. In the same way there were "Apache-Mojaves" and "Mojaves proper."

I was soon able to satisfy the complaints, written and verbal, of the aged chieftain and his companions, and to provide for their immediate wants, though spending but a single day upon their grounds. As a rule these Indians had defective sight, owing, I presume, to the torrid heats, the constant smoke, the excessive dust, and the oft-recurring torment of terrific sandstorms. A sandstorm seems to rise far away on the horizon. It approaches steadily and finally bursts upon the village, the garrison, and the Indian camp; but there is no rain in it and none to follow. The blackness comes from the dense clouds of sand and alkali dust, and there is no comfort to anybody exposed to the blast until the storm has spent its fury and passed.

The first accounts we have of these Indians, given by the Spaniards who visited Arizona, show them to have been unusually large in size. The early visitors called them "giants." Habitually at that time they were altogether without clothing. They were athletic in build and possessed great strength. "A log," says our writer, "that six Spaniards could not carry, a Yuma would pick up and carry on his head with little apparent effort." They would bear off a load of two or three hundred pounds without a show of fatigue.

Soon after the Mexican War, some twenty-five years before my visit, the Yumas, then about two thousand strong, had shown themselves averse to our taking possession of the country. I heard a staunch old army officer, Colonel Heintzelman, say that he had encountered those Indians in the outset and had conquered them in battle, and that ever since they had been well behaved, gained a reasonable self-support, and given the government no trouble. Heintzelman stoutly averred that the true way to keep Indians good and peaceable was to begin by whipping them soundly. The old chief, Pascual, was of great age and very infirm, and in himself and his surroundings he exemplified the poverty and degradation of his people. He had just a vestige of the pomp and pride that had once been his. I could not help thinking that there was a better way to deal with Indians than to begin with the conquering sword and follow it up with starvation, and justify every species of neglect and mismanagement in our dealing with them. In spite of our prolonged Florida conflicts with the Seminoles, we have dealt in a better way with them and their descendants than with the Yumas.

# CHAPTER VIII.

## CAMPAIGNING IN ARIZONA — JOURNEYING ACROSS THE "ALKALI DESERT" — LIFE AMONG THE PIMAS AND MARICOPAS.

Disagreeable Effects of Alkali Dust — A Ration of Raw Onions — "Oh, Pshaw! The General Would Eat a Boiled Crow!" — A New Way of Obtaining Self-control — Trailing the Apaches — Tales Told by "Dismal Jeems" — A Dry and Barren Country — My Pima Indian Interpreter — Civilizing Wild Indians with a Melodeon — A Man with a Remarkable History — A Queer Missionary — "Let the Parson Preach!" — Religious Service in a Frontier Saloon — Taking up a Collection — An Arizona Bull-train — Pima Women — Oddly Constructed Houses — A Missionary Bride.

EARLY the next morning, after my council with the Yumas, our party, using the six-mule team, with "Dismal Jeems" for a driver, proceeded across the long stretch of country then called the "Alkali Desert." An army paymaster, Major Sprague, set out at the same time for Fort McDowell and accompanied us all of the first day. We halted for the night at a cross-road, a place near which there had been a silver mine, which, after opening, proved of little value, so that the small hamlet called "Gila City" had been reduced to a single house and stage station. The ride through the alkali dust had been an extremely disagreeable one, and it was difficult to cleanse our faces and hands from the grime without increasing the usual poisonous effect. One young man's eyes became so sore and swollen that he could scarcely see.

Major Sprague that evening invited us to dine with him around the "mess chest." I had been trying to discipline my friends so that their faces would be immobile when in the presence of Indians, never betraying any feeling of anxiety, vexation, or anger, and I had annoyed my aide-de-camp by insisting that he should eat any sort of food without hesitation or question, that might be placed before him. That night in the presence of all our party at Major Sprague's entertainment he tried to turn the tables upon his general. He knew that I was not fond of raw onions. Before him he saw a large plate of them. Without a smile, and with an innocent look on his face, he passed the onions to me. Instantly comprehending his purpose I took a couple of them and, with apparent relish, quietly ate them. His expression is better remembered than described when he exclaimed to Sprague: "Oh, pshaw! the general would eat a boiled crow!" It was not long after this that the aide-de-camp realized the benefit of self-control and self-command as never before, when several of the fiercest Apaches were narrowly watching his face, which, in spite of a mighty effort to appear unconcerned, ill concealed his profound disgust while eating an article of their food.

We passed several places on that journey that had an eventful history. One was where a few houses had stood and the Indians had raided them, killed all the people and driven off their stock. At another two or three men were upon a hill surmounted by a flat rock, from which point of view they saw a woman separated from her group

ON THE MARCH.—UNITED STATES CAVALRY CROSSING THE GREAT PLAINS.

and a quarter of a mile away. One of them proposed to see if he could "wing" her with his rifle. He took aim and fired, whereupon, to the astonishment of everybody, she fell upon her face, and before they could get to her had bled to death. The man who fired the rifle was her own husband. It was with such tales as these that "Dismal Jeems" regaled my companions and myself, as by turns we took a place by his side on the high seat.

At last, through hours of unceasing heat and dust, we arrived at Sacatone, the stage station nearest to the Pima agency. "Jeems" had already filled my mind as full as possible with wild tales of the barren region through which we had passed; poor man, he could not tell of one pleasant incident to redeem it. He seemed miserable himself, and had a strange relish for making other people miserable with his distressing stories.

The Pimas at that time were estimated to be five thousand strong. They were for the most part of the Pueblo class and well disposed toward other Indians and toward white men. According to the information which I brought in my pocket they had a very serious grievance against the white settlers who were crowding them and taking up land above them along the Gila River. This river is very remarkable. You may find a stretch of it for a mile or more where there appears to be an abundance of water and a reasonably rapid current, but above this opening there is only the semblance of a river, apparently a river bed of nothing but dry sand. The surface has no moisture and has a barren look. As you proceed you find the same conditions repeated. I thought there must be some underground connection to keep up the flow of water which here and there was exposed, though I was told that the sand really absorbed the water and let it in above and out below without greatly hindering its current.

The Pimas, by a system of irrigation, succeeded in raising crops of grain and vegetables. But when the white men, imitating them, made ditches far above the Pima territory, the quantity of water was so diminished that they could hardly succeed in cultivating a crop. What an exhibition of selfishness! Many expedients have been resorted to to relieve the situation. For years there has been a hope that the government would construct for them a dam and a reservoir, so that in the flood season in the mountains there might be stored up water enough to satisfy all the dwellers along the banks and valley of the Gila.

The agent, a young man with a family, Mr. J. H. Stout, met me at Sacatone with his buckboard and took me comfortably over to the agency buildings.

The first Indian I saw at Sacatone was introduced to me as "Louis," the interpreter. I looked upon him with admiration. He was five feet and eleven inches tall, with a perfect figure. He had large dark eyes that were changeable according to his mood, lustrous and winning when he was pleased, but full of quick flashes and repellant when he was angry. His very black, thick hair was combed back, slightly parted in the middle, and plaited in two braids which extended below his knees behind. While at the agency I never saw him wear a hat. He did not need any. He was always on hand to translate from English into Spanish, but usually from Spanish into the Pima tongue. It was a pleasure to hear his melodious voice roll out Spanish with a measured accent. Louis was with me a long time during the summer of 1872, and traveled with me many miles, and I became very fond of him.

Louis was the helper to the agent, but more so to the teacher, Mr. C. H. Cook (his name was Koch when he came to America, but he had it changed to Cook when he enlisted in the army). Mr. Cook had a remarkable history. During the Civil War his regiment had been sent into New Mexico and along the borders of Arizona to quell Indian outbreaks. After he was mustered out he became greatly interested in religion, making public confession and uniting with the Methodist church. While recalling his past life and experiences, he thought of the Apaches of New Mexico and Arizona, and became possessed with the idea that it was his duty to go as a missionary to them. When he had laid by a small amount of money he concluded to start for the Apache country. He bought a small melodeon which he could use to accompany him in his singing, packed it in his trunk, and started from Chicago for Santa Fé. The journey cost him so much that he had but a few dollars left, not enough to reach the Apaches whom he had in mind. After prayer and consideration he concluded to take the stage and go as far as his money would carry him.

One Sunday morning he arrived at a cross-road in New Mexico where there was a little hamlet and a single liquor saloon. While thinking what he had better do next he noticed a number of rough men coming from different directions to spend the day in and near the saloon. He leaned against a log by the roadside and watched the different parties as they rode races, while others sat in groups to play cards, throw dice, or gathered in the saloon to treat one another. Taking his Testament and hymn book from his pocket Mr. Cook arose and went into the saloon and said to the bartender that he would like to hold a religious service. The astonished bartender was making some strenuous objections when a queer-looking man, with a tall hat, much the worse for wear, pulled down over his face, suddenly took it off and said to his boon companions: "Let the parson preach!" Accustomed to this man's whims the crowd laughed and jovially consented, taking a chair or bench with mock solemnity, or backing up against the counter with smiling expectancy. The bartender, making no further objection, entered into the fun himself and said: "Parson, go ahead!"

Mr. Cook, not abashed, began at once to read a hymn, then he started a tune, and to his astonishment several of the roughs joined in the singing. He went on to read the Scriptures and preach and pray, and closed with another familiar hymn. At the end of his service the strange man with the tall hat said: "This thing will not be complete without a collection," and passed his hat around. Everybody contributed, and in this way our friend obtained thirteen dollars and fifty cents. The next morning he joined what was called in that country a "bull-train." It was a train of wagons loaded with merchandise and hauled by small oxen, several yokes of them being attached to each wagon. He was charged simply the price of his food, and went on with the train to its destination, which proved to be Tucson, at that time the capital of Arizona.

In Tucson then there were few Americans, but many Mexicans. The Pueblo Indians, the Pimas, Maricopas, and Papagoes, came and went, making such small purchases as they could afford. The governor and his friends took a great fancy to Mr. Cook and persuaded him to give up his idea of going to the Apaches as a missionary and to establish himself among some of the more peaceable Indians.

He yielded to their advice and went to the Pima agency, where for more than a year before my visit he had labored among the Pimas and the Maricopas. I had heard of him and was glad to meet such a man. Antonio, the hereditary chief of the Pimas, with whom I had many interviews, told me of the invaluable services which Mr. Cook had rendered. He said: "We did not know anything about you Americans or the government we were under until Mr. Cook had gathered the children in classes and taught them. The children told their parents what they had learned. So the Indians had knowledge." Mr. Cook's method was first to learn the Pima language so that he could understand the children and the children could understand him. Then he instructed them in English; and it was amusing to hear them speak English with an unmistakable German accent which they had caught from Mr. Cook, who could not fully overcome it in his own speech.

Mr. Stout, the agent, had constructed for Mr. Cook a rough schoolroom with boards. But among the Maricopas, thirty miles distant, he had been obliged to improvise a schoolhouse. As there was no timber of any size, he managed to put up a square frame with a few small joists, the top being horizontal, and then wattled the sides with reeds, bushes, and poles, such as the country afforded. Thus the scholars, when inside, were sheltered from most of the dust and sand which the unobstructed winds often drove in clouds through the Indian village. No roof was needed, for rain was almost unknown in that region.

Antonio, the chief of the Pimas, was rather short and stout, and his son, Antonito, the prince of the tribe, was even shorter than his father. Antonio appeared to be about fifty years of age, and Antonito thirty. These Pima Indians usually dressed as the Americans did, using showy blankets on their horses and to protect themselves in the chill of the evening or morning, and also for cover at night. Though the weather was warm, I do not believe I saw an adult Indian without some kind of clothing. The women were not ill-looking, usually having their hair cropped behind around the neck, wearing it combed back over their heads and behind their ears. It dropped down over their faces as they ground the corn with a pestle or bent over their tubs when they were washing near the Gila.

Their houses were so situated as to make continuous villages, yet no two nearer each other than forty or fifty yards. The Pima house was usually made of ordinary adobe material, was oddly constructed, and appeared, a little way off, like a globe perched on a cylinder, with one door for entrance. There was a hole in the center of the top for proper ventilation, but no windows. Its size was similar to that of one of our old-fashioned Sibley tents, and had just about as much space and comfort as I obtained from mine when on the Rappahannock during the winter of 1862 and '63. I had constructed the cylindrical part of logs driven side by side like spiles, and the tent was stretched over the tops of the logs.

The children, in later years, were represented at Hampton Institute by quite a number of boys and girls selected by the agent and sent there under the care of Antonito. At one time I visited my son, Lieutenant Guy Howard, while he was a student in the artillery school at Fortress Monroe, and saw Antonito sitting outside of his basement quarters upon a rustic bench. He arose and smiled pleasantly as Guy and I spoke to him. I asked how he came there and my son said: "He is studying with the boys and girls from his native village, but without making much progress. He comes over here very often and silently watches me pass in an out, after which he returns contentedly to his school and his charge." He had seen me, and later my son, in his own far away country, and it did his simple heart good just to gaze silently upon us.

Antonio once said to me, through the interpreter Louis and Mr. Cook, as follows: "Many of my women behaved badly when the teamsters and trainmen came along and camped near us; sickness has come from it, so you see the bad condition of many children." Mr. Cook said that quite a number of children of the Pimas and of the Maricopas were afflicted with scrofula as never before.

The Pimas did not practice polygamy. It was a tradition among them that Montezuma had told their ancestors that a man should have but one wife, and the Pimas had followed that teaching. Mr. Cook's instructions had been most wholesome. Louis called himself a Christian and was very angry one day when Mr. Cook told him, on account of the impatience and anger he suddenly exhibited, that he was no Christian. The Pimas, at the time of my visit, were trying to understand what it was to be Christians, and they had good examples before them in Mr. Stout and his family and Mr. Cook. A little later Mr. Cook brought to them his German bride, a woman of great beauty of person and character; so that the Indians had before them a good specimen of a genuine Christian household.

# CHAPTER IX.

## IN AND AROUND TUCSON — INTENSE FEELING AGAINST THE INDIANS OF ARIZONA — A TRAGIC AND REGRETTABLE INCIDENT.

A Typical Frontier Character — A Much Armed Sheriff — A Walking Arsenal — Among the Papagoes — Indians Who Embraced the Roman Catholic Religion — A Mexican Dancing Party — An Attractive Indian Maiden — A Harmless Flirtation — Ludicrous Mistake of my Aid-de-Camp — "Good Pigs, Senorita!" — Hospitality of an Army Post — Trying the White Man's Ways — My Mexican Half-breed Interpreter — Capable but Dirty — My Devoted Friend, Chief "Santo" — Outrageous Attack on Indians While Feasting and Dancing — Wounding Little Indian Boys and Girls — Carried into Captivity — Arrangements for a Great Council.

WE went next to Tucson, then the capital of Arizona, a beautiful little city situated in the southern part of the territory, and occupying an oasis in the wide desert which here extends in every direction. Grant's "Peace Policy" was then very unpopular in all that country over which the hostile Apaches roamed. Still, as I represented the President himself, and at the time outranked all the military officers, including the department commander, Governor Safford and his friends showed us all the respect and attention we could desire. The governor extended to us his hospitality and we soon had comfortable apartments in roomy adobe structures. The editor of the local newspaper, a man of unusual acuteness and native talent, attacked the "Peace Policy" with severity, but wrote kindly of my friends and myself in spite of his political bias.

There was in Tucson a character frequently met in frontier towns, in the person of a rough sheriff, Major Duffield, who protected himself against his numerous enemies by having about his person loaded revolvers, and a loaded rifle upon his shoulder which could discharge sixteen continuous shots without hesitation or delay. At night these implements of authority were laid upon his table and kept always within easy reach. More than once he had defended himself successfully against what he called " Mexican robbers and frontier sports."

Nine-tenths of the people of Tucson were Mexicans. For them the Roman Catholics had a very respectable church edifice full of images and pictures appropriate to their faith. There being no other church in Tucson, my friend and companion, Rev. E. P. Smith, was asked to hold a Protestant service. He did so in a hall, where during the first Sabbath the English-speaking people, almost without exception, gathered to listen and participate.

Indians, for purposes of trade, came to Tucson every day. The Pimas, though living far away, mounted upon their hardy little ponies, made the journey thither in groups and families. They encamped near at hand until they had gathered in such articles as they wished from the traders, then they returned as they came. No liquor was allowed to be sold to them and they made no disturbances.

About ten miles south from Tucson was an old Catholic mission. This mission had been extended to the Papagoes who had gathered in villages within easy distance of church and mission house.

They were like the Pimas in most respects. The difference was not in their houses, or in their habits, dress, or manner of cultivating the soil, but in their being Roman Catholic Indians, having the characteristics of uneducated Catholic people everywhere, with a perceptible retention of Indian customs and superstitions. These Indians were uniformly peaceable and well-disposed toward the Mexicans. Our friends at Tucson, including the governor, invariably spoke highly of the Papago chief and his people, and wanted me to do all I could to secure for them more land and more privileges in the way of schools and irrigation.

When I was with the Pimas I secured a delegation to join me at a meeting to be held with the Aravipa Apaches in about twenty-five days. The place to assemble was near Aravipa Canyon, where the army post was then called "Old Camp Grant." A similar delegation was promised by the Papago chief. The governor and several of his officers, among them the United States district attorney, also promised to go to Old Camp Grant, taking with them as many of the Mexicans as possible, particularly those who had Apache children held as servants in their households. The reasons for these preliminary arrangements will soon appear.

While staying a few days at Tucson we attended dancing parties, which were peculiar to the Mexicans. They were pleasant little gatherings that seldom continued till very late in the night. My aide-de-camp, Captain Wilkinson, and other young officers who were stationed near Tucson, enjoyed the dances, especially the efforts of the

Mexican girls to please them, and their willingness to teach them their soft and musical language. The most famous beauty of the place was "Chica," who lived with her widowed mother, and gave pleasant little "salons" every evening while we were there. She was beautiful and in every way charming and was always obliging when asked to play her guitar; she sang melodiously and sweetly. Wilkinson was fond of music and soon delighted in making visits at Chica's home.

One night, after he had acquired a smattering of Spanish, he made an effort to bid Chica good-night when he was taking his departure. It may be remembered that "*noches*" signifies night, and "*coches*" means pigs. In his bashfulness and imperfect knowledge of the Spanish tongue my aide-de-camp, while bowing politely, said: "*Buenas coches, Señorita!*" This created a laugh among the Mexicans and the story found its way to the fun-loving Louis of the Pimas. So Wilkinson was often reminded, during our subsequent journeys, of how he had bidden a young lady farewell by saying, with deep expression: "Good pigs, Señorita!"

Bidding our friends adieu we hastened on over the forty miles to Old Camp Grant. The last eighteen miles our spring-wagons, hauled by mules, dragged heavily in the coarse, deep sand, but for that distance there had been a constant descent till the country finally opened out into a beautiful and broad plateau. It was a grassy valley, with a winding stream called the Aravipa, coursing through what looked like eastern meadowland. There were deep ravines and mountain ranges not far off, and rugged, rocky canyons within a few miles. This post had only rough barrack buildings which were not adequate for the four companies stationed there, so that tents had to be used. The garrison was under the command of Lieutenant-Colonel Crittenden. It is always like coming into civilization for a campaigner to find and visit an army post, the more so when it is remote from educated and intelligent people. Hospitality is always offered, and is never narrow or restricted, but charming and generous. So it was here.

The Apache Indians whom this post was intended to watch were called Aravipas or Aravipa-Apaches. They were, in contrast with the Pueblos and Papagoes, comparatively wild. Various tribes furnished them with additions, not of the best but, as a rule, of the worst individuals of the tribe from which they came. Doubtless there had been depredations committed by these Indians. They often helped themselves freely to horses, mules, and cattle, when they could find them, and without so much as saying "By your leave." But for some time prior to my visit peace had existed and they had been trying the white man's ways. There was a United States agency within a mile of the garrison, with Mr. Jacobs, the agent, in charge. The headquarters of the agency consisted of a few temporary structures to house the employees and furnish an office in which the business of the government was transacted.

Among my first acquaintances at the agency

was the interpreter, a Mexican half-breed named Concepcion Equierre. His father was a Mexican and his mother an Indian. He spoke the Apache language glibly and English with great facility. It sometimes required extraordinary attention, however, to understand him. He was short of stature and thin of flesh, with hair and eyes as black as coal. Usually he wore an old jacket, well-seasoned trousers that looked like leather, a Mexican straw hat, and a shirt with a collar opened at the neck. His garments were never washed, and his hair was never combed, but it was straight enough withal and worn back behind his ears. When sober he was a capital interpreter, who heartily sympathized with his Indian mother's people.

Another acquaintance I made at the agency was "Santo," the old hereditary chief, and father-in-law of Eskimenzeen, then chief of the Aravipas. He had married the daughters of Santo — three in number — all at the same time. Two of them were too young for brides, but Eskimenzeen could wait to consummate the marriage till they became of sufficient age for Indian wives. The eldest was a very presentable young woman who loved her father and mother and was proud of her husband.

I took a glance at Santo as he sat upon a small bench looking at me. He had rather a long body, short legs, and a very large head. His face was so honest that it occurred to me to try an experiment. Accordingly I told Concepcion to say to him: "You have a Father up yonder," pointing upward. He seemed pleasantly to assent. "Say next, 'I, General Howard, have a Father up there, too. Your Father and my Father the same. Then if you and I have the same Father we must be brothers.'"

Santo arose at once and came to me and put his hand in mine. He was so sincere that from that time until his death he was my devoted friend. Without him I could not have accomplished what I did in behalf of the Aravipa Apaches.

Lieutenant Royal E. Whitman, belonging to the garrison, had taken a great interest in these Apaches and had written to the Indian bureau at Washington much of their story, ill treatment, and suffering. His story was substantially that the inhabitants of Arizona, both Americans and Mexicans, had falsely accused Eskimenzeen and his followers. They had been misrepresented, he said, as guilty of various robberies and murders which had been perpetrated by others at considerable distance from Old Camp Grant. The crime of horse-stealing, in particular, had been charged against them, and the young chief, Eskimenzeen, was declared to be the worst of his race.

The feeling against Indians at Tucson and round about, especially on the Mexican border, had become so intense under current rumors that a volunteer force of some two hundred or more, consisting of Mexicans, with a sprinkling of Americans, had been organized. They marched out from Tucson and arrived, as they had planned, at the mouth of the Aravipa Canyon just before the break of day. The Indians had had one of their characteristic feasts and dances. In the dance the

Indian men had separated from their women and children, and, as was their custom, had lain down to sleep on the dancing ground. At dawn the Tucson contingent had come upon them, firing into the bivouac of the men and of their families simultaneously. Many women and children were killed and more were wounded. The men suffered from the attack, but not so much as their families, as they ran quickly to shelter, and with the few arms that they could seize upon began to return the fire. The Indians scattered and the affray was soon over. In spite of the excuses given for it, the American part of the force was much ashamed of the outrageous massacre which had taken place.

Lieutenant Whitman was unsparing in his comments and reports, and implied that the governor, and even the department commander and many of his officers, sympathized with the attacking party. The little boys and girls, some wounded and some unhurt, were carried off by the Mexican families and distributed to households, many in places far beyond the limits of Arizona. It was these children that the governor and others promised me should be brought back by the Mexicans on the day which I had appointed.

After making all the preliminary arrangements for a great council to be held soon near Aravipa Canyon, to which were invited all the Indians I have named and the Tontos besides, I set out for Prescott to deliver my letters from the division commander and the President to General Crook, who was in command over the territories of Arizona and New Mexico.

## CHAPTER X.

### MEETING GENERAL CROOK — AN IMPORTANT COUNCIL — INDIANS PLEADING FOR THE RETURN OF THEIR CHILDREN — HOW A MOMENTOUS QUESTION WAS DECIDED.

A Great Indian Fighter — General Crook's Attitude Toward the Indians — Roads Infested by Hostiles — The White Flag — Hungry and Tired of Fighting — Lieutenant Ebstein's Experience — Results of Kind Treatment — Dress and Ornaments of the Apaches — Endurance and Speed of Indian Runners — A Wonderful Journey on Foot — Gathering of the Apaches — A Council Made up of Hostile Factions — Anxious Hours — Indians Present their Grievances — How I Matured my Plans — Praying for Guidance — A Wonderful Scene — Return of Captive Indian Children to their Relatives.

AT Prescott General Crook invited me to share a room in his house. Mrs. Crook long before this, with her brother, had joined him. The visit afforded me an opportunity to become better acquainted with the man who was called the greatest Indian fighter in our army. I had known him at West Point, but as he was two years ahead of me in that institution we had but a casual acquaintance. His reputation as a division and corps commander during the Civil War was well known to us all, and on account of his extraordinary merit General Grant had him promoted from a lieutenant-colonel to a brigadier-general in the regular army.

Crook was a peculiar man. He was six feet in height, never fleshy, of very light complexion, with light hair, wearing when I saw him a thin moustache. He was even more reticent than General Grant, carefully keeping all his plans and thoughts to himself. He was very temperate in eating and drinking, and at the time I saw him he was so strong and muscular that he appeared never to be troubled with fatigue. He was indeed a favorite with the Indians, and though terrible in his severity when they broke out and made war, and perhaps at all times distrustful of them, yet he believed in keeping his word with an Indian as sacredly as with a white man, and in all his dealings with them he was uniformly just and kind.

The general had that art which some men possess of saying very little to you in conversation, being at the same time such an attentive listener that one was unconsciously drawn out in discourse. The time passed pleasantly and swiftly. It was a delight to a fellow-officer to find himself at his table, particularly when his genial wife presided at the head of it.

Here I met Lieutenant Frederick E. Ebstein of the Twenty-first Infantry. He had been sent by General Crook, at the request of the Indian bureau, to take command at an Indian station or gathering called "Date Creek." During my stay at Prescott I paid him a visit.

A letter just received from Ebstein tells something about the Indians under his charge, and how interested he was in their welfare. They were Apache-Yumas and Apache-Mojaves, numbering about six hundred and fifty souls, and inhabiting the country lying east of the Colorado River agency. They were not true Apaches, but offshoots from the Yumas and Mojaves who had not gone on reservations with the remainder of their people, but went to the mountains instead. They lived as best they could on the country, getting a sort of subsistence from incursions into neighboring settlements and attacks upon wagon trains which traversed the roads from the Colorado River to Prescott. They assumed the name "Apache." The two people kept up distinct tribal organizations, having, however, much intermarried, and both spoke the same language.

When Ebstein went to his post in 1869 these Indians, being hostile, made the roads and the vicinity of the post so unsafe for individual travelers, or small unescorted wagon trains, that the troops were constantly engaged in scouting for and fighting with them. In 1870 a small party of them approached the post with a white flag and said they were hungry and tired of fighting and wanted to come in. A few days later six hundred and fifty of them, including men, women, and children, came in and camped about a mile from the soldiers near the Date Creek bottom. "Then it was," writes Ebstein, "I took charge under orders from the department commander and afterward issued daily one pound of beef and one pound of flour to each Indian."

Ebstein encouraged the Indians to begin work, paying them by additional issues of flour. The women supplied the military post with fuel; they gathered wood in the canyons, sometimes miles away, bringing it in on their backs. For each load so delivered one quart of flour was given. For clothing they mainly depended upon the skins of deer which they killed, and upon the cast-off uniforms of officers and soldiers. Ebstein says: "I never had a cent of money for the use of these Indians until you (General Howard) came to the post in 1872 and gave me, upon my request, fifty dollars for the purchase of garden seeds." I also authorized an increase in the rations by adding some coffee, beans, and soap. That helped out materially. The Indians now began gardening in a primitive way, and were sufficiently successful the first year to encourage them to continue planting. Ebstein remarks: "I remember with what pride they presented me with some of the first melons raised by them."

The clothing of the men in the summer time consisted of a breech-clout of unbleached muslin, but after coming to the post they picked up soldiers' discarded uniforms and blankets, which they freely used for dress. The women wore a picturesque short skirt made of successive narrow strips of bark of trees intertwined with red flannel. This skirt extended to the knee. They wore leggings of deer-skin, often fancifully trimmed with beadwork, and also moccasins. The body from the waist up was nude except for a deer-skin apron just under the breast, held by a string of beads, or bones of birds threaded on a cord about the neck. In cold weather a Navajo blanket was drawn over the shoulders, the older women using a gray army blanket. Ornaments of brass, silver, and shells in the shape of necklaces, finger- and ear-rings, were common. Married women had a straight piece of sharpened bone piercing the flesh just under the lower lip. Their hair was combed out straight, left unbraided, and banged across the forehead just above the eyes. Men tied their hair into a sort of queue with pieces of red flannel. Frequently the queue was braided. In summer the men were accustomed to braid their hair close to their head and plaster it with mud. They had an idea that the hardened mud kept their heads cool.

Lieutenant Ebstein regards these Indians as fine specimens physically of their race. They excelled as runners, "being able to go on a dogtrot all day." Once an Indian brought Ebstein a message from the River agency a hundred miles distant, completing the journey between sunrise of one day and noon of the next. When young, the girls were comely, but aged rapidly after marriage. Among them strict chastity was the rule.

At last my party turned back from Prescott, this time being accompanied by General Crook and some of his officers, and on the 21st of May we were again with the garrison at Old Camp Grant. It was on this day that we succeeded in bringing together in the broad shady valley the delegations from the various tribes of Indians already named. The Aravipas were largely represented. Some of the Tontos put in an appearance, and the northern bands were early on hand. There were many Pimas and Papagoes. The Mexican residents who had captured and still held the Apache children were induced to come bringing the children with them. There were also present a large number of white men who had been more or less emancipated from the restraints of civilization, and who particularly enjoyed raids against Indians wherever assembled. Here came the civil functionaries of the territory, including the governor. The commissioned officers from the neighboring garrison also honored the occasion by their presence. Probably there was never an assembly of men more thoroughly made up of hostile factions who had all their lives been more or less at war one with another.

We had for interpreters the superb Louis of the Pimas, the singular-looking Concepcion of the Aravipas, and Mr. Cook, the Christian teacher, whom I could use as a chaplain or as a faithful adviser. In a beautiful glen-like spot, on ground a little above the river bottom, the remarkable council came together. A few chairs, some rough benches and camp stools, with small logs drawn together in regular arrangement, gave the dignity of order to the occasion. Indians as well as Americans always desired to have councils conducted with proper formalities. They choose somebody to speak for them, usually a chief, who, though he spoke in the first person, always meant to embrace in it all his tribe or band.

On this occasion we had to wait some time for Eskimenzeen and his people to assemble. Like many consequential white people the Indians seemed to fancy that it added to their importance to come late to church or to council. That day all parties became anxious while waiting lest there should be trouble, but at last the Aravipas, led by their chief, filed into their place. The chief was not at all prepossessing; he stammered in his speech, and was inordinately proud, though he exercised a fierce leadership over his tribe. That day and the next all parties were listened to patiently and attentively.

The Indians presented their grievances. Several of them, after Eskimenzeen, made speeches. They pleaded for the return of their children. Most of the parents were dead, but the relatives wanted them back. The Mexicans then told how much they were attached to the children whom they had carried away. They said they were kind to them, and were bringing them up well in Christian families. The governor gave us his views, which agreed with those of the Mexicans, and the district attorney from Tucson explained what was the law.

Before dismissing the council the second day, I told them that my decision would be to return the children to their relatives. Against this, however, the district attorney made such strong objections and gave so many reasons that I thought it better to reserve final action for a meeting on the morning of the 23d of May.

The Aravipas went off six miles to their bivouac, as they did every night, into a narrow canyon very defensible against attack. The others were grouped here and there where they could talk together, prepare their food, and sleep comfortably. The Pimas, with Mr. Cook amongst them, selected a pleasant grass plot near a group of trees, and there they sat together and talked over the doings of the day until sleep overcame them.

That evening I went over to their ground and found Mr. Cook already sound asleep with his head pillowed upon his saddle and his horse blanket under him. I awakened him and laid before him my troubles, and then said: "Mr. Cook, what would you do if you were in my place? What would you do about the children?"

He answered rather gruffly: "I would give them back to the Indians." I said: "Few of their parents are living and the Mexicans seem to have taken good care of them." "I know that," he answered, "but they use them as servants — as slaves — and the children have relatives among the Aravipas. They were carried off by force, some of them badly wounded. It is right to give them back, and I would do it."

After I left him to resume his sleep, I said to myself: "But that will not bring peace among the tribes." I then wandered far away from the bivouacs and sat down upon a log. Here the whole subject was carefully thought over, and, as I have been accustomed in all emergencies, I earnestly prayed for help and guidance. After that I lay down and fell into a sound sleep.

The rising sun shining across the bright water and through the beautiful canyon awakened me, and instantly I realized that I had a matured plan of settlement in my mind. Just as soon as I could wash my face and adjust my clothing, I walked to the commanding officer's quarters. His wife, Mrs. Crittenden, met me at the door, and I asked her if she knew of a woman in the whole garrison whom I could employ to take care of some Apache chil-

WAR AND CEREMONIAL TOMAHAWKS, CLUBS, SLUNG SHOTS, WAR WEAPONS, ETC.

*For Description see page 14*

PHOTOGRAPHED AND PAINTED FROM THE ORIGINAL OBJECTS EXPRESSLY FOR THIS WORK.

dren. I wanted one who would be kind and patient, and one on whom I could depend to carry out instructions. Mrs. Crittenden thought a moment and then said: "Yes, I know of one, Mrs. ———, the wife of a sergeant, who himself is a good soldier. She has an invalid daughter of whom she has taken the most tender care, and she is a woman of infinite patience." I declared at once that this was the woman I wanted. After I had found her and her husband at their tent I was not long in making arrangements.

To the governor and General Crook my course had not seemed wise, and the district attorney was outspoken in his opposition to any peace policy. The Indians were restless and could see no good likely to come out of my long talks. But they all came together, as they had promised the evening before, and I sat for a while hearing over again the pleas already made — pleas which the interpreters were trying to make plain in different tongues. At last I arose and stood before them, and in my earnestness began to speak so rapidly that nobody could interpret my words. Most of the Indians, however, seemed to understand what I said. This was the substance of the speech:

"Yesterday I decided that it was right to return the children to the parents and relatives of their tribe. From this decision the district attorney has made an appeal and wants the matter referred to Washington. I have determined to listen to his appeal. His superior authority is vested in the United States Attorney-General; mine is in the Secretary of the Interior. They two have a common head, the President of the United States, General U. S. Grant. He only can decide this matter. Now, I will take the children and place them at the agency under the care of Mrs. ———, a good Catholic woman, who will care for them kindly and permit Mexican friends to visit them during the time of their detention, and also permit their Apache relatives to come and see them. This detention will continue until the whole case is laid before the President himself and decision had thereon."

The district attorney then sprang to his feet and said: "We wish to keep the children and will give bonds to bring them forward according to the President's decision." I instantly answered: "No bonds are necessary. General Crook, with his army and authority, will see to it that everything is carried out to the letter as I have decided."

Thereupon a wonderful scene followed. The Indians of different tribes doubly embraced each other—Apache and Pima, Papago and Mojave—and even the Mexicans participated in the joy that became universal. I said to myself, "Surely the Lord is with us."

In due time our differences were laid before President Grant, and I need hardly say that he sustained me in my decision and that the children were returned to their relatives.

# CHAPTER XI.

## SELECTING A DELEGATION OF WILD APACHES TO VISIT WASHINGTON — GREAT FEAR OF THE JOURNEY — CALLING UPON THE PRESIDENT.

Close of the Great Council — A Visit from Tribe to Tribe — Midnight Visit to an Indian Camp — A Rough March — Arranging Details of the Journey to Washington — Getting the Party Together — Parting Scenes between Chiefs and their Families — First Lesson in the Use of Knives, Forks, and Spoons — Trust Begets Trust — Loud Murmurs in a Discontented Camp — First Glimpse of a Railroad — Indian Amazement and Curiosity — First Ride in the Cars — Crouching Upon the Floor in Abject Terror — Calling Upon the President — Opening their Hearts to Him.

AFTER the close of the great council I determined to go from tribe to tribe, according to my instructions, and, if possible, reconcile all differences. Here at Camp Grant I began to select members of various bands to take with me to Washington. The object of these eastern visits was twofold: first, to cement the ties of good will, and, second, to show to them the hopelessness of resisting a government as powerful as ours. That very night I made a midnight visit to Eskimenzeen's convenient and safe lodging-place in the narrow canyon. The shrill savage cry that met my small party as we approached was frightful to unaccustomed ears, but Concepcion, throwing loud " back talk " to the clamor, conducted me safely to the chief's lodge.

The Indians had never seen a railway or a telegraph, and at first I could not get one of them to go. The risk seemed too great. It was here that Santo began to show his friendship for, and his great confidence in me. He arose, his face animated by a new resolve as he spoke to the interpreter and told him to tell me that he, Santo, old as he was, would trust himself in my hands and would go with me to Washington. He made a capital delegate for the Aravipas.

A little later two Pimas, Louis and Antonito, one Papago chief named Ascencion, two Date Creek Indians called in English Charlie and José, Mr. Cook, the Pima teacher, and Concepcion, joined Santo and constituted the party that was to leave Old Camp Grant for the White Mountains (Sierra Blancas), which lay near the eastern borders of Arizona. We set out on the morning of the 25th of May.

By short journeys I accomplished the roughest march that I ever undertook, of a hundred miles over jagged hills, rocky trails, and through deep canyons furrowed with stony cross-gulleys. True, Santo, placing a flinty specimen on the ground, had promised that the mountains would now be level and the canyons filled up, but his prophecy for that portion of Arizona between Camp Grant and Camp Apache had not yet been fulfilled. Camp Apache was in an opening in the forest, in as beautiful a stretch of country as one can well depict. The barracks and houses and sutler's store, dotting the green plateau, were built of rough logs and newly-sawn lumber. It was truly a pretty village in the wilderness, and most acceptable to us weary travelers.

Here I found three bands of Indians sometimes called the "Sierra Blancas," but usually known as White Mountain Apaches. After a visit to each band and a consideration of their special complaints—for each had some trouble to present—I persuaded them to add a representative to our delegation. We agreed that the principal chief should go and represent his band. The eldest was Es-kel-te-ce-la, who enjoyed the reputation of loving peace. The next, and the one best known to the whites, was one-eyed Meguil, who had been a famous warrior, and the other, who constantly longed for civilized life, was Pedro.

From Camp Apache I made several vain attempts to communicate with the Chiricahuas, who were the real warriors to be pacified. While waiting for scouts and messengers to go and come I was entertained in the most hospitable way by Major Dallas, who commanded the garrison; but in time the messengers returned, having been unsuccessful, and I decided to set out for the long journey eastward through New Mexico.

The parting scenes between the chiefs and their families were affecting. Indians from the three bands had come up to Camp Apache for rations. They were seated on the ground upon a gentle grassy slope in the forest opening, waiting, as multitudes have ever done, for the distribution of bread. The Indians were troubled and manifested great apprehension, which showed itself often in tears over the last adieus. Old Es-kel-te-ce-la made me look into his large clear eyes to assure me that there was no badness in him, then took me by the hand and led me to his wife and daughter, and made me, by Concepcion's help, explain and promise that the journey would surely be safe and that I would bring them back. Santo, who was now the best lieutenant I had, praised me over and over again to the children of Meguil and Pedro, and so reassured their troubled hearts. It was no light thing — this going to Washington!

My aged Bowdoin professor, Cleveland, a chemist of world-wide reputation, in 1845, saw at Brunswick, Maine, the first railway carriage which passed through that city. His eyes sparkled behind his slightly-colored glasses and his face wrinkled into smiles at the novel sight, but he shook his head and said: "I am too old; I'll not risk it!" So never would he enter a railway coach, but always journeyed, when occasion required it, in his own chaise from Brunswick to Boston. Just think of it! What was the professor's risk compared with that of those untutored Indians of the Southwest as they started upon their first trip of three thousand miles over vast regions to them unknown? Their fears were natural, but their confidence in a white man's promise of a safe return was simply marvelous.

There was added to our company the Indian superintendent of Arizona, Major Bendel. His title was one popularly given to Indian agents and superintendents. My friend Rev. E. P. Smith had gone back by the way of California. The Indian party of ten, Cook, Bendel, Wilkinson, the drivers of the ambulance and baggage wagons, and a few soldiers, constituted my caravan. For our conveyance, besides a few saddle horses, we had a high-bowed six-mule wagon, a common army escort carriage, and our six-mule ambulance.

When we rode out of Camp Apache there was considerable style in our improvised chariots with Indian outriders. June 1st we made a fair march, — all the day in a continuous forest. I called a halt before the sun had disappeared as we were emerging into our first glade-opening.

"Apache chiefs must not work!" so said half-blind Meguil while his evil-looking eye rested upon me as I began to gather firewood. "We must all work!" I said through Concepcion, repeating the words for Meguil's benefit. "Take the hatchet, Meguil, and help me; we must all work!" "*Tatah* no work—white *Tatahs* no work," he murmured, as I glanced at his twinkling eye. "I am as big a *Tatah* as you are," I laughingly replied. Apparently in sport he joined me in dragging sticks and bushes to the camp fire. Soon all the rest of the party were doing the same. That was our first work lesson. It was not long before the Indians would spring forward and anticipate me in such chores.

At the table I played the host. We had a square piece of canvas stretched on the ground, and a plate, knife, and fork were placed for each guest. Some of us sat cross-legged like tailors, some of the Indians leaned on elbow like the disciples of old, while some squatted as they were wont to do at council fires. After the food had been put on the canvas it was hard to resist our appetites until a short grace had been said, but we soon learned.

The preliminary reverent uncovering of the heads became a potent sign. It was very awkward at first for the Indians to use those knives, forks, and spoons. Pedro, who acquired polite manners quickly, speared bread with his fork and took meat with his fingers, while Louis, who spoke four languages and whose shining braids hung below his knees, and the determined Santo, wedded to old habits, required considerable extension of the meal hour to do things rightly and to satisfy hunger.

My Sabbath restraint was at first as irksome to the Apaches as to children. At the end of the first day, it being Saturday, I halted and rested till Monday. Sunday morning Meguil mounted his pony and said to me: "Meguil go — his horse — come back!" Mr. Cook shook his head doubtfully as he looked at his receding figure, and Louis said: "No more Meguil!" But three days later, after we had left the forest and were traversing a treeless wilderness, we caught sight of a couple of horsemen off to our left gracefully loping toward us. I was glad to hear Louis' Spanish as he pointed and said: "He *aqui,* Apache Meguil!" It was he, true to his word, and his return was an earnest of the confidence that I had desired to establish between us all. Trust begets trust.

By another Sabbath we had made good progress. That was a day to be remembered. We were near the Rio Puerco. A small abandoned hut, the only sign of past habitation in the neighborhood, was quickly freed from the rubbish and dirt left by former occupants; a few sticks, after much search, were found for firewood, and our provisions were unpacked and brought in. Soon, however, the drivers of our wagons rushed to the door and cried out excitedly: "The water of the river is bad, the animals won't drink it!" Our white men from the very first were vexed with me for halting just there. Was not the Rio Grande only a few miles ahead? Wasn't there a ferry, and a town just beyond the river?

I understood the cause of their dissatisfaction. The place was full of liquor saloons and I dreaded more than I can tell two nights and a day with such extraordinary temptations for our rough drivers, soldiers, and Indians. I persisted in remaining at the Rio Puerco. The water once drawn in pails I believed would speedily settle and become clear, but in this I was mistaken, and amid murmurs of growing discontent we passed a hard night. Sunday morning the pails filled at evening contained the same clayey porridge; nobody could drink it. The thirsty horses pawed the brink of the river and caught up the hateful water in their lips, and, without swallowing, raised their noses high in air; thus they made their indignant protest against such stuff. But just as necessity appeared to compel a resumption of the march, Concepcion and Antonito, the young Pima chief, ran to me with good news. Wandering over the ledge not a hundred yards away they had found a natural basin of clear, good water. My heart was glad. Our discontent and anxiety vanished.

That day we had a brief religious service. Captain Wilkinson was a good singer, and at the close of the exercises he sang the hymn entitled

"The Cleansing Fountain." This is the last verse:

"When we've been there ten thousand years,
Bright shining as the sun,
We've no less days to sing God's praise
Than when we'd first begun."

Pedro, who certainly could not have comprehended the words, was in tears. He arose from his half-kneeling posture, went straight to the captain, folded him in his arms, and with a softened voice said: *"Bueno! bueno!"*

On this Sabbath at the Puerco, Louis, having been drawn into a dispute with some of our party, after a time became fretful and impatient and then sulky. For this conduct Mr. Cook reproved him with severity. At this Louis became angry. Noticing his temper I called the young man to me and asked: "Why, Louis, what's the matter?" He replied: "I am going back!"

"What for?"

"Teacher don't treat me right. He insults me; he says, 'Louis no Christian.'"

Major Bendel, who was a Jew, inquired into the trouble that was becoming so serious, and was able to adjust all matters amicably. Poor Louis' contribution to Christian progress was rather meager and doubtful. Still, it was something gained for an Indian to feel insulted at being called "no Christian."

In spite of the attractions ahead there was considerable dread of the great obstacle across our path, the Rio Grande. One of the most vigorous of my West Point classmates was Lieutenant

Davant of South Carolina. In 1855 he attempted to cross this river on horseback and was carried off by the swift current and drowned. Among army officers the difficulties of the passage of the Rio Grande at high water were proverbial. Before our approach the river had risen over its banks and was as swift in its flow as the Mississippi in flood-time.

We came to the western shore opposite Albuquerque. The Indians were full of wonderment and gazed up and down the fierce waters. Presently they caught sight of a large flatboat coming toward us from a point farther up on the other bank. The boat swept past us oblique to the current, but held by strong hands, and, at last striking the shore, landed far below. It was then dragged by ropes back to us. It took close packing to get our party, wagons, ambulance, animals, and all else on board.

"Dismal Jeems," tall, lank, and somber, had little fancy for the prospective voyage. One of his mules, a quiet, handsome little creature, he called "Lucy." When she was on the road and became tired she would put her ears back and not pull a pound. Two or three times, sitting by Jeems' side and noticing that he could not reach her with the whip, I tossed some pebbles which hit her back, an action that Lucy naturally imputed to the driver. When, last of all, I stepped upon the flatboat I saw Jeems standing near Lucy's heels. Never for one moment would one suspect trouble from this quiet little mule, so demure was she with her upright ears. However, at just the last push from shore, nobody could tell how, two hind feet struck poor Jeems in his stomach and he made a quick somersault into the water. Jeems went down with a plunge, but, luckily, on the land side, so that coming to the surface he was caught and lifted to the boat, where, with dripping garments, he sputtered aloud with terror and indignation. The Indians were not yet civilized enough to restrain their mirth. Clapping hands, they bent their flexible bodies forward and back and laughed remorselessly, saying: *"Jon-dai-sy-ton-judah!"* i. e., "Mule very bad!" This incident added another link to Dismal Jeems' chain of misfortunes. The flatboat, shooting across the torrent, brought up against an island. Here we had to disembark and wade to the eastern shore. Our mules wallowed in the muddy bottom, and now and then sank in quicksands, so that we had trouble to save them, and our staunch army wagon was so broken and mired that it had to be abandoned.

Sad as was our plight when we came into camp above the town, our misfortunes were aggravated by the very disaster which I had feared. Some of the men were made crazy with liquor, but to my great joy the Indians, including the interpreter, kept their promise and did not drink.

On June 12th, after refitting—the men having become reasonably sober—we took the road again. At Santa Fé we finished what I regarded as the first important division of the journey, and so I ordered a brief rest before taking the stage for Pueblo. The stay was too long for Concepcion. Intolerable thirst for strong drink overcame his promise. He was in a terrible plight and passed from spasm to spasm, screaming, crying, and laughing by turns. The rapid transitions from maudlin good nature to fierce anger, and *vice versa*, terrific and ludicrous as they were, became object lessons to the Indians. The interpreter's final phase of besotted stupidity was a relief to Meguil and his Indian helpers, who had constantly watched and held him till the drunken sleep came on. In time we neared the new city of Pueblo. The Indians had greatly enjoyed the jolting journey of two hundred miles in a four-horse stage. None of them had ever passed beyond Santa Fé, and only the "Sierra" Apaches had been so far.

The 17th of June we suddenly came upon the narrow-gauge railroad just outside of the city, which had been only recently completed to that point. I enjoyed the Indians' manifest surprise. Hurriedly leaving the stage they ran to the railway and sat down upon the strange framework. With great curiosity they felt of the cross-ties and fingered the spikes which fastened the iron rails. They looked long and wonderingly at the freight and cattle cars, which were standing near, and then, like children surprised with new gifts, they clapped their hands with glee. A train soon backed down to take us. Our party slowly filed into the small coach to take seats two and two. I was astonished at the evident fear of the Indians. They crouched in abject terror upon the floor between the high backs of the seats and covered their dark faces with their hands.

"What's the matter now, Es-kel-te-ce-la?" I

asked.. The interpreter gave me the old man's affrighted reply:

"We've said we'll go with you. We've given you our whole hearts, and we'll go where you go!"

"But what makes them hide their faces and keep so quiet, Concepcion?"

"Why, sir, they are afraid!"

Their terror did not last long. After a few miles of safe and easy riding they lifted their heads one by one and began to count the high hills and mountain peaks. The first fear had given place to other emotions. There were new wonders for them as towns became larger and more frequent, and the variety and size of the buildings increased.

Before we had crossed Colorado, Meguil told me with a sigh that he could not count the mountains any longer, but must rely upon me to get him back.

The climax of surprise was reached in New York City, not in the magnitude of the metropolis nor in the throngs on the streets, nor in the magnificent buildings, nor in Central Park, whose collections of natural objects delighted them, nor in the forest of shipping, the like of which was beyond their dreams; no, it was in beholding Meguil clothed and in his right mind, having two eyes, the lost one having been so restored as to look precisely like the other.

In Philadelphia I took the Indians to Fairmount Park, to Girard College, to several manufactories, and—what delighted them especially—to a magic entertainment. Everywhere they were made particularly happy by the cordiality of the people. I shall never forget our visit to the Moyamensing Penitentiary. The Indians walked up and down the great galleries, which branch out like the spokes of a wheel; as they sauntered along, stopping to gaze through the gratings, they were filled with compassion for the inmates. Before leaving, Meguil came to me with the interpreter. He had a solemn look. With much feeling he asked:

"Is there one man in confinement here who is innocent?"

"Why, Meguil?"

"If there is one I want to speak to him, for I was once a prisoner and kept a whole year, in a prison like this, in Santa Fé. I was innocent of any crime. I was very lonely and sad, and I don't want another man to be so unhappy."

In Washington nearly two weeks were spent to good purpose. As it was vacation at Howard University and my own house was near the dormitories, it occurred to me to use the latter for sleeping rooms for the Apaches. I gave the Indians glimpses of curiosities in the Capitol and in numerous other public edifices. By appointment they went to see President Grant, accompanied by the Secretary of the Interior and the Commissioner of Indian Affairs. To them they opened their hearts in set speeches and received pleasant rejoinders. They looked through the navy yard, and the arsenal, where the large guns and numerous small arms powerfully impressed them. But nothing imparted richer enjoyment than our visit to the College of Deaf Mutes. The bright, active boys, who could not hear a sound, at once established sign communications with the Indians, and the Indians rivaled the boys in the variety of their imitations. The cat, the dog, the horse, the bear, and other animals, tame and wild, were successively characterized. Again and again the Indians spoke of these young people as "the boys who talked with their hands and arms."

All the Indians of my party, after leaving Santa Fé, wore the white man's clothing and had made wonderful progress in the ways of civilized life. They visited my family freely and all took their meals with us; but I am sorry to say that agents from Washington were secretly sent to them and they were offered as high as one hundred dollars apiece if they would only leave me and insist on being entertained at a city hotel. Of course this was a bribe and a decoy to have them visit the lowest places in Washington and subject themselves to the vilest doings. I was told that other Indian delegations had been dealt with successfully for the purposes of gain. But my party, thoroughly loyal to me and keeping rigidly to their promises, stoutly said: "No, we will not go! Apaches stay with General Howard."

# CHAPTER XII.

## RETURN OF THE APACHES TO THEIR ARIZONA HOMES — I SET OUT TO FIND THE NOTORIOUS CHIEF, COCHISE.

Great Assembly of Relatives and Friends to Meet the Returning Braves — Chief Meguil and his Glass Eye — Some Astonished Indians — Following the White Man's Ways — Determined Efforts to Find Cochise — "Snake, General, Snake!" — Close Call from a Rattlesnake — Meeting with "Tom Jeffords" — "He's a Bad Egg" — Agrees to Take Me to the Camp of Cochise — Starting on the Journey — A Strange and Suspicious Group — Threatened by Angry Miners — Adventure with a Desperate Prospector — Following an Apache Trail — Communicating Signs by Smoke — Arrival at Cochise's Stronghold — Meeting One of His Wives.

IN keeping with General Grant's peace policy, the Dutch Reform Society of New York nominated the agents in Arizona. Leaving Washington July 10th on our homeward journey we paid a visit to that society in the metropolis. One seldom sees an assemblage of men more dignified and impressive than were those who gathered in a large room to welcome our delegation. When the Indians were ushered in the assembly rose *en masse* to receive them. Vincent Colyer, whom they knew, was present, and it greatly relieved their embarrassment to meet him. Every chief was encouraged to speak, and so one after another recited grievances to sympathetic ears, and received in response such comfort and cheer as loving hearts could suggest.

In the evening we were transferred to a large

Presbyterian church, and the Indians were again asked to speak and to tell the people about their condition and their wants. Though addressing a large and civilized assemblage for the first time, and through interpreters, these rude men fresh from savage life commanded undivided attention and received ringing applause. On this occasion Pedro, every day growing in ideas, said:

"You have schools, churches, places where clothes are made, houses filled with wealth; you have wagons, horses, cars, and more than I can speak of. We have nothing. We are very poor. I have been thinking hard. We had long ago all the land; the Indians were once as one man. Now they are divided and the white men have all the land and all things. Now I am going to be a white man. I shall wear the white man's clothes. I shall cook and eat the white man's food, and I want my children to go to school and learn to be white men. I am done."

Each Apache followed suit, and that evening many of the hearers were satisfied that the seeds of civilization which had been sowed were already springing up and bearing fruit.

A conservative army officer present at this meeting was not so hopeful. He whispered to me: "When a chief returns from Washington to his tribe his Indians do not follow him. They declare that he has been bewitched, or had 'bad medicine,' and they do not believe anything he tells them." Doubtless this is in part true. It requires constant work and perennial faith to produce permanent results. We ought not to expect too much from a chief like Meguil or Pedro, returning from his surprises and new convictions to the tepee and its old gypsy ways, where roaming is more attractive than labor and light-hearted indolence preferable to perplexing thought. All good effects are lost when a chief, by liquor and the baits of passion, is made more savage than before in consequence of his visits to us. But at any rate, our party of Indians was carefully guarded against such drawbacks.

At New York we divided. The two Pimas, the Date Creek Indians and the Papago chief went with Major Bendel *via* California. The other five accompanied me through Colorado and New Mexico, pursuing substantially the same route by which we came — the railway to Pueblo, stage to Santa Fé, and the saddle horses, with wagons for baggage, to Camp Apache. I took Captain J. A. Sladen this time as an aide, and also my eldest son, Guy, then in his seventeenth year and enjoying a college vacation.

In fulfillment of the promises made at Washington by the Department of the Interior, I was obliged to purchase at Santa Fé some horses and equipments for the Indians. When we passed beyond Santa Fé we were well mounted, and we had a delightful enlargement of our company in the persons of Major Pope, the Indian superintendent of New Mexico, his good wife, and the Rev. Dr. McFarland, an aged missionary. Without hindrance or accident we went on some two hundred miles to Fort Wingate, located on the border of the large Navajo reservation.

The Apaches and Navajos had long been hostile to each other and bad feeling existed between them. The old policy of government officials was to foster enmities and mutual hatred in order to weaken the Indian tribes. Having a different conviction, it was the burden of my efforts to settle all the troubles and introduce terms of peace and good will. Hostile relations of one tribe to another had kept up a warlike spirit, and their internecine strifes usually brought terror and disturbance to white settlements.

As I had arranged, the Navajo leaders were on hand at Fort Wingate upon our arrival. An unforeseen difficulty resulted because neither the Apaches nor the Navajos were willing to make the necessary advances. At first I took all our white people with me and went to the place appointed for the joint council, but not an Indian—Apache or Navajo—would come. So much for Indian pride.

Next I tried the experiment of seeing the hostile parties separately and engaging them to meet each other at a given time and at a particular spot, coming up simultaneously. On this occasion I went again, alone, to a meeting-place which all the Indians could see. Then I beckoned to each party to come. They came on slowly, solemnly, arriving at the same instant, and arranged themselves for a talk. The Court of St. James could not have been more ceremonious.

After the usual method of such councils there began a recapitulation of wrongs. Then promises for a better understanding were exchanged. The eloquence, native grace, and show of deep feeling were very marked. Soon their faces lighted up and their tones changed from accents of complaint to those of reconciliation, heartiness, and joy. As was done at the Aravipa council, the Indians embraced each other in that curious double manner peculiar to them. They began to talk and laugh freely like old comrades, and continued their festivities throughout the night. Here I scored another victory, because peace makes peace. Neither whites nor Indians can long exist by war measures alone. When peace by mediation is obtained even the mediating party has a share in it.

We found a crying evil existing along the borders of the great Navajo Reserve. Frontier stockmen, who had but a single cabin to live in and a very small corral, were nevertheless accustomed to take vast stretches of the unoccupied public domain for pasturage. They naturally lost much of their stock, both cattle and horses. They sometimes found signs of stock-killing, and their horses suddenly disappeared as if stolen. The owners and herdsmen cried out that they had been robbed, and, whether right or wrong, they stoutly accused the Indians.

After meditating upon this state of things, I gave them a wholesome preventive measure. I established an Indian police, the members of which were to have the same pay as our soldiers, and put their proud war chief Manuelito, with his consent, at the head. That police was very efficient while it lasted. It prevented all good Navajos, who were in the majority, from being involved by their evil brethren in troubles which invariably followed the commission of crimes. The greatest disturbance arose from being obliged to give up Indians to white men for punishment. The police, being loyal to those who paid them, very quickly arrested the criminals and delivered them up, and this was done so quickly that Indian hospitality to the accused was not violated.

Leaving the Navajos we continued our long journey to Camp Apache. Here we again met brotherly greetings, generous hospitality, and home comforts. As we emerged from the continuous forest the rough quarters appeared elegant, the grass plot greener than ever, and even the deep-cut river close at hand seemed to murmur sounds of peace and good will. As Mrs. Dallas gave me her hand in greeting I said: "What a cosy nest you have made here among the protecting hills!" It was hedged in by countless trees.

"But, General," the lady answered, "it is *so lonely!*" That was true; however beautiful the situation, it alone is insufficient to compensate for the society which cultured minds desire.

A large body of Indians had assembled from the three tribes to meet our returning braves. There were lively demonstrations. Each chief was a hero. But Meguil, with an eye in his sightless socket, took the palm of attention till the home-brewed *tizwin** obscured the vision of himself and friends by its relentless effects. Poor Meguil was

* Among the Apaches and kindred Indians, an intoxicating distilled liquor similar to the Mexican mescal, made from the yucca or Spanish-bayonet.

no longer under a pledge. Es-kel-te-ce-la, with his people, laughed heartily and talked rapidly; he was, no doubt, telling to wife and children and a crowd of listening Indians most wondrous tales of adventure and sightseeing too grand for him to portray.

Pedro, the most civilized of all, began at once to introduce into his lodge such practical measures as he could. He visited Major Dallas and asked his aid in building a new house. No persuasion could induce him to put off that shirt, once white, which, unfortunately, had become too much soiled by travel. To the major he discoursed with great particularity, through the interpreter, upon the changes he proposed to make in his housekeeping, in his supplies, and especially in the cooking and in new observances at his table. We smiled at Pedro's enthusiasm, but he has lived on and continued to improve, while Meguil and Es-kel-te-ce-la, a few years after that, perished in a petty Indian outbreak.

Santo all along had been my favorite. On the return stage, when near Santa Fé, I ventured to tell the Apaches that the earth was round and turned on an axis. Santo was grieved, and, showing much feeling, said: "General Howard, you have been like a father to us. You have told us the truth, and never deceived us. We are on our way home. Now do not talk that about the earth. Nothing can make us believe that. Indians do not think that way. We want to keep you our friend."

Santo parted with me at Camp Apache. Years after an officer told me that the old chief always slept with a New Testament which I had given him under his head. Though he could not read, Santo was ever after loyal to the book and to the giver!

As my son Guy must soon return to college, I sent him *via* Camp Grant over the hundred miles of rough journey in charge of an expedition to take the Aravipa Indians, with some from San Carlos, to their reservations. This party consisted of Rev. Dr. McFarland, Santo, a few Indians besides, and a detachment of soldiers from the garrison. It was, as we know, a dangerous journey over a rugged, rocky trail. The young student, to my joy, acquitted himself with honor and carried through his company without loss, though the aged missionary came near giving up his life from fatigue and exhaustion. He insisted that the tender care that he received from the young commander saved him.

For another attempt to negotiate with the wild Chiricahuas, Concepcion and several other messengers were dispatched in different directions toward the south. Cochise's men were reported to be still roaming and robbing; they appeared to have no fixed dwelling place. Meanwhile, Captain Sladen and I, with a small escort of cavalry, visited the lodges and farm patches of all the different bands of the Sierra-Blancas. The captain, then young, was of medium height, straight, stout, and broad-shouldered. He had a short neck, a countenance ruddy and full, a shapely head and large hazel eyes, now with a sad expression, now sparkling with humor. His hair was straight and black and so was his heavy moustache. He had been my companion in many battles, — always genial, fearless, and intelligent. Of late years he had employed his leisure hours in the study of medicine, and was at this time admitted to practice.

As we passed on, lodge after lodge revealed to Sladen the squalor, the diseases, and the sufferings of those neglected Indians. With his small assortment of drugs and his sympathetic voice he became to the Indians during that journey an angel of light and deliverance.

We went as far as San Carlos. The bottom lands in that quarter were largely used for Indian planting, and white men averred that the Indians made it a starting point for their thieving raids. One night I camped near the Gila River. Captain Leib, who had charge of a local cavalry guard, and I were occupying an open space for our bivouac. We were sitting upon logs some four or five yards apart reading, when an enormous rattlesnake, coming from Leib's left, suddenly coiled, and, with head in air, made ready to spring at me. Leib cried out, "Snake, General, snake!" He seized a good-sized stick and struck him a heavy blow across the tail just as the snake's head reached my knee. The blow so quickly delivered was enough. His snakeship coiled again and Leib soon dispatched him, while he remarked: "That was a close call!"

The next day we turned back and made a circuitous trip by the way of canyons, wild, jagged, and precipitous trails, and among numberless buttes and rugged mountain crags. The scenery everywhere was picturesque, but our paths were ugly and often fear-inspiring. Two hundred and fifty miles of circuit and inspection brought us again to Camp Apache, where we rested for two days. Our messengers, led by Concepcion, had made their journeys far and wide in vain, and returned without finding even a trace of the wily Cochise.

My several efforts to complete this most important part of my mission had been thus far unavailing, but I was not ready to give up the chase. I determined to seek for some one of Cochise's various trails to the east and follow that back till I could uncover his hiding-place. We had a glimmer of light to aid us — some vague stories from the wife of a half-breed living near Camp Apache. She was a Chiricahuan. She was sure the old chief would not let us go directly to any of his strongholds, but she knew that he occasionally went eastward, crossing New Mexico as far as the Rio Grande.

I resolved to go first to a camp of soldiers and Apaches in New Mexico which my instructions required me to visit. These Apaches were kindred to the Chiricahuas. The camp was at Tulerosa, in the western part of New Mexico. On my arrival I found there Victorio's Apache band, which had been recently brought from the Rio Grande. The home they came from bore the musical name of Cañada Alamosa. All were full of discontent at the transfer, and the officers of the garrison said that these Apaches had been sorely ill-used. At the first interview they pleaded: "Oh, take us back home to Agua Caliente on the Rio Grande! we are dying here. At Cañada Alamosa there is good land, good water, and good food." Patiently I heard the Indians' complaints and promised a visit to that salubrious Cañada, i. e., if Victorio would send with me a proper delegation; and, further, I would carry this petition for the Indians' return to the Rio Grande directly to the President.

While I was interviewing the Indians and the officers of the garrison, a returning troop of cavalry that had been chasing some wild Apaches brought in as its guide a singular character of whom I had frequently heard but had never seen. Everybody called him "Tom Jeffords." I may say that frontiersmen, though this was not much to his discredit, gave him a bad reputation. "Tom Jeffords! He's a bad egg; he trades with Indians, sells them whisky, powder and shot. They don't kill him 'cause he's bought 'em up."

At one period while the stage was running regularly on the Tucson road, Jeffords, living in that neighborhood, had managed to keep the good will of the Apaches. On one occasion, when the driver and other passengers were killed, Jeffords, who was on the stage, was spared. Whenever after that he had fallen into their hands he had always escaped. Major Pope told me that he had once managed to reach the Chiricahua chief through Jeffords, and that he was confident that the man had dealt honestly with him. I believed it a good providence which now threw him in my way.

Learning that the cavalry troops had actually arrived, I went to their camp to find Jeffords. The first tent I entered a tall, spare man, with reddish hair and whiskers of considerable length, rose to meet me. He was pleasant and affable, and I was in the outset prepossessed in his favor. Giving my name I asked:

"Is this Mr. Jeffords?"

"Yes, sir, that is my name."

"Can you take me to the camp of the Indian Cochise?"

He looked steadily and inquiringly into my eyes and then asked:

"Will you go there with me, General, without soldiers?"

"Yes," I answered, "if necessary."

"Then I will take you to him." Something in his brave face and decided manner made me believe that he could and would do as he said.

With those Tulerosa Indians was a young chief called "Chie," the son of Magnus Colorado, Cochise's brother, a notorious chief captured and killed by our people in 1863. Jeffords said: "Chie must go with us as a guide and friendly witness." By giving a horse to him and another to his young wife, who was to stay behind, after some delay he was induced to go. The officers of the garrison trusted Chie and spoke well of him. He had often been a hunter for them.

Jeffords seemed in no haste. He favored our making the expedition, which I had promised, back to the Rio Grande. He declared that he must find Ponce, another young chief, who with a roving band had recently fled from Fort Stanton and was somewhere near Cañada Alamosa depredating on the country. Ponce's Apache father had been in his lifetime Cochise's friend. Ponce knew Spanish and would be a true interpreter. Of course, like a good general, Jeffords planned to have everything possible in our favor. "Ponce is a favorite friend of the old man," he averred. "He and Chie will make us welcome to Cochise's stronghold."

We made the expedition to Cañada Alamosa and attended to all Victorio's wants, and enabled him to renew his petition for a return to that favored land. We then began a diligent search first for Ponce's band.

This was the make-up of my party which left Cañada Alamosa the 20th of September: Captain Jeffords, Jake May, an Anglo-Spanish interpreter, two packers leading their pack-horses, Chie, Captain Sladen, and myself. We were all well mounted. I had besides our pack-horses a good four-wheeled ambulance, and a driver who was also a passable cook. The ambulance had to keep on wagon roads, but the rest of us could follow the trail at will and so shorten the distances in each day's march. It was only at long halts that we had the ambulance with us at all.

The first day after leaving Cañada Jeffords and I rode on ahead. We were jogging along over a trail that took the tributaries of the Rio Grande transversely — a trail that was naturally up and down with few level stretches — when the quick eye of Jeffords detected the fresh track of an unshod horse. The rider had ridden to the brow of the hill, seen us, and turned back. We followed the track of this horseman till we reached an abrupt descent. It led to a deep cross-canyon. At the bottom flowed the Rio Cochinillo Négro. We could descry that river's tortuous course for miles toward the Rio Grande. The valley afforded many rich fields for cultivation. At intervals waving corn glistened in the sunlight and gave picturesqueness to the view.

Immediately before us were Indian children at play, women around camp-fires at work, and a large group of men, not far off, squatting upon the ground. Indian ponies, quietly grazing along the river, completed the picture. Without hesitation we descended the zigzag trail a mile or more and approached the strange group. Many men were playing cards, the remainder looking on; all were deeply absorbed. At first nobody in the card party took the slightest notice of our coming. Jeffords left me a few rods back with the horses. As he neared the Indians, walking, he saw Ponce among them. He motioned to me that all was right, and went and sat down beside a thick-set, pleasant-visaged young Indian and spoke to him. They exchanged a few words in Spanish, then Ponce, for it was he, went on with his game.

After it was over the Indians arose and some of them took favorable notice of me, calling me *Tatah*, a term with them meaning chief, like *Tyhee* among northern tribes. Some came very close and examined my clothing and our mounts with evident admiration and curiosity. Ponce was intelligent, speaking Spanish with readiness — a big hearted, lazy fellow in camp, but quick enough on a scout or a hunt.

Ponce made two objections: First, he asked: "Who will take care of these Indians?" and, second, "I have no horse." Our soldiers from different posts were out scouting and hunting for this very tribe of renegades, which had escaped from a reservation and were feeding upon corn which they did not plant. His first objection I removed by taking the whole band to the nearest Mexican hamlet where there was a store of general merchandise. I furnished their gypsy-band with thirty days' supply on condition that they remained there and did not depredate. I met the next objection by presenting Ponce with a horse for the journey. But the next day, as we drew out on the trail, I noticed that Ponce was on foot. I exclaimed: "Where is your horse?"

With a mysterious look he pointed back to the Indian village. On the eve of starting he had given his horse to his wife. I could not get another for Ponce, but told him that I would "spell" him now and then with my own. Sometimes on easy trails he rode behind my saddle and a portion of each day I walked and let Ponce ride. This arrangement greatly pleased him.

Taking the routes directly toward the Arizona border we were able to spend the 23d and the 24th of September at Fort Bayard. Here we received hospitable welcome and replenished our stores. Silver City, a small mining village, came next. In its outskirts the rough miners, seeing our Indians — Ponce and Chie — barred their doors from fear. In the town a crowd acting like a mob pressed closely upon us and so persistently insulted the

Indians by threats and gibes that they became alarmed. By keeping Ponce and Chie as much as possible in the background out of sight, and by conciliatory speeches, Sladen, Jeffords, and I managed to quiet the villagers. Nobody there believed in the peace policy, but fortunately there were present several sensible men who helped us to remain through the night without suffering violence, and to get on the western trail at the first peep of day.

Ten miles beyond the village we ran upon a prospecting party who were searching for mines. The leader, a big burly man, had had a brother killed by the Apaches; he was far from cordial. When the two Indians came near him he saluted me with a fierce oath and swore he would kill the scoundrels on the spot. As he raised his rifle I stepped between him and the Indians, and, looking him steadily in the face, said simply:

"You will kill me first." He dropped his rifle and rode away cursing a "damnable peace policy which permitted savage brutes to go at large!"

Not long after that Ponce was walking by my horse in a lazy fashion with his eyes on the ground, when of a sudden he became animated and cried in Apache, "A deer! a deer!" and then sprang up the side of the hill with alacrity. Having Jeffords' rifle in his hand, he followed the track like a trained dog and soon brought back a small deer. A few days later Ponce was lying prone on my horse, patting his neck as he bore him along the beaten trail, when a horse's single hoof-print in the sandy soil caught his attention. He instantly took the trail, which bore off at an angle. In a few minutes he galloped back, calling out, "Apache! Apache!" I asked Jeffords how Ponce knew it was an Apache horse. Ponce laughed at my simplicity as he answered: "Feet small, pony no shoes; Indian horse goes all around like Apache." By this I understood that an American would ride straight ahead from hill to hill, but not so the Apache.

This one trail led to others. Soon we found the footsteps of men, women, and children near a large log where they had dismounted and stopped to cook and eat. Both of our Indians said at once, "Cochise Apaches!" No others shod their horses with deer skin tied above the fetlocks.

The trail now became full and plain. We put ourselves upon it, and wound around among the sand hills and through the wastes of southwestern New Mexico till the Peloncillo Mountains began to rise and stretch themselves across our path. The trail, reaching harder ground, suddenly spread into several dim paths and then vanished altogether, but we kept moving toward the range. At the foothills the Indians made us keep together and follow the lead of Chie, who ran some two hundred yards in advance. There were no trees of any size, but here and there were some resinous shoots, straight and tall, having blade-like leaves, with about the firmness of a cornstalk. Chie set fire to eight of these, ranging in a large circuit, — then to eight more, and repeated the operation; the fire would shoot up quickly and leave a peculiar little cloud of black smoke. I asked: "What does he do that for?"

Ponce answered: *"Paz, humo paz,"* that is, peace, peace smoke.

Shortly Chie began to bark like a coyote and was answered by a bark like his own from the mountain side. He then ran up the slope to meet a fellow Apache, while we went on slowly.

The danger to miners, prospectors, and soldiers while crossing arid wastes arises from long droughts. Indians also suffer for want of water when their well-known springs dry up. We were very thirsty, but Ponce assured us that there was one good fountain up there among the trees where Chie had gone. Our disappointment, however, was great to find the source almost exhausted, there being hardly water enough for the men to drink.

While we sat beside the spring Chie and the stranger joined the party. The latter ate some crackers, drank some water, and smoked a pipe in silence, then turning toward Chie he said: "I must go." He immediately started off and ran farther up the mountain. After a moment's delay Ponce ran after him without remark.

Cochise's scout, for such was the stranger, very soon returned. He was mounted on an Indian pony with a child behind him, while his obedient spouse followed on foot. Ponce, now coming from another direction, led in a small company of ill-dressed, dirty-looking Indians, some mounted, and the rest leading their ponies. Evidently the spring water had not been wasted in ablutions. An old woman, wrinkled and haggard, was introduced to me as one of the wives of Cochise. We had come upon an outpost of the famous chief, but his stronghold was yet more than a hundred miles distant. Soon the ponies of sixty Indians and our own horses and mules were feeding together along the foothills of the range, while the Indians and white men were eating bread and drinking water from the same fountain. Luckily for the animals, before night another spring was discovered, where a few at a time were permitted to get a good drink.

The next morning Cochise's scout told me frankly that I must diminish my party or never see his master. I then turned off three more men to meet the ambulance at Camp Bowie and remain there till called for. Camp Bowie was a garrison post in Apache Pass, a few miles south of the Indian trail which we were following.

# CHAPTER XIII.

SCOUTING FOR THE APACHE CHIEF, COCHISE — ENTERING HIS MOUNTAIN STRONGHOLD — FIRST NIGHT IN A WILD CAMP.

Setting Out to Find Cochise — "General, Aren't You Doing Wrong?" — Marching Under a Cloudless Sky — A Camp Without Water — An Offer of Whisky in Place of Food — A Midnight March — An Ideal Camp — Little Savage Guides — In an Apache Camp — No Word from Cochise — "Will it be Peace?" — "He is Coming!" — The Apaches Prepare to Receive their Chief — Arrival of Cochise — "This is the Man" — His Appearance — I am Asked to Explain the Object of my Visit — A Long and Interesting Interview — Some Startling Questions — A Midnight Scare — My Return Through a Dangerous Country.

JEFFORDS, Sladen, myself, and the two Indians went over the mountain and across the valleys in a southwesterly direction. While ascending the Chiricahua range along a blind trail, Sladen rode to my side and said: "General, aren't you doing wrong? Don't you think you are taking too much risk? Eight could have made some resistance, but now there are only five of us."

"The risk is indeed great," I replied, "but I have thought the matter over carefully and am determined to proceed."

For some time we rode along in silence. I was troubled and anxious about Sladen. At first I meditated sending him back, but I knew that the bare mention of it would make him indignant. But it is one thing to lay one's self on the altar of sacrifice, quite another to put there a faithful friend. Suddenly I turned to Sladen and looked him in the face and said aloud: "Captain, whosoever will save his life shall lose it, but whosoever will lose his life for my sake, the same shall save it." Without another word Sladen dropped back upon the trail and the danger was never again referred to between us.

That first day's ride of forty miles over the Chiricahua range was tedious indeed. The atmosphere was dry, the sun scorching, and there was no water in any of the usual places. The animals suffered even more than the men from increasing thirst. Ponce and Chie had told us of a beautiful spring on the western slope of the mountain we were crossing. About sunset Chie, who had ridden off the route, came back shaking his head: "*No agua!*" Not one drop—all dry. We still pushed on, fearing and hoping, while we examined every semblance of relief in the ravines and deep gulches. Just as the twilight was fading into night we discovered some high, perpendicular rocks. When we came closer the welcome sound of water trickling down over their surface caught our ears. Imagine the joy of our little party! The animals were quickly there — at a well-filled basin hollowed out in the bottom ledge. How glad we were to drink at that fountain and, like Rebecca, let the animals drink also!

Under the same cloudless sky the next day we toiled on for thirty miles across the San Simon valley, in Arizona. It was a broad, dry, sagebrush stretch of country which reaches the foothills of the Dragoon Mountains. These, all that day, ragged, gray, and lofty, intercepted the western view. At last, weary enough, we struck the road at Rodgers' ranch, twenty-five miles west from Camp Bowie. The Bowie garrison had sent out a small guard to protect this stage station. Rodgers and the soldiers were much surprised as we approached them from the desert. I said to Mr. Rodgers, who ran out to meet us: "Can you give us something to eat?"

"No, no," he answered, "but I have some whisky to drink."

"But we don't want whisky!"

"Why not?" he asked in astonishment, "it is good whisky!"

The little guard of enlisted men kindly shared their bread and bacon with us and fetched excellent water from the sulphur springs — the salty impregnation was very slight. Here we staid, a group mysterious to the guard, till the twilight had disappeared and the upper dome was never before more thickly studded with stars. Rodgers had three or four large dogs, who were particularly hostile to Indians. They were unwilling to make any allowance for Ponce and Chie. As I lay down upon a bear skin I asked Chie to come and sleep with me. He approached, and looking at the bear skin, said: *"Shosh no bueno!"* *"Shosh"* was the Apache word for bear. Chie was more afraid of the dead bear's skin than he was of the living dogs, but I put away the bear skin and used only our overcoats, so then he came and was protected from both dangers.

Shortly after midnight we saddled up in silence and quietly moved away, going southeasterly toward the outer slopes. The grass was tall and nutritious, but there was no water. Coming to a level space Jeffords had us halt and said: "Let us make a dry camp." We did so, resting till daylight, and then without stopping to eat we began to thread a cross-canyon of the lofty range, going on steadily till we came to the western slope. The sound of a stream flowing from the mountain gave us fresh delight. In a few minutes we were upon its banks. It came from an abundant spring which produced a rivulet of clear, cool, most acceptable water. Near at hand, beneath a scraggy oak with branches low, broad, and thick, we made our bivouac, while the animals, quickly freed from their loads, ran to the stream and drank their fill, after which they busied themselves for hours feeding upon the sweet grass around them.

North of the halting-place was the rough gap which, Jeffords said, led to Cochise's ordinary abode. Chie had hardly placed his saddle and blanket under the tree when, without a word, he bounded over the rocks and crags, ever upward in the direction of that gap, till lost to view. All the day, under Ponce's direction, we were setting five fires in circular order. This meant peace and five comers. We watched in vain for a responsive smoke. There was not even the footfall of a horse to indicate the nearness of Cochise or any of his clan. Chie had disappeared behind the high rocks, and probably gone into the deep canyon beyond, and as yet there was no sign from him when we gathered around the canvas for supper. Ponce, apparently not anxious, was stolid. We had written our letters and notebooks and spent the long day trying to while away the time as patiently as possible.

Just as we finished eating supper we beheld two Indian boys of perhaps ten and fourteen years approaching from the west. Both were on one horse. As they drew near we saw that the horse was without saddle or blanket, and for bridle they had a small rope tied to his under jaw, with the loop thrown over his neck. Coming near, the lads dismounted, looked us over carefully, scarcely speaking, and then sitting on the ground regaled themselves with the crackers and coffee which we offered. The repast finished, the larger of them pointed toward the gap, and told Ponce that Chie had come to their lodges and wanted us all to come in and join him.

In a trice we understood the message. We caught up our blankets and supplies, saddled our mules and horses, and hastened away. The boys acted as our guides, keeping our party ahead of them along the trail. One of them took a great fancy to Captain Sladen. He examined his clothes, admired his pistol and belt, and minutely inspected his horse and equipments. The good-natured little savage doubtless coveted those luxuries, yet he showed no enviousness either in look or act.

Winding around the foothills to the left we found a crooked stream flowing westward from the gap. By a moderate ascent we followed that up through the western pass into the heart of the

RED CLOUD'S BUCKSKIN WAR SHIRT, ORNAMENTED WITH HUMAN SCALPS AND BEADS; BEADED LEGGINGS AND MOCCASINS.

*For Description see page 15*

PHOTOGRAPHED AND PAINTED FROM THE ORIGINAL OBJECTS EXPRESSLY FOR THIS WORK.

range. The sun had set, but there was still sufficient light to get glimpses of our environment. A small band of Apaches — mostly women and children — were sitting and waiting under some trees. Chie, as well as a sub-chief, had risen to meet us, and the children were flocking around. Almost encircling the party were the walls of an enclosing natural fortification; the bottom was a rolling plat of thirty or forty acres of grass land; a *ceniga* or small swamp near the middle was fed by abundant springs; out of this flowed the clear creek which we had ascended; stunted trees were growing here and there. This plat was protected on the north and south by sandstone cliffs, rough and irregular, rising in places to two hundred feet; there was considerable débris at their base. The whole space was shut in except where the narrow canyon afforded entrance or exit. It was a veritable *cul de sac.*

We made our bivouac near the creek under a tree, amid a throng of those wild people who, in the outset, appeared curious and happy, not hostile. That evening Tygee, a sub-chief, paid us a visit, courteous enough, it is true, but he himself was gloomy and reserved, and had no word from Cochise. Even Ponce and Chie were troubled and silent.

"Will it be peace?" I asked.

Ponce shook his head and answered demurely: "*Quien sabe?*" i. e., "Who knows?"

When I had spread out my blanket and placed my saddle for a pillow, and was lying down for much-needed rest, the children came and nestled at my feet, laying their little heads upon my blanket. I turned to Captain Sladen and said: "This does not mean war"; so without particular apprehension I slept comfortably till morning. The Apache band had made their bivouac under the small trees at a distance near the débris of the great walls.

After our breakfast the following day we began to be uncertain as to our next step. I asked: "What shall we do now, Jeffords?"

"Pack up as if we could go where we please," he replied. Therefore, to show our independence, not very real, we were packing up and making ready, when suddenly the sound of many voices arose and echoed through the canyon. Ponce said: "It is he; he is coming!"

Immediately preparations were made by the Indians to receive their chief. The circle of sitters was enlarged on the higher bank of the creek, and a folded blanket placed for his seat.

First there appeared in advance, riding rapidly down the ravine, a single horseman, short, thick-set, and much painted with stripes of black and vermillion. He had a fierce look and carried a long lance in his hand. He dismounted and embraced Jeffords, while I asked: "Is that the man?"

"No," said Jeffords, "this is Juan, his brother." The Indians never say Cochise, but in Apache *"Shi-ca-she,"* and in Spanish *"Mi Hermano,"* meaning my brother.

We had hardly been made acquainted with the warlike Juan, who was diligently inspecting our personal possessions, when a mounted party appeared. It consisted of a fine-looking horseman, a younger Indian, and two women. The party proved to be the old Chief Cochise, his son Natchez, his sister, and his young wife. His elder son was absent.

Having ridden up to us Cochise dismounted and saluted Jeffords in Spanish as an old friend. He then turned to me as Jeffords was saying: "This is the man." The chief was fully six feet in height, well-proportioned, with large eyes; his face was slightly colored with vermilion, hair straight and black, with a few silver threads. He warmly grasped my hand and said pleasantly: "*Buenos dias, Senor!*"

Having returned his salute I began to study his face. His countenance was pleasant, and made me feel how strange it is that such a man can be a notorious robber and cold-blooded murderer. In after interviews I observed that upon ordinary occasions he showed courtesy and simplicity, but, as the Chiricahua chief, when in council or mounted, leading his tribe, if Apache wrongs were touched upon, he was terribly severe in aspect.

As soon as Cochise's sister met Ponce he said something evidently very afflicting to her, for she sat down, and for some minutes uttered a loud and continuous Indian wail. Everybody stood still till she had finished, then Cochise and I passed up to where the blanket was placed and took seats. Already the Indians — men, women, and children — had arranged themselves about us in a large semicircle, giving due form and interest to the proceedings. Cochise now turned to Ponce and Chie, who were seated upon his right, and proceeded to gather from them what he could of my history and designs. Both Ponce and Chie were now my strong friends and their story evidently created a favorable impression.

Next Cochise turned to me and said something in Apache. Jeffords gave the substance in English: "Will the General explain the object of his visit?"

"The President sent me to make peace between you and the white people."

"Nobody wants peace more than I do," he replied.

"Then," I answered, "as I have full power we can make peace."

He then continued: "I have done no mischief since I came from Cañada Alamosa, but I am poor,—my horses poor and few. I might have brought in more by raiding the Tucson road, but I did not do it."

Cochise, however, acknowledged later that he had recently sent out twelve captains in different directions in Mexico and Arizona to get their living. He next recited at some length his own story of the Apache wrongs.

I answered that I knew of these things; that there were two parties in the United States—one friendly to the Indians, and the other hostile to them; that the friends of the Indians were now in power, with General Grant at the head. I then broached my plan of making, on the Rio Grande, a common reservation for the different bands of Apaches, including his own.

"I have been there," Cochise replied, "and I like the country. Rather than not have peace I will go and take such of my people as I can, but that move will break up my tribe." Then he asked suddenly: "Why not give me Apache Pass? Give me that and I will protect all the roads. I will see that nobody's property is taken by Indians." As he said this his eyes flashed and he lifted his chin proudly.

I answered: "Perhaps we could do that, but it would be vastly to the interest of the Chiricahuas to go to Alamosa. Five rivers are near there: the Rio Grande, the Alamosa, the Negro, the Palomas, and Puerco; in their valleys are fine planting grounds and good grazing for thousands of cattle; plenty of mescal plants are there, and there is good hunting in the mountains."

He quickly turned the subject. "How long, General, will you stay? Will you wait for my captains to come in and have a talk?"

These were startling questions, considering that our lives were at his disposal, but I answered promptly: "I came from Washington to meet your people and make peace, and will stay as long as necessary."

"It will take ten days," Cochise said. He appeared to be pleased at my answer and ordered his messengers to the captains to get ready; then his whole manner changed and he went into a complaining and sometimes fierce recital of the bloody history of the Apaches.

"We were once a large people covering these mountains; we lived well; we were at peace. One day my best friend was seized by an officer of the white men and treacherously killed. . . . The worst place of all is Apache Pass. There, five Indians, one my brother, were murdered. Their bodies were hung up and kept there till they were skeletons. . . . Now Americans and Mexicans kill an Apache on sight. I have retaliated with all my might. My people have killed Americans and Mexicans and taken their property. Their losses have been greater than mine. I have killed ten white men for every Indian slain, but I know that the whites are many and the Indians are few. Apaches are growing less and less every day. . . . Why shut me up on a reservation? We will make peace. We will keep it faithfully. But let us go around free as Americans do. Let us go wherever we please."

I answered that all this country did not properly belong to the Indians; that all God's children had an interest in it, and therefore to keep the peace we must fix metes and bounds; that such a peace as Cochise proposed would not last a week. "Suppose," I said, "some rough prospectors should fire upon and kill a portion of your band, or suppose some of your wild young men should take the life of a citizen, the peace would then be hopelessly broken."

After considerably more plaintive pleading he said: "You Americans began the fight." I replied, as before: "I know that. A large number of your friends fully believe what you state and they wish to see war, murder, and robbery cease."

He smiled and in a different tone added: "I

am glad you have come, but will not the soldiers fire upon my Apaches as they come in?" To this I answered that I would send Captain Sladen to Camp Bowie to notify that garrison and to telegraph to other posts. Cochise shook his head doubtfully:

"The soldiers may not obey Captain Sladen. They will obey you. I want you to go. Jeffords and Captain Sladen can stay here."

Looking around upon the people with a smile he added: "Our young women will look after the young captain." Thereupon shouting and laughter, with clapping of hands, came from all the women in response. I hardly think Sladen enjoyed the alternative, even though he had evidence of such popularity.

I decided to go back over the Dragoon mountain fifty miles or more to Camp Bowie, and therefore asked for a guide. None of Cochise's people dared to go. They answered the chief as he spoke to them: "There is no peace yet. We might be killed." At last Chie stepped forward and said: "I will go, if Jeffords will give me his mule."

Then, the mule being given, Chie and I prepared to make the journey. We mounted and rode westward to the mouth of the canyon. Our friends, accompanied by Cochise and several Indians, went with us that far. Stopping on high ground and leaning against a large smooth-faced stone we gazed around. Before us was a magnificent landscape. As Cochise raised his eyes and took in the view he exclaimed: "*Shi-cowah!*" i. e., "My home!"

Chie and I set out together, moving northeast and ascending the western slope of the Dragoon range. We followed a faint trail till night obscured it; we then scrambled on as best we could over ragged heights and through deep gulches. I tore my coat in shreds, pricked my legs with thorns, and withal made such poor headway that for a time I was sure we should be obliged to remain on that mountain all night, but the young Indian did not falter. Occasionally he cried back to me: "*Camino no bueno,*" i. e., "Road not good." Then he would stop and push out in another direction. I leaned forward and hugged my mule's neck as he ascended a height, pulled him up after me along the sides where it was too steep to stand still, and sometimes I slid down a deep ravine by holding his tail and pushing him before me. My Spanish was meager and Chie's no better. His only English was "yes, sir," and "milky-way"; but "*Camino bueno,*" oft repeated by Chie's cheery voice at last brought me out upon the foothills, where each of us showed his joy by whistling and singing.

Obtaining a lift in Rodgers' lumber wagon over the last twenty-five miles, we came in sight of Camp Bowie when the sun was an hour high. We passed through Apache Pass, where Chie's father, Magnus Colorado, was slain. Here Chie lost his usual cheerfulness and seemed in distress. Once previously the young man had asked Jeffords: "Why did the white men kill my father?" Jeffords answered: "Because those were bad white men." This answer doubtless kept him from holding all white men responsible.

On our approach to Bowie through the woods the outpost men took us for Apaches and came near firing at us, but my American voice, shrill enough then, reassured them.

At Camp Bowie I found the son of my old general, Major S. S. Sumner, in command. His good wife helped put my wardrobe in better condition. After I had given all necessary orders I took those of our party who had been detached with us and we turned back and by sunset of that day were once more at Rodgers' ranch.

The next morning, after a much-needed rest, we followed the Tucson road till we had passed the Dragoon mountains, and then turned southward by the way of Dragoon springs. Cochise and Captain Sladen, from a high point fifteen miles south of the springs, were eagerly watching for the first sign of our coming. As we neared them they all descended with joyous speed to meet us. The night previous, the Apaches there in Cochise's stronghold had had a great fright. Some rumor came that soldiers were nearing them; they changed their ground to a place of easier defense. "We lay," said Sladen, "the rest of the night on the sharp rocks of the mountain side." Behind them was a rough bridle path practicable only for leading horses and mules up to the summit of the mountain. Instantly upon actual approach of soldiers the women, children, and luggage would pass to the height and be off, while the warriors could easily destroy any small force that should rashly undertake the ascent and the attack.

## CHAPTER XIV.

### MY EXPERIENCES IN A WILD APACHE CAMP—FAREWELL TO COCHISE.

Getting Acquainted with Cochise—A Dance of Welcome—Becoming Conduct of Indian Women—Apache Mothers—Inviting Cochise to Dinner—Some Ludicrous Table Manners—Eating from my Plate and Drinking from my Cup—A Sudden and Startling Alarm—Cochise Becomes Intoxicated, Unruly, and Violent—Disquieting Rumors—Managing Rough and Troublesome Customers—A Strange Ceremony and Weird Performance—An Embarrassing Offer—A Chief Covets my Mules—Offers to Exchange Two of His Wives for Them—Declining the Trade Without Giving Offense—Farewell to Cochise.

I WAS now to live with the Indians for some time. The new camping ground to which Cochise took us was north of the entrance to his stronghold, well up on the foothills where were clusters of oaks and several acres of grass land. Six miles off stood a globular height, springing three hundred feet from the plain, with the San Pedro River at its foot. On this hill, at the request of Cochise, Jeffords and Sladen had planted a white flag. Sladen told me how the Indian women and children clapped their hands when they first saw this emblem of peace. Jeffords had understood them when in one compound word in Apache they cried: "The-flag-of-peace-I-love!"

A stunted oak, with broad branches, covered my bivouac; thirty yards away was Cochise's. His was made by a couple of boughs leaned against a scrub oak which had grown near a high rock. A place for sleeping was hollowed out in the earth beneath. The furniture consisted of several buckskins dressed with the hair on them, a few blankets that had seen long service, some bows and arrows, a rifle in prime order, and four sets of saddles and bridles thrown together with as many sets of hide horseshoes; also a number of knives, a small tin vessel for coffee, a water bucket, and an *olla* or earthen water-jar. Our provisions, consisting of some fresh and some jerked venison, were hung on a branch of the oak. Mescal plants were abundant, and sundry esculent seeds whose names I could not learn were lying in heaps close at hand.

Every night after my return Cochise sent his sister, a woman of at least forty years of age, with a few helpers, to guard our animals and protect our supplies. The first evening, in the dim starlight, without a camp fire, the Indians gave us a dance of welcome. They used a simple contra-figure. The women stood in line and opposite to a line of men. Two women then stepped forward, keeping time to the rough music of a tom-tom, as they moved toward one man. He followed them as they retired. At given times the men crossed over and all formed one line, the men and women facing different ways; then going forward and back the women faced about and the men followed suit, without losing step; occasionally, at a word, all moved in a circle. The drum was the ordinary tom-tom made of buckskin stretched over an *olla*, and the drumstick was a flexible rod.

When I was invited to dance I did so. As I

passed into line an Indian woman held my left hand and another my empty right sleeve, chatting and laughing all the time, but I could not understand what they said. After each dance the men were expected to make a present to both women; it was the rule for every man. Any little thing answered the purpose, such as a penny or a pencil. One tall packer by the name of Stone, who had come with me from Bowie, delighted the Indians beyond measure when he joined the dance, for he spoke Apache a little and was full of fun. But one night he had nothing in his pocket with which to pay the tax. Ponce suggested: "You have two shirts, give them one," and so he did. Ponce shouted in Spanish: "A man who gives his last shirt is sure to prosper!"

The conduct of the women during our visit was uniformly good. Most of them were industrious. They tanned deer hides, did all the camp work, attended to the cooking, and cared for the children. As soon as I let them have some *manta* (cotton cloth) they worked busily enough making new garments. All had short skirts, with loose sacques hanging over them, and wore moccasins ornamented with beadwork. Nearly all wore strings of beads around their necks. There was no wantonness, and not one woman in that entire camp bore the dreadful mark given by Apaches for adultery, which was the cutting off of a part of the nose. I had seen one case of it in the first Apache party we met.

I was careful to maintain the good footing I had established with the children on that first night when we were in Cochise's stronghold. The babies were each bound to a board, the head usually sheltered by basketwork. I saw mothers dip their little ones in the clear cold stream and immediately wrap them in numerous bands of cotton cloth and fasten them to the boards, leaving the head and feet free. A strap enabled the mother to swing the little one upon her back, supporting it by the strap against her forehead as she walked or ran. Until they were twelve years old the boys seldom wore any other clothing than the breech-cloth. A bit of cracker or lump of sugar overcame the shyness of the children. Day after day I noticed them happily sporting upon the huge rocks in innocent play. Boys and girls gathered around me when I was writing and did their best to imitate the "copy" that I wrote for them. Cochise's son Natchez, a lad of fourteen, learned from me to write his name. For a diversion they tried to teach me the Apache language,—laughing at my queer pronunciation and at my evident dullness in learning Indian speech.

The Apaches could go many hours without food, but in times of plenty they had food always ready. Whenever one of them was hungry he proceeded to help himself, for there was no regular meal time. I introduced the three-meal-a-day system, using in lieu of a table my canvas spread on the ground. When the first meal was served I invited Cochise to sit at one end and beside me. After the invited guests were located the sub-chiefs and other Indians were asked to occupy the vacant places. As soon as we were seated boys and men crowded into every interval. I had, while squatting on the ground in tailor-like position, an Indian at my left elbow and a child astride of my right leg, both eating from my plate and drinking from my cup. The white man's table etiquette was not closely followed.

Only once did we have anything like an alarm. Cochise and several of his Indians had had a *tizwin* spree. They made the liquor from the mescal plant. It was not very strong, but they kept pouring it down until the inevitable result followed—they became much excited. Suddenly I heard sharp screams from Cochise's wife and sister, and I saw them fleeing in terror from his bivouac. He was striking and scolding them, and his voice was loud and harsh. With some trepidation I said to Jeffords: "What shall we do now?"

"Oh, General, sit down! sit down!" replied Jeffords.

I did so, while Jeffords ran to Cochise and placing himself beside him managed to entertain him. Crazy drunk as the man was at first, he soon became more quiet, and in a short time the extreme violence of intoxication had passed. Indians when sober may be managed, but with Indians drunk no one can predict the consequences.

The first Apache captain to come into camp was Nyle-shie-zie, a man over thirty,—Cochise's brother-in-law. He brought a rumor that soldiers, in spite of my orders, had been sent against the Chiricahuas. The whole camp seemed to be running to me, and all were frightened. The scare was caused by Indians getting a distant glimpse of

Navajo Boy.

Comanche Girls.

Kiowa Girls.

COMANCHE, KIOWA, AND NAVAJO CHILDREN.

*From photographs supplied by United States Bureau of Ethnology.*

Captain Sladen, and Jake May, our interpreter, who were returning from a food and mail trip to Bowie. This incident, like that of the night camp-moving, showed in what constant apprehension these Indians lived.

Other Apaches continued to come in until nearly all were in camp. Many of the newcomers were rough and very troublesome, and an adjustment of all vexed questions was hard to bring about. I was forced to abandon the Alamosa scheme, and to give them, as Cochise had suggested, a reservation embracing a part of the Chiricahua mountains and of the valley adjoining on the west, which included the Big Sulphur Spring and Rodgers' ranch.

The evening after the council a strange ceremony for consulting the spirits was observed by the Indians. It took place on a separate plateau near my bivouac. I was not to be present at the beginning of the performance. I could, however, hear the muffled sound of voices of a multitude of women apparently imitating the low moaning of the wind. Then all—men and women—sang with ever increasing volume of sound, and the women's voices rose higher and higher. It was a wild, weird performance.

In due time the roughest-appearing Apache that I had ever seen, tall and muscular, his long hair hanging in braids down his back, ran toward me. His manner was not as fierce as his appearance would indicate, for he now spoke gently and invited me and all our white men to join the band on the plateau. Arriving there we sat outside the women's circle,—the male Indians being seated within it. As soon as the singing ceased the men kept on talking, but without rising. An authoritative voice now silenced all the others. It was Cochise speaking in a mournful recitative. More than once I heard him use Jeffords' sobriquet, "*Stag-li-to*," meaning Redbeard. Our whole case was evidently being discussed at the meeting. Those were solemn moments to us, for we could not determine on which side of the Styx their superstitions might land us.

Fortunately, the spirits were on our side. Their answer to the Indian incantation was rendered through Cochise, who said: "Hereafter the white man and the Indian are to drink of the same water, eat of the same bread, and be at peace." I felt that the object of my mission was now accomplished.

The day following the spirits' favorable declaration we all set out to meet, by appointment, the officers from Camp Bowie. We were to assemble at Dragoon Springs. During the journey I rode a stout mule, carrying double; Cochise's Indian interpreter, with his supple arms encircling my waist, was my companion. Cochise, with his face freshly and hideously painted with vermilion up to his hair, had a fierce and repellant aspect. The wild yells of his mounted warriors seemed to excite him almost as much as the *tizwin* had done. On the way they made several wild charges at imaginary foes, and I could see how wagon trains of mules could easily be frightened and stampeded almost beyond recall.

Arriving at Dragoon Springs Cochise located his men with such skill that every one of them could in two minutes have been safely under the cover of a ravine, and in three minutes more have escaped behind a protecting hill, and so have passed to the mountains without the least hindrance.

Cochise now said to Jeffords: "I know your party and I trust you, but those people from Apache Pass (Camp Bowie) I do not know. How long have you known them?"

"I never saw them," said Jeffords. That was all the conversation that occurred between the Indians and ourselves before our arrival and their quick formation near the Dragoon Springs.

Major Sumner, with several officers and a few civilians, came out to meet us. We immediately entered into a council with the Indians which lasted four hours. It was substantially a repetition of those which I have already described. The metes and bounds of the reservation were fixed, the agency at Sulphur Springs established, and Jeffords was appointed as the agent of the Indian department. It was arranged that all Apaches when off from a road were to show a white flag, and all on a road were to meet people, as white men do, without any manifestation of fear.

One day while in Cochise's camp I noticed a beautiful rifle, a breech-loader that had been the property of Lieutenant Stewart whom the Indians had killed in battle. As I was thoughtfully looking it over, the old chief, who was intently watching my face, suddenly said: "*No trieste,* General!" I was thinking of the young officer's sudden death and how he was mourned at home. Cochise interpreted my thought and said in Spanish: "You know, General, that we do things in war that we do not do in peace." It was hard to comply with the old chief's admonition and not keep a sad countenance, but I did my best and told him that as I had been in war myself for many years I knew that what he said was true, but I longed for the time to come when all people would make peace and there would be no more war.

Cochise had said in the spirit council to his fellow Indians: "Hereafter the white man and the Indian are to drink of the same water and eat of the same bread." Soon afterward one of his wildest captains came to me with the interpreter and tried to buy my four magnificent mules. After offering me everything of value which he possessed, and receiving my answer, ofttimes repeated: "I cannot sell them; they are not mine; they belong to the United States government," he went away with an incredulous look that plainly showed he did not quite believe what I said. Had I not declared in council that General Grant had given me all necessary power to make peace with the Indians? Was not the power to give him those four handsome mules necessarily included?

After a time he returned with the same interpreter and two young Indian women. They were dressed in new *manta,* their hair was neatly combed, beads hung around their necks, and the moccasins which met their pretty dresses were fresh and clean. I said to myself as they approached: "These are very presentable girls."

They smiled when they looked in my face as if they had interpreted my thought.

Now judge of my surprise when the young brave, looking at them and then at me, said through the interpreter:

"General Howard, I will give you these two girls for those four mules. They are my two wives, and I shall be glad to let you have them for your wives if you will let me have the four mules."

I stammered out: "Why, I am married already."

The girls then said something to the interpreter and smiled sweetly upon me while he said: "The women say that will make no difference. They don't mind your having a wife already; they will do everything they can to please you and will go anywhere with you."

This flattering answer puzzled me more than I can explain, but I remembered an incident that had occurred the night before, and of which I had been told. One of our packers had approached the sister of Cochise during her watch over my camp property—a duty which Cochise had required of her, and made to her an improper proposal. She answered him indignantly: "Sir, that is not the custom of our people!" The packer could speak their language, and their conversation was in the Apache tongue.

I thought that as an experiment I would try the same phrase, if the interpreter could add a little to it and translate it into Apache, thus: "It is not the custom of our people for a man to have more than one wife."

As soon as this was translated the young women turned away and went back to their husband's lodging-place, apparently satisfied with my rejoinder.

Just as I was leaving for home *via* San Francisco Cochise looked at me a moment, then stepping forward and putting his arms around me, said in plain English: "Good-bye!" Thus we separated.

On Monday evening we were in Tucson. Here a lively opposition was shown to what I had done. The people and the local newspapers declared that I had protected Cochise against deserved punishment. Nobody believed that he would keep the peace beyond the ensuing winter months. Still, in spite of the clamor, the citizens gave those Indians a fair chance to keep their word.

Six years after the above events a letter from an Indian inspector, who had been among these Apaches to learn their condition and needs, said that they told him I had made a good peace, adding: "General Howard placed the stone on the *mesa* and told us that as long as that stone should last so long would the peace continue. The stone still lies on the *mesa* and we are still at peace."

Cochise kept his promise while he lived, and his eldest son preserved the peace until his death. On a visit to Washington in 1876 this son was attacked with a fever which resulted fatally. I happened to be in that city at the time and attended his funeral.

As a matter of fact, the entire tribe kept faith as long as our government did, but at last, on recommendation of a new agent, they were taken by force and put with the San Carlos Indians. The consequence was that a part of them went off under the notorious Geronimo, and among them was the boy Natchez, Cochise's son. An Indian war of the worst sort followed.

Military operations in 1887, in which Generals Crook and Miles participated, finally captured a remnant of this band, including Natchez. They were sent as prisoners to Florida and taken thence to Mount Vernon barracks, Alabama, and were kept at one of my posts for six years,—the last years of my active service in the army.

On my visits of inspection they always exhibited confidence and great affection. From them were formed two Indian companies that did themselves credit while we were permitted to have Indian troops.

# CHAPTER XV.

## ASSIGNED TO THE DEPARTMENT OF THE COLUMBIA, EMBRACING ALL THE NORTHWEST — THE MODOCS AND THE MODOC WAR.

An Arduous Task — Ordered to Report to General W. T. Sherman — Assigned to the Department of the Columbia — A Field Embracing Oregon, Washington, Idaho, and Alaska — My Arrival at Portland, Oregon — The Modocs and their Chief, "Captain Jack" — Causes that Led to the Modoc War — Old Hostilities Revived — Attempting to Arrest the Leaders — The Modoc Strongholds in the Lava Beds — Massacre of General Canby and of Dr. Thomas — Defeat and Capture of the Modocs — "Scar-faced Charlie" — End of the Modoc Campaign.

IMMEDIATELY after the close of the Civil War I was engaged for nine years in matters pertaining to freedmen and refugees; the latter were whites disturbed by the operations of war in the regions between the Union and the Confederate armies. My work embraced the payment of bounties and claims, particularly the back-pay of soldiers. This period extended from the 12th of May, 1865, to August, 1874, having, as we have seen, an interruption of about one year, which was devoted to the settlement of Indian difficulties in Arizona and New Mexico. Of this period all that concerned the freedmen and refugees, the colored soldiers and the white population, has been treated of by me in a separate volume entitled the "Period of Reconstruction."

The famous bureau of which I had charge began with an extension to all the functions of gov-

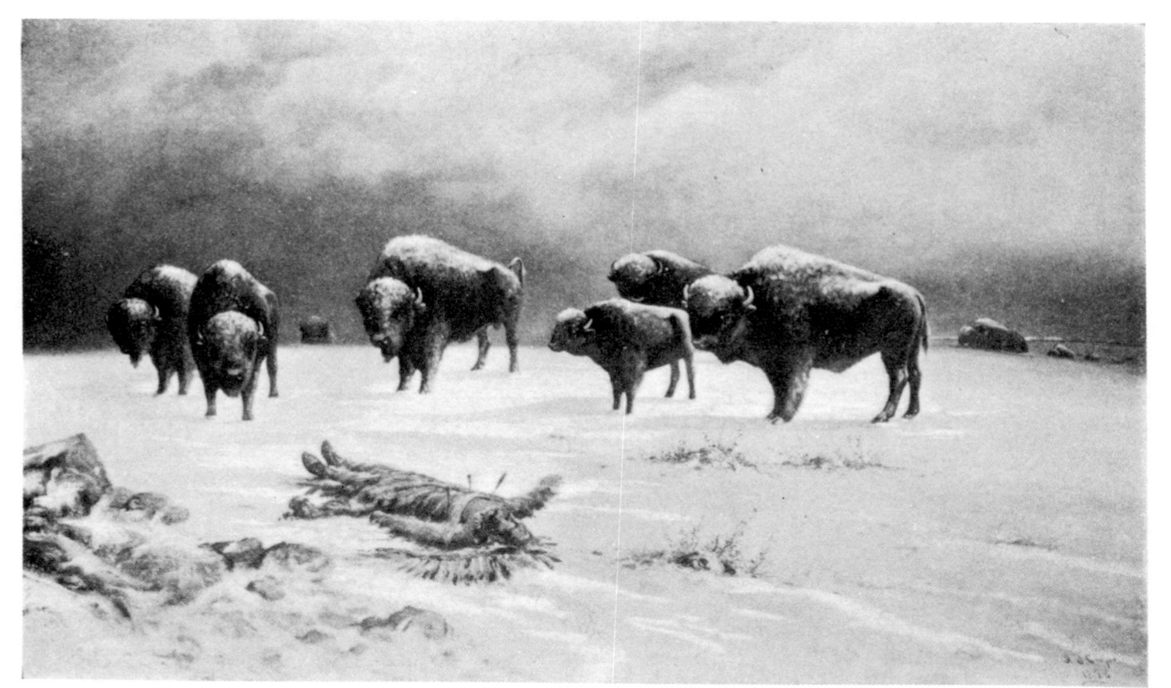

THE INQUEST.—A WINTER SCENE ON THE GREAT PLAINS BEFORE THE DISAPPEARANCE OF THE BUFFALO.

ernment, and touched every subject where the welfare of the people, without distinction of race, was involved. As it proceeded it was able to throw off one function after another until during the last three years it devoted itself to little else than the development and regulation of the schools under its charge, and the payment of bounties and back-pay to colored soldiers. When at last the bureau was closed all payments devolved directly upon the Adjutant-General's Department.

Being relieved from this duty, I reported back to General W. T. Sherman, then commanding the army. I endeavored to exercise some choice as to a position, thinking that my rank and previous hard service entitled me to express a preference. But Sherman wrote me that after so much duty at Washington—which was regarded by officers of the army as easy and desirable—I must not presume to pick and choose my department. Really, the bureau labor was the most onerous of any ever imposed upon me. Fortunately, however, he sent me to the farthest corner of the Republic, namely, to the Department of the Columbia, with headquarters at Portland, Oregon,—a department that embraced Oregon, Washington, a large part of Idaho, and Alaska.

Arriving at Portland the 25th of August, I assumed command September 1st, relieving Jefferson C. Davis, who from a major-general on reduction of the army had become colonel of the Twenty-third Infantry.

Davis was hurt at being displaced after the distinguished and loyal service he had rendered, especially in the Modoc campaign, which had then just ended. The Modocs were located in the southern part of my department, and with them I had very little to do except to send a remnant of them, escorted by my aide-de-camp and a few soldiers, to the Indian Territory.

The treachery of "Captain Jack," the Modoc chief, and his followers, the massacre of General Canby and his companions, the prolonged strife which a few Indians had waged against our many troops, the efficient work of General Davis in grandly closing up the campaign, executing Captain Jack and a few guilty leaders by hanging,—all this was over, and peace, for a time, reigned throughout the immense territory where the troops in Alaska and those in Idaho were more than a thousand miles apart. Davis and I, though he was much disappointed, had no personal feeling, for he gracefully yielded his command and went back to the sole charge of his regiment.

I had the opportunity more than once to visit Fort Klamath and go over the rough lands occupied by the Modocs, and to observe many of those that remained after the removal of the tribe.

There were in the Modoc country three general groupings of Indians. In eastern Oregon, north and south of the line which separates Oregon from California, the country was largely inhabited by the Klamaths. East of the Klamaths and west of the Cascade range of mountains, over a similar extent of territory, were the Modocs and a tribe known as the Snakes. The latter were not the same as the so-called Snakes of the interior. These tribes were at war with each other long before white men came to share their possessions and little by little to displace them.

As early as 1865 a sufficient number of Indians from these three tribes were brought together for a council. Those in conference, assuming to represent all the Indians (as they did not and could not), made a bargain with the United States. Our people gave them a reasonably large reservation, and procured as a *quid pro quo* from the Indians from fifteen to twenty thousand square miles of the rough land of that region. For this an appropriation of seventeen thousand dollars was to be made. At no time did the government agent succeed in gathering about his agency even a majority of the Modocs. A part of the tribe, who had suffered at one time a terrible massacre at the hands of white men, were hostile to going upon any reservation, and in fact were hostile to the white men themselves, and to all Indians that had traded lands for such a paltry compensation.

The Modocs' original location was in the roughest sort of woodland and pasturage, among the Lava Beds, a wild region in northern California and southern Oregon, near Tule Lake. It seems strange that anybody should have desired to take from them their old habitations, which occupied about forty square miles of as dreary and uninviting a region as men could inhabit and live upon. Probably it was the hope of those who were prospecting for mines to find some favorable indications among the volcanic and basaltic heaps of stone and lava which strew the open fields for miles and miles north and east of the lake—a hope that always promotes a covetous disposition.

After some of the Modocs had made a trial of life upon a Klamath reservation difficulties arose, old hostilities were revived, the government's promises were unfulfilled, and the pledged money long delayed, so that suddenly every Modoc rushed away and all went back to their former desolate homes. A new agent made requisition for the troops at Fort Klamath to go out and arrest the leaders and bring back the Indians. Against this the Indians protested, Captain Jack being their spokesman. He begged for peace and peace measures, but declared that the Indians would not yield to force. Of course the troops persevered and bloodshed followed. Then the Indian captain led his people to the stronghold of the Lava Beds, and stayed there fighting our troops till forty soldiers or more had been killed and wounded. On the way to the Lava Beds, passing a white settlement, white men and boys were slain by the Modocs, but for once the white women and younger children were spared.

At no time did Captain Jack's soldiers exceed a hundred warriors, yet for months they held an army six times their number at bay. Among their last acts was the massacre of General Canby and of Dr. Thomas, an Indian commissioner, effected by treachery. A few weeks passed and these Indians were conquered. Captain Jack and three others were tried for murder by a military commission, found guilty, and a few weeks later were executed at Fort Klamath.

My aide-de-camp took charge of about a hundred of those who were banished and ordered to the Indian Territory. He handcuffed several of the men who had been in the fights, and for a while kept these irons upon them as they journeyed by rail to the east, but their disposition was so evidently good, and they were so thoroughly obedient, that he ventured to remove their uncouth bracelets. After that all the Indians of his party showed themselves grateful for his kindness and helped him in every possible way to make the journey agreeable to him as well as to themselves.

One strong reason why the Modocs struggled so hard to remain near Tule Lake was what has been recorded as their special superstition, — "To live, die, and be buried where they were born." One of their favorite leaders, usually called "Curley-headed Jack," when he was about to be taken to Fort Klamath by the soldiers shot himself with a pistol and died in the arms of his mother. Though the other Indians of his party felt the same repugnance to leaving their territory and mourned deeply for him, yet they did not go so far as to take their lives.

It was the custom to bury with a deceased Modoc whatever belonged to him and could be so disposed of, such as clothing, ornaments, and at times even coin. They also put into the grave some kind of food to sustain him on his journey to the Happy Hunting Grounds.

## CHAPTER XVI.

### THREATENED HOSTILITIES — A TRIBE THAT CAUSED TERROR TO THE WHITE PEOPLE OF THE NORTHWEST.

Twenty-five Distinct Tribes of Indians in my New Field — The Nez Percés — Their Dress and Appearance — Decoration of Their Horses — Fondness for Bright Colors and Picturesque Attires — Fanciful Dress of the Children — The Famous Nez Percé Chief Joseph — An Indian Feud — Chief White Bird and His Band — Indian "Dreamers" and "Tooats" — A Lazy Interpreter — A Message from Chief Joseph — A Dignified Procession — A Ceremonious Call — Clinging to Old Haunts — "We Want Nothing from You" — Efforts to Avert the War.

WITHIN my northwestern military jurisdiction I soon found that I had twenty-five distinct tribes of Indians. They were under the care of nine agencies, five of which combined several tribes in their charge. Each of the remaining four had charge of a separate tribe, as follows: The Simcoe Indians, under Mr. Wilbur, were north of the Columbia River and just east of the Coast Range of mountains; the Warm Spring tribe, under Captain Smith, was far south of the Columbia and amid the foothills of the same range; the Nez Percés, under J. B. Monteith, were above Lewiston, Idaho, and occupied a large country; and the Skokomish bands, under Mr. Eels, were on Puget Sound. Mr. Cornoyer, who had married a Cayuse wife, managed the Umatilla agency, but had various other tribes besides the Cayuses under his care. General Milroy, who achieved fame during the Civil War for almost reckless bravery, had his headquarters at Olympia, and looked after various tribes up and down the coast.

These Indians were particularly fond of ornament and display. I have often watched them at Indian gatherings on feast and council days, and noticed how careful the men were of their personal appearance, and how painstakingly they decorated the manes and tails of their horses with bright-colored strips of cloth. The women were dressed in the gayest clothes they could command for such occasions. When passing in review the men and women rode separately, and all intoned an Indian song or chant that no doubt gave expression to their feelings.

In illustrated newspapers the Nez Percés were frequently shown in the old stereotyped manner usually followed in portraying wild Indians. They were represented as being mounted on sleek and prancing chargers, naked above the waist, hair as stiff and bristling as porcupine quills, long lances poised high in air and ready to strike, and so on. Neither in peace nor war do they so appear. In these days the Nez Percé prefers the rifle and usually he has the best. Those of them who remained at peace during my stay in the Northwest dressed like the white people as near as they could, though their dress varied according to the degree of civilization to which any body of them had attained. The men averaged about five feet eight inches in height, and perhaps one hundred and forty pounds in weight. They wore their hair cut short. They looked, when on foot, like the Spanish-speaking inhabitants of Arizona; when mounted they sat upon their horses firmly and naturally and were more graceful in their motions than the Mexicans or our own frontiersmen.

The women wore their hair long enough to reach down the neck, sometimes banged in front, and sometimes tied back with bits of ribbon. Their skirts, even for young girls, were never short. They had a fondness for bright shawls, and wore them pulled over the head so that the face was half hidden. At the Lapwai agency, on gala occasions, I noticed an almost universal use of handkerchiefs of bright colors, which seemed to take the place of shawls. To the beholder the effect was picturesque in the extreme.

Some families dressed their children as fancifully as whites do, but usually the little ones had only such plain, cheap garments as the traders furnished. When our people first met the Nez Percés a century ago, they were then comfortably clad in dressed deer-skin and furs, and took pains, as our soldiers did, to keep the old white belt ever white and new by the use of chalk. They are just as painstaking today in their manners and dress.

In a rich valley called Imnaha I found two young men—Joseph and Ollicut. Their father, who had not been long deceased, was called Joseph, but usually in later years "Old Joseph." For a while, when the famous missionary Mr. Spalding held his mission and school on the Lapwai reservation, Old Joseph and his family went there to get the advantages offered by the mission. The boys succeeded in obtaining a smattering of knowledge, and the family was inclined to accept the conditions of civilization, including the use of the plow and the hoe; but a feud sprung up between Old Joseph and another hereditary chief, forcing the old man to leave the Lapwai reservation and go back to settle in Imnaha Valley, just over the boundary in Oregon, there to occupy the Grande Ronde country. Joseph had under him a large band of followers and they owned many horses. At Imnaha they found great abundance of grass of the best sort (the bunch grass), and fertile ground for their corn whenever their superstitious inclinations would permit them to plant it. It was declared by most of them that they could find enough fruits to subsist upon, which grow of themselves, without disturbing the soil to raise others.

Other bands had gone off to the east, to the south, and to the west from Lapwai; indeed many of them had never come at all within the boundaries of that well-chosen government reservation.

In 1876 and 1877 the Nez Percés were the cause of a reign of terror among the white people, followed by great expense to the general government. It is not difficult to trace the causes which led to the subsequent disaster. The Nez Percés, before Joseph's war, prided themselves upon never having shed white men's blood, and their steady purpose was to live at peace with them. They, mingling with the Flatheads, had early heard about the white men, and sent messengers to learn the truth and the causes of our civilization. After the return of these messengers, they had always welcomed our people, whether coming as "Bostons"—a term they applied to white soldiers—as English fur traders, or as missionaries. Mr. Spalding and his saintly wife, always beloved and trusted by the Indians, had succeeded in increasing their regard for the white men of the east.

In 1855, when Governor Isaac Stevens made a treaty with them, which was confirmed by the Senate of the United States, he defined the boundaries of a Nez Percé reservation. The immense territory set apart for them was so extensive as to take in Old Joseph and his people and all the other bands which bore the name of Nez Percés. It embraced an area half as large as the state of New York, a diversified and rich country of rivers, valleys, woodland, mountains, and mines of various descriptions. Even then one might have predicted that the time would surely come when white men would insist upon the reduction of those ample limits.

The time was not long in coming. As soon as Oregon was secured to our people a flood of immigration set in, and in due time encroachments were made on Indian lands; indeed, white settlers never could be made to understand the reasons for treaties with Indians, nor the justice of protecting them in their reservations against the encroachments of the whites.

Eight years after the first treaty, another bargain was made with a body of Nez Percé Indians gathered in council. The new treaty left out Imnaha, Wallowa, and all the Grande Ronde Valley, now occupied by several thriving cities. True, a majority of the Indians agreed to the new treaty, but this caused a fatal division among the Nez

Percés, which eventually brought about dreadful results. Two parties opposed each other from that time on. Those within the reservation at Lapwai were the "treaty Indians"; all the others were known as the "non-treaty Indians."

Of the non-treaty chieftains White Bird had the largest band. He dwelt in the Salmon River Valley, and his followers occupied that valley and its feeders. The White Bird Canyon was a favorite gathering place for these wild Nez Percés, who were rich in cattle and in horses. Between the Salmon and the Snake Rivers, for the most part a rough, mountainous fastness, dwelt another band under a strange leader called "Too-hul-hul-sote." He was not a real chieftain as the Indians reckon it, but a "Dreamer," named by the Nez Percés a *Tooat*.

South of the Snake River, above the mouth of the Grande Ronde, a river full of rocks, rapids, and falls, comes in a famous stream called "Asotin Creek." Along this creek was another small band which made common cause with the non-treaties.

Off to the westward was still another roving set of non-treaties. They fished in the Snake River and hunted far and near in the rugged country south and east of Lewiston. Hush-hush-cute was their young chieftain, pleasant and courteous in deportment, but never considered by white men to be reliable. He was a favorite associate of young Joseph.

On the reservation itself was to be found a majority of the Indians whom I have described as treaty Indians, i. e., the Nez Percés proper. They were divided into Protestant and Roman Catholic Indians, and had a United States agency near Fort Lapwai, and a sub-agency at Kamiah on the Clear Water about seventy miles from Lewiston. James Lawyer, an intelligent farmer, had been elected as the chief of the tribe. The Catholic Indians lived on Little Mission Creek, some eight miles from Lapwai. Here they had a village to themselves to which they were greatly attached because it was near their mission. A sub-chief, with whom I had much to do, was named Jonah. James Reuben, the son of a former head chief, a very scholarly man who had translated the gospel of John into Nez Percé, was for two years my interpreter, friend, and helper. The whole number of these reservation Nez Percés when I first met them was estimated as between two and three thousand.

Early in 1875 I visited Umatilla and there met Mr. Cornoyer, also Mr. McBean, the interpreter. Mr. Cornoyer, a light-hearted Frenchman, introduced me to his three beautiful daughters,—the Indian mother we seldom had a glimpse of,—and I was royally entertained. McBean had a great reputation as an interpreter. He was stout and inclined to be lazy. Whether his interpretations were always correct was better known to himself than to anybody else.

Not long after my arrival McBean came in and said: "Here is a messenger from Joseph. He and ten of his Indians are at Young Chief's camp. Joseph and his *tillicums** want to have a talk with the agent and with the new commander."

* *Tillicums* signifies Indian people.

Soon eleven of these Nez Percés made their appearance. They were strikingly tall, much more so than the average Nez Percé, were in good flesh, and clad in Indian costumes such as I have described. Each one had a blanket on his shoulder or near at hand. They came on, one at a time, in dignified procession and took first the agent's hand, afterwards mine. Young Joseph opened his dark eyes upon me and studied my face with care. His fixed gaze did not annoy me, for I had a feeling that he not only wanted to read my thoughts but in some way to show me his own good disposition. For a long time after that interview the young man and I were apparently the best of friends.

At this first meeting his message was short. It is, as I recorded it at the time: "I heard that Washington had some message for me. I came to visit my friends among the Cayuses. Young Chief told me to speak to the agent. That is all." I simply told him that there were no new instructions from Washington, but that I was glad to see him and make his acquaintance.

The eleven then immediately retired with the same formal ceremony and dignity that had characterized their coming, and after remaining a short time with the Cayuses, went back to their home in Wallowa.

This visit fulfilled the prophecy made by General Davis the previous year concerning the nontreaties in the Imnaha valley. He reported, in effect, that a collision with Joseph would come sooner or later, that the Indians were very restless, and that the real cause of their discontent was that their beautiful country was being more and more encroached upon every year by enterprising and covetous white settlers.

As no order for the Indians' removal had been enforced they had hoped to stay permanently where they were. They were clinging to their old haunts and herding their ponies upon the rich grass lands of Wallowa, whilst white men who were gathered in settlements near at hand were taking up land as fast as it could be surveyed, erecting houses upon it, and putting up extensive fencing in plain sight of the protesting and irritated Indians.

Governor Grover of Oregon naturally took the side of the settlers, and had succeeded in getting their petition heard at Washington, so that all the lands that had belonged to the Indians in that quarter (Oregon) had been secured by a presidential order in favor of the new farming and stock-raising settlements, and against Indian occupancy.

After all these statements concerning the relations between Indians and white men, and the favor shown to the whites by government officials, I will repeat here what I have previously asserted, for it is my conviction, that the main cause of the bloody Nez Percé war that followed lay back of ideas of legal ownership, back of savage habits and instincts; it rested in the natural and persistent resistance of independent or "dependent" nations to the authority of other nations. The non-treaty Indians denied the jurisdiction which the United States claimed over them. Everything that they might want was offered and extended to them if

INDIANS RETURNING TO THEIR CAMPS FROM A FALL BUFFALO HUNT.

they would submit to governmental authority which the United States agents exercised. They answered, sometimes very roughly: "We want nothing from you. We have not given you our land. You have no right to take it from us. Washington cannot divide up the country and give it to anybody." Too-hul-hul-sote, one of the confederates whom Joseph trusted, always rough and ugly, said to me in council: "We will go where we please, and when we please, and do as we please. Who gave Washington rule over me?"

In 1876, after an Indian had been killed by a white man in a dispute concerning some stock, I entreated the President to send a good commission with sufficient power to settle these Nez Percé difficulties. At last the commission came and held its session at Lapwai in November, 1876. No better men could have been selected for that purpose. They tried their best to get the consent of Joseph, Ollicut, and the other non-treaty Indians to a settlement of all their troubles. At one time the younger men, seemingly influenced by a spirit of peace and good will, were on the point of yielding to the persuasion of the commissioners.

Just then the "Dreamers" came in with their characteristic talks and prophecies and turned the tide against the measures of adjustment. The Dreamers asserted that if the Indians would continue faithful to old teachings "a leader would be raised up in the east who would restore all the dead Indians to life, and who would unite them in expelling the whites from their country; then they would repossess the lands of their ancestors."

It must be remembered that Joseph and his confederates set up an absolute title to the lands and claimed an independent sovereignty; so that any adjustment that the commission could have effected would have been, like so many other compromises, simply temporary.

The commission recommended that Joseph be required to come on the Lapwai reservation and reside permanently within its limits.

In process of time orders came from Washington to carry out the recommendation of the commission. They were directed to the United States Indian agent, J. B. Monteith, and, I being in command of the troops, instructions were sent to me to coöperate with and aid the Indian agent. Monteith at once, early in January, 1877, sent messengers bearing an order to Joseph and to the other outside chieftains: "Come on the Lapwai reservation." Instead of heeding the message the Indians, who were in constant communication with each other, were vigorously preparing for war. In March, Mr. Cornoyer visited me in Portland and told me that Joseph wanted to make him a visit, because he was sure that the interpreters of Lapwai had not properly spoken for him.

I answered: "Encourage them to come and I will send my aide, Major Boyle, a judicious officer of long experience with Indians, to represent me at the council, and to hear and report what they have to say."

The council was held, but Joseph's brother Ollicut, not Joseph himself, came. He had great influence with Joseph, and when he spoke in a public council Joseph immediately accepted Ollicut's promises as his own. In private Ollicut urged war measures, taking the side of the more reckless of his tribe. To him the prospect of battles with white men had a charm which he could not well resist. No fruit came from this conference except a promise from me to have another interview with Joseph and his people the 20th of the ensuing April.

# CHAPTER XVII

MY ARRIVAL AT FORT LAPWAI — GROWING DISCONTENT AND INSOLENCE OF THE INDIANS — FEARS OF AN OUTBREAK.

An Important Indian Council — Happy "Medicine Men" — A Picturesque Indian Procession — A Suspicious Gathering — A Fear-inspiring Song — My Plain Talk to Chief Joseph — His Reply — "They Treat me like a Dog" — Growing Excitement — Defiant Attitude of the Hostiles — Ominous Signs — Efforts to Conciliate the Indians — An Immediate Uprising Threatened — A Fierce Rejoinder — "I am the Man" — An Obstinate and Angry Indian — Thrusting a Mischiefmaker out of the Council — Averting the Crisis — A Distrusted Indian Chief.

TAKING Captain Wilkinson with me, I left my headquarters April 16, 1877, and was at Walla Walla by the 18th. Colonel Grover, a brother officer in Civil War time, took me to his house on my arrival, where he and his good wife extended a generous hospitality.

The Indians did not appear till about 6 P. M. of the 19th. Ollicut came to the western gate and stated in the most courteous manner that Joseph was ill so that he, Ollicut, had come to represent him. I promised to give him an interview the next day in the presence of his Indians, and he turned away to select a camp for the night. It was arranged that the council should be held in the band quarters, and we gathered in the large, low-ceiled room at about 10 o'clock in the morning. It was soon well filled, the Indians being seated on rough benches to the right, while officers of the army and some citizens were upon the left. I took my seat, with my aide for a secretary near at hand, beside a large table. There was a sprinkling of ladies among the officers and near the doorway.

After all the preceding formality and remembering that the appointment had been made long in advance, I was much disappointed when the council closed. The Indians were outwardly pleasant, and as dignified as usual. Again the wishes of the government were explained to them. They answered that they were only delegates and could make no binding promises. They begged me to fix a date and place for another interview in order that Joseph, his people, and other malcontents might meet me. I promised that the desired interview should take place at Lapwai in twelve days. The whole appearance of the "medicine men," of Young Chief, the Umatilla friend and advocate, of Ollicut, and every Indian present seemed to bespeak good will. Yet it may have been a ruse on the part of the Indians, particularly of Ollicut, to observe how many troops there were at Walla Walla, and the character of our armament. They had an opportunity before they left of seeing a review of the small garrison, and the testing of our Gatling guns for different ranges and rapidity of firing. We shall see by and by that they learned some other things which were to our disadvantage.

Before the twelve days had expired I was at Fort Lapwai. The council appointed for the 3d of May for Joseph and his people began on the day designated. There were present the agent, J. B. Monteith, with an interpreter, then Joseph and

Ollicut, with about fifty of Joseph's Indians. The council assembled out of doors under some awnings carefully arranged. The guard-house was on one side of the awnings and the barracks, with soldiers at hand, not far off on the other. I did not distrust the Indians, but when one makes a preparation it is better that it should be complete.

Before the council assembled there was an Indian procession, consisting of a column of men followed by women and children, all mounted on Indian ponies. This time the Indians were freshly and hideously painted, the bright red color passing up into the parting of their hair; the hair of the men was braided and tied with colored strings, and their bodies were ornamented with decorations of different kinds. They had an odd variety of hats, some blankets, leggings of buckskin, and moccasins, some of them covered with beads; the women wore bright shawls or blankets, with skirts to the ankle, and high moccasins. The effect was very picturesque. As Indians do, they kept us waiting long enough in their mind to produce an impression, finally moving up slowly from their camp to the vicinity of the soldiers' garden.

As soon as they had made careful announcement of their purpose they struck up a song and slowly moved on. The men were armed with tomahawks and knives, but did not bring many firearms from their camp. The wild sound of their singing did indeed produce upon every one of us a marked effect. I was glad myself that the Indians were so few. Their voices were shrill and penetrating, now dying away to a plaintive wail, then bursting into a mighty volume of sound that was fear-inspiring in its finish. The Indians kept on outside of the fences until they had made the entire circuit of the garrison, ever repeating the blood-curdling refrain of their song as they rode. At last Joseph, Ollicut, and other leading Indians came to the garrison from behind Colonel Perry's quarters. They were thus attempting to do honor to the commanding officer.

At the council tent I found two interpreters, Mr. Whitman and James Reuben, also two aides, Captain Wilkinson and Major Boyle. Many officers and ladies of the garrison had come to the conference. There were numerous treaty Indians gathered about. Father Cataldo, a priest from the Roman Catholic mission, was also present. As soon as the Indians with Joseph and Ollicut came in and occupied the benches and chairs prepared for them, the Catholic father opened the proceedings with a brief prayer in the Nez Percé tongue. Then, speaking to Joseph as the chief, I remarked:

"I heard from your brother Ollicut twelve days ago at Walla Walla that you wished to see me. I am here to listen to what you have to say."

Joseph replied that Chief White Bird was on the way and already in the Craig Mountains, and that he would be present the next day. Joseph wanted all the Indians to hear. I told him that we would wait for White Bird if he wished us to do so, but if he would immediately comply with the wishes of the government he could have his pick of the land. I told him further that the instructions to White Bird were the same as to himself.

The old Dreamers already present now spoke up boldly, and charged the interpreters to tell the truth. They intimated that they wanted to talk many days about their land and deprecated any hasty proceedings.

I answered them as quietly as I could and assured them that they could have all the time they desired, but that they might as well understand first as last that all the Indians would be required to obey the instructions of the government. Mr. Monteith, the agent, slowly read aloud his orders from Washington, which were interpreted to them, and added with considerable show of firmness: "I sent out Reuben and some others to your camp and invited you to come in. (They had not heeded this message.) Now you must come and there is no getting out of it. Your Indians and White Bird's can pick up your horses and cattle and come on the reservation. Joseph can select the place he wants, if he will do it at once. General Howard will stay until matters are settled."

Next Ollicut spoke: "We must think for ourselves—whites and Indians. We have respect for the whites, but they treat me like a dog and I sometimes think my friends are different from what I had supposed. There should be one law for all. If I commit murder I shall be hung, but if I do well I should not be punished. Our friends will be here tomorrow and I will then tell what I think." Of course I had to tell them that whatever the government commanded us to do must be done. I urged them to come on the reservation, and explained that the privileges to hunt and fish in the

Imnaha Valley might be granted to them; that if they hesitated, the government had directed that soldiers be used to coerce them; that Joseph and Ollicut knew that we were friends to them, and that if they complied there would be no trouble.

Joseph then put forward the Dreamers. They were as rude in their manner as in their speech. I deemed it best to meet their insolence with severity of manner and brevity. For this I have been blamed, but I noticed that the commission's action the year before at Lapwai, on account of the kindness and long-continued patience of the members, was interpreted by Joseph and the other Indian chieftains as indicating weakness and fear. My own idea may be expressed in this way: in dealing with Indians we must neither fear nor hate them; after instructions are given by the proper authority see to it that the Indians are made to understand the orders; afterwards see to it that they are carried into execution without hesitancy or delay. Everybody present understood that that was the position of the Indian agent, and of myself as department commander, when we adjourned the council until the morrow.

The next day was exceedingly mild and beautiful. The sun shone brightly and gentle summer breezes swept the valley of the Lapwai. As usual, the Indians were very deliberate in coming to the council. They went through the same showy parade and procession as the day before, but with very much larger numbers. At last they came in again by the colonel's back way and took their places. Ollicut crouched at the feet of Joseph,

White Bird took his position a few yards away, and his followers sat on the benches or on the ground near him. He kept a large eagle's wing in front of his face.

The discontented Dreamers, or *Tooats*, were made as prominent as on the day before. As soon as we were ready Alpowa Jim, a treaty Indian, opened the meeting with a fervent prayer in his own language. Mr. Monteith then repeated the instructions which we had received from Washington. Joseph, as soon as Monteith had ceased, glancing toward him, said to me: "This is White Bird. I spoke to you of him. This is the first time he has seen you and you him. I want him and his Indians to understand what has been said to us."

I made all necessary explanations as before, whereupon the Indians made for this occasion Too-hul-hul-sote their principal spokesman. After he had stopped talking Joseph, first, and White Bird after him, endorsed what he had said. I saw that the Indians were getting very much excited, and was glad when the young chieftain asked for a postponement of the council. The postponement would enable me to get some troops into place that were coming from Alaska and Oregon. Indeed, the Indians at this meeting gave clear evidence that they did not intend to comply with the instructions from Washington. The next day being the Sabbath we adjourned the council until the following Monday.

It was plain to be seen that the treaty Indians were frightened. As their opponents, the non-treaties, increased in numbers it was noticed that they were fully armed with modern weapons. They put war paint on their faces and their manner was insolent, defiant, and hostile. The ladies of the garrison instinctively comprehended the situation, and in evident fear kept asking: "Is Joseph going to fight the troops?"

The Sabbath was as peaceful a day as we could desire. At the agency the gathering was so large that the hall used for a church would not hold the people. The Nez Percé women and children were dressed in their best, their picturesque attire giving at a little distance the bright effects of a holiday assemblage. Many of the non-treaty people mingled with the worshipers, and the service was in every respect a good one. The only thing that marred the occasion was that in Joseph's camp some of his warriors went through with a weird dance, accompanied by the incessant beating of tom-toms, and other ceremonies characteristic of their heathen worship. Notwithstanding this diversion, at the close of the day a happier feeling seemed to pervade all parties.

The most important council, at which I felt sure matters would come to a climax, assembled on Monday, the 7th of May, 1877. All the different non-treaty bands from the south, the east, and the west were there. Indian runners gave Joseph to understand that our soldiers were already in the Wallowa country. Again there was the same marching and singing. The Indians had evidently gained in courage, and all those who wanted war were bolder in their attitude. Monteith, the agent, appeared this morning to be very kind to the Indians. He wished, he said, to remove a false impression that had somehow gotten abroad. He assured them that their religious rites would not be interfered with, but he added that if a teacher counseled insubordination and disobedience to the clear instructions of his department such a teacher would have to be restrained.

Again Too-hul-hul-sote took the floor. He asserted that the earth was his mother, that it should not be disturbed by any instrument of husbandry, that men must eat what grows of itself. He had much to say of chieftainship; that it came from the earth and was inherited, and so on. I answered: "We do not wish to interfere with your religion, but you must talk about practical things. Twenty times over you have repeated that the earth is your mother, and that chieftainship is from the earth. Let us hear it no more, but come to business at once."

Too-hul-hul-sote replied with another speech in which he denied the jurisdiction of the United States, and disowned the binding force of the treaty already made. His manner was so surly and disagreeable that I could see plainly that he was exciting an opposition which might result in an immediate outbreak, for every Indian appeared to have, just at that time, some weapon ready at hand for use.

"But," I replied firmly, "you know very well that the government has set apart a reservation and that the Indians must go upon it. If an Indian becomes a citizen, like old Timothy of Alpowa, he can have land like any other citizen outside, but he must leave his tribe and take land precisely as a white man does."

Too-hul-hul-sote made his fiercest rejoinder: "What person pretends to divide the land and put me on it?"

I answered: "I am the man. I stand here for the President, and there is no spirit good or bad that will hinder me. My orders are plain and will be executed. I hope the Indians have good sense enough to make me their friend and not their enemy."

The hostile spirit then manifested could hardly have been stronger, and I knew that the crisis had come and that something must be done to relieve the situation. So after listening for a short time and hearing the old chief say that he had never given anybody a right to sign away his lands, I demanded: "Do you speak for yourself alone?"

He replied, with additional emphasis and anger: "The Indians may do what they like, but I am not going on the reservation!"

Of course this was intended, as is the Indian custom, to voice the purpose of all the non-treaty people. I told him that it was bad advice, and, trying to drive a wedge between them, I said: "Joseph and White Bird seem to have good hearts, but yours is bad. I will send you to the Indian Territory."

Indeed, Monteith and I had feared that this Dreamer, who hated every approach to civilization, would make trouble. He did not claim to be a medicine man, but he talked all the time like one. We knew well that he had not spoken a conciliatory word, that he had advised all the non-treaty Indians to fight. So I said: "You counsel them to resist, to go to war, to lose all their horses and cattle, and have unending trouble."

Then suddenly I turned to the others and asked: "Will Joseph and White Bird and Looking-Glass go with me to look after their land? The old man shall not go. He must stay with Colonel Perry."

"Do you want to scare me with reference to my body?" exclaimed Too-hul-hul-sote.

I said firmly: "I will leave your body with Colonel Perry." Then before anybody could act, with the help of Colonel Perry, I seized the cross-grained Dreamer and led him out of the council and delivered him to the guard. At that instant some of the Indians were on the point of plunging their knives into my breast, but Joseph and White Bird both counseled delay. They could have killed me and the few other white men in the council, but they knew they could not pass out of the enclosure without large loss to themselves, for our men, with rifles loaded, were ready at the guard-house on the one side and at the barracks on the other.

The crisis had now passed; the Indians changed their tone and were pacific. They readily agreed to go with me over the Lapwai reservation to its remotest boundaries, where they could find fertile lands for cultivation, if they would condescend to cultivate them, grassy hillsides for their ponies, and a well-wooded country. With this understanding the council adjourned.

We came together again after several days spent in riding over and inspecting the reservation, Joseph, White Bird, Hush-hush-cute, and others in turn jogging along by my side and talking to me through James Reuben, or another interpreter, while my aide-de-camp, Captain Wilkinson, Rev. Mr. Thompson of Olympia, Mr. Monteith, the agent, and Whitman, the interpreter, mingled with the other Indians, conversing pleasantly with them. Looking-Glass took a special fancy to Captain Wilkinson, and indicated great delight at the peace prospects. We all firmly believed that the Indians had at last made up their minds to obey the instructions of the government and come on the reservation.

Joseph at the last meeting presented a petition that I would release Too-hul-hul-sote from guard. This petition I granted. Joseph then promised solemnly to be on the reservation by June 14th, and he was to go to the region of the Clear Water River for his allotment of it. That gave Joseph and his people just one month to break up at Imnaha.

Hush-hush-cute asked for thirty-five days. He was the Indian most distrusted at the time, but nobody supposed he could make war alone.

There was a general satisfaction among the white people at Lapwai and Lewiston. The peaceful treaty Indians had no doubt of Joseph's good intention, and even now I think that he then believed the best thing to do was to heed the instructions of the Indian department, and take up his abode along the fertile grounds of the Clear Water.

# CHAPTER XVIII.

## AMONG THE COLUMBIA RIVER INDIANS — INCIDENTS AND PERSONAL EXPERIENCES — "CUT-MOUTH JOHN."

Up the Columbia River — Smohollie, a Pompous Indian of Important Manner — Standing on His Dignity — Treating Him with Indifference — Changing His Mind — Sending for an Interpreter — Renegade Indians — Wild and Fierce to the Last — The "Skookum-house" — An Insubordinate Old Chief — United Against the Whites — An Odd Character — A Sea-sick and Disgusted Indian — "Cut-mouth John" — How He Acquired His Name — Introducing Himself to Me — His Dirty and Comical Uniform — His Personal Appearance — A Ludicrous Spectacle — Trying to be a White Man.

SOON after our return to Portland from the Lapwai council, while waiting for the time to arrive when Joseph and his people were to go upon their designated reservation, I made a trip up the Columbia River, arriving late one afternoon at crumbling old Fort Walla Walla, which stood near the river where the hamlet of Wallula is now situated. The proprietors of the hotel were very hospitable, though they had but a poor, rickety house, wretchedly built, with partitions hardly thicker than pasteboard.

They had made the perilous journey over the plains and across the mountains from the Kansas and Nebraska frontiers to the Touchet River, and finally settled at Wallula, rich in personal experience, and with a fund of stories to relate of adventures with Indians, hairbreadth escapes, of danger, exposure, plenty, and want, enough to interest strangers for hours.

Here we spent the night. The next day, in a large tumble-down storehouse, I brought together several bands that we called the " Columbia River Renegades." In accordance with a previous promise, I had sent a message to Smohollie, the leader of the Indian spiritists, who was at the time in a large combined camp, higher up the Columbia than Wallula, and on the other side.

Smohollie, who could not be exceeded by any earthly potentate in assumption of power or importance of manner, had upon my arrival sent me word by a messenger that I must go to his camp. I informed the messenger that I had come all the way from Portland, by appointment, to meet Smohollie at Wallula, which was an arrangement of his own seeking, and that if the chief had anything to say to General Howard he must come to Wallula and say it.

Smohollie sent a second messenger who was to find out and report to him what I intended to say to the Indians. The messenger intimated that he would carry back the tidings promptly, whatever they might be, and then Smohollie and his followers would act.

I replied that I had nothing whatever at this time to say to Smohollie, and that it was not important whether I saw him or not. This was, of course, rather ungracious, but there was no apparent reason for this attempt to draw me across the river. It might mean personal harm. A little after noon Smohollie, having changed his mind, and having mustered all the people he could, including women and children, crossed over the river just above Wallula. They approached the village, freshly bedecked with paint and feathers, and the cavalcade filed in with all the pomp and circumstance characteristic of Indian conceit. As many of the Indians belonged to the Umatilla agencies I had arranged to have their friend Mr. Cornoyer with me. The council was at last held, and there were at least two hundred and fifty men present, besides fifty women with little children. All gathered in and around the building, eagerly waiting for some communication from me.

How some days everything goes awry! We held an unsatisfactory conversation by using the Chinook—that meager and inadequate language through which it is extremely difficult to convey information. Our interpreter, McBean, had been taken ill while on his way to us from Umatilla, and a messenger brought word that he could not come. Some of the bystanders made feeble attempts at interpretation through signs and the Chinook language, but I was obliged to adjourn the council until we could bring to us an old and famous frontiersman, Mr. Pambrum, who lived near Wailatpu, where Dr. Whitman, who was slain by the Cayuses, was buried. I knew Pambrum to be a remarkably good interpreter. He could speak the different Walla Walla dialects, which the Cayuses, the Walla Wallas, and the Umatillas well understood.

He arrived at last, late in the evening, when we immediately called a smaller council. There we had Smohollie, Young Chief, the best leader of the Umatillas, Homily of the Walla Wallas. and Old

WAR AND SACRED SHIELDS; BEADED BLANKET BAND; WOMAN'S BELT
WARRIOR'S DISK STRAP, HEAD DRESS, ETC.

*For Description see page 15*

PHOTOGRAPHED AND PAINTED FROM THE ORIGINAL OBJECTS EXPRESSLY FOR THIS WORK.

Thomas, a refractory chief who had led his band to some lands beyond the Snake River.

The statements made by all these Indians were the same that the non-treaty Nez Percés continually repeated. They said they wanted peace, but they desired much more to roam at large whenever and wherever they pleased. They really belonged, as the white men averred, on some reservation, and so the word "renegades" described them well. I believed that they were combining and meditating resistance the instant I should attempt to carry out the instructions of the Indian department at Washington, and that they were further waiting to see what the non-treaty Nez Percés, under whose wing they proposed to act, would finally do. Should they alone precipitate war they understood well enough that they would soon be annihilated. However, I carefully explained the wishes of the government and exhorted them to run to the shelter of the reservation as soon as possible. Mr. Cornoyer strongly endorsed my words.

The roving Indians had now obtained what they wanted and we separated with apparent good feeling. Old Thomas, whose hunting ground was near some of the non-treaty Nez Percés, was an exception. He was wild and fierce to the last, and wanted to know why I had been sending troops to Wallowa, and denounced the action and wishes of the United States government in unmeasured terms.

Every Indian left the little town before midnight. Old Thomas' people, going with him, rushed northward up the Snake River, making better time than the steamboat. They were crossing their hands and stating to every one they met that I was going to make slaves of them, and was going to put them into the "skookum-house," meaning the guard-house or military prison.

"Father Wilbur," the Yakima agent, had previously brought us an insubordinate old chief, Skemiah, and we had him still confined in a guard-room at Fort Vancouver. This fact the renegades had learned during our interview, therefore the "skookum-house" loomed up as a possibility to them. As soon as they heard of it, these renegades, though two hundred miles from the old captive, pleaded his case with me and begged for the imprisoned Skemiah's release. The renegades were thus connected by a common feeling and sympathy against all the white men, even though they did quarrel and fight with each other.

Old Homily of the Walla Wallas was a singular character. His village was along the Columbia, not far from it, north of Wallula. A more rocky, gravelly, forbidding, and unfruitful patch of land I never saw. It was always windy there and often so dusty as to make it doubly disagreeable. Yet Homily enjoyed that wild country of his. At one time, with some other chiefs, he went to Washington. On the way back on the steamer just below the mouth of the Columbia he was very seasick, and begged the captain to stop the steamer and send him ashore. "Oh," he said, "me much rather heap walk!" He told me afterwards, shaking his fat sides, that some people might like to live in such a place as Washington city, but it had no attractions for him. He would "a heap rather" live in his own home among the abundant rocks and stones above Wallula.

Among the Umatillas was a distinguished character who rejoiced in the name of "Cut-mouth John." He was brought to the city of Portland when I was there in 1876. He came as a witness in connection with some law cases where white men of bad repute had been selling liquor to the Indians of the Umatilla agency. When John introduced himself to me he had on a lieutenant's cast-off coat, with shoulder-straps, a red sash around his waist, a pair of dirty white gloves, and a slouched hat. He appeared in my room, and as I looked up he asked: "Mr. Howard?"

"Yes," I answered.

"Me Cut-mouth John," he said.

True enough, the right side of his face showed a deep and continuous furrow, which ran from where the corner of his mouth should be over and beyond his eye, leveling teeth, skin, and bones, and making his expression a constant and unsightly grimace. Major Boyle, who knew all the Umatillas, told me that Cut-mouth John had always been true to the white man. He was a scout for General George S. Wright. In one of his skirmishes an Indian, who was hostile to the whites, put his pistol on his arm, aimed sideways, and shot John, thus disfiguring his face dreadfully. Since then he had borne his present descriptive name.

After giving his testimony in Portland, Cut-mouth John came to bid me good-bye. He took plenty of time to silently look at everything around me. He felt much ashamed of his poor shoes. He declared he had called the Indian agent's attention to this sign of poverty; then he shook his head, with an indescribable grin upon his disfigured face, and said: "No potlatch" (no present). John's soiled white gloves were full of holes and his uniform was old and rusty. Poor fellow, in his shabby finery he presented a truly ludicrous spectacle! Yet I had a feeling of great compassion for him when I looked at the sad disfigurement of his visage, and remembered that it was a wound received from a hostile brother on account of his fidelity to the white men who have never been very faith-keeping to him or his people.

In their own native attire the Indians usually appear well. The dress of skins and feathers, however variegated, befits them. But when they put on our clothing and strut about in it their appearance is sometimes comical. A chief in an old shabby uniform, with perhaps a plug hat picked up on the dump pile of a fort, thinks he is pleasing and honoring the white man who in reality is pitying him, or laughing at his senseless vanity. Poor Cut-mouth John was trying to be a white man.

# CHAPTER XIX.

## BIDDING ADIEU TO MY FAMILY FOR WHAT PROVES TO BE A LONG ABSENCE — ON THE VERGE OF A BLOODY INDIAN WAR.

Chief Joseph's Bad Conduct — Robbing a Missionary's House — Miraculous Escape from Bloody Hands — Resting in Comfort, Peace, and Hope — My Fourteen "Commanding Officers" — An Old Comrade of the Civil War — Chief Joseph's Unconverted Heart — Guarding Against Indian Treachery — Release of Old Skemiah from the "Skookum-house" — His Grievances and Plea to go Back to the Reservation — Bidding Adieu to my Family — It Proves to be a Long One — On the Verge of a Bloody War.

THE date agreed upon when the Nez Percés were to come on the reservation was drawing near. We had returned to Portland from the council at Lapwai with a feeling that a great work had been accomplished. One of our Union generals always said to me at the close of a successful engagement: "*Fait accompli.*" Such seemed to me the closing interview with Joseph's people. We felt confident that there would be no serious difficulties with the Nez Percés. All their past history and their traditions favored this thought.

I have since learned, however, that Old Joseph had behaved badly toward the missionary Spalding as soon as he heard of the massacre of Marcus Whitman and his family—which I shall describe in another chapter—and that during the absence of Mr. Spalding's family he had robbed his house, destroying such goods as he could not take away. Besides, young Joseph and Ollicut, his stalwart sons, had in them Cayuse blood. I well remembered that the fierce Cayuses had perpetrated the horrible massacre of the early missionaries at Wailatpu, a very few of whom miraculously escaped from their bloody hands. Yet after all that may be said nobody can make me believe that young Joseph, at the time I left him, was planning treachery and murder.

The days came and went in Portland as usual. The spring rains had nearly ceased and were followed by gentle summer showers, which make the heart of an Oregonian glad. How many things come back to memory when a resting-time is over and the old perpetual conflict is renewed! My military family and myself were enjoying comfort and peace, and looking hopefully forward to the future, when one day Colonel E. C. Watkins, the inspector of Indian affairs, came into my office. How glad I was to see him!

I often declared that I had fourteen commanding officers, being obliged to obey the call of fourteen different Indian agents. It is not scriptural to obey so many masters. Colonel Watkins was senior to them all, so I transferred my allegiance at once to him, and placed him over all the agents. He was an able official and very congenial to me—the more so perhaps because he had been a comrade in the Civil War. He was a large, wholesome man, possessing genuine courage that never failed in any dangerous situation. We looked over the vast Indian field and concluded that Joseph, should he be inclined to treachery, might be tempted to take that course if he could induce the numerous Columbia River tribes to join him. We knew well enough that his heart was not wholly converted to our civilization. We therefore planned to anticipate any messengers sent from Joseph to tribes north of the Columbia.

To carry out our plans we made a brief visit to that part of the Indian stamping-ground. At Fort Vancouver we participated in the exercises of Memorial Day. Old Skemiah was still in the guard-room of the fort. He wanted to see me, and, still more, Colonel Watkins as soon as he heard of his presence and his office. Immediately we had a formal interview with him. He was chief of one of the small bands that should have gathered upon the Fort Simcoe reservation.

Having seated ourselves in General Sully's office, a soldier brought in poor old Skemiah, who had a clay-colored, expressionless face, a fat body and waddling gait. A sergeant, acting as interpreter by using the Chinook language and a few Indian signs, poorly made, managed to learn from Skemiah that his heart was good, had always been so, and that his people had gone to Fort Simcoe already, and that he would be very glad to go there too, and do all we wished him to do henceforth. "Only let me go back!" he pleaded.

After a brief consultation Watkins and I answered him favorably. "Tomorrow you shall go to Fort Simcoe under the escort of a sergeant." We were sure Father Wilbur would release him if he behaved well after reaching the reservation.

On the 31st of May we again set out from Portland, leaving there by the Dalles steamer at five o'clock in the morning. I little thought as I took my valise in hand and bade adieu to my drowsy family that I should pass through a terrible Indian war and be absent five months before I could look upon their faces again. Such, however, was the truth.

We picked up Skemiah and the sergeant on the way. The old man was happy, and his dull face suggested eager anticipation that was not unpleasant to look upon. I felt glad for him.

We left the Columbia transport forty miles above the Cascades and began to ascend the mountain range to the northeast. We passed up the north bank and turned our eyes back from time to time to look down the beautiful valley of the great river, and southward to catch glimpses of twice ten thousand hills and the grand old mountains beyond them. Slowly we wound our way to the top of the Simcoe range. Near the crest, where the weather was cold enough for a fire, we camped for the night. A large number of Indians had now joined my escort. Skemiah's little son of four years, dressed in Indian finery and well mounted, was with them, and all seemed happy to receive provisions from us. Indians who smoke in a circle with a white man, and condescend to eat the white man's food, as a rule, wear, whether real or assumed, an expression of remarkable contentment. Anyway it is hospitable and politic thus to eat and smoke or let them do so. It makes friends.

We had an early breakfast and arrived at the agency on the Simcoe River by 11 A. M. of that day. The Simcoe is a branch of the Yakima, a river which passes into the Columbia above the mouth of the Snake. The confluence is quite a distance above Wallula. The name "Yakima" is also given to the handsomest Indian reservation west of the Rocky Mountains. The agent, Mr. Wilbur, was away when we arrived attending to that interesting and exciting operation of branding cattle. There is only one thing that Indians enjoy better, and that is killing them with firearms.

In the evening Mr. Wilbur and his wife returned. How tall and strong he looked, standing six feet in his shoes, a broad-shouldered, thick-chested, large-headed, full-voiced, manly man! Still the advancing years had begun to tell upon him. Mrs. Wilbur said: "We had to stop by the way for my husband to lie down a while." I did not wonder, for he had the care of a nation on his shoulders and was himself the whole government, though Mrs. Wilbur, a motherly woman, appeared to be an efficient prime minister.

Monday we sent messengers to all Indians far and near, some of them hundreds of miles away, with an invitation to come to Fort Simcoe for a council. While waiting Watkins, Wilkinson, and I went over the extensive reserve. For a while we watched the branding of cattle and saw how the Indians marked wild steers. After being thrown down the animal was held flat and still, while a strong Indian seized and applied the hot and heavy branding iron. To repeat that operation throughout an entire herd was a trying ordeal.

When we returned to the agency good news was brought to us, to wit.: Joseph, Ollicut, and White

Bird had been gathering in their cattle and ponies preparatory to entering the Lapwai reservation as they had promised.

Fort Simcoe was built by Major Garnet, under whom I had been when he was commandant at West Point, and who fell in battle on the Confederate side during the Civil War. The post was constructed for three companies of infantry. The quarters of the officers were picturesque and all the buildings good, and showy fences surrounded well-kept gardens. Years before this time everything had been transferred to the Indian bureau, and Fort Simcoe was now the headquarters of the Yakima Indian agency.

The agent, the head chief, Joe Stwyre, and the Indian police were ever ready to help Colonel Watkins perform his part. They were to assemble the renegades and nomads of the Columbia and start them, like the Yakimas, on the road to civilization. White people said to Joe Stwyre: "You'll be killed if you go to Smohollie!"

"No, no," he answered, "I will not be killed; I will go. I will go and carry the good message!"

Smohollie received him gladly and hastened with his leading Indians toward Simcoe. So also did Moses, whom the messengers found at Priest's Rapids, far up the Columbia, and so did other wandering tribes along the river valley. Pambrum, the interpreter, who spoke a language that all Walla Wallas and Cayuses could understand, came to us from his home near the Touchet River.

By Saturday the 8th of June all the Indians far and near, north of the Columbia River, had come together to meet us. We had a large tent-fly stretched in a beautiful grove, and this together with the trees afforded a grateful shade during the intense heat. There is nowhere so much formality as in an Indian council. There were Colonel Watkins, Agent Wilbur, and our military selves—white men and ladies—all occupying comfortable seats; facing us were the Indians seated on benches or chairs. In the first row, from right to left, in order of their supposed rank, were Moses, Smohollie, One-eyed John, Calwash, Skemiah, Thomas, and others. Other renegades came in behind, sitting or squatting as Indians do. The background was studded with women and children clothed in bright and contrasted colors, with straight black hair and black, flashing eyes, and some of them had clean hands and faces. The friendly Indians were mixed up everywhere with the newcomers and treated them with persistent kindness.

After the opening prayer Colonel Watkins followed in a brief address, which was rather mandatory in style for an Indian council. "First, the government requires that you shall all come on this or some other of its reservations.

"Second, in every possible way of looking at this matter it is better for you to come. Third, the commander of the military forces will enforce this requirement."

Agent Wilbur argued the second proposition. He strove to influence Smohollie particularly, because Smohollie ardently fostered and openly advocated the Dreamer religion, and was believed to be the special cause of the restlessness of the

Columbia tribes. He kept alive the hope of supernatural intervention; relief was to come, so he taught, through a general Indian resurrection. Without making much reply that day the Indians desired to postpone the council until the following Monday.

All the Indians were cordially invited to be present Sunday in that very grove for a religious service. I enjoyed that occasion greatly. The Christian Indians seemed to plead the cause of the great Master with earnestness. They spoke in the Indian tongue, so that I could not follow them closely. Smohollie behaved well that day and answered all appeals with apparent sincerity.

On Monday, June 10th, we again assembled in council at the same place. Moses forcibly intimated that he would do his best to comply with the wishes of the government, not only for himself and his own tribe, but for many other bands.

Smohollie, with his hunch-back figure and big head, apparently fearing that Moses was getting ahead of him in our favor or in diplomacy, stood up and answered with loud voice: "Your law is my law. I say to you, yes. I will be on a reservation by September. I have but two or three hundred people." The difference between Moses and Smohollie was that Moses would keep his promise and Smohollie could not be relied upon. With the Dreamer this may have been to some extent from want of actual authority with his people.

The oldest chief present was Thomas, a spare, tall man afflicted with a nervous trembling. He said: "I have about fifty Indians in all. I will go to the Umatilla reservation by the 1st of September." He evidently took no exact account of time, for he did not get there till the ensuing November. All the others, Skemiah, One-eyed John, and Calwash, made similar promises, each naming the number of his Indians. The five Indians who spoke thus strongly in the council were considerable chiefs, and it was gratifying to us that they made these promises. They did not join the non-treaty Indians who subsequently went to war, and but very few of their followers behaved badly after that council.

It was an impressive story that we told them about Joseph and his discontented Indians, how they had already yielded to the persuasions of government officials and had abstained from preparations for war. We thought so then.

The next day, in a spring wagon drawn by mules, which were as lively and more enduring than horses, our party followed the Yakima down its southeasterly course. The majority of the Indians had separated and gone back to the people whom they represented, but there were still with us the interpreter and many mounted braves. They afforded our wagon a good escort, constantly riding before, behind, and on our flanks.

We arrived at the Columbia fatigued by the heat and hard traveling through leagues of sand, and it was yet twenty miles to our destination—Wallula. It occurred to me that Indians in the vicinity might take us down the river in a canoe, and messengers were sped on ahead to secure one. We were at the mouth of the Yakima at sundown.

Wilkinson had become alarmingly ill and begged to be left at a half-civilized ranch near that place. It was very important for Watkins and myself to be at Wallula to catch the Lewiston boat, and yet we were unwilling to leave Wilkinson behind.

It was now dark. We ran to the bank of the river and called loudly for the canoe that the Indian messengers were to have in readiness at that place. After waiting a short time two of Smohollie's Indians pushed out from the other side in the darkness and silently paddled over to us in a long, partly-decayed dugout. We laid Wilkinson on a narrow bed in the middle of the boat. Pambrum and the Indians managed the boat, while Colonel Watkins and I sang songs and told stories till Wilkinson, to our surprise, brightened up a little and insisted upon joining us. Past the islands, past the Homely Rapids, frightful to our small boat, past the mouth of the Snake River, we sped along for over twenty miles, wind, current, and Indian paddle all in our favor.

By two o'clock in the morning, just as dawn was appearing, we pulled up at the Wallula wharf. The gangplank of the up-river steamer was about to be drawn in when we stepped upon its deck. "Fifteen minutes for telegraph messages?" I said to the captain.

"Yes, yes," he answered, "but hurry." The messages were sent, and in less time than I asked the plank was drawn in and we were on our way to Lewiston.

# CHAPTER XX.

## OPENING OF HOSTILITIES — BATTLES OF WHITE BIRD CANYON AND THE CLEAR WATER.

A Disquieting Message — Starting for the Front — Rendezvous of Chief Joseph and the Hostiles — Discovering the Indian Camp — Guarding Against Surprise — Murdering a Husband in the Presence of His Wife — Women and Children at the Mercy of Savages — Indescribable Brutalities — The Battle of White Bird Canyon — Slaughter of the Troops — Death of Lieutenant Theller — Defeated by the Indians — Burial of Our Slain Comrades — A Forced March — An Indian Ambuscade — Battle of the Clear Water — Flight of the Indians — Preparation for a Long Chase.

THE thirty days given to the Nez Percés to come on the reservation had now expired, and I was again at Lapwai. My former aide-de-camp Boyle was now a full-fledged captain in command of an infantry company at this place. Perry, who was a colonel by brevet, was a captain of the First Cavalry, and his troop and Captain Trimble's completed the garrison. Parnell, also a colonel by brevet, was really a lieutenant in Trimble's company. Lieutenant Theller was serving under Captain Boyle in the infantry. The command of the whole garrison at this time devolved upon Colonel Perry.

Everybody was happy and predicted that the war-cloud had passed over. But we sometimes arrive at conclusions too soon! I had hardly stepped inside of Perry's doorway when a messenger, who had evidently ridden fast and far, handed him a letter, dated that very day, and signed by a prominent citizen, L. P. Brown of Mt. Idaho, a small village sixty miles distant to the southeast and not far beyond the limit of the Lapwai reserve. One sentence in the letter was this: "They (the Indians) say openly that they are going to fight the soldiers when they come up to put them on the reservation." The letter reported that the non-treaties were gathering ammunition and had taken a strong position in a rocky canyon, evidently expecting General Howard with his troops.

Another sentence in the letter was significant of the feeling of the whites, to wit.: "Sharp and prompt action will bring them to understand that they must comply with the orders of the government. We trust such action will be taken by you as to remove them from the neighborhood and quiet the feelings of the people."

That rocky canyon to which the letter referred was near the corner of the Lapwai reservation, just beyond the boundary. The impression I gained from the general tenor of the letter, and from my knowledge of the locality, was that the Indians were hesitating just what they had better do. As a matter of fact they were hesitating just then because they had in their own bands divided counsels.

I at once dispatched a scouting party with instructions to reconnoiter and report the facts in the case as soon as possible. The scouts, quickly on the road, met a couple of friendly Indians and turned back with them on account of an alarming rumor. The friendly Indians declared that four of the malcontents—restless young Indians of the war party—had committed a murder near Slate Creek, forty miles beyond Mt. Idaho. It appeared that a man named Larryott had previously killed an Indian, and that they had begun hostilities by making him the first victim.

Joseph's father-in-law, then with me, was a treaty Indian. He insisted that Joseph would not fight and, he volunteering, we sent him to the front with a few other friendly Indians, hoping to secure better news. Not long after their departure all came rushing back at full speed, bringing with them a half-breed whose name was West. A brother of Looking-Glass accompanied him. West bore the second letter from L. P. Brown. This letter stated that some settlers about eighteen miles from Mt. Idaho had been attacked and the whole party killed or wounded. The writer's entreaty was: "Don't delay a moment! We have a report that some whites were killed yesterday on the Salmon River. . . . Mr. West has volunteered to go to Lapwai; rely on his statements."

By the same messengers came another letter which probably the brother of Looking-Glass had received later and with it had overtaken West while on the road. It said: "Since that (letter) was written the wounded have come in,—Mr. Day mortally, Mrs. Norton with both legs broken, Moore shot through the hips, Norton killed and left in the road six miles from here." This letter ended with these words: "Hurry up! hurry! rely on this Indian's statement; I have known him for a long time. He is with us."

This is my reply of June 15th:—

"Mr. Brown.

Dear Sir:—Your two dispatches are received. I have sent forward two companies of cavalry to your relief. They leave tonight. Other help will be *en route* as soon as it can be brought up. I am glad you are so cool and ready. Cheer the people. Help shall be prompt and complete. Lewiston has been notified.

"Yours truly,

"O. O. Howard."

As my letter indicated Colonel Perry was ordered to take his cavalry, consisting of ninety men, and proceed at once to Mt. Idaho, and do what was necessary for the protection of the people. Perry needed one lieutenant more, so Theller was detailed and furnished with a horse to accompany the detachment. I had no more men to send, as the other company was, of course, needed for defense of the garrison. It was a great risk to send but ninety men; I knew it, but it was the best that could be done. One never saw two finer troops of cavalry than those which set out for the front on the evening of the 15th of May.

Reaching the vicinity of Mt. Idaho a company of volunteers under Captain Chapman, less than fifty strong, reported to Perry, and urged him to go on at once some eighteen miles further and attack the Indians and drive them across the Salmon River. The idea of the volunteers and of the citizens was that the Indians would be afraid of the troops and would rush off. They were, in fact, assembled in White Bird Canyon—a deep and

PURSUED.—A BAND OF INDIANS CHASING A PONY EXPRESS RIDER.

broad valley—and very strongly posted in complete readiness to meet any body of troops that did not exceed their fighting men in number. They probably had at that point as many as five hundred Indians bearing arms. Many young Indians from other tribes had joined them, delighted to take a hand in the war that Joseph was going to conduct.

It is said, and it is now generally believed, that Joseph himself was away from the Indians at the time the first massacre began, and that the first intimation he had of the actual state of things was when a lot of young braves came racing back into his camp and showed him evidences of slaughter and of capture. Admitting this to be true, he now decided to fight, and was present to command the whole Indian force, which was standing on the defensive in White Bird Canyon.

At Grangeville, a small hamlet four miles from Mt. Idaho, Perry gave his men a short rest, and then set out to follow the Indians, strengthened by the few volunteers, who appeared very eager for the conflict. Marching all night they arrived at early dawn on the high crest of White Bird Canyon. Four miles away they could just discern in the dim light of the morning the faint smokes of Indian camps. All the signs, such as the movements of herders, of horses, of sentinels on the watch, and the extent of the ground occupied, indicated only a small number of Indians present. Surely this was not the whole combination of dissatisfied non-treaty Indians. The citizens were more confident than ever and declared that what they saw was only a rear-guard of Joseph's outfit.

Perry, though not wholly convinced of the favorable nature of the situation, and hoping to surprise the camp, whatever it was, put his force into as good order as possible. The infantry officer, Lieutenant Theller, riding a good horse, was sent out some hundred yards to proceed in advance, with eight cavalrymen for guard and skirmish. Perry followed with the volunteers and his own troop. Trimble, with Parnell, led his men after Perry with a short interval. With horses now quiet, more so from the night march than anything else, all in column of fours, the handsome young commander began the descent of the steep trail.

They had not gone over a half mile when poor Mrs. Benedict came up, leading a little girl, and carrying her baby in her arms. Her husband had been murdered in her presence, and she had suffered indescribable outrage, but by the help of some compassionate acquaintance among the Indians she had at last succeeded in escaping from further brutalities. Believing that troops would come to meet the Indians down that canyon road, she, worn out with fatigue and distress, had been awaiting them, lying hidden in the bushes by the wayside. The commander, after hearing her sad story, provided an escort from the volunteers to take her and the children to Mt. Idaho, and then pushed on into the valley.

No commander could have located his men better than Joseph had done for a defensive battle. The ground was rough and there were stony buttes along his front, and his entire force was completely hidden by the formation of the ground. His flanking parties, particularly those under White Bird, had their ponies in readiness. Lieutenant Theller began the action by skirmishing straight up toward the occupied buttes, while the citizens ran to the left hillock with a hope of getting beyond the Indians in that direction.

Trimble deployed his troops and followed Theller straight forward, while he himself bore off to the right to watch his exposed right flank.

Soon Perry's men also were deployed to the left of Trimble's, and the Indians were firing sharply all along the line. Our men fired as best they could over their horses' heads, many of which became so excited as to be beyond control. Parnell was doing his duty near the center, and Perry, with a trumpeter by his side, was doing his best to keep a fighting line unbroken. One instant, looking to the south, they saw some of the Indians running their ponies to high ground just off to their right and rear. Six men and a sergeant flew to the threatened knoll and repulsed them. Perry, turning to the left, noticed that two of the citizens were limping with wounds, and that the remainder of the volunteers were fleeing to the rear. Just then his bugler fell dying from his horse.

At this decisive juncture of a fierce battle Perry saw that the Indians had at least three to one against him, and that both his flanks were turned. It was evident that he could not go to the Salmon River nor stay where he was many minutes, so he ordered the command back to the foothills of the canyon whence he had come, but amid the yelling of the Indians and the rapid firing of rifles and carbines there was no longer any order whatever, so that a confused mass, *sauve qui peut,* started to the rear, the swifter horses having the lead.

Chief White Bird and his flankers ran their ponies with all speed to get to the crest of the canyon before the troops, and starting so soon, just after their first check at the knoll, they had the advantage. Indians also pursued and kept within easy rifle range of Perry's rear, so that all along the way horses and men were falling. Every white man that fell was slain.

Up the foothills of the canyon were ravines and ridges, and our remaining men under Theller were trying to ascend first a ravine and then a ridge. So many Indians came upon him that soon horse and rider fell; Theller and the majority of his cavalrymen were slain. All our men that reached the crest were quickly reorganized and covered by skirmish rear-guard; turning to the right they pursued their way, slowly retreating and beating back the Indians without further disaster for the next ten miles. After that the Indians gave up the chase and returned to Joseph's position in White Bird Canyon.

Before night of that eventful day, June 16th, 1877, I had received the terrible news at Lapwai. I shall never forget a message in Perry's note to me: "Please break the news of her husband's death to Mrs. Theller." When I opened her door she anticipated my tidings and cried out: "Oh, my husband!" They had no children; he was her all, and her heart was broken. Thirty-three out of the ninety that had left Lapwai in health and strength, all in the buoyancy of young manhood, were slain, and Perry was humiliated. A defeat is hard to bear.

At the time I had only one small company of infantry with me at Lapwai, but my men, responding to telegrams, were on the way from every part of the immense Department of the Columbia. When I had gathered not to exceed two hundred of them I moved forward, taking command in person, setting out at noon, June 22d.

Meanwhile Joseph had succeeded in picking up small parties of soldiers and citizen scouts, and had slain them all. We moved with care until we joined Perry at Grangeville. When I thought my command was sufficiently strong I began active pursuit of the Indians. At Mt. Idaho we met women and children who had been outraged and wounded. We passed into White Bird Canyon and there buried our comrades. We then crossed over the Salmon River, at that time foaming and tumbling like a boiling caldron, and ran down all the trails and recrossed the Salmon at its widest point not far from its mouth, for the Indians had gotten over on their skin rafts, hauled by their swimming ponies, and had turned back eastward between us and Lapwai, crossing the broad prairies to the west and north of Grangeville.

I had managed at last to gather a force of between five and six hundred in number, with two field-pieces (small cannon) and a Gatling gun. Locating the Indians as well as I could in the wild forest southeast of Kamia, near the head waters of one of the branches of the Clear Water, I made a march in one day of forty-four miles, using country wagons to carry about a third of the infantry at a time, while the remainder marched on foot.

On the 11th of July we discovered Joseph as we were descending the right bank of the Clear Water. He and his men were waiting for us; his women and baggage were on the other side of the river. It was a woody country, full of rough knolls and transverse ravines. In one of these the Indians lay concealed until my troops had passed them. They then sprang out and ran to close in my command between themselves and the river where there was a considerable bend. We faced them, deploying our lines and putting all our supplies and ammunition, carried by our pack-mules, between us and the river. At first we had a spring of water in our possession, and also a small, muddy pond of bad water.

The battle began and was so fiercely contested that the Indians at night had us completely hemmed in and were in possession of our spring of water. The other water neither our men nor the animals would drink. The Indians were very confident, but the next morning, using my artillerymen, Colonel Marcus P. Miller commanding them, I first recovered the spring, then everybody had breakfast. After that Colonel Miller with his artillerymen broke through the Indian line and met Jackson's troop of cavalry, which was bringing to us fresh supplies.

Miller, after meeting Jackson, caused him to

rush across the Indian line with his supplies while he himself made a quick movement, which I had ordered him to try, turning to the left and rolling up the Indian lines. They were surprised and fled in a panic, and swam the river or waded it where the water was not too deep, and set their whole body quickly in full retreat. I do not think that I had to exercise more thorough generalship during the Civil War than I did in that march to the battlefield, and in the ensuing battle with Joseph and his Indians on the banks of the Clear Water.

We immediately took up the pursuit and followed the hostiles as far as Kamia. There the Indians, still numbering between six and seven hundred, according to an estimate made at the time, recrossed the Clear Water. We had skirmishes with them, and tried the metal of our Gatling gun, but our foes easily kept beyond its range and were very cautious about engaging in battle again. I sent out Colonel E. C. Mason, my chief-of-staff, with all the cavalry I could muster, to press the Indians' rear as they were retiring by what was called the Lolo Trail, which led through the forest toward Montana. Mason overtook Joseph's rear-guard, had a skirmish near a forest glade not far from Kamia, and then returned in haste to me. Meanwhile I was getting ready for what I believed would be a long chase.

## CHAPTER XXI.

### PURSUIT AND DEFEAT OF THE INDIANS — SURRENDER OF CHIEF JOSEPH.

Marching through a Rough Country — Word from General Gibbon — An Experienced Scout and Frontiersman — The Fleeing Indians Turn Back Upon Me — A Vicious Night Attack — Half-breed Bucking Ponies — Arrival in the National Park — Murdering a Party of Visitors — Lost in the Forest — "The Howard Road" — Unwearied and Relentless Pursuit of the Indians — An Adroit Indian Chief — Running the Gauntlet — Slim Chances of Success — The Surrender.

I HAD with me a few troops from California, but my main dependence was upon the artillery acting as infantry, a majority of the Twenty-first Infantry as a battalion under Captain Evan Miles, the greater part of the cavalry under Major Sanford, and a company of volunteers under Captain McConville. It was necessary to divide my command, leaving a portion at Kamia under the command of Colonel John Green to guard against the return of the hostiles or any further outbreak in the department.

Captain Spurgin of the Twenty-first Infantry was put in charge of a select body of fifty citizens employed by my quartermaster, who were able to do some sort of engineering work. They took with them the necessary axes, picks, and shovels, but owing to the character of the trail from Oregon to Montana we could take no wagons, so all that we had in the line of supplies was borne by pack animals. Another small volunteer force, called "The

Scouts," was added under the charge of Captain Robbins. Among them we had a few Indians from the friendly Nez Percés, and later some from the Bannocks, with quite a number of selected frontiersmen. This body, well organized, varied from day to day—never, all told, exceeding fifty men.

From Kamia a long and tedious march began on the 26th of July, 1877. The Indians were already a hundred and fifty miles ahead, and yet over the Lolo Trail the first day we made but six miles. A rougher country one could hardly imagine, and the short march looked discouraging even to our experienced officers, but I knew that muscular endurance would develop as we went on, and that our men would be untiring. The Indians generally make their greatest distance the first day and then slacken and rest when they are not closely pursued. General Gibbon opposed the hostiles with volunteers and a few regulars at the Montana end of the Lolo Trail, but they easily, by the help of friendly Flatheads, turned his flank and escaped battle there. Then, notifying me, he pushed on after them as rapidly as he could until he overtook them at the mouth of Big Hole Pass.

As we were pushing on with all our might, horses getting weak and weary from overwork and underfeeding, we were met by a second messenger from General Gibbon. His message apprised us that he had had a battle, beginning at daylight on the 9th of August, at first successful, "but they (the Indians) then turned on us, forced us out of it (the camp), and compelled us to take the defensive." Gibbon had a number of wounded who needed medical attendance, and his men seemed to be in pretty bad condition, as it was difficult for them to cover themselves against the Nez Percé rifles. The general closed with these words: "Hope you will hurry to our relief."

As quickly as it could be done I made the march to the vicinity of the Big Hole, when Joseph, hearing of my coming, made off eastward with his Indians. General Gibbon had been wounded in the leg, but notwithstanding this was able to ride with me over the battlefield.

At Junction Station, Montana, a place where the stages halted before continuing their journey, our cavalry was so weak that we were obliged to stop and rest for a few hours. Here another company of volunteers joined us with fresh horses, and remained with us a couple of days. From this point I sent Lieutenant Bacon in command of two troops of cavalry, giving him for a guide a wonderfully skilled frontiersman by the name of Fisher. He was very deaf, but possessed extraordinary sharpness of sight, and was a capital scout. He took with him a few Bannocks, among whom was the famous Buffalo Horn. Bacon was to move rapidly away from the Indian trails and strike in by Henry Lake in the vicinity of Tacher Pass, a gateway to the National Park. He was to head off the Indians and detain them by his fire till we could come upon them from the rear. Bacon got into position soon enough, but did not have the heart to fight the Indians on account of their number.

While he was gone the Indians turned back upon me, on the Camas Meadows, where there were piles of lava covered with vegetation, and offered battle in the night. They fired into our camp, ran off our mules, having first cut the strap of the bell-mare, so that she ceased to be their leader, then ran from our cavalry and attacked one of Captain Norwood's companies, which had strayed far to the front during the rapid advance. We succeeded in recovering most of the mules and setting Joseph and his people again in rapid motion. He went straight toward the National Park, where Lieutenant Bacon let him go by and pass through the narrow gateway without firing a shot.

Buffalo Horn was disgusted because we did not follow the Indians with more energy, and he wanted me to kill Captains John and George, our favorite Nez Percé scouts, because, as he insisted, it was they who cut the strap of the bell-mare and betrayed us to the Indians. After this night fight, in which some of our volunteers became badly demoralized while wading a deep creek and losing some of their arms and ammunition, a number of them took final leave of our expedition and went back to their homes.

At this place, Henry Lake, I encamped for three days, as I was obliged to halt for supplies. I thought perhaps we had gone far enough and that the troops of other departments would complete what we had so well begun; but hearing from General Sherman that I should continue the pursuit of the Indians until relieved by some other officer of sufficient rank and energy, I took Lieutenant Guy Howard, my aide-de-camp, with me and went north seventy-five miles for the supplies, riding night and day to what was called Virginia City, then a small mining village. I bought nearly everything that the village could furnish in the way of provisions, clothing, and fresh animals. The horses were pronounced "well broken," but subsequent experience proved this to be untrue. As I wrote at the time, "such a pitching and plunging, hooting and yelling, running and falling, made one think of danger ahead from something besides Indians." The bucking of a half-broken half-breed pony is always exciting and frequently dangerous.

My aide and myself returned within three days and the command was again set in motion. In the National Park the Indians had killed or wounded all the men of a party of visitors, but had spared the women, and finally sent them to their homes. We met one man who was deranged and nearly starved; another had been left for dead,—him we rescued and returned to his wife, already in mourning; a third was also badly wounded, but finally recovered and returned to Bozeman.

Joseph had gone on through the park and beyond the Yellowstone and, fortunately for us, had become lost for a few days in the entangled forest of that region. The road that we made for a hundred miles across the park is still pointed out to tourists as "The Howard Road." Of course we had a view of the geysers and hot springs, and of Mary Lake; we marveled at the falls, which exceed Niagara in height. High up that river we built a bridge, using the logs which, already suited to our purpose, we had found in a deserted house.

Thinking I was too tired or too old for such an extraordinary march, General Sherman dispatched Lieutenant-Colonel Gilbert, an officer much older than I, though of less rank, with a body of cavalry from Fort Ellis to overtake me, relieve me from duty, and take my place; but it was not to be. The stern chase was so hard that after ten days' trial Gilbert and his worn-out horses gave up the chase and returned to the fort.

Everybody will remember the Custer massacre, that took place June 25, 1876. Taking as a nucleus the remnant of the Seventh Cavalry, that suffered so heavy a loss at the battle of Little Big Horn, a new Seventh Regiment had been organized. Colonel Sturgis was commanding it in the vicinity of Hart's Mountain. We knew that the Indians, following the usual Nez Percé trails, would probably pass over the top of that mountain. I had sent word to Sturgis to head them off, as he had a full regiment of well-drilled cavalry in good trim for campaigning and ready for a quick march. We had reason to believe that our campaign was about to end in a great victory. But Joseph's scouts, aided by a few wily Crow Indians, succeeded in deceiving Sturgis and in getting the Seventh Cavalry some forty miles off the trail.

Joseph and his Indians passed on over Hart's Mountain and, with my command, I was not far behind. He deviated from the usual path after clearing the mountain, and went through a strange canyon, where the rocks on each side came so near together that two horses abreast could hardly pass. After clearing this canyon, Joseph, feeling himself comparatively safe, allowed his band to rest by making shorter marches. But soon Sturgis, finding himself behind them, turned back and overtook my command. Adding something to his force, I encouraged Sturgis to make a forced march and overtake the Indians, who were now not far ahead. He was glad enough to do this to allay in a measure his chagrin at being outwitted by them.

The next day I had made a march of some twenty-five miles when a message came from my aide-de-camp, Lieutenant Fletcher, who was with Sturgis, that they had had a running fight with the hostiles, and that there was a prospect of a decisive battle before I could reach them. I rested for three hours; then, taking fifty cavalrymen with me and ordering my chief-of-staff to follow with the command in the early morning, I marched all night. At sunrise we found the upper waters of the Yellowstone before us. Crossing over I was on the battlefield a little after ten o'clock.

Finding that the wily Indian chief had again escaped after small loss, I gathered up my forces and, retaining Sturgis' cavalry with me, moved along more deliberately toward the Musselshell. There was little hope of overtaking the Indians by direct pursuit. Information led us to suppose that they were running the gauntlet of the Judith Basin across the Musselshell and then the Missouri somewhere above Carroll, and that they would probably push on rapidly into the British territory. They, in fact, did this, defeating a guard of regular troops and capturing a wagonload of supplies at the Missouri crossing, but I did not yet know of that encounter. My only hope of striking the Indians lay in apprising Colonel Miles (afterward Lieutenant-General of the Army) of the situation, and asking him to make a diagonal march across our front and take Joseph unawares.

Colonel Miles was said to be near the mouth of Tongue River. I sent one dispatch to him by messengers riding overland and another by a boat down the Yellowstone. These messages reached him and he replied, telling me what he would undertake, and that he would start immediately upon the expedition. Sturgis and I slowed our marches for fear of causing the Indians to hasten too rapidly, but Miles with his mounted infantry made rapid and extended marches, crossing the Missouri near the mouth of the Musselshell. The first news I received from the front came in a remarkable way. Colonel Mason, Dr. Alexander, and myself were riding together. I told them that I had asked the great Master for success, even if the credit were given to another, and that I believed we should yet have a favorable ending to the campaign. The doctor rallied me concerning my conviction, for which he could see no reason, and Mason replied pleasantly, but seemed to lack faith in the possibility of such an outcome. A very short time after this conversation two messengers came riding rapidly, and reported that Colonel Miles had overtaken the Indians and that an engagement was imminent.

We now pushed on as rapidly as possible to the Missouri. In plain sight of Carroll was the steamer *Benton* ready for my use. Leaving

Mason, my chief-of-staff, to move my command proper and Sturgis' Seventh Cavalry over the river to a designated point between Miles and what was called the permanent camp of Sitting Bull on the British side of the line, I steamed up to the Indians' crossing near Cow Island. I had with me two aides, Lieutenant C. E. S. Wood and Lieutenant Guy Howard. I had also the two Nez Percé scouts, Captains John and George, and several American scouts. We promptly took up the Indian trail, plain enough now for anybody to follow, and on we went, meeting now and then messengers who apprised us of the situation.

Miles had had a battle, but it had not been altogether decisive. It was near what was called "The Little Rockies," a part of the upper portion of the Bear Paw Mountain.

One night we camped on the trail, where we had wood enough—which we much needed on account of the extreme cold—but the water was alkaline and caused much sickness among my men. Still none were left behind. During the day we met some scouts, who reported that Indians were between us and Miles' bivouac. They said that they could not go on and had turned back, but we found the supposed Indians to be friendly hunters and so pursued our way.

It was early in the evening when we came upon the crest of a hill and saw the campfires of our troops. We heard firing, and some of the bullets whistled over our heads, and as I thought that our party had been mistaken for savages I cried out: "What are you firing at us for?"

Just then Miles himself with a small escort met and took me to his headquarters. That night we consulted together; he showed me how the Indians had dug deep holes instead of ordinary entrenchments; that part of the herd of Indian ponies had been captured and a part was still in the possession of the Indians; that he was very anxious for a speedy surrender. He had sent in a brave and capable officer, who had been for a while detained by Joseph, but at last had returned, having been unable to bring matters to a decision. I proposed to send in my two Nez Percé scouts, Captains John and George, bearing a white flag. I believed that they could secure a prompt surrender of Joseph and all his people who were with him.

The next day this was done. Miles and myself sat side by side upon the slope of a hill in plain view of both contestants, when "Captain John," accompanied by George, moved off on foot swinging his white flag.

We did not have very long to wait. The scouts returned and bore Joseph's message to the effect that he had done all he could and that he left his people and himself in our hands. Some of the Indians violated the promise they had made to Joseph, creeping out of camp in the night and escaping. One of them was Chief White Bird.

It was rather a forlorn procession that came up out of that Indian bivouac. They were covered with dirt, their clothing was torn, and their ponies, such as they were, were thin and lame. A few of the Indians preserved their dignified bearing and had attired themselves as best they could for the occasion. When Joseph appeared he extended his rifle to me and I waived it over to Colonel Miles, who had planned and made a swift diagonal march, and so bravely fought the last battle.

That night Miles and I slept again in his tent. He made his report to his department commander, and a little later I made mine. I had been instructed by McDowell to send the Indians back to the Department of the Columbia, and I so gave Joseph to understand, but I was overruled from Washington, and Miles was ordered to keep them for the time being and finally send them to the Indian Territory.

All this was done. My own troops were brought back to the Missouri, sent down that river in steamboats as far as Omaha, and thence taken back by rail and ocean steamers to Oregon and Washington Territory. I returned to my headquarters in Portland, Oregon, reaching home the last of November. From the last day of May until the last of November I had been under the severe strain of an arduous campaign. We had marched one thousand three hundred and twenty-one miles in seventy-five days. Joseph's loss during the entire period was over a hundred. Too-hul-hul-sote, Looking-Glass, and Joseph's brother Ollicut perished in battle. Our own losses in all the battles included several valuable officers, and nearly as many men as were lost by the Indians.

# CHAPTER XXII.

## STARTING FOR ALASKA — EXPERIENCES WITH ALASKAN CHIEFS AND TRIBES.

Reservation Indians of Puget Sound — Evil Results of Dissolute White Men Mingling with Indians — Indians as Coal Miners — Wonderfully Picturesque and Varied Scenery — Arrival at Fort Wrangel — Some Dejected Indians — Listening to their Grievances — Influence of Strong Drink — Presenting a Tribe with the Dead Body of their Chief — A Dance of Satisfaction — A Pantomine Show — Begging for a Teacher — Hideously-painted Faces — Sitka Indian Chiefs — Extreme Poverty and Vicious Indulgence — Results of Missionary Efforts — Brief Sketch of Colonel Guy Howard's Career.

WHEN I first assumed command of the Department of the Columbia Alaska was within my jurisdiction. I had already visited several reservations on Puget Sound, for example, the Skokomish, the Swinomish, the Tulalip, and the Neah Bay. The Indians upon these public lands were substantially of the same description, differing a little in dialects. They were not so tall as the Indians of the interior, and they had no horses. Their bodies were long and their legs short, as one would expect from a people that spent more than half their time in canoes and paddle-boats. Those on Puget Sound were, for the most part, dressed in citizens' clothing.

On each reserve, however, there were two groups: the larger dressed as we do and lived in small houses, but the smaller group adhered tenaciously to old Indian customs. They usually wore leggins, moccasins, breech-cloth, and blanket; they painted their faces more or less, often hideously, using deep colors. Some of the uncivilized people of the Coast tribes were very low in their habits of life and in their morals; where dissolute white men from the logging camps and mills and from incoming vessels mingled with them, scrofulous diseases were coupled with other signs of degradation.

The civilized Indians on the Tulalip and nearly all on the Skokomish reservations, the former Roman Catholic and the latter Protestant, have been educated in a Christian way and encouraged to marry early in life. Their lives are simple and exemplary. The men have become useful in cutting timber and in working in the numerous mills along the Sound, while the women are fairly good housekeepers. I found some of their houses very neat and tidy throughout, with all the essential appurtenances of civilized life.

In the early summer of 1875 the members of a court-martial were to sail for Alaska on the steamer *California,* and I thought it would be an excellent opportunity to accompany them for the purpose of making a tour of inspection in that distant portion of my department. I also took advantage of this official visit to give an outing to my wife and children. We left Portland, Oregon, on the 2d of June, proceeding by railroad and a Sound steamer as far as Victoria, and thence by the regular transport, the *California.* The steamer sailed from Portland by way of the Columbia River and the Pacific Ocean to Victoria, thence by "the inner passage" to Wrangel and Sitka.

At "Nanaimo," an English post, I accompanied the officers of the court-martial to some extensive coal mines where many Indians were at work with other employees. The Indians in the neighborhood did not exceed two hundred. They were fairly well dressed in civilians' clothing, and had clean faces; there was no regular school; a small mission of the Methodist persuasion was active among them.

The voyage from Nanaimo to Wrangel was very pleasant. The gulfs and sounds were connected by straits and bays, which seemed like a succession of beautiful rivers. Wonderfully picturesque and varied was that "inner passage." At times there was on the right and left a wall of magnificent mountains rising from two to three thousand feet, snow-crowned and covered with trees; glistening cascades falling hundreds of feet; streams coursing like silver threads down the mountain sides; mighty glaciers and extensive snow fields; every natural feature that travelers go beyond the ocean to see here meets and delights the eye.

We had heard and read enthusiastic descriptions of the Alaska journey, but could never have imagined half the wonderful beauty of this sheltered and safe inland passage from Port Townsend to Sitka.

Soon we were safely at anchor near Wrangel Island. Fort Wrangel was on one end of the island and was occupied by a small detachment of troops, hardly a platoon, under command of Lieutenant John A. Lundeen of the Fourth Artillery.

He had with him Lieutenant Macomb as his second in authority. Buildings sufficient for the detachment were protected by an old-fashioned stockade. The garrison being small, Lundeen occupied only a part of the stockade enclosure. He reported successful attempts by unprincipled white men of the neighborhood to manufacture strong drink, which was sold to both Indians and whites, and the lieutenant was annoyed because he did not have quick rowboats to reach the liquor stills and destroy them. I authorized him to hire a canoe for this purpose.

As soon as my inspection was over, the Indians from "the ranches," the name given to the long rows of houses built and occupied by them, came with extremely dejected countenances to have an interview with me. Fortunately, our interpreter, Alexander Choquette, spoke English well and the Stickeen or Thlinket tongue with equal facility. The complaint laid before me was that white men had some time before taken away their favorite chief Fernandeste by force; that our people (some accursed liquor dealers who were prisoners with him on the steamer *California*) had so frightened Fernandeste as to excite his apprehension of the consequences of his detention and journey to Portland, so that in extreme terror he had taken his own life; that his immediate relatives were worried and goaded almost to madness by the sneers and gibes of other Indians, who called them cowards because they did not seek revenge or obtain a settlement. I learned that under the influence of this passion, increased and stimulated by strong drink, these same relatives had made more than one attempt to kill a white man. The Indians had received a letter from me, as department commander, which contained a promise to provide for a complete "settlement," and relying on this promise they were patiently awaiting my coming.

Now that I had come the Indians felt certain that I would soon make everything all right. They went on to make several urgent propositions, but finally settled upon the condition of a *potlatch*, which was to consist of one hundred blankets and the dead body of Fernandeste. Luckily I had been amply forewarned and so had brought the body of Fernandeste with us (it having been disinterred at Astoria and put on board the *California*). I had also obtained the formal permission of the Secretary of War at Washington to make the issue of the necessary blankets. Thus prepared, I graciously yielded to the Indians' fervent entreaty and gave them evidence of the blankets intended for them and of the body which we had brought.

By the end of our first interview the appearance of these Stickeen Indians had wholly changed. That night they gave a characteristic dance of satisfaction, participated in only by the men and lasting for hours, in which they depicted, in rude pantomime, the departure of Fernandeste on the steamer, his suicide, and the return of his body; they also portrayed our visit and the satisfactory settlement which I had just promised.

These Indians had heard about our schools, and their children had been taught to some extent by members of officers' families, who had been previously stationed at Wrangel. They begged for a teacher, such as they had heard of at Fort Simpson and at Metlakahtla. Their houses were surprisingly good. They were constructed of thick slabs, sometimes very long and broad, with a large door in the middle. The roof had a broad opening at the center, under which was a portion of ground enclosed by logs partly sunk in the earth, used as a fireplace and for cooking. All around the inside of the best houses was a banquette conveniently high and well built. It served for sleeping places and for such bedding and clothing as they might have. Many of the Indian women wore their hair in a natural way, cut off just below the neck and parted in the middle, but they painted their faces with something that looked very much like lampblack.

The totem poles interested me very much. Some of the carvings of different animals on the posts and at the top of the totem staffs were so well executed as plainly to indicate a bird, a bear or some other animal. The totem pole may have carved upon it the tribal emblem, or the personal history of a chief and the names of distinction given him are indicated by its curious devices.

From Wrangel we journeyed northward in the night and reached anchorage near Sitka Thursday evening the 10th of June. An old friend and comrade of mine, Major J. B. Campbell, was not only commander of the troops, but the Indian agent for the territory. I went ashore so as to make my military inspection early Friday morning. Having been troubled for some time by numerous newspaper charges against the major's management of affairs at Sitka, I gave those who called themselves citizens, comprising Russians, Aleuts, half-breeds, foreign traders, and Americans proper residing in the town, an opportunity to meet me, as they desired, separate from the officers of the garrison. We met at the house of the United States collector, who kindly briefed the complaints for me. These I carefully considered and acted upon as far as possible. The complaints did not prove to be of great importance. I remedied the real ills by having Major Campbell introduce a little home-rule and a few police regulations. He established a general hospital and raised sufficient revenue to meet necessities. One of his most humane officers acted in the capacity of a police judge. Major Campbell could under the law do those things with the powers vested in him as Indian agent.

During the afternoon of Sunday, June 13th, I met the Indians who lived in the neighborhood of Sitka and had a long interview with the chiefs who were present, and with their people. The famous "Sitka Jack" was absent. He had gone away with his long canoe filled with men using the paddle, while he, having hoisted his flag, sat in the stern and steered the craft. I was sorry not to see him, as he controlled at that time over one-half of the Indian households. In each house there was one family and some branches, often numbering twenty or thirty people.

Anahootz was the chief who governed the other households; this time he spoke for all the Indians.

He first came to me in a dignified way and submitted the numerous and fairly well preserved recommendations which he had received from prominent officials, both Russian and American. He told his story and concluded by saying: "My people are just beginning to arrive at what I have long desired—amity with the whites and with each other under the protection of a good commander. I have had many battles to secure this and my people are just beginning to see that I was right."

After his speech I spoke to him of the advantages of education for the children, and told him that was the best means of bringing about a mutual understanding and of acquiring knowledge of the white man's ways, and advised him to lay this subject before his people. Anahootz heartily approved of my suggestion and said: "I have spent sleepless nights thinking for the interest of my people. I want a good teacher; I will build him a schoolhouse. A teacher once came, but he did not stay."

In reply to Anahootz I tried to address all the Indians, urging education and industry and constant coöperation with their good chief. There was a universal response, hearty and happy, to my suggestions.

The Indians at Sitka showed many evidences of extreme poverty, and some of vicious indulgence, but the desire for a good teacher was universal. I presented this desire, not only from Sitka but from Wrangel, to the different societies in the missionary field, but for a time without result. At last, under the pleadings of the Rev. Dr.

Lindsley of Portland, Oregon, the Presbyterians added that part of Alaska to their mission field, and great results have followed their efforts. I may here add that the widow of the Rev. Dr. McFarland, whom it will be remembered my son, Guy Howard,* so tenderly nursed when ill and brought in safety to Old Camp Grant, was the first missionary at Fort Wrangel. Her sucesses there and at Sitka was phenomenal.

* General Howard's son, Colonel Guy Howard, entered the service in 1876, as a Lieutenant of Infantry. He was long a Captain in the Quartermaster's Department, and became Corps Quartermaster with the volunteer rank of Colonel during the Spanish War. He was sent to the Philippines, there became General Lawton's Chief-Quartermaster, and fell in action on the Steamer *Oceanica*, October 22, 1899, while hauling barges of supplies to General Lawton. Colonel Howard, when mortally wounded, sprang to his feet and cried to his men, "Whatever happens to me keep the launch going."

# CHAPTER XXIII.

## OUR JOURNEY TO ALASKA CONTINUED — A VISIT TO THE CHILCATS, THE SUMDUMS, AND OTHER PACIFIC COAST TRIBES.

Pacific Coast Indians — Their Domestic Life — A Patient Indian Sufferer — A Contrary Old Woman — "Sitka Jack" — Among the Chilcats — A Faithful Watcher — Home of the Sumdums — Icebergs, Glaciers, and Picturesque Scenery — Celebrating the Battle of Bunker Hill — Describing the Battlefield of Gettysburg — Homeward Bound — A Methodist Missionary's Home — Religious Service in an Indian Village — How it was Conducted — Publishing Marriage Banns — Extraordinary Changes in Indian Life — A Skeptical Officer — Ascending the Columbia River — Arrival at Portland.

WHILE the court-martial was performing its duties at Sitka I visited different islands and promontories in the vicinity, including timber lands where the Alaska cedar grows in great abundance, and mines which were more or less productive. We proceeded northward as far as we could in the five days that were left to us before the *California* would have to return to Oregon.

We stopped at Koutznous Bay, where we found a band of Coast Indians of that name. They were peaceably disposed, and watched us curiously while we rowed a small boat around a point and went on some four miles to the north of our anchorage. We had run along by Admiralty Island.

In a pleasant little nook we came upon their village. The ground was low and fertile; potatoes were planted in high rows like celery in eastern gardens, and there were growing crops of turnips, cabbages, beets, and parsnips. The Indians seemed to be happy, living substantially in the same sort of houses as those at Wrangel, with a pitched roof, quite broad and rather flat, and one door under the gable just big enough to crawl through. One had to ascend a few steps to enter it. The frame was made of very large beams and the planks were of great size. I measured single planks four feet broad, six inches thick, and sixty feet long. The houses were fifty or sixty feet broad and often eighty feet in length.

In the best of the houses was a paved square for the fire directly under the opening in the roof; around this square the banquette was terminated inward by a handsome single plank three feet wide standing on edge. This plank was sometimes carved and colored, as were those on the inside of their canoes. Skins and furs of different kinds were thrown upon or against the banquette. Over the fire were pots, kettles, and horizontal poles on which salmon were drying and smoking. Here also were square waterproof casks for fish oil, and well-made watertight trunks used by the Indians in their canoes on long voyages.

In one house we found an old Indian of commanding appearance, who had a finely-shaped head and high forehead. He had been wounded in the leg in an Indian skirmish years before and the wound had never healed. His leg was kept straight by props, his knee was swollen to three times its natural size, and his uncut toenails had grown long and pointed. His sufferings must have been intense, but he made no complaint. Oh, the infinite patience of that poor fellow! His wife seemed ill and was moaning with pain as she sat at the doorway.

The Koutznous complained of a settler by the name of Sullivan, and his partner, who ran a small schooner into the bay with liquor for the Indians of their village. They said they did not want them there. One old woman, however, took the liquor-sellers' part and scolded the other Indians vehemently for telling about them. Among settlers may be found crafty traders who understand the game of getting Indians partly drunk before they buy their furs and oils; after that they get all they want at their own price.

Continuing our journey we anchored at the mouth of the Chilcat River. The strong cold wind was furiously lashing white-capped waves and everything was bleak and dreary. As our anchor fell a number of Chilcat Indians paddled about the steamer. They were noticeably thin, but tough and hardy, not so well clad as those at Sitka, but in language, size, and features much like them. Here I was glad to find "Sitka Jack" with his long canoe, thoroughly equipped with paddles and manned with expert paddlers. At this time he carried a handsome United States flag in the stern of his boat and came up to us in grand style. As he clambered on the deck of the *California* he was welcomed like a prince. We descended into a row-boat and Sitka Jack was delighted to pilot us to a small Indian village located under the shelter of a high mountain four miles up the Chilcat River.

All their buildings, totem-poles, and customs were like those of the other Indians we had visited.

Here we found an enormous meteorolite and tried to purchase it for the Smithsonian Institution, but some bold prospector then on a voyage up the Chilcat had engaged it, and the Indians, faithful to their promise, were determined to keep it for him.

After leaving the mouth of the Chilcat the *California* turned eastward, and at four in the morning we were in plain sight of another Indian town. Choquette and I, with a boat's crew, here left the steamer and rowed along a rough and wooded shore toward the town. Suddenly a small dog appeared barking and moaning piteously. From this circumstance I feared that the Indians had left the village, but on going ashore we found the poor animal in a starving condition, but faithfully watching a *cache* at the edge of a wood.

When we were again on board, the steamer headed toward the Tacon River and reached its mouth in a few hours. Here was a village occupied by the Tacon Indians, who were kind and hospitable and did not differ from the Koutznous in any material respect. A very old man, blind and feeble with age, was being tenderly cared for by his children and grandchildren, and I learned that it was the custom with the Tacons to care for the aged and helpless. This trait is seldom found among Indians.

Just after noon, as we were approaching an island inhabited by the Sumdum Indians, we encountered some large icebergs, and also caught sight of some remarkable glaciers working their slow way between the hills toward the strait. One glacier extended from the top of a mountain, two hundred and fifty feet high, along a gentle slope for miles. It was about three hundred yards broad, but was narrower near the base. It was near this glacier that we found the home of the Sumdums. A young chief named Foust Chou met our boat at a halfway island. He was greatly pleased because I showed so much confidence in him as to get into his canoe and have his people paddle me back to the steamer, beating the steamer's boat by many lengths.

After a formal interview he asked me for "a paper" for himself and for the old chief "Harteshawk," whom he had left at the village. On Choquette's recommendation I acceded to his request. Choquette, in his own tongue, read to him the contents of my paper, which briefly stated that I had met him; that I was strongly opposed to the liquor trade of the settlers with his people; that I hoped they would some time have a good teacher and keep abreast of other Indians in knowledge and in good behavior, and so on. Such papers strongly influence not only the chief who holds them, but all who, through frequent talks, become familiar with their contents.

Two hours before the sun touched the horizon, where it skimmed along for a considerable time, we found ourselves in Prince Frederick's Sound. I estimated that it was twenty miles wide. It was calm and smooth as a mill-pond, with shores of irregular outline, and mountains of different shapes rising in the distance like ghosts. The glaciers in the dimness of the evening light looked like the mists of Niagara, while the islands and nearer shores were as clearly defined below as above the water's surface.

The steamer moved almost noiselessly toward Prevontet Island, whose distance proved to be four times greater than it had seemed. The whole scene was indescribably grand and beautiful. Captain Hayes, who commanded the steamer, had come from Massachusetts in his youth, and, remembering that it was the anniversary of the battle of Bunker Hill, loaded his small cannon, putting in as large a charge as he dared, and fired it, while two of his men dipped the flag.

We had with us five of our children, the youngest being but four years old. Daylight continued so long that it was difficult to get the children into their berths at a reasonable hour. That evening from nine to ten I marked the outlines of the battlefield of Gettysburg on an improvised blackboard which was hung against the mast of the steamer, and described the battle to the people assembled on deck. The outlines in red chalk were clear enough to be distinctly seen when I finished my description. In fact, there was scarcely one hour from the end of twilight to dawn of the next day.

We soon entered a snug little bay called Saganaw. The Cakes, a band of Indians living near the shore, had, previous to my coming, undertaken to revenge themselves for the loss of several of their tribe at the hands of certain white men. How far they had succeeded in carrying out their plans of revenge I do not know, but one of our gunboats had visited the bay and "the avengers" had been demanded of the tribe. They not being delivered up the gunboat opened fire upon the village, completely destroying it. After that, either from timidity or suppressed hostility, the Cakes had up to the time of my visit kept aloof from the whites. Such was the story told me by Choquette.

As soon as we were at anchor a Sitka Indian and a child appeared in a canoe. By this man I sent for the chief of the Cakes, who soon appeared, coming toward us slowly, and with apparent reluctance came on board the steamer. After getting a little acquainted he gave me some reasons why he had not visited Major Campbell at Sitka. He had been warned by a Sitka woman not to do so, fearing we were against him still and that he would not be kindly treated. He declared that the next time he visited Sitka he would report directly to the commanding officer. This chief, a very young but dignified man, was well dressed and showed good sense in all he said.

We were now obliged to turn southward and homeward. I had visited many tribes of Indians from Wrangel to the mouth of the Chilcat River and found them much the same, usually well fed and kindly disposed, but prone to believe the abundant superstitions of Indians, and still depraved, most of them, by the grosser vices of savage life.

Quite a contrast to all this was presented at Fort Simpson, British Columbia, and a more marked one at Metlakahtla, eighteen miles south of that place. We touched at Simpson on Sunday,

June 20th, very early in the morning. After breakfasting on board the steamer, officers, ladies, and children went on shore. We passed by numerous Indian houses built like all the others on the coast, but with a little more care in their construction. Many had in them two small glass windows. The fort, which once had contained an old Hudson Bay garrison, consisted of a single dwelling-house and several storehouses built inside of a high stockade.

Mr. Morrison, the Hudson Bay agent, who had been there many years, looked like a thorough British seaman. He had married an Indian woman. He gave us a very cordial welcome to the fort, and showed us the way to the temporary home of the Rev. Mr. Crosby, a minister of the Methodist Church, who had come up from Victoria. His little house was newly finished, and close by was his church, which was then in process of construction. He told us he had been at Fort Simpson only eleven months, and that he had been much helped by the good influence of those Indians who had come to him from the Episcopal Mission at Metlakahtla. Having been introduced to his family we tarried a short time and then proceeded to the Indian village to attend a religious service which was to take place in one of the largest Indian houses.

Soon after we left the parsonage a great bell rang, when instantly not less than five hundred Indians, well dressed, some with shoes and some without, many women carrying babies, old men and young men, boys and girls, came flocking from all directions, obedient to the summons. They had quietly remained in their homes until they heard the sound of the bell. We joined the throng, and going into the Indian house found seats ready for us near the desk. Mr. Crosby had not arrived. After I had sat down and while waiting for Mr. Crosby I said to the teacher:

"Shall we sing a hymn?"

"Oh, no, sir; we do not sing till Mr. Crosby comes," he answered.

When the second bell sounded Mr. Crosby came, his young wife following with her little baby named "A-he-shime," which is the Indian word for "Sunbeam." Mrs. Crosby was glad enough to meet Mrs. Howard and Mrs. Wilkinson. She said at once that she had not seen a white woman for eleven months.

The Indians quickly filled the house and the few benches reserved for them were soon occupied, but the majority sat upon the floor, with their heads raised in an attentive and expectant attitude. One could hardly find a better behaved congregation. Mr. Crosby read the Scriptures and an Indian woman interpreted them sentence by sentence; then all joined in a hymn. It was a strange and plaintive sound that arose from that assembly. Mr. Crosby took as his text: "Dost thou believe in Jesus, the Son of God?" As he preached, the same young Indian woman stood at his elbow and translated his speech into the Indian tongue, and it seemed as if no one in that house missed any part of the sermon, except perhaps when the faint cry of a little child was heard.

On this occasion the minister published the

banns of matrimony between two Indian people, and, as this was the second publication, the wedding would soon follow. It reminded me of the same custom in my native town, where, in my childhoood, I had seen the town clerk stand in the gallery and read aloud for two Sundays in succession the intention of two young people to wed.

The Simpson mission had been in operation less than a year. The origin of it is worth recording. Some young Indians had gone down on a steamer to Victoria for a frolic, and ran the risk, as many others have done, of falling into bad company, and subsequently leading a sinful life; but certain Methodist Christians met them and, as Mr. Crosby said, "they were soundly converted to God." Among those who found the new experience was the young woman whom we saw acting as an interpreter for the minister. Mr. Crosby told us that many Indians had already become consistent Christians, and many more were seeking the way of salvation.

As soon as the more public service was ended a number of young people, those who could read a little and had Bibles, stopped awhile to go over their lessons with the interpreter. I enjoyed listening to this performance. First, a word pronounced by her in English was repeated by all in concert, then two, three, and four at a time; soon a whole sentence. Over and over they repeated a passage until it was thoroughly mastered by all.

A few years ago the quarrels and fights among these Indians were dreadful, often ending in bloodshed and death. They were at one time so savage and brutal as to eat a slain enemy, but quarreling had now altogether ceased, order and cleanliness prevailed, and there were no more blackened and disfigured faces. They were very careful to keep the Sabbath. At certain times in the year they went up the Stickeen River to the mines, going all the way in canoes. If the Sabbath intervened they would tie up their canoes and wait patiently till Monday morning. Of course they had not at that time attained to a very high Christian life, but vast and rapid progress had been made in the short space of eleven months.

When I first met Mr. Duncan, the head of the Metlakahtla Mission, I was accompanied by an officer who was very skeptical with regard to the truth of the Scriptures. He had heard of the manner in which Mr. Duncan had brought a large tribe of perhaps the worst Indians on the coast from gross ignorance and superstition to a high degree of civilization. After we had shaken hands with Mr. Duncan my skeptical friend said: "Mr. Duncan, how did you do it?"

Mr. Duncan made prompt answer, which I have never forgotten. It was this: "I first learned their language, then I put the Word of God into their minds, and you now behold the results."

We returned all the way by sea, having a safe and pleasant voyage. When we were passing Astoria we recalled the scenes at Wrangel and the poor Indians who were such natural actors there, for it was from the Astoria wharf, during the up trip, that the dead body of Chief Fernandeste had been taken on board.

# CHAPTER XXIV.

## THE STORY OF MARCUS WHITMAN AND HIS LABORS AMONG THE OREGON INDIANS — THRILLING ACCOUNT OF HIS PERILOUS OVERLAND JOURNEY.

The Story of Doctor Whitman's Life — The Remarkable Journey of Four Flathead Indians — The Quest for "The White Man's Book of Life" — A Brave Methodist Pioneer — Open Hostilities of the Great Fur Companies — Starting on a Perilous Journey — His Return and Marriage — Organizing Another Expedition — Dangerous Journey for Brides — Toils and Privations of Frontier Missionary Life — Circulating a "Bad Medicine" — Instigating a Massacre — An "Indiscreet Conversation" — Whitman's Remarkable Journey to Washington — Unspeakable Hardships — Mutterings of the Coming Storm — A Man of God and a True Patriot.

IN a previous chapter I alluded to the massacre of Marcus Whitman and his family. The scene of his missionary labors and tragic death was in the country that was now the theater of my operations against Indians, and as his noble life and services are worthy of more than passing mention I will tell the story here.

Marcus Whitman was born in Rushville, New York, September 4, 1802. When he was eight years of age he was sent to Plainfield, Massachusetts, and lived at the home of his grandfather for ten years that he might receive such fundamental education as that town afforded. At eighteen he returned to Rushville and continued his studies under the direction of Rev. David Page for two or three years, afterward completing a course in medicine at Fairfield, New York, in 1824. He soon entered upon the practice of his profession in Canada, continuing there about four years, when he again returned to Rushville, and remained till a favorable opening appeared at Wheeler, New York. Here the young physician practiced his profession four years more, until the spring of 1835, when he received his first call from the American Board.

With regard to the occupation of Oregon, and especially the rich valley watered by the beautiful Willamette, as missionary ground, our Methodist brethren were a little ahead of the Presbyterian and Congregational bodies then represented in the American Board. In 1834 the Methodists sent Jason Lee and his helpers there to establish a mission among the Indians. That was done in answer to the report of Mr. Catlin, in which he told the story of the four Flatheads who journeyed all the way, over two thousand miles, from Oregon to St. Louis, to find "The White Man's Book of Life." Only one of the Flatheads lived to return to his people. An American trapper, whose expeditions had led him to the far-off camps of these peaceful Indians, had first told them of the wonderful book and something of its teachings. The story was published in a New York Methodist journal in March, 1832, and in the editorial comment was the thrilling call: "Who will respond to go beyond the Rocky Mountains and carry the Book of Heaven?"

The Willamette Valley was not hard to reach by way of the Columbia River, because Astoria at its mouth, and Fort Vancouver but six miles from the nearest point of the Willamette Valley, were then securely held by the American Fur Company and the Hudson Bay Company. Jason Lee, that Methodist pioneer "of strong nerve and indomitable will," with a tender, loving heart, was in that valley, and all around him were Indians, and numbers of white *voyageurs* who had already to some extent demoralized them.

A missionary to the Sandwich Islands had once visited the northwestern coast and the Columbia Valley, either in going to or coming from his distant station, and had reported the evil ways and teachings of many of the fur traders, and had convinced the secretaries of the American Board that American missionaries would not be welcome in Oregon Territory. The Northwest was all Oregon then.

The need of missionary work among the Indians on the one hand, and the fur traders' hostility on the other, caused the American Board first to hesitate, then at last to make a tentative effort. Early in 1835 they decided to send the Rev. Samuel Parker of Ithaca, New York, a highly-educated man of power and purpose, to explore that country, and report upon the practicability of establishing a mission there. The enterprising young physician, Dr. Marcus Whitman, was chosen to accompany Mr. Parker on this expedition. One who knew the young man well has furnished a sketch of his character, which is photographic in its details. He said: "He was a man of easy don't-care habits, that could become all things to all men, and yet a sincere and earnest man, speaking his mind before he thought the second time, giving his views without much consideration, but correcting them when good reasons were presented for a change; yet when fixed in the pursuit of an object he adhered to it with unflinching tenacity."

He further describes him as generous in the extreme, kind and self-denying, giving his whole mind and thought to the accomplishment of the work in hand; a character without excessive apprehension of danger, animated in conversation, earnest in argument, and of indomitable energy. As a physician he was successful.

Parker and Whitman set out together and had accomplished more than half their perilous journey when, at a halting place near a trader's post called Fort Independence, at Green River in the Rocky Mountains, a serious difference arose between them, which has never been satisfactorily explained. Dr. Whitman's ability to "rough it," as the soldiers say, was marvelous, and Parker was feeble in that regard. Opposite opinions supported by various reasons were asserted and obstinately adhered to.

It is evident that their tastes, habits, and daily life were different, and that neither could adjust himself to the ideas of the other. At Green River these two men of God, in some vexation and perplexity, were considering these untoward things, when a Nez Percé Indian chief, with his hunters, fortunately appeared. He agreed to safely guide Parker over the long trails to Fort Walla Walla, and did so with much display of savage pomp and with but small discomfort to his guest. He delivered him safe and sound to the secretary of the great British fur company and asked for no payment.

The Nez Percés did more: they allowed two of their boys to go, as guides, with Dr. Whitman, he having resolved to return to the East and report to the American Board, with the intention of returning with means and men to plant a mission, not in the Willamette Valley, but in Oregon east of the Coast range and among the Nez Percé Indians.

It is delightful to see how easily Dr. Whitman won the hearts of the rough American fur traders, and of all the Indians that he met. His own warm heart and ready help for body and soul lightened the hardships of his long homeward journey. He reported in person to the American Board, obtained the sanction of the secretaries, and soon was preparing to return, greatly reinforced, to plant his important mission.

We have glimpses of Whitman's dramatic homecoming. On a Sabbath evening in November, 1835, without previous warning, he and his two young Nez Percé guides marched down the aisle of the Rushville church, startling his mother, who, in spite of the solemnity of the place, cried out: "Well, there's Marcus Whitman!"

In February, 1836, a wedding occurred at Prattsburg, New York. Narcissa Prentiss, "the adored daughter of a refined Christian home," the sweetest singer of the village choir, greatly beloved by all who knew her, there became the wife of Marcus Whitman. The last hymn she sang in the church before starting for Oregon, "Yes, my Na-

20

tive Land, I Love Thee," was sung in her usual voice, "clear, musical, and unwavering," and profoundly impressed a sympathetic and weeping congregation and seemed to emphasize the sorrow all felt at her leave-taking.

Of this mission band the principals were the well-known missionary H. H. Spalding and his equally notable wife, then also a bride, Dr. and Mrs. Whitman, and W. H. Gray of Utica, New York, who was chosen by the American Board as business agent, and "solicited to join the expedition." The two Nez Percé Indian boys and two teamsters made up the little party. Three wagons, eight mules, twelve horses, sixteen cows, and Whitman's extra wagon and team completed the equipment. This vehicle is mentioned in Gray's history of the Whitman family, which states that "the journey was commenced in an old wagon." Everyone said it would have to be abandoned, but the irrepressible energy of the doctor overcame all obstacles and the practicability of crossing the mountains in a wheeled vehicle was established. The fact gave much encouragement to those who were considering the possibilities of emigration. About the middle of May, when they were well on their way, a young English nobleman, Captain Stewart, joined his wagon and outfit to theirs.

Pawnee Indians in Nebraska, astonished and pleased to see such women on the western march, escorted them part of the way. The hardships of that journey of more than two thousand miles cannot be told. But on they went, overcoming all obstacles, until in the far West, after traveling for a month alone, they joined the American Fur Company's caravan, then moving up the great Platte Valley. At the place on Green River where Parker and Dr. Whitman had parted, a wonderful and characteristic scene at first terrified and then pleasantly surprised them.

The Green River encampment was a great meeting-place for all the different fur companies, and Indians came from every quarter to barter their furs and other goods for the white man's merchandise, which often, I am sorry to say, consisted of nothing but beads, baubles, and useless trinkets. "Two days before we arrived at our rendezvous," wrote the business agent, "and some two hours before we reached camp, the whole caravan was alarmed by the approach of some mounted Indians and four or five white men, whose dress and appearance could scarcely be distinguished from that of the Indians. As they came in sight over the hills, they all gave a yell, such as hunters and Indians only can give; whiz! whiz! came their balls over our heads, and on they came in less time than it will take to read this account. The alarm was but for a moment; our guide had seen a white cloth on one of their guns, and said: "Don't be alarmed; they are friends," and, sure enough, in a moment here they were. It was difficult to tell which was the most crazy, the horses or the riders; such hopping, hooting, running, yelling, jumping over sage-brush, and whirling around; for they could not stop to reload their guns, but all of us, as they came on, gave them a salute from ours, as they passed to the rear of our line and back again."

I myself in later years often had just such experiences on the plains, and with my companions have suddenly passed from a state of apprehension to that of relief and satisfaction.

The frontier forts, especially in all that long-disputed territory, in the mountains and beyond, were not in 1836 our military posts, but were trading stations defended by strong stockades and well-armed employees of the fur company to which they belonged. Our two beautiful brides appeared at these posts like angels of light. They awakened the chivalric spirit and gentle behavior of the the roughest frontiersman and of all peaceable Indians. The 2d of September they arrived at Fort Walla Walla, not where the city of Walla Walla and Whitman College, named for Marcus Whitman, now is, but thirty miles farther west: a stockaded fort in charge of one of the principal agents of the Hudson Bay Company.

The agent and employees of the fur company met the newcomers with every show of courtesy and generous hospitality. The women were sent, for a time, more than a hundred miles down the river, beyond the snow-capped mountains, to enjoy the welcome and protection of the chief of the great English monopoly. Meanwhile our missionaries reconnoitered what was called the Nez Percé territory from the Umatilla below them to the Lewis and Clark forks of the Snake River. Along the borders of the great Columbia, which cuts its way through a long stretch of prairie country from the Rocky Mountains to the Coast Range, where it bursts through seemingly impassable barriers to

Circling around a Wagon Train that has Gone into Corral for Defense.

Lying in Ambush While Watching an Approaching Wagon Train.

INDIAN METHOD OF ATTACKING OVERLAND WAGON TRAINS.

find its way to the Pacific Ocean, we have on the southern bank for a hundred miles a broad belt of barren, sandy land. From Wallula eastward, after passing that belt, Dr. Whitman examined and selected a fine rolling country bordering on Walla Walla Creek, which is now known as Wailatpu. Many times have I visited this spot. There are trees, a rich valley of cleared land, and choice knolls for buildings, but even now the region has but few inhabitants.

Dr. Whitman thought Wailatpu the finest spot in that region, and the one best suited for a mission to the lower Nez Percés. Besides a sprinkling of that tribe it included three sub-tribes, the Walla Wallas, Cayuses, and Umatillas. It was convenient for supplies to Fort Walla Walla, and a fine meeting point for all the Indian bands that roamed between the Columbia River and the Blue Mountains.

Dr. Whitman did not know, and no scientist seemed to have then discovered the fact, that the vast open country, apparently covered with alkali deposits, hills, knolls, mounds, foothills, and long belts of mountain sides, had a soil unsurpassed in fertility. Forty years later I stood on the Blue Mountains and beheld more than sixty square miles of the finest wheat land, covered with waving crops, that I had ever seen. The soil was apparently so dry, deep, and shifting, and the dust in the roadways so superabundant, that it did not occur to the early settlers to test anything beyond the narrow valleys of the abundant streams which were finding their way to the Snake and the Columbia.

Dr. Whitman chose Wailaptu for his home and slowly built up his mission. Meanwhile Mr. and Mrs. Spalding settled among the Nez Percés proper amid the hills in the beautiful Lapwai valley, more than a hundred miles to the northeast.

For seven years these good missionaries, sometimes slightly reinforced, endured all the toils and privations of frontier life. They established schools for Indian children and extended their acquaintance among the various tribes round about them. Dr. Whitman himself was apparently much beloved by the Indians. He visited and ministered to them in sickness and generally with success. One scourge, however, among the Cayuses, for which they had no remedy, was an attack of the measles, which went from lodge to lodge until the whole tribe was in terror. Many deaths occurred in spite of Dr. Whitman's faithful attendance.

As it now appears, some of the worst of the Hudson Bay Company's employees took advantage of this state of alarm and fanned into flame the smoldering embers of superstition by impressing the Indians with the idea that the Whitmans, notwithstanding their devotion and apparent kindness, were circulating a "bad medicine." There was also the old religious opposition to all newcomers by the Roman Catholic people, especially the Jesuit Fathers, because they themselves had come to the country and started a mission of their own; but it must always be remembered that the Roman Catholic could not be a pronounced friend to other denominations, because his fundamental religious principle was that they were wrong in the faith. It does not appear that Catholic opposition promoted a massacre, but it does appear that a few Hudson Bay employees endeavored to saddle upon them the responsibility of stirring up the Indians. The missionaries found that arms, ammunition, and liquor were freely sold to the savages by British occupants of the territory, and against this evil the missionaries exerted every possible influence.

One day an "indiscreet conversation" by these British employees was held at Walla Walla in the presence of Dr. Whitman, in which new plans to hold the country against all American commerce and at all hazards, were made known to him. This was in October, 1842.* Without waiting for permission from the American Board, the impulsive Whitman suddenly decided to brave the perils of a winter passage over the mountains in order to reach Washington before Congress adjourned. That resolve was made and he started on his long and dangerous journey only twenty-four hours after his ears first heard the fur company's prematurely triumphant cry: "Hurrah for Oregon, America is too late! We have the country!"

More than once the doctor's winter party nearly perished in the deep snows, but every obstacle was overcome by his indomitable courage and fertile expedients. March 3d, 1843, after a five months' journey in the winter season, through hardships

* This conversation is denied by several writers, but as I knew Dr. Gray, who wrote the "History of Oregon," and have the greatest confidence in the truthfulness of Mr. Spalding, I adhere to the belief that my account of what took place at Walla Walla is correct.

unspeakable, he reached Washington.* To Daniel Webster, then Secretary of State, he told his story. Webster discouraged him, but, providentially, President Tyler, after hearing him through, said: "Your frozen limbs and leather breeches attest your sincerity. Can you take emigrants across the mountains in wagons?"

Here is the glorious answer of a patriot who had faith in himself and faith in God: "Give me six months and I will take a thousand emigrants across."

The President replied: "If you take them across, the Ashburton Treaty (which would have given Oregon to Great Britain) shall not be ratified."

Now comes the record: Dr. Whitman's party, then about a thousand strong, in June, 1843, gathered on the banks of the Missouri River at the small town of Westford, and set out for Oregon. In good time, and after great trials which called for incredible pluck and endurance, the party safely arrived at Fort Walla Walla.

It is said that the anger of the Hudson Bay Company knew no bounds, and we can easily see the reason. It was a little more than four years later that the dreadful storm, which had been slowly gathering and darkening the skies between

* That Whitman did reach Washington is proven by a recorded correspondence with the then Secretary of War. There is no direct evidence of the doings of Webster or the sayings of the President at that time. It is, however, the story of the intimates of Whitman who were with him in Oregon. What was Whitman in Washington for but to carry out his purpose of interesting the administration in the populating of Oregon by our people and holding it for our government?

the Cascades and the Rockies, broke upon them. The tragedy that followed is more fully described in the next chapter. November 29, 1847, Dr. Marcus Whitman, his wife, and seven others were cruelly massacred and their home destroyed, but the recorder adds: "Whitman's work had, however, been accomplished, and the foul deed only recoiled upon its instigators."

As I have said, as soon as the instigators perceived their mistake and its consequences they tried every conceivable plan to saddle the whole blame upon the missionaries themselves and the Cayuse Indians, but the evidence of plotting, of craft, of ambition, of avarice, and of diabolical instigation is too plain for the historians of today to relieve all of the white men of Oregon who were then hostile to the American republic, and to our type of Christian work and development, to escape the scathing denunciation which they deserve. Savages are bad enough, but savagery in alliance with such white generalship is incredibly wicked and cruel.

I have just seen a likeness of Dr. Whitman, probably taken after he had passed his fortieth birthday. It bespeaks a glorious character—one of nature's noblemen. Generous, hearty, frank in statement, thoroughly educated, abreast of any in his profession, he devoted his life to the service of his fellow-men, and through them to the service of God. No personal exposure, no toil, no prolonged endurance, no opposition of men, not even that of the great Webster, then Secretary of State, could abate Whitman's patriotic fervor.

It should make every lover of humanity happy to see a glorious college, erected on the banks of the Walla Walla, which watered Whitman's gardens and received Whitman's blood of sacrifice and that of those so precious to him. Let that college prosper, and bless the rich valley that his eye first fell upon! I am glad to know that the fertile knolls and hillocks that so long remained covered with weeds and thistles, and that the grave so long surrounded by a decaying picket fence, without even a headstone to mark the places of burial, have at last been looked upon by patriotic and Christian eyes, and been cared for by tender hearts and grateful patriots.

Yes, my countrymen, Dr. Marcus Whitman, an American type of Christian manhood, heroically planted the first mission of the American Board in eastern Oregon and Washington, for it was his energy that carried the devoted party of missionaries thither into that vast domain. His example and his work have stimulated every effort to raise up the lowly and to redeem the savage. More, still, that one heroic man, seeing the imminent danger of losing to our country priceless regions of magnificent domain, with a heroism never surpassed by anybody on earth, made one of the most remarkable journeys on record, with a purpose to save to us our rightful land.

So let us, who can appreciate high achievement, give all honor to the memory of Marcus Whitman —the man of God and the true patriot!

# CHAPTER XXV.

## A FRONTIER TRAGEDY — THE COLD-BLOODED MASSACRE OF MARCUS WHITMAN AND HIS FAMILY.

Scene of the Brutal Massacre — Unsuspecting Settlers Engaged in Peaceful Avocations — Hovering and Watchful Indians — Sudden Appearance of Indians at an Open Door — Dr. Whitman Asked to Come into the Kitchen — The Deadly Tomahawk — Fighting for Life — Ghastly Scenes — "Oh, the Indians! the Indians!" — The Infamous Murderer "Joe Lewis" — Death of Dr. Whitman — Heroic Efforts of His Wife to Save His Life — Discovering the Hidden Children — Dreadful and Heartrending Scenes — "We Will Now Burn!" — Assassination of Mrs. Whitman — Desperate Struggles for Life — Escape of the Few Survivors.

I HAVE frequently visited Wailatpu, the scene of that cold-blooded massacre of devoted Christian people. It was past noon November 29, 1847. Joseph Stanfield had driven an ox from the pasture to Wailatpu and Francis Sager had killed it for beef. Kimball, Canfield, and Hoffman were dressing the same near the mission buildings; Sanders was in the schoolroom just beginning an afternoon session; Marsh was at the mill grinding; Gillan sat on his tailor's bench in the adobe "mansion"; Hall was busy laying a floor near Dr. Whitman's dwelling; Rogers was working in the garden; Osborn and his family were in the Indians' room, next to the doctor's sitting-room; young Sayles was lying ill with the Canfield family, who resided in the blacksmith shop; Bewley, a young man, was ill in the doctor's house; John Sager, convalescent from measles, was sitting in the kitchen; Dr. Whitman, his wife, and three sick children, and Mrs. Osborn with her sick children were in the dining or sitting-room of the Whitman house. Such is the historian's presentation of the domestic and peaceful situation at Wailatpu on that fatal day.

It is not easy to give a sketch of the buildings. Dr. Whitman's dwelling was an adobe structure, sixty-two feet long and eighteen feet deep, with a half story above. The long building faced west and probably had three doors opening that way. In the north end was the large Indian room, in the middle was the sitting and dining-room, and in the south ĕnd a library on the front, and behind it a bedroom. Behind the dining and sitting-room, probably one and the same, was a kitchen of large size, and abreast of it was the schoolroom. Due east from the Whitman house was the blacksmith's shop, partly used for a residence, and south of the kitchen and some little distance from it was the extensive building that is named in the accounts as "The Mansion." To the south and east and some way from the mansion was the mill. Near the mill, on the rapid creek which afforded water for all, was a small lake or pond made by damming the creek. The water from the mill flowed into a ditch, which passed on the north side of all the buildings, and furnished water for irrigating purposes.

Dr. Whitman's house was the most complete structure yet finished. That day the man whose name we revere was sitting in the midst of his family reading the Scriptures. Several Indians, who had been hovering about and watching the killing and dressing of the ox, entered the kitchen by a door from the outside. One of them stepped to the open door which led to the dining-room and requested the doctor to come into the kitchen. He rose, and, carrying his Bible in his hand, went into the kitchen, closed the door behind him, and took a seat. Edward Sager, not feeling well, at once sat down beside him to take some medicine; then, while these two were talking, the Indian Tamsaky, who had some time before promised to give the bishop at Walla Walla the doctor's station, silently came up behind him and suddenly drawing a tomahawk from under his blanket struck the doctor on the back of the head. The first blow stunned him and his head fell forward upon his breast. A second blow followed instantly upon the top of his head and brought him senseless, but not yet lifeless, to the floor.

Young John Sager then sprang to his feet and attempted to draw a pistol; the Indians in front of him rushed to the outer door crying: "He will shoot us! He will shoot us!" but the Indians immediately behind him seized his arms, and, after a desperate struggle, threw him upon the floor and fired into his body several shots from Hudson Bay rifles, hitherto concealed under their Indian blankets. Moreover his assassins gashed him with knives; his throat was cut and a woolen tippet thrust into it,—still he lingered. Two of the murderers were accidently wounded by each other in the struggle.

The moment that Mrs. Whitman heard the tumult in the kitchen she understood the cause. She wrung her hands in agony, crying out: "Oh, the Indians! the Indians! That Joe (referring to Joe Lewis) has done it all!"

To digress a little: Joe Lewis had but recently come from the East, from Canada, with a party of priests. He afterwards claimed to be a Cherokee. On his way west, not long before the massacre, he told the people at Fort Boise that there was going to be a "great overturn at Dr. Whitman's, and in the Willamette." He came to Dr. Whitman's quite destitute and the doctor showed him great kindness. Finding that Lewis was making mischief the doctor sent him away with some emigrant families as a teamster, giving him a good outfit. He was gone only three days when, having abandoned the emigrants, he came back to Wailatpu. He spent most of his time in Nicholas Finlay's lodge, close to the station, the resort of Stanfield and of the Indians engaged in the massacre. Finlay was a half-breed, an employee of the Hudson Bay Company, and the counsellor of the Indians. Joe Lewis was really the leader in the whole affair. Several times before the massacre Mrs. Whitman had seen him coming to a window with a gun and had asked him: "What do you want?" At the sound of her voice he ran away.

To resume my story: Mrs. Osborn, seizing her child, ran into the Indian room, where Mr. Osborn immediately followed and managed to hide all of them under the floor.

The Indians next began their destruction outside the Whitman house. Just then, assisted by Mrs. Hayes, who had hurried in from the mansion, Mrs. Whitman dragged her dying husband into the dining-room, and placed his head upon a pillow, and did all she could to stay the blood and to revive him, but without avail. All he said until he breathed his last was, "No," repeating the word in a low whisper in answer to several questions.

Just then the women saw Mr. Kimball come in through the kitchen and run upstairs with his arm broken and hanging by his side. Mr. Rogers followed him with a wounded arm, his head covered with blood from the cut of a tomahawk. Rogers assisted the women in making fast the doors and in carrying the sick children upstairs.

Out of doors were heard the screams of frightened and fleeing women and children, the groans and struggles of the dying, the roar of musketry, the whistling of balls, the blows of the tomahawk, and a furious riding about of naked and hideously painted Indians, who gave unearthly yells characteristic of infuriated savages maddened like tigers, at the sight and smell of human blood. It would seem hardly possible that there could have been so much noise and terror where there were so few to be slain.

Mrs. Whitman saw two Americans fall under the Indians' blows outside her window, and, as she looked, an Indian who had always been treated most kindly by her, leveled his gun at her and fired. The ball penetrated her right breast and she fell forward, uttering a single groan. Presently she revived, rose, and went to the settee, and was heard by some one who escaped to pray for their adopted children (the Sager family, who had lost their parents in crossing the Plains), and also for her aged father and mother back in the East, that they might be sustained under the terrible shock that would follow the news of this tragedy. Soon after this prayer she was helped into her chamber, where were now Mrs. Hayes, Miss Bewley, Katherine Sager, Messrs. Kimball, Rogers, and the three sick children,—nine persons altogether. The rooms below were then being plundered and the furniture smashed in pieces, Joe Lewis leading in the work of destruction.

The famous Cayuse Tilokaikt, seeing Dr. Whitman still breathing, deliberately chopped his face, but still death did not come. John Sager was similarly cut.

Joe Lewis now made his way into the schoolroom and, finding the hidden children, brought them into the kitchen to be shot. As Francis Sager passed his mangled brother he removed the tippet from the wound, when John, attempting to speak, immediately expired. Francis said to his sister: "I shall soon follow my brother."

Eliza Spalding, the missionary's sweet daughter, who was among the children, understood every word the Indians said while they were pointing their guns at them and yelling: "Shall we shoot?" Eliza, in anguish of mind, leaned upon the sink and covered her face with her apron that she might not see them shoot her.

From this place the children were taken out of doors by the side of the Indian room. The Indians next called to Mrs. Whitman and Mr. Rogers to come downstairs. On receiving no answer Tamsaky started to go up, but discovering the end of an old gun desisted. He urged them to come down, saying that nobody would hurt them. Mrs Whitman answered that she was shot and had not strength to come down, besides she feared they would kill her. Tamsaky expressed much sorrow and promised that no one would be hurt. Mrs. Whitman answered: "If you are my friend come up and see me!"

"No," he replied, "there are Americans with arms who would kill me." Mr. Rogers, near the head of the stairs, told him there were none, so he came up, sympathizing with the sufferers and assuring them that he was sorry for what had taken place. He urged Mrs. Whitman to come down and be taken to the other house, where the families were, intimating that the young men might destroy her house in the night. Just then Joe Lewis cried out: "We will now burn!" and proceeded to execute his threat.

They came out, Mrs. Whitman being carried on a settee. They heard the command not to shoot the children. Mr. Rogers perceiving their treachery, dropped the settee and raised his hands exclaiming: "Oh, my God!" when a volley was fired from within and from without the house at Mrs. Whitman and himself. He fell upon his face pierced with many balls, and Mrs. Whitman was instantly killed. An Indian near by caught Francis Sager and held him, while Joe Lewis, exclaiming: "You bad boy!" deliberately shot him.

Mr. Kimball, Katherine Sager, and the three sick children remained in the chamber all night. Mr. Osborn remained under the floor till the Indians retired; he then made his escape to Fort Walla Walla with his family. The three men who were dressing the beef were shot early in the massacre and all were wounded. Mr. Kimball ran to the house, Mr. Canfield to the blacksmith shop and thence to the mansion, where, strange to say, he managed to hide till night, when he fled for Lapwai. Mr. Hall wrenched a loaded gun from an Indian and ran for the bushes; he, too, reached the fort the next day, and was carried across the Columbia but was never heard from again. Mr. Gillan was slain upon his bench. Mr. Marsh, pierced with a ball, started toward the Whitman house, but expired before he reached it.

Mr. Saunders emerged from the schoolroom, and, being seized by several Indians, was thrown upon the ground and wounded with musket balls and tomahawks. Being a strong and active man he rose, though wounded, and ran some distance, but was at last overtaken, surrounded, and murdered. Hoffman was also cut down after a desperate fight, which he made with a knife; his body was cut open and his heart and liver taken out.

Joe Lewis took the two Manson boys and a half-breed Spanish boy, whom Dr. Whitman had raised, and soon arranged to send them to the fort. Whoever this Joe Lewis was, or wherever he came from, he acted faithfully his part in the great "overturn" which he had predicted. It is said that he afterward killed a guide who belonged to a company of United States troops and was himself shot for his crime.

The facts which I have given of this frontier

tragedy are substantially those narrated by Mr. W. H. Gray, who went to Oregon with Dr. Whitman, and who has left us this sifted story of the terrible massacre. The Cayuse Indians led by Joe Lewis perpetrated the murders, but they were only the executioners of a dreadful plot whose authors are not even yet fully known. Surely it was a contest primarily aimed against United States immigration and settlement, and fomented by the old contest of one religious faith endeavoring to supplant and destroy another. The executioners may have gone beyond the design of those who planned the crime, for savages when used as instruments by civilized men cannot always be controlled.

# CHAPTER XXVI.

## CAMPAIGNING ON THE UPPER COLUMBIA — EXPERIENCES WITH MOSES, WAR-CHIEF OF THE SPOKANES — HIS OWN NARRATIVE.

Moses, the War-Chief of the Spokanes — His Personal Appearance — A Diplomatic Indian — Some Hostile Threats — Fears of an Outbreak — My Letter to Chief Moses — His Reply — The Gathering War Clouds — Efforts to Pacify Moses — Starting for His Camp — Moses and Sixty Painted Warriors Advance to Meet Me — Hunting for the Murderers of the Perkins Family — Arrest of Moses and His Imprisonment — The Story of His Experiences Narrated by Himself — " Our Hearts are One " — How Misunderstandings Arise Between Indians and Whites — Release of Moses.

THE first time I met Moses, the war chief of the Spokanes, was the 8th of June, 1877, a date previously mentioned, when he came to meet Colonel Watkins and me at Fort Simcoe. It then took our messengers three days to reach his camp, a distance of one hundred and twenty miles, but not half that time for him to come to us.

Moses had been informed that the government at Washington required him to go upon the Yakima or some other reservation. He came to the council to represent his own band, the Methuse Indians, the Okanagans, and other nomadic tribes located near the upper Columbia waters; probably every one of these bands had belonged in a general way to the Flatheads. Moses was a large, muscular, and handsome Indian, neat in his dress, head carried well up and with a proud pose. His eyes were red, caused by the smoke from Indian camp-

GIRL'S BUCKSKIN BEADED CLOTHES BAG; GARTERS; TOILET AND TOBACCO POUCHES; MOCCASINS, NEEDLE CASE, FIRE BAG, ETC.

*For Description see page 16*

PHOTOGRAPHED AND PAINTED FROM THE ORIGINAL OBJECTS EXPRESSLY FOR THIS WORK.

fires, and by the wind and alkali dust that he had met on the way. His first speech was: "My Indians are scattered over a large country. I cannot say what they will do. I am ready to go on any reservation, except this at Fort Simcoe. Several tribes of the Indians above the Spokane have invited me to become their chief, and if they shall have a reservation I would like to go with them."

When an Indian answered me warily and like a diplomat I always tried to match him, so I answered that a council would be held near Spokane Falls in about twenty-five days, where the tribes and bands to which he referred would be brought together, and should they express to me such a desire I would consider it. Moses assented to this agreement and gave it his approval by making his mark upon a formal paper.

General Frank Wheaton attended the next council, held near Spokane Falls on the 16th of August, 1877, where he expected to meet Moses, but in a letter that I afterward received from him he wrote: "I regret that Chief Moses was not at the council." Colonel Watkins informed me that it was doubtful if Moses received notice to appear. As a matter of fact the message sent to him by Colonel Watkins was duly delivered to Moses, but indirectly and through an Indian woman, whereas he had expected a white messenger. Moses claimed that he did not think he was in reality called to the council, and even declared that he did not receive word in season, and so forth. By such irregular proceedings his dignity was much offended, but he still remained friendly to me.

Near the beginning of the Pi-Ute and Bannock war I received the following message through the commandant at Lapwai: "Moses' people want to fight, but against his wishes. Seven villages who have joined the hostiles threaten to begin a war."

From the knowledge I had already gained of Moses, directly and indirectly, and knowing the great extent of his influence, I deemed it best to use every exertion to persuade him to keep the peace, for I feared an outbreak in the upper Columbia, where he lived, more than in southern Idaho, and I knew that more mischief would be done should it occur. Here is a copy of the letter I sent to this dignified old chief:

"Moses, Dear Sir:

"I have sent you word about the Bannocks. I send again. The Bannocks are giving me trouble, so that I cannot meet you as I promised at Spokane Falls. When I come back from the Bannocks we will arrange a meeting somewhere. I depend on you to keep the peace. I am glad you have good crops where you are."

Previous to this a letter had come from Moses, substantially as follows:

"General Howard:

"I, Moses, chief, want you to know what my *tum-tum* (heart) is in regard to my tribe and the whites. Almost every day reports come to me that the soldiers from Walla Walla are coming to take me away from this part of the country. My people are excited and I want to know from you the truth, so that I can tell them, and keep everything quiet once more among us. Since the last war (the Nez

Percé) we have had up here rumors that I am going to fight if the soldiers come. This makes my heart sick. I have said I will not fight and I say it to you again, and when you hear white men say Moses will fight tell them 'No.' I have always lived here upon the Columbia River. I am getting old and I do not want to see my blood shed on my part of the country. Chief Joseph wanted me and my people to help him. His orders were many. I told him, 'No, never!' I watched my people faithfully during the war and kept them at home. I told them all, when the war broke out, that they must not steal. If they did, I would report them to Father Wilbur (the Indian agent at Simcoe).

"It is time for us to begin spring work. We all raise lots of vegetables, and wheat and corn, and trade with Chinamen to get money. I wish you would write me and tell me the truth, so that I can tell my people that they may be contented once more and go to work in their gardens. I do not want to go on the Yakima reservation. I wish to stay where I have always lived and where my parents died. I wish you would write to me and send your letter by the bearer of this, and be sure I am a friend and that I tell you the truth.

his
"(Signed) Moses X Chief."
mark

The following May a prominent citizen, Mr. John A. Shoudy, who lived about thirty miles from Moses' resort, while in Yakima City sent the following statement to me: "There are about three hundred people whose lives would be in immediate danger should Moses' Indians break out. We think the Indians are now peaceably disposed and would prefer that they should stay where they are, as the land they occupy is of no material value to the whites. We believe that if Moses is let alone he will not disturb the people nor commence hostilities anywhere. I translated General Howard's letter to him, and he was glad enough to get it, and said as long as the one-armed man was his friend he feared no trouble. But if the Indian bureau should insist upon putting Moses upon the Yakima reserve his band and several others will certainly resist and then run for the British line. Somebody keeps telling him that General Howard is going to force him upon some reservation."

Shoudy's friend added: "Shoudy has gone home. He will see Moses immediately and report. As the lives of members of his family are at stake, and as he thinks he can safely keep them within thirty miles of Moses' lodge, it shows that he (Shoudy) believes that the Indians up there are peaceably inclined."

Other letters came from Moses. In one he said: "I want to live the balance of my days in peace with all. I do not think we ought to be like dogs all the time. My *tum-tum* is to quit this way of doing."

Later, somebody sent me a telegram to this effect: "Moses hopes General Howard will visit him and his people soon, as he promised to do." Moses wished to be reassured that the Indians connected with him would not be disturbed in their habitations. At this time I was so absorbed in other matters of vital importance that I sent an aide-de-camp to meet Moses. The aide telegraphed after a personal interview: "Moses met me at Kititas Valley Monday, riding all night. His message to you is satisfactory."

Notwithstanding the Indian bureau's urgent desire to gather all the Indians on reservations, in order to satisfy timid or greedy white men, I deemed it judicious to secure a delay in the case of Moses. Thus matters remained till near the close of the Pi-Ute and Bannock war. A few renegade Indians engaged in that war succeeded in crossing the Columbia from south to north, and murdered a white family by the name of Perkins. The murderers then pushed on and encamped near Moses, doubtless hoping to incite him to rebellion. The renegade murderers failed in this, but continued to skulk around somewhere in the big bend of the Columbia.

At last, with an escort and plenty of troops, I went to Moses' camp, both to fulfill my promise and to form a correct judgment with regard to all the upper Columbia Indians of whom sundry white inhabitants were suspicious. Moses and sixty warriors, freshly and handsomely painted, all armed and well mounted, rode eighty miles to meet me. We had a council of two days' duration. The Indians agreed to deliver up the murderers of the Perkins family, if they came to them, and any stolen horses which they could discover. Then, through Moses, they made a formal request that the big bend of the Columbia should be set apart as their home, and that they might have some territory on the other side of the river. I made a note of their request and promised to forward it to the President and to convey to them his reply. This was the President's answer through his secretary:

"Agent Wilbur believes that he can bring Moses and his people, without trouble, on the Yakima reservation. Let this be done if possible. Second, should Agent Wilbur fail in this, then the Indians' request will be granted."

Upon invitation of Agent Wilbur in the early part of December, 1878, Moses came again to his agency for a conference, and agreed to furnish an Indian contingent to act with the Yakima Indian police in the arrest of that small band which was charged with the murder of the Perkins family, and also with horse stealing. This conference was supplemented by a meeting of citizens at Yakima City, a hamlet near Wilbur's reservation.

Moses was present at that meeting. It resulted in an agreement on the citizens' part to furnish twenty volunteers, armed and equipped, to act jointly with Moses, whom they agreed to meet at or near Priest's Rapids on the Columbia.

Uniting and crossing there the combined party were to proceed to what was called the Crab Creek country for the purpose of arresting the fugitive criminals. Moses, with his followers, was on hand, but the volunteers were diverted by some subsequent report to a place twelve miles below, where they heard that the Perkins' murderers had been seen later. The failure to meet him very naturally excited in Moses' mind a suspicion of bad faith. Informed by an Indian runner that the whites had crossed the Columbia far below him, he hastily called together all Indians of his vicinity and proceeded to that crossing. Uneasy and fearful of treachery, Moses, meeting the whites, confronted them in what they considered a menacing attitude. There was, however, no firing or outbreak. A parley ensued between him and the captain of the volunteers, and, after some wordy altercation, both parties withdrew without positive collision.

On reflection, after returning home, Moses concluded to go in quest of the malefactors independently, so with nine picked men he set out for Crab Creek, and encamped there. On the 20th of December, while asleep in his camp, a bright fire burning, and his horses turned out to graze, Moses and his small escort were suddenly surrounded by the volunteers and the Yakima Indian police. He suffered himself to be captured and disarmed without resistance. Six of his men were subsequently released upon giving a promise to continue the search for the murderers, while Moses, with the remainder, was hurried off to Yakima City and shut up in jail.

Then Mr. Wilbur, the agent, fearing violence from the citizens, assumed the responsibility for Moses. He bailed him out and took him to his agency at Fort Simcoe, and held him in confinement there. The other six Indians succeeded in arresting one of the murderers, another committed suicide, and two more were subsequently taken and placed in jail to await the action of the civil authorities.

The volunteers now returned to their homes.

No indications of an outbreak among the Indians followed these proceedings. Moses was confined in the Yakima City jail for a few days, and while there, under date of December 25, 1878, made the following statement:

"When Agent Wilbur sent Eneas* for me I came at once. I arrived at Simcoe and was informed that he wanted me to go after the Perkins' murderers. The proposition was to send fifteen men of the agency police. I said: 'No; these murderers are strong; fifteen men are not enough.' I promised to send five of my best men, making twenty in all.

"The conference then broke up and I started to go home. On the way one of the horses of my party broke down and I told the man to go to a camp near the river, but to say nothing about our arrangement, so that the friends of the murderers would not hear of it.

"I reached the Columbia River in the night; my people were at the one house. I told them all to stay there and not go away; that tomorrow or the day after the Bostons † would come with the agency Indians, and to watch for them, and when they arrived to take their boats to the place agreed upon for the crossing. I directed my people, when the party reached there, to send a man to my house, eight miles distant, and let me know. I then went home and slept there. A young man came to my house as directed and said the Bostons had come on the west side of the river, but they did not come

* Eneas was Wilbur's Indian scout.

† A term frequently applied to white troops.

to the place he was watching, where the boats were waiting. They had gone below.

"After this I stayed at my house one night and told my young men to go and get their horses and we would go and see the Bostons. Forty or fifty of my people went with me. I did not go with a disposition to fight or with a warlike purpose. My people wanted to see, and, from custom, took their guns. My young men went along laughing and talking. I went on until I could see the agency Indians and the others, a little below the Indian house. Just before arriving I met Eneas and told him to go back to his party and I would come on.

"When I came near the Bostons' camp I saw them getting on their horses excitedly, but I went right on close up to them. Billie Splawn, the captain, came out and shook hands with me and wanted to know what this meant, so many Indians coming there with guns in their hands, and horses. I answered that it was because the young men wanted to see. My people were not far away. Splawn wanted to know if all of us were going with him after the murderers.

"I said: 'No, but I will send some of my *tennas* (picked) men.' My guns were all pointed up to the sky, not one toward the Bostons. As Splawn and I stood together I called to Eneas and asked him if he had a bad heart toward me, and what I had done that he should have bad feeling? I told him then that my heart was all straight and that I did not know why we should be bitter toward each other.

"Not long after this the Bostons and agency

Indians, separating from us, went down the river. With my people I went back and stayed at my home three nights. Mr. Simbley and five other Bostons then came to my house. One of the mules they rode had become tired. I told him to leave the mule, and I replaced it by one of my horses.

"This is the way my heart has been all the time with the whites. Is it for this and for other kindnesses that I now have these shackles on my limbs? Mr. Simbley wanted to know where the party of Bostons were. I said at White Bluffs. He and his men then went down the river, staying where the volunteers crossed two nights, and then made for White Bluffs, but Crab Creek was some twenty-five or thirty miles distant. The next day an old man came to me and told me where the volunteers were. I made my young men hasten, taking nine with me, and went to help arrest the murderers. I made up my mind at once that I would give four more than I had promised. For fear of any misunderstanding I went myself. My intention was to keep on with the nine till I met the volunteers, let the nine work with the others, and return myself to my home.

"The first day we kept on our march until into the night. I said as we halted: 'Here we will stay until the sun rises, so as to see where the Bostons are.' We lay down to sleep around a large fire; there was a hill on one side of us and a road not far away, which led over the hill to White Bluffs. There was a stream of water over there where I thought the whites were encamped. They came to the top of the hill in the night and saw our fire. As they approached I thought it was cattle running, but it proved to be the tramp of horses, and it was the volunteer party coming. They came up with a rush and surrounded my camp. I ordered my people to lie still and not get up. Somebody cried out three times: 'It is Moses! Moses! Moses!'

"I then got up and found them around us and their guns trained on our people. I thought we were all to be killed, so I wrapped my blanket around me and prepared to die. They dismounted and I called out: 'Do not do so. We have come to help you!'

"They then disarmed us, we making no resistance. They took our knives as well as guns. They were very strong—a good many had been drinking whisky, and we came near being killed. I gave up my own knife, pistol, and gun. I told them we were not to quarrel among ourselves, or with Mr. Wilbur's men, but that our only business was to get the murderers. All this occurred about four in the morning. The whole party next went on to Crab Creek, myself and nine men being held as prisoners. We stayed there one night and when the sun arose started back to White Bluffs.

"I then said: 'Give back the guns, the nine men shall go with you to capture the murderers; I will go home.'

"They answered, 'No,' and took away also our provisions and went on to White Bluffs. I advised them not to go back there; that going there would take us in the opposite direction from the criminals. I then proposed that three of my men should go with three of the Indians and two or three of the Bostons in pursuit of the murderers.

"They said: 'No.'

"Again I proposed to the whites to send six. I had good horses and wanted them to go, but said: 'You must return their guns.' They answered no to this, but consented to let them have pistols. With this outfit I let them go.

"I have watched my people, not only those about me, but all around the country, and if they had done badly I would have caught them and put chains on them as you have put them on me. If my people had caused the trouble for which I am held I would not feel so hurt about it, but it is in consequence of the acts of renegade Umatillas that I have these irons on and am made to suffer. The Bostons in the Kititas Valley have a good heart toward me and treat me all right, but here everything is dark. I have a thick bundle of papers from General Howard and other *tyhees*. I shall not throw these away and go to fighting.

"When the sun comes up one day I do not talk one way and the next day another. I only have one straight way. When the Bostons, one, two, or three, no matter how many, pass through my country my people do not disturb them. My mind is not to die by violence in war, but to die when I get sick or old like other people. I do not know who brought these irons upon me, whether Eneas or some other, but it is the lying that has done it. These chains are working a lie against me.

"When General Howard and I had the talk at Priest's Rapids last summer about a reservation I did not expect an answer right off. After the talk my mind was at rest until he should give me an answer. I believed all the time that he and I were friends.

"While he was fighting last year and the year before I was holding my people back so that they would do nothing bad. General Howard did exactly right, and I am trying to do the same. We have been a good way apart,—General Howard and I,—but our minds have been together—our hearts are one.

"While the Bostons and friendly Siwashes (police) have lied about me and brought the chains on me, if I am liberated I do not mean to have a bad heart toward them. My mind is to go along the road with good men — those that tell the truth and do not lie. In staying here I am getting very tired and I would like to hear from General Howard very soon, so that I can go to my own house."

When pushed by questions as to bringing his people upon the Yakima reservation Moses' manliness was apparent. He said: "I prefer not to answer that until after the question of reservation is finally settled, and until after I have seen my head men and understand their minds."

A physician by the name of Kuykendell has given the citizen's view of Moses. He says that the Indian Eneas, Wilbur's scout, represented to Captain William Splawn, the commander of the volunteers, that on the scout's visit to him Moses was grum and sullen and had but little to say; that he refused to furnish the men as he had promised and was not disposed to do anything. Eneas feared he meant fight. When Moses met the captain he had nearly a hundred men, all painted, feathered, and yelling like excited savages. Again, when Captain Splawn spoke to Moses he at first made no reply. He asked him if it was necessary to have all of those Indians to find the thieves and murderers. Moses said: "No." The doctor thinks that Moses at last sent the six men as helpers merely with the hope of getting himself released.

In all this we can see how easy it was for two men not speaking the same language, and for white men, full of suspicion and fear of an Indian outbreak, to misunderstand each other.

Fortunately Mr. Wilbur appealed to me and I released Moses from confinement and took the whole responsibility of his subsequent conduct upon my own shoulders, and he never disappointed me.

During the fall of 1878 and the early part of the winter following the Indians, who had scattered over a large territory in the upper Columbia, had not yet been gathered upon a reservation. Some of them, however, hád wandered away from different agencies and continued nomadic, being constantly involved in troubles with the whites, especially in the thickly settled parts of the Yakima country. We succeeded in bringing a few of them upon the Yakima reservation. The release of Moses from prison did not allay the excitement. There were terrible threats on the part of both whites and Indians, and at last Agent Wilbur, fearing an outbreak, made a formal requisition for the presence of troops. I answered him favorably and placed a good camp in Kititas Valley near the headwaters of the Yakima River.

In consequence of these difficulties and others of a worse sort among the Umatillas, where some Indian murderers had been tried and executed, and where the Indians were divided between the friendly and helpful and the secretly hostile, it was thought best to humor the Indians by sending certain chiefs of the Umatillas to Washington, where their pleadings could be heard. Agent Cornoyer was to be their mouthpiece. I sent also Chief Moses and a member of his tribe. In order to give confidence to Moses and some other non-treaty Indians that they would have a safe journey and return, I sent with them an officer in whom they had confidence, Major Boyle of the Twenty-first Infantry. This measure of sending the chiefs had a good effect upon all the Indians left behind.

Quite a tract of country had been set apart between the Columbia and the Okanagan Rivers named the Colville reservation. Upon it was a large Roman Catholic agency for the Colville Indians proper, but few of the Indians themselves had ever gone upon the reservation to dwell; a few small bands, however, nominally under this agency, were on and near the big reserve. Moses begged of me to let him take his people into the same territory, that is, into unoccupied parts, and if we would extend the lines to the Methow River he could surely get all the Indians who had made common cause with him under reservation cover.

A very good agreement was made with Chief Moses while in Washington, but when he returned there seemed to be some doubt about the limits of the lands intended in the promise; however, Major

Boyle promptly made a careful affidavit to the agreement actually made. To settle all difficulties and to relieve apprehensions, Governor Ferry of Washington Territory and myself, with considerable force, made an expedition to the Colville country. Chief Moses and other chiefs, representing a large number of Indian tribes, met us at a frontier store, the only inhabited place near the Wenatchie. Here we held very satisfactory councils with the Indians. So peaceful and complete were our arrangements and settlements that I took my large force no further. The peace then entered into settled matters finally between the whites and Indians, so that there has been no disturbance of any consequence from that day to this.

The Washington authorities overruled General McDowell and myself in not sending the remnants of the non-treaty Nez Percés back to Oregon. Instead they dispatched them to the Indian Territory proper, south of Kansas, where they remained fretful and discontented until their entreaties for a return to the Northwest, through humanitarian influence, at last secured permission to that effect. Joseph and all that belonged to him were then transported to that part of Washington Territory where Moses was, and placed as neighbors to him upon the great Colville reservation.

# CHAPTER XXVII.

## ADVENTURES AMONG THE BANNOCKS — A MIDNIGHT WAR DANCE AND ITS SEQUENCE.

The Bannocks — Their Good Mounts and Equipment — A Shocking Incident — My Bannock Scouts — Mysterious Disappearance of Twenty Horses — How I Made the Indians Recover Them — A Distrusted Chief — An Exciting Midnight Scene — War-Dance of the Bannocks — An Uneasy Night in Camp — Demanding Permission to Kill Three of My Scouts — Getting the Best of the Bannocks — Execution of an Indian — Surrounding the Indians — Fair Promises but Hollow Hearts — Plans for Revenge — An Old Indian Legend — Looking Forward to a Resurrection.

DURING my Nez Percé campaign the Bannocks were mostly confined upon the great reserve in eastern Idaho, usually called the Fort Hall reservation. At that time it is said that there were not to exceed five hundred of these people who came under the charge of a government agency. In 1877 about a score of them accompanied the troops for the entire campaign from Idaho to the Missouri River. The men were fairly good-looking, had good blankets, and their mounts were in prime condition and well equipped with good saddles and bridles.

It was difficult at times to restrain them from what white men call criminal acts and insubordinate conduct. Once the Bannock scouts came suddenly upon one of Joseph's abandoned camps. Finding in it an old woman too ill to keep up with the hostiles they instantly killed her and took her scalp as a token of victory. Again, on Gibbon's battle-field, the dead, including women and children, had been buried close to the water under the bank of a stream. The Bannocks found and disinterred their bodies, robbed them of clothing and ornaments, then pierced and mutilated the naked bodies in a shocking manner, carrying off their scalps. Our men came upon this field too late to prevent the mischief, but they carefully buried the dead again, more deeply than before. The Bannocks acted here just as all wild Indians had been taught to do for a century. For a while Buffalo Horn, their war chief, behaved well and sided with me in my attempts at discipline.

At the foot of the mountain near Mary Lake forty horses belonging to citizens' teams, which were doing the transportation work for us, were turned out to graze. During the night these horses disappeared. The rough and indiscreet language of the Bannock scouts aroused my suspicion that a party of them had taken the horses. I arrested ten and held them as prisoners. Their leader, Rainé, a half-breed, was surly and disrespectful. I had them all disarmed, their horses and rifles taken from them, and sent them as prisoners to the guard tent. The brave scout Fisher, who had come to help us in controlling the Bannocks, was on the front scouting line, almost deserted, for the Bannock scouts had found something to do besides hunt other Indian trails. Soon an old Bannock chief came and begged of me to release the prisoners, earnestly assuring me of their innocence.

I answered: "What you say may be true, but Indians are good to hunt horses. They follow

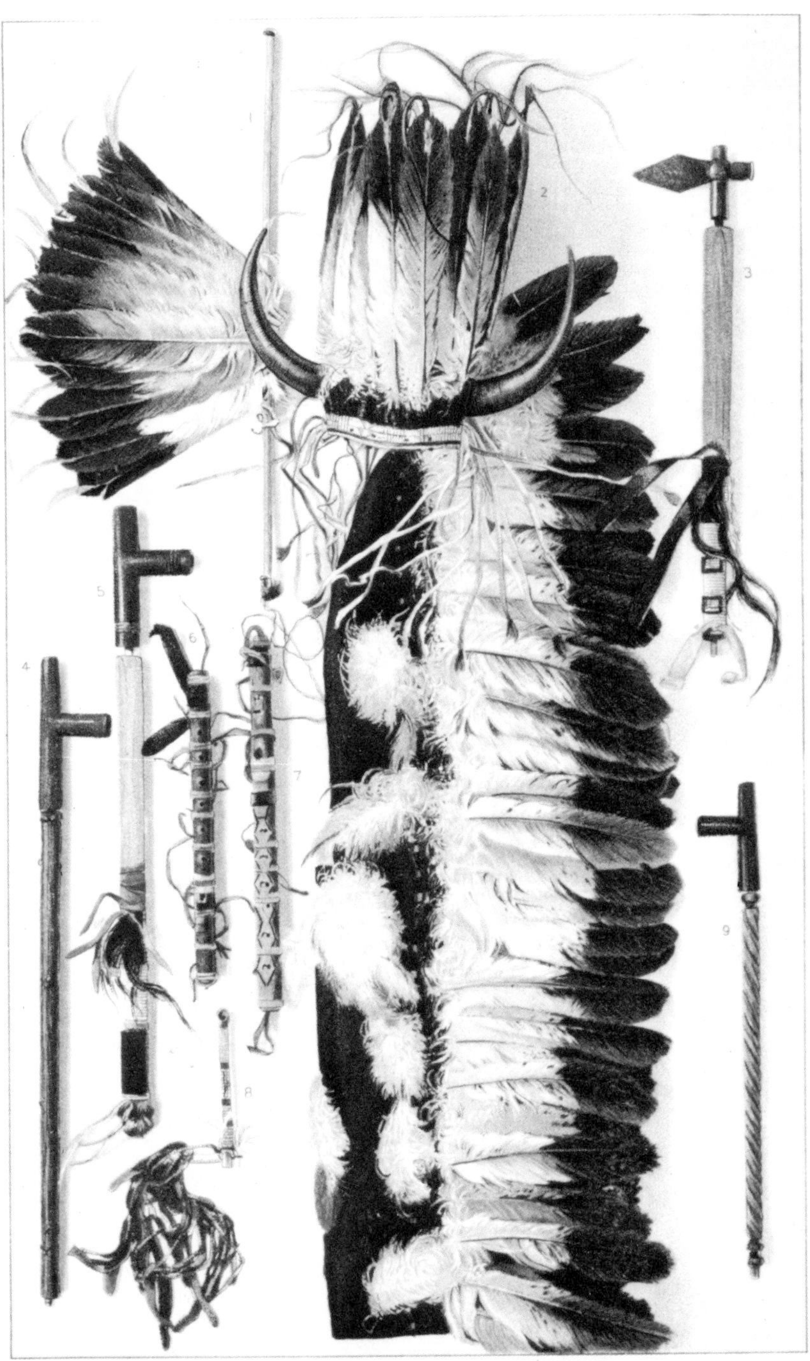




WAR BONNET OF RED FLANNEL ORNAMENTED WITH SCALP LOCKS, EAGLE FEATHERS AND BUFFALO HORNS; PIPES, FLUTES, ETC.

*For Description see page 17*

PHOTOGRAPHED AND PAINTED FROM THE ORIGINAL OBJECTS EXPRESSLY FOR THIS WORK.

blind trails better than white men. Send some of your young men and bring back the lost horses. When they do that, let me know."

"Yes, Indians good to hunt horses," said the old man, "I will send them."

In a few hours twenty of the horses came galloping into camp, chased by the young Indians. Again the old man came to me and declared that twenty were all they could possibly find.

I said: "All right, I shall not let the prisoners go until I see the other twenty horses."

The old chief gave a grunt of dissatisfaction and a shrug of his shoulders when he left me. This time he went himself with the searching party. That night the remaining twenty horses overtook us, and all the prisoners were released except Rainé, whom I could not trust. He, at least, understood that horse stealing was a crime to be punished.

One night we had an exciting scene in which Rainé figured. It occurred in a beautiful glade near the head waters of the Snake River. The Bannocks had their tepees on a slight knoll not far from my bivouac and near the water. Buffalo Horn asked permission to have a war dance, and I consented. The unearthly din of their wild wailing and singing, the weird shapes of the dancing Indians silhouetted against the blazing camp fires, and the sense of actual danger seemed to impress my whole command with a feeling akin to awe. Elsewhere there was an unusual stir of preparation to start our march by two o'clock in the morning. The neighing of the horses and the braying of the mules sounded ten times louder than usual. It was a night to be remembered. At midnight, after the war dance and a brief council, Buffalo Horn and Rainé came to my headquarters and demanded authority to kill my three Nez Percé scouts, "Captain John," "Old George," and one other comrade of the tribe. Rainé insisted that they were traitors, that they had rejoiced at Joseph's success in the late Camas Meadow fight, and at his surprising and stampeding our mules. He asserted that Old George, in particular, ought to die.

I made George face his accusers. He was so frank and evidently honest that I did not for a moment distrust him, and Buffalo Horn was denied the small favor he had asked. He was very angry at the time and never quite forgave me for the refusal. The third Indian may have been the one that cut the strap of the bell mare and produced confusion in the herd of mules. At any rate he was so terrified at the talk of the Bannocks that he escaped that night into the forest and I never saw him again.

All of the Bannock scouts left me after the last battle near the Rockies and returned to their agency. Buffalo Horn, puffed up with pride and self-confidence, hoped in the future to do better than Joseph and his warriors. So he fomented the causes of dissatisfaction in and around Fort Hall, and stimulated the Indians to seek revenge for real and fancied wrongs.

After the Bannocks had been given a reservation, as far back as 1869, it was determined by the

Indian department to put all roaming Indians in that neighborhood upon the same reservation. As long as the Bannocks were the most numerous there was very little trouble. They had thousands of ponies and were nomadic themselves, and were really under but little restraint. They simply came to the reservation for their annuity goods and departed at will. But little by little the roaming Indians, mostly Shoshones, came upon the same reservation to stay; goods, subsistence, and clothing intended for the Bannocks were issued to the Shoshones, as they were always near at hand and docile, and before long they outnumbered the Bannocks two to one. This was the main cause of the restlessness and bitter complaints of the Bannocks. They not only hated, but robbed the more industrious and more favored Shoshones.

There was an immense stretch of camas meadows between the great Fort Hall reservation and Boise, Idaho. The Bannocks insisted on this as their own special province, and regarded the white settlers generally as their enemies. In August, 1877, the positive work of revenge began. A Bannock near Fort Hall killed two white teamsters. Next the authorities, with a view to punishing the guilty, began to look into the matter. The Indian agent sent his interpreter to the Bannocks with an order for them to come in to his office and bring with them Petope, who was believed to have slain the teamsters. The Indians appeared to obey. They brought the suspected man and delivered him to the marshal, who conveyed him to prison at Malad City to await trial. But the Indians were feigning. They despised the white man's justice. They believed they were merely squaring old scores when they, through Petope, had killed the two teamsters.

Within an hour after the marshal had gone the suppressed wrath of the Indians began to show itself. Alexander Rhodan, a young government employee, was killed by Nam-pe-yo-go, and other mischief was done. Captain Bainbridge, the commander of Fort Hall, was quickly on hand with a detachment of troops. He demanded the murderer of Rhodan at the hands of the Shoshones and the Bannocks. The former replied that if a Shoshone had committed the crime they would have arrested the criminal at once, but that this arrest now belonged to the Bannocks.

The Bannocks feigned acquiescence and started off as if to make the arrest of the guilty Indian, but when night came the pursuers returned without Nam-pe-yo-go. They said he had escaped to join his father and brothers far beyond the Snake River.

It was plain enough that the Bannocks were hostile. They had armed themselves well and supplied their band with tough ponies, possessing great endurance, and well trained for actual use. But Nam-pe-yo-go did not escape. White men in the vicinity found him, and he was tried, condemned, and executed with extraordinary dispatch.

General John E. Smith, who commanded one of my divisions in the Army of the Tennessee, was a thorough soldier, stationed at Fort Douglas. He had charge of that district. At dawn on the 16th of January, 1878, his troops surrounded two Bannock villages which were evidently preparing for conflict. Though the Indians were armed, both villages were surprised and captured, and upwards of fifty warriors and three hundred ponies were escorted to the agency. The father and two brothers of Nam-pe-yo-go were sent to the garrison for detention. The remainder, after General Smith had given them good counsel, were allowed their liberty, but their ponies and their rifles were kept for them. Again the Bannocks feigned acquiescence, but at heart were angry enough and vexed at the loss of their mounts and weapons. They had all-night talks among themselves and were constantly hatching plans for revenge.

As soon as spring had produced abundant grass for animals the Bannocks one dark night fled from the reservation. Many of them had put in their crops, but even these were abandoned to their Shoshone rivals.

These wild Bannock warriors shrewdly and secretly negotiated with other and even distant tribes of Indians. They took advantage of a discontent which they found quite extensive in the Department of the Columbia, and sent delegates to the malcontents. The Pi-Utes gave them the most abundant sympathy and aid, and were their first allies.

There is a strange story, a very old Indian legend, told by Sarah Winnemucca, daughter of the Pi-Ute chief Winnemucca, to the effect that there was a set of cannibals who occupied the

Humboldt River country at the time the Pi-Utes were living by Mud Lake in Nevada. The cannibals laid ambuscades for the Pi-Utes and other more civilized Indians, and killed and ate them. Of course this provoked wars, in which the cannibals were as fierce and reckless as were the followers of the Mahdi. Sarah's ancestors at last made effective war upon them, killed large numbers, and drove the remnant into the thick forest north of Humboldt Lake. They then set fire to the forest, but the cannibals rushed from the flames to their bulrush boats and succeeded in making a landing on the eastern border of the lake, and sought refuge in a large cave not far off. The Pi-Utes followed them and set a watch at the mouth of the cave.

As it took too long to starve them out the Pi-Utes began to pile up wood at the entrance to the cave, while the cannibals withdrew farther and farther within it. Then suddenly the Pi-Utes set fire to the wood and made an oven of the cave, and the last remnant of this ferocious tribe was destroyed. Such is the legend.

There was something remarkable about the Pi-Utes. When the white men began to cross their country they enjoyed being at peace with them, but little by little their extensive possessions were diminished as the white settlements increased. The lakes from which they took fish in abundance were claimed by frontier occupants of the good land, and their hunting grounds were circumscribed and at last taken from them. One writer says of them: "They are quite harmless and subsist upon fish, game, roots, and the like. They show some disposition to be industrious." The same article calls them "a tribe of degraded Indians of the Shoshone stock." Neither description is fair.

I may say of them that, as a rule, they have shown a love of peace and exhibited good qualities. Both men and women have been willing to work and often made great progress in imitating their civilized neighbors. Under advisement they opened an *acequia* (irrigating ditch) near the railroad on the Pyramid Lake reservation and by hard labor extended it a mile. They had a flume and power to propel a saw and gristmill, which had been promised them by the agents of the government, but the saw and gristmill never came, and the lumber for houses was never sent. The *acequia* became lost to them and is now used by Anglo-Saxons for purposes of irrigation.

Again, in 1865 a cry arose among the white settlers around Harney Lake that the Indians had stolen some of their cattle. That might have been true, but the Pi-Utes were not the Indians engaged in the theft. Chief Winnemucca's tribe was at that time far away in Nevada. Many were at Mud Lake fishing. A detachment of soldiers were sent over there from Camp Harney to answer the settlers' cry. They came suddenly upon these peaceful Indians in Nevada, fired straight into their camp and killed old men, women, and children. Chief Winnemucca and his young men were, fortunately for the future of the tribe, away on a hunting expedition.

After this terrible catastrophe, whoever was to be blamed, it is not at all strange that the Pi-Utes became apprehensive and suspicious. They were indeed ignorant and full of superstition, so that when some *tooat* arose and made predictions many were ready to listen. A favorite idea, similar to the "Messiah craze," carried by these Dreamers from tribe to tribe all through the Northwest country, was that there would soon be a resurrection of Indians. All the whites were to be killed, and the Indians' wrongs would then be righted.

# CHAPTER XXVIII.

## PREPARATIONS FOR ANOTHER CAMPAIGN — OPENING OF THE PI-UTE AND BANNOCK WAR.

The Noted Pi-Ute Chief Egan — An Indian Princess and Her Interesting History — An Anxious Night in Camp — Some Wakeful Hours — Fresh Troubles with the Bannocks — The Discontented Pi-Utes — The Promised Resurrection of Indians — Anticipating an Outbreak — The Lava Beds of the Modocs — A Desolate and Sterile Region — An Ideal Place for Ambush — Preparations for Another Campaign — Constant Murders and Outrages — Weakening an Indian's Courage — Terrified and Fleeing Settlers — The Wary Chief Buffalo Horn — "Pi-Ute Joe" — An Indian Woman's Loyal Service.

AFTER the close of several conflicts inaugurated by a massacre in one of Chief Winnemucca's tribes in Nevada, another band of Pi-Utes, led by an able chief, Egan, was brought upon a fairly good reserve of public land not far from Harney Lake. It was named "The Malheur Reservation." It was here, in the summer of 1876, while on a tour of inspection, that I first met the Pi-Utes. At that time they had a favorite agent, Mr. Sam Parish; and Sarah Winnemucca, sometimes called the Indian Princess, daughter of the Pi-Ute chief Winnemucca, was their interpreter. I had long before heard something of her history. She spoke English perfectly, was very neat and tidy in her dress, and at that time maintained an air of great self-respect.

During the night, as I had no guard or escort, and in fact nobody with me except my aide-de-camp, Captain Sladen, and my daughter Grace, who had then recently returned to our home at Portland, Oregon, from Vassar College, and was accompanying me on this tour, I felt no little anxiety about the situation. This anxiety was increased when the Indians assembled and held a council, accompanied with singing, beating of tom-toms, and dancing through the whole night, so that I spent many wakeful hours. However, they appeared to be contented with their agent at that time, and the *tooat* was not predicting an immediate resurrection.

Soon after this a new agent, a Mr. Rhinehart, was sent to the "Malheur" by the Indian bureau. The Indians were intensely opposed to the change, for they loved Mr. and Mrs. Parish and had begged for their retention. Rhinehart was a political appointee. In giving the causes of the trouble that followed, he said that the Bannocks had been there as delegates some time before; that they were particularly angry because some of their horses had been taken from them, and because of a story spread among them that all Indian horses and ponies were to be seized and given to the soldiers. Sarah Winnemucca gave an account of this affair. She said: "Some Indians of Bannock Jack's band had got drunk and shot two white men. One of these Indians had a sister who, with other women, was digging some roots, and these white men had caught this poor girl and abused her. The other women had run away and left her to the mercy of these brutes, and it was on her account that her brother and others had shot them." That was the Indians' version.

It was while these Pi-Utes were in a state of unrest and extreme discontent that the Bannock messengers had come among them. The outbreak seemed so extensive that the old *tooats* suddenly had a new inspiration to the effect that the time was at hand for the great, long-promised resurrection of Indians. This news was carried from tribe to tribe. With some reluctance the great majority of the Pi-Utes decided to join the Bannocks and other discontented spirits and make common cause with them, because surely, if combined, they could defeat all the white troops and destroy all the troublesome white people in that part of the Northwest.

I will now develop the campaign of 1878 which followed; it was my last active one in the field: I very early learned, by corresponding with various Indian agencies, that Indians who were friendly were coöperating and giving unmistakable signs of danger at hand. These statements were made by white men who were living in the vicinity of the plotting warriors, and were often exaggerated. I was anticipating an outbreak, expecting it from the Columbia renegades who had escaped from their reservation and were causing a constant ferment among the scattered white settlements. The declared policy of the Indian department, which was to put every one of them on some reservation, was everywhere resisted. The Indians were evidently waiting for me to send troops against them, which would give them a pretext for carrying out their war policy. Then they would strike, beginning, as usual, to kill white settlers.

The stockmen who pastured their horses and cattle upon the public domain made at this time unending complaints against the Indians; their stallions were found among the Indian herds, some of their cattle and horses were lost, and so on. In the fullness of time a terrible war began, but not on the Columbia, where I had predicted it would occur.

On June 2d, my commander at Boise said: "Bannock Indians have been making serious threats and ordering settlers off Big Camas Prairie. A man from there this evening reports two settlers shot by Indians this morning, both wounded, ninety miles to where Indians are camped between Big Camas and Snake River in the Lava Beds. Number of hostiles two hundred, well armed and supplied with ammunition; settlers counted sixty lodges, and twenty more with Buffalo Horn who has just joined them."

At this time there was a daily stage line running from Fort Hall to Boise. It will be remembered that previous to this time the Modocs had chosen the Lava Beds for the scene of General Canby's massacre, and Joseph, in 1877, had found the place favorable to his boldest plan. So, doubtless, Buffalo Horn, following suit, had placed his lodges among the Lava Beds to favor his campaign already begun. It was a desolate and sterile region, the "beds" being simply knolls of igneous rocks, upon which débris and drift had gradually formed a soddy loam, and the surface was grown over with briers and bushes. The knolls were scattered here and there without regularity, alternating with spaces of prairie grass land. There is such sameness of surface that it is difficult to find one's way, and people are lost easier than in the forests. Still, the region is well adapted for Indian tactics in war time, because all trails disappear, and the knolls are favorable to ambush, where Indians may lie perfectly concealed until their enemy is within good range of their rifles.

On the last day of May, 1878, I sat in my house at Portland, Oregon, amid my family, when telegrams came pouring in saying in substance: "An Indian war is upon us; come, we entreat you; come to our help!" I said to my wife: "Is it possible that we must go through another such ordeal as that of last year?" I referred to the Nez Percé war.

A soldier's self-conflict is not much prolonged. A moment later the proper spirit of decision came, and within an hour the troops of my department at the various posts, hundreds of miles apart, were holding themselves in readiness to go by water, by rail, or by marching, toward the scene of strife.

The governor of Idaho sent this dispatch the 2d of June: "The right to Big Camas Prairie evidently the cause. Sheriff Hays informs me that one hundred and fifty Indians are in Jordan Valley; King Hill Station, overland (stage) road, raided; horses carried off."

Captain Reuben F. Bernard, a soldier of experience and ability, with his troop of fifty cavalrymen, was the first to reach the prairie. He found two herders wounded. They were shot while in their tent by two Indians without apparent cause or provocation. The Indians then robbed the place of everything valuable and drove off thirty horses. There were signs that many warriors had combined for murder and plunder.

When Bernard had gone a little farther he discovered that the Indians had abandoned their camps and fled, evidently not being quite ready to meet his troop. A surprise is apt to weaken an Indian's courage even more than that of a white man. Captain Bernard now pressed on to the eastern portion of Big Camas Prairie and came into the lava country, where he deemed it too dangerous to operate with a single cavalry troop. He turned to the stage road. At King Hill Station ten more horses had been stolen by the Indians. After this theft, the Bannocks for some reason abandoned the Lava Beds and crossed over the Snake River southward at Glen's Ferry, where they robbed a store and house, turned the ferryboats loose, took everything they could carry off from some freight wagons, and stole all the horses in the region far and near, in stable or pasture, which they could find. Farmers, terrified by the first rumors, had quickly abandoned their homes, and fled to the larger settlements, where they set up defensive barricades. Our soldiers found the body of a stranger who had been killed and thrown into the river; several well-known persons, then away from home, never returned.

A few Pi-Ute and Columbia River Indians were present with the Bannocks before the first blow was struck; the Lemhi agency supplied some, and a few came from elsewhere. An offensive league had been formed among these Indians, and the agreement was to move in such a way as to get the most plunder possible, gradually passing from tribe to tribe in a large circuit, and by working westward they hoped to increase their forces, like a snowball that increases in size as it rolls. They especially needed to increase their supply of horses. By carrying out this plan the Indian force would soon be so large that it could cope with all my troops. Such was the Indian hope and expectation.

Bernard wrote me: "This is the strongest outbreak I have ever known. They give no reasons of any kind for their actions, except the Bannocks, who make objections to white men coming on Big Camas Prairie with stock."

All our Indian friends in the East wanted us to have "talks" and try to settle difficulties without war. But I knew from experience that whenever our officers had in the past attempted to parley after hostilities had once begun,—and they had often tried it,—the attempt had never been successful. Indians laughed at such efforts and attributed them to weakness. I believed it was too late to attempt a council. There were many valleys leading to that of the crooked Snake River, and the Indians sped on from one of these valleys to another, killing and destroying as they went.

Captain Patrick Collins of the Twenty-first Infantry, mounting his small company at Boise, succeeded in joining Bernard near a big bend of the Snake River. On the way he found Bruneau Valley fortified. One man had been killed; cattle, horses, and mules had been stolen and driven off.

On the 5th of June, Collins joined Bernard, turned over his force to him, and returned to Fort Boise. Bernard, thus strengthened, crossed the broad and swift current of the Snake River, took the trail of the raiders, and by marching most of the night reached a spot in the morning where the white settlers had assembled and protected themselves by a unique fort,—a sort of stockade. He escorted these settlers to a larger and safer settlement.

In addition to Collins' company Bernard had gathered some citizen scouts, mounted upon fresh horses, and placed them under an experienced frontiersman by the name of Robbins. Bernard instructed them to push ahead in pursuit, ascertain where the Indians were, and let him know. By the 8th of June the scouts had succeeded in locating the hostiles' bivouac not far from Battle Creek.

As Bernard thus watched the Indians and protected the citizens, Buffalo Horn became very wary and endeavored to avoid battle with him. But that very day, in the afternoon, a small company of volunteers hurried up from another direction, coming from Silver City toward Battle Creek. They succeeded in heading off Buffalo Horn, who had with him at the time about sixty Bannocks. The women and children had taken another route. The place was seven miles from a small village called South Mountain. The Indians at once attacked the volunteers with fury, killed four white men and two friendly Pi-Utes, and wounded another.

Pi-Ute Joe, a scout who went out with the volunteers, gave an account of this engagement which was slightly different from theirs. He said that the

DISMOUNTED UNITED STATES CAVALRY REPULSING MOUNTED WARRIORS.

UNITED STATES TROOPS AND SCOUTS SURPRISING A BODY OF INDIANS.

two Pi-Utes who were killed were guides conducting the volunteers to South Mountain, where they proposed to annihilate the Bannocks, and that the volunteers ran off at the first fire, leaving behind the poor old schoolmaster of Silver City, who had joined them. He had been badly wounded by the savages, and being angered by their desertion he cursed his retreating friends while he was bleeding to death. Pi-Ute Joe further stated that he himself had killed Buffalo Horn; that the fall of their leader had checked the Indians so that he, having a swift horse, succeeded in escaping.

I was not able thoroughly to verify the story about the volunteers, but Buffalo Horn did fall in that skirmish at South Mountain, and after his death the hostiles pushed on as fast as they could with a view of joining the Malheur Pi-Utes at the Juniper or Stein's Mountains.

Sarah Winnemucca left the agency when her friend Sam Parish ceased to be agent. At the time of the Bannock outbreak a man by the name of Morton had hired Sarah to drive him and his daughter in her wagon from the John Day Valley in Oregon to Silver City, Idaho. She was making that journey when, on the 11th of June, she met some volunteers and Pi-Ute Joe at Fort Lyon, an old abandoned army post, then a station on the stage line. The next day, with Pi-Ute Joe, she went on to another station called Sheep Ranch. I arrived at Boise that day and received Bernard's report. The Indians had gone toward the Juniper Mountains. They had captured the stage bringing military supplies from the railroad, seized two boxes of Winchester rifles and much ammunition, and had besides their mounts four hundred horses in a herd. This band numbered sixty warriors. He added to his report: "Sarah Winnemucca is in my camp; she wants to go to her people with any message you or General McDowell might desire to send; thinks if she can get to the Pi-Utes with such message she could get all the well-disposed to come near the troops, where they could be safe and fed; says there is nothing at the Malheur agency with which to feed them."

I answered: "Send Sarah with two or three friendly Indians straight to her people, and have them send a few of their principal men to you. I will see that all who behave well and come in are properly fed. Promise Sarah a reward if she succeeds."

Sarah, on horseback, with two friendly Pi-Utes, immediately set out from Sheep Ranch in the direction of Stein's Mountains, a distance of over one hundred miles through the roughest part of Idaho.

# CHAPTER XXIX.

## IN ACTIVE FIELD SERVICE AGAIN — SARAH WINNEMUCCA'S REMARKABLE RIDE — NEARING THE INDIAN STRONGHOLD.

Planning the Campaign — Active Field Service — Sarah Winnemucca's Ride — The Story She Brought — Fresh From the Hostile Camp — Incidents of Sarah's Remarkable Journey — Scenes Along a Bloody Trail — "Who Are You?" — Climbing Steep and Rocky Mountains on Hands and Knees — "Oh, Sarah, You Have Come to Save Us!" — An Old Indian Chief's Advice — Escaping from the Hostile Camp — Followed by the Bannocks — Some Brave Women and their Escort — A Strong Force of Indian Warriors.

IN suppressing Indian outbreaks a commander is apt to be impatient; he chafes at exaggerated and sometimes conflicting reports as they pour in from every quarter. But the experience of the Custer massacre and of the Nez Percé war had taught me never to send out, if I could possibly avoid it, an inadequate force against Indians after they had had time to get ready.

As the troops were hastening forward, a frontier garrison at Camp Harney dispatched McGregor's troop of cavalry and Downey's company of infantry. With many misgivings they left but a small guard at Harney to protect their women and children. At the same time, and from all directions, other detachments were hurrying to the scenes of disturbance by water and by overland roads from California.

Now, to follow my own course, the reader will find me on the 9th of June consulting with Colonel

Frank Wheaton and Colonel Cuvier Grover at Walla Walla. Wheaton had come from Lapwai to meet me, and Grover had been in command at Walla Walla. I ordered the latter at once to Boise to take charge of everything in that vicinity and keep me informed of important matters by telegraph. Wheaton was to take up his station at Walla Walla and guard the home district with small reserves, while the rest of us were endeavoring by active field service to arrest the depredators in Idaho and southern Oregon. I promised to speedily beat them in battle or take them as captives.

Pushing on with my staff officers, Major E. C. Mason and Lieutenants Wilkinson and Wood, I arrived in Boise on the morning of June 12th, just in time, fortunately, to render Sarah Winnemucca's expedition effective.

A brief dispatch to General McDowell at San Francisco from myself will indicate the plan I had in mind: "Arrived here this morning; sent force under Grover, including Major Sanford with cavalry (coming from Kelton), to clear up scattering Indians, eastward toward Fort Hall. Please ask commanding officer Fort Hall to work toward Grover, to detain the Bannock families reported going to Hall, particularly relatives of those on war-path. I am concentrating other troops against Bannocks and Malheurs at Sheep Ranch, six miles from O-wy-hee Ferry on Winnemucca stage road, taking charge of this column myself."

At that time companies coming from Walla Walla and farther west,—cavalry, artillery, and infantry,—were marching through stifling clouds of dust along the Baker wagon road, aiming for Sheep Ranch. I supposed that the force sent from Camp Harney was then somewhere near us.

As soon as my work at Boise was in operation I hurried down the stage road and reached Sheep Ranch on the 14th of June. The next day, while waiting for the scattered companies to come together, I was sitting with Captain Bernard at about 5.30 in the afternoon, in a little room at the stage station, when a mounted party was reported in sight. It proved to be Sarah Winnemucca and her companions. She was well in advance of the party and riding very rapidly. Hastily dismounting she burst into tears and was so fatigued and excited that for some time she could hardly speak. As soon as she was sufficiently recovered to talk intelligently, Bernard, Wood, and Pitcher being present with me, I received her account of her remarkable journey; she had ridden over two hundred miles and met with some thrilling experiences. My comrades thought her statements at the time were exaggerated, but I had sufficient confidence in her story to change my whole plan of movement —a change which afterwards proved to be for the best.

Sarah had ridden to the hostile camp and brought out her father and brother. Others followed them, but were pursued, overtaken, and forced to go back. She heard firing, and feared that her brother Lee was killed. Natchez, another brother, aided the white men to escape from the camp and went with them. Oytes, the Pi-Ute

Dreamer, and Egan, the chief, with their bands, were still detained, although arms and plunder were offered and threats and coercion made to induce them to join the hostiles. She located the camp near Juniper Lake, just north of Stein's Mountains, giving the number of Indians at about seven hundred. She brought her sister-in-law Mattie with her, and implored help for her father, whom she had left behind with a few men and guns guarding fugitive women and children.

Sarah said: "We (Sarah, and the Indians—i. e., George and John, Pi-Utes), followed the trail down the O-wy-hee as much as fifteen miles, and then we came to where they (the hostile Bannocks) had camped, and where they had been weeping and cutting their hair, so we knew that Buffalo Horn, their chief, had been killed." She saw articles of clothing and numerous beads broken from their strings and strewn around. They found on the trail the whip of the stage driver, who was killed, and other articles from time to time which made the trail over the rocky beds easier to follow. She and her friends paused for the briefest rest at Mr. G. B. Crawley's farm. Everything combustible had been burned; the fire was still smoldering and fresh human tracks were everywhere.

Having rested, they followed the freshest of several branching trails, which led them straight toward Stein's Mountains. That day they picked up a clock and a fiddle on the road. Pi-Ute Joe shot a mountain sheep, some strips of which were added to their supplies; now they were near Juniper Lake; then five miles farther on they caught a glimpse of two people on the slope of the mountain dressed like Indians. Sarah's account of this meeting is pathetic: "As we came nearer to them I said to Pi-Ute George, 'Call to them!' He did so. I saw them rise to their feet; I waved my handkerchief at them, as I had done before, and one of them cried, 'Who are you?'

"I said, 'Your sister, Sarah.' It was my brother, Lee Winnemucca, who had spoken. Coming nearer Lee said, 'Oh, dear sister, you have come to save us, for our people are all prisoners of the Bannocks!'"

Her brother told her that her father had been badly treated; that his friends had been stripped of their guns, horses, and blankets, and that there was great danger ahead for Sarah and her companions, "because," said Lee, "they will surely kill you as they have threatened to kill every one who comes with messages from the white people; for they say Indians who bring messages are enemies. Every night they repeat these threats."

Sarah was not intimidated. Up to this time she and her companions had been dressed like white people, but they now changed to Indians dress, effecting the transformation by using blankets and putting on war paint, as they knew well how to do; then, still keeping together, they went on and joined the grand encampment beyond Stein's Mountains. "The mountain we had to go over was rocky and steep," said Sarah. "Sometimes it was very hard to climb on our hands and knees, but at last we were up there and looked down into a great hostile assembly. It was a sight to see. It was beautiful; over three hundred lodges and four hundred and fifty warriors."

A little later Sarah succeeded in working her way into the hostile Bannock camp, and then into her father's lodge, where she found several Pi-Ute men and women. "Every one in that lodge whispered, 'Oh, Sarah, you have come to save us!'"

By concerted action some seventy-five stealthily crept out of camp in the night. When they were well on the way they heard a horse behind them. "We lay close to the ground," said Sarah, "and the horse came up to us and stopped. Oh, how my heart did beat! He stood still until some one whistled, and the whistler cried out, 'Where is my father?'" The horse's rider proved to be Mattie, Lee Winnemucca's wife.

After that Sarah and Mattie rode and tented together during the entire campaign. Lee, being with the party, turned back to get more Pi-Utes, and to act for them as a scout and guard. The old chief said: "Ride two and two! Keep close together. Men, look after your wives and children! Six men keep well back for fear we may be followed!"

Thus Chief Winnemucca's family and friends escaped from the hostile camp and rode for six hours, reaching Summit Springs at the break of day. While stopping there for rest and food, one of their rear guard came riding furiously toward them. "We are followed by the Bannocks!" he cried. "I saw Lee running and they fired at him. I think he is killed."

Winnemucca's party, thus warned, mounted at once and rushed on again, tired as they were. But Sarah, finding her friends too slow to suit her impatient spirit, took Mattie and two Indians and said to her father:

"Come, father, give me your orders, for I am going forward to the troops. What shall I tell General Howard? I am going to where he is this very day."

Winnemucca answered: "Tell General Howard to send his soldiers to protect me and my people." With this message these brave women and their escort sped on to Sheep Ranch and reported to me, as I have said. Robbins was immediately dispatched with his well-mounted scouts to meet the old chief and his party and bring them speedily under the protection of the troops. To facilitate this, Sarah sent Pi-Ute Joe back as a guide, and in due time Chief Winnemucca was rescued.

Sarah said of this extraordinary journey, rather boastfully, but nevertheless with perfect truth: "I went for the government when the officers could not get, for love or money, an Indian or a white man to go."

According to the reports that came to me the aggregate number of the hostiles varied from seven hundred to fifteen hundred warriors. They had a strong defensible position and expressed fierce determination to give me battle at Stein's Mountains.

I received a sad report that McGregor and Downey, finding the Indians so strongly posted, had turned back to their families at Camp Harney.

From every consideration Stein's Mountains were just then our objective point. The different columns coming toward me were stopped *en route* and ordered there; they were to take every precaution; carefully scout the country; pick up Indian men, women, and children, and avoid all ambuscades; were warned not to attack the enemy separately except where there was a reasonable prospect of success, but when an attack was determined on it must be delivered at once and be quick and vigorous. The columns were to keep up constant communication with each other by scouts and couriers, so as to give one another the readiest information and the promptest support in case of need. Colonel Wheaton at Walla Walla was instructed to watch with great care the Cayuses and other Columbia Indians in his district, particularly the Umatillas, and to guard against the successful return of renegades at all times.

After putting everything in motion, my staff officers and myself, taking Sarah and Mattie as guides and interpreters, drove rapidly from Sheep Ranch to Fort Lyon, resting there a short time. We then made a quick drive to the Baker road and joined our right column under Major Stuart. His men were pressing forward as fast as they could march toward Stein's Mountains.

At Rhinehart's corner was a large brick house and other buildings filled to repletion with families that had rushed in for mutual safety from the valleys and cattle ranches. My aide, Lieutenant C. E. S. Wood, who was in charge of the scouts, hired all the men in the vicinity to go out and skirmish for the government. Every man was mounted upon a Cayuse pony—a half-breed animal, swift enough, but often ugly. A woman cried out in anguish to me: "What, send away our husbands? Who will care for us? Who will protect us?"

Wood replied laconically: "Their going is your protection."

"Oh," said one in tears, "let the soldiers do that; let the soldiers do the fighting—it is their business!"

"Why, yes," the humorous lieutenant remarked, "the soldiers will do the fighting—your friends will only have to help them find something to fight."

By the 19th we were within striking distance of the great Indian stronghold. When the Indians caught sight of Bernard's mounted men they lost courage, and rushed eastward and southward, running with great speed, as only Indians can, for over a hundred miles, escaping into a very hilly and heavily wooded tract southwest of Camp Harney. The instant Bernard found that the Indians had fled from Stein's Mountains he pressed after them, following their trail, and putting his own troops to their utmost speed.

# CHAPTER XXX.

## INCIDENTS AND HARDSHIPS OF AN INDIAN CAMPAIGN — THE BATTLE OF BIRCH CREEK — FLIGHT OF THE INDIANS.

A Chosen Indian Leader — Panic in an Indian Camp — Indian Women for Guides — Alarming Rumors — The Battle of Curry Creek — Camp of the Renegades — An Innocent-looking Log — Pulling an Old Indian Squaw Out of It — Pursuing the Indians — Picking up a White Man's Scalp — A Couple of Unreliable Guides — A Steep Descent of Four Miles — Finding a Column of Pack-mules — A Word of Warning — Locating the Indians — Getting Ready for Battle — How a Soldier Feels Before a Battle — Indians Abandon Their Stronghold — "Come on, You White Dogs!"

CHIEF EGAN had now become the Indians' chosen leader. He had been very reluctant at first to join the Bannocks, but under threats and persuasions he concluded to take Oytes, the Dreamer, as his counselor, and become the military head of all the tribes represented. In former years Egan had successfully fought General Crook and other officers, and had won quite a reputation for heroic valor among both white men and Indians.

He never risked everything in a pitched battle. As soon as he heard that I was coming with three separate bodies of fighting men and plenty of guns and ammunition, he decided to move rapidly westward to his old stamping ground, where my columns would be separated; while the Indians would have the protection of extensive forests, and could scatter at will and deceive their pursuers by numerous trails. He hoped also that as he drew nearer to the resorts of the Klamaths and the Umatillas some of them would join his ranks, and that these new allies would bring fresh supplies.

The heart of old Oytes himself began to weaken when the Indian scouts rushed in crying that more than a thousand mounted men were moving to attack them. Notwithstanding the panic that followed, Egan steadily continued the march, with his warriors heavily encumbered with women, children, and baggage. Their march was phenomenal. No white caravan of like size could stand such tremendous strain and fatigue.

Meanwhile, I sent Lieutenant Wilkinson, with two soldiers and the two Indian women for guides, to make their way by the stars to Camp Harney. The air was full of alarming rumors and one was that McGregor's troops outside of that post had been met by Egan and annihilated, and that Harney was in great danger of capture and massacre.

It was the 23d of June. I was with the head of the foot column. We had gone late into camp and an extraordinary quiet reigned. Suddenly, at about eleven o'clock that night, Wilkinson startled the outposts by coming back with his Indian guides, and rode rapidly into camp. He had ridden forty-five miles that day from Camp Harney. He brought good tidings. McGregor was united with Bernard; a battle had occurred the day before, but instead of being defeated they had won a victory. This was the battle of Curry Creek, ninety miles from us, and forty-five beyond Camp Harney.

After unusual resistance the Indians had fled

from that field, but had rallied again not far off and continued their flight. Bernard had managed to get four troops of cavalry into the Curry Creek engagement, but, owing to their forced marches over rough ground and long distances, his soldiers were exceedingly weary, and he now called strenuously upon me for reinforcements. That battle was not decisive enough to end the campaign.

Before eleven o'clock the next morning the advance, with myself, entered Camp Harney. Taking but two hours for food and rest, Lieutenant Wood and I rode on toward Captain Bernard, reaching Captain Evan Miles' company of infantry at Sage Hen Springs. Captain Miles was hastening from Harney to support Bernard. Early the following morning we were on the battle-field, and pushed forward to join Bernard, who was still following the trail of the largest body of Indians.

We learned from some prisoners that the Klamaths, some Columbia River Indians, and a small body of Umatillas were about to join the Bannocks and Pi-Utes. These renegades had gone into camp not far from the John Day Valley, sixty miles south of the Umatilla reservation, and Egan had turned his march northward in that direction. The Indians had to cross a rough range of mountains to get into the John Day Valley, and they were then executing this movement. What a diversified country! Jagged rocks, precipitous slopes, knife-edged divides, deep canyons with sides steep and difficult, the distance from a crest to the mountain stream that tumbled over the rocks far below being sometimes four or five miles.

It was on the north side of this, the John Day divide, that the Umatillas and other Indians under suspicion were waiting for Chief Egan and his raiders. Along one of the trails we came upon a large, half-decayed log. This log, like so many in veteran forests, was at one end simply a shell. From the very center of it we pulled out an old and decrepit Indian woman clad in tatters. At first she was almost speechless. She was without food, and had crawled into the log to stay there until she died. I gave orders to have her brought to my next night encampment, where Sarah and Mattie took charge of her. She was fed, clothed, and treated with great kindness by all. As soon as she recovered her senses she cried bitterly, and said that her nephew, Buffalo Horn, was dead. She believed old Oytes had been put in his place.

Sarah and Mattie won her confidence and were rewarded by a full statement of what the Indians had done, and of some of their future plans.

The 30th of June was an eventful day. On the two preceding days we had experienced the cold of winter in the mountains, and considerable snow had fallen. As we went from Indian camp to Indian camp we found hundreds of pine trees stripped from the bottom up as high as one could reach. Sarah said that the Indians used the inner bark for food. The outer bark helped them to cover the frosty ground for beds, and also added to their fuel. From the camp signs we estimated their numbers to be about fifteen hundred. On a stump near the remains of a lodge we picked up the scalp of a white man.

That morning we met two men—mine prospectors—who wanted employment. Upon their declaring that they were familiar with the country I engaged them as guides. As we went deeper and deeper into the forest and ascended the slopes of the mountains one of the guides, becoming conscience-stricken, deserted, and not long after the other, having halted the train, came back to me and confessed in broken English that he had lost his way. I was greatly puzzled what to do; every man near me was an utter stranger to that region. After a moment's delay I galloped to the head of the column closely observing the country as I went. I saw plainly by the formation of the ridges that if I could go from hog-back to hog-back I would finally gain the crest.

The hostile Indians, having no wagons, had been able after crossing the divide to descend by a narrow river canyon. At the risk of finding the northern slope impassable I decided at once to take the chances of advancing. Ordering the wagons to follow me, without uttering a word of the uncertainties that oppressed me, I led the way from ridge to ridge until I gained the summit. There I discovered a spur, a steep one it is true, with a slope not too difficult for wagons. The spur ran northward, and then down into the very country we wanted to reach. That night we were happy to find ourselves in a good camp in a land more familiar to some of our own men.

The next day had its own trials. Looking down into the deep canyon of the John Day we discovered signs of an old emigrant wagon road. A spur similar to that of the mountain, only steeper, led from us to the bottom. One can judge of the depth of that canyon when I say that there was a steady down-hill descent of at least four miles. It took from two P. M. until ten o'clock that night to worry our train down those difficult steeps into camp. The hill was so precipitous as to cause a constant sliding of the wagons. This sliding was checked by dragging chains, by fastening limbs of large trees to the axle-tree, by hitching a pair of obstinate mules behind the wagon body, and by other emergency contrivances. The most successful experiment was the tying on of long ropes and manning them with soldiers, who watched the wagons in their descent and prevented their capsizing.

In the valley, the next morning, we saw where another company of volunteers had rushed upon the Indians and been driven back, leaving the dead bodies of two of their number to be buried by our advance.

We steadily kept on northward until our different columns appeared to be in position to hem in the Indians upon all sides and force them to battle. I was warned by some experienced officers who said: "Ah, General, Chief Egan is 'great' on hiding and running. He always takes to the wooded mountains. He is wary and swift."

I had come to Pilot Rock, a little hamlet north of the famous Blue Mountains, near the charming little town of Heppner. There were two streams rising in the Blue Mountains a few miles southeast of Pilot Rock. They ran northeasterly and emptied into the Umatilla River. The mouths of these two streams are miles apart, but their head waters are near together, so near, in fact, that numerous little rivulets can hardly determine which creek to take, till a chance knoll or rock has decided their course.

It was between these streams near Birch Creek that two of our diligent scouts the night before had found the Indians. Chief Egan had chosen a broad and rugged height for defense. The slopes in front of his warriors, after the detached hill was reached, were steep, stony, deceptive, and extremely difficult. Egan had woods on his right a few hundred yards away, and hills as good as the one he held and other woods behind him.

At sunrise, July 8th, I was talking hopefully and looking toward that rugged hill, when Sarah Winnemucca said: "No, they will not stop long. The timber is near and the Pi-Utes will get away."

The sun came up bright and clear, and my columns were soon in motion. Throckmorton, with a well-reputed guide, having some artillery, infantry, and volunteers, took the Butter Creek route; Bernard, with seven troops of cavalry, and Robbins, with his scouts and a Gatling gun, accompanied me. We went up the foothills, passing rapidly from knoll to knoll, and struck as directly as possible for the rocky height. There is always a feeling of dread just before a battle. It takes but one bullet to kill you. The thought of death to a comrade is not a happy one, and even the blood of your country's foe is not attractive. The distinction, the glory, the reward — they are no compensation.

As we reached a high crest we saw the Indians

and their ponies among the rocks. They did not act as usual, but kept moving about, some jumping up and down as if in defiance. Their conduct was like Joseph's Nez Percés' at the Clear Water the year before, when with blankets tossed high over their heads they danced around, looking and acting like howling dervishes in their frenzied capers, doubtless hoping to inspire terror in our breasts.

Bernard, taking the trot, began the ascent. The cavalry sped from hill to hill until it reached the vicinity of the enemy. The Indians from between the rocks began to fire at Bernard's soldiers as well as they could down such an unpropitious grade. Our men veered to the right and left as they went up different sides; several soldiers were hit; several horses fell under the men, who with difficulty extricated themselves from their stirrups. Soon we saw them clearing the summit. It was speedily done; wave after wave striking the Indians' position—front and flank—in quick succession.

But Egan and his warriors carried out their plan. They were too quick for our breathless horses. They had already abandoned their stone-crowned hill, leaving to us only some old horses and played-out mules, which were filling the gaps between the dark rocks, while the Indians themselves appeared triumphant on the next height beyond. Bernard was vexed; yes, disgusted. Like a flock of birds they were on this pinnacle; and, like them, they had flown to the next. In a book Sarah Winnemucca has written she says of us:

"Dear reader, if you could only know the difficulties of this wilderness you could appreciate the soldiers' royal service. The fight commenced at eight o'clock, under a hot sun and with no water. The whole of it was watched by the general commanding. The bullets were whistling all around us and the general said to me and Mattie: 'Get behind the rocks; you will get hit.'"

At one time we heard an Indian's shrill call. It was from Oytes. Sarah interpreted it as meaning: "Come on, you white dogs; what are you waiting for?" We strained our ears to catch more words, but they did not come.

Bernard endeavored this time, after a short rest for his horses, to cut off their retreat while he ascended the next height, but the rough country and the great exhaustion of the horses and men made it possible for the Indians to elude his next charge, and they soon disappeared from his front altogether. Not many Indians were killed and wounded. Their women, children, and best horses, in droves, were beyond danger before the battle began.

I felt that night tired and chagrined. This experience reminded me of a hunter chasing an antelope all day with several beautiful chances in his favor, but the animal's quick ears and native fleetness divined the hunter's approach and enabled it to elude all his shots. Unlike the hunter, my object in pursuing these Indians was not to kill, but — like my dear father chasing bees — to hive.

# CHAPTER XXXI.

## A LONG AND EXCITING CHASE — THE ENGAGEMENTS THAT FOLLOWED — THRILLING INCIDENTS OF THE CAMPAIGN.

Stumbling Upon Fresh Indian Trails — Catching Up With the Hostiles — "See the Enemy!" — Indian Tactics in Battle — A Brutal Cayuse Chief — The Murder of Chief Egan and His Companions — Searching for Indian Hiding-places — Six Hundred Indian Prisoners — Charging the Indians Across a River — Murder of a Nez Percé Scout — A Remarkable Death Scene — Surprising a Crowd of Indians — Breaking up Indian Camps — Results of the Umatilla Council — A Burly White Ruffian — Efforts to Provoke a Quarrel With Me — Sarah Winnemucca's Criticisms — Death of Mattie.

PLACING my chief-of-staff, Major E. C. Mason, in my place at Cayuse Station, I hastened on to Walla Walla to communicate with General McDowell at San Francisco, and to inaugurate a new pursuit. Some Umatillas, professing to be friends, came into Mason's encampment the first night after I had left and were kindly received. They gave false information concerning the hostiles and gathered knowledge from us that they ought not to have had. Their reports fortunately caused Egan to turn back against us.

Meanwhile, Mason changed his headquarters to the vicinity of the Umatilla reservation, and was gathering our scattered forces into a common camp for rest and recruitment. In executing this movement Captain Evan Miles, having nearly all the Twenty-first Infantry Regiment with him, ran upon fresh Indian trails, which he at once followed.

On the 12th of July he made a march of thirty-five miles, and camped at two A. M. on the 13th. While in camp Captain Rodney of the Fourth Artillery arrived with two companies of his regiment, and he also had with him a troop of the First Cavalry, under Captain Bendire. Miles' camp, though made in the night, proved to be a good point for observation, and daylight revealed groups of Indians in plain sight who took no pains to conceal their position.

At first a band of Umatillas, seemingly about to join the hostiles, sent one of their number under cover of a white flag to Captain Miles and had a talk with him, with the result that they wisely remained neutral and were passive spectators during the conflict that followed. Miles made a slight change of location for the convenience of his command in getting coffee and breakfast, but the fires were hardly lighted when the Pi-Utes and Bannocks were seen coming stealthily toward him in large force. Without waiting a moment Miles deployed his men, Rodney's companies being on the left and facing southward, while some companies of infantry formed a semicircular line from Rodney's position westward, putting Bendire's cavalry upon the extreme left. The remaining companies of the Twenty-first Infantry were held in the rear in reserve.

Captain Miles had two small howitzers which he brought into action near his center. The Indians, as usual, stopped just beyond the zone of immediate danger. They ran into deep and crooked ravines, and concealed themselves as completely as they could, like our skirmishers, the difference being that if our men heard a call such as "See the enemy!" every individual soldier would spring up and jump upon a log to see where the enemy was, while the Indians would remain motionless or secrete themselves still more effectually. From their hiding places the Indians fired briskly but irregularly, and our skirmishers returned the fire, aiming at puffs of smoke. This kind of fighting lasted a long time and much ammunition was expended with small results, especially upon our side.

About two o'clock in the afternoon Miles ordered Rodney with his battalion to gain ground to the left and then push forward and clear a ravine in his vicinity. Rodney's men sprang forward with enthusiasm and promptly set the Indians in motion. Seeing this Miles made a charge along his entire curvilinear front. Chief Egan did not expect this, for he was intently watching other chances in the game of war. His Indians at once mounted their ponies and swiftly rushed for the foothills behind them. Egan went with them, pursued by the excited troops, who for the time had forgotten both breakfast and dinner. The chase continued for more than three miles up the mountain steeps and into the thick forest. At last, worn out with fatigue, our men at dark went into camp where they were.

Meantime, Mr. Cornoyer, finding that many of his Umatillas had been treacherous, sent a hurried dispatch to Captain Miles to return at once, saying that he feared the agency and everything connected with it would be destroyed. Tired as the soldiers were with the terrific march of the day and night before and an all-day battle, they silently but hurriedly turned back and were soon at the agency, where their commander made thorough preparation for defense and then gave his men needed food and rest.

After this defeat the renegade allies—Cayuses, Umatillas, and Columbias—came to Captain Miles and proposed to act on his side. Their real leader was Umapine. He was a Cayuse Indian about six feet in height, having a closely-knit frame, thick chest, and broad shoulders. When not on the war path he had a friendly eye and not an unpleasant smile, yet the impression he left upon you was that he possessed a fierce animal nature. When he ate he consumed twice as much as any other strong man; when he fasted he could go a long time without food. In war he displayed profound treachery and postitive enjoyment of murder. Even his mates shuddered at his brutality. After commiting atrociously wicked acts he would strut with pride and boast of his brutal prowess.

The Pi-Utes and Bannocks had leaned upon him as a friend. After the interview with Miles, the day following the battle, Umapine, with a few followers, overtook Chief Egan and his fleeing warriors. The next day he brought back to the agency ghastly signs of his terrible work. He had murdered Egan and some of his companions.

The talk of Natchez, Sarah Winnemucca's brother, to the Umatillas in a subsequent council tells its own story. After showing the Umatillas

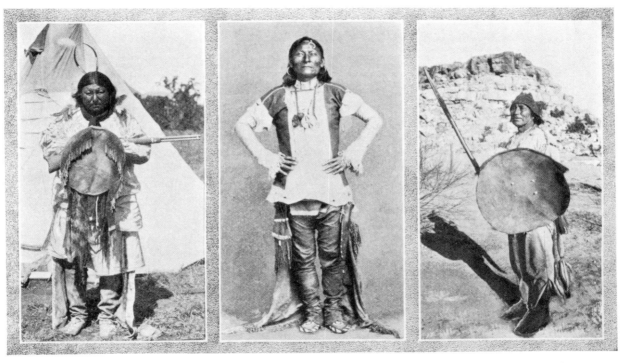

"White Horse."—Kiowa, a Notorious Raider Killed in 1893.

"Always Riding."—A Ute Raider.

Old Navajo Warrior with Lance and Shield.

NOTORIOUS INDIAN RAIDERS AND FREEBOOTERS.

that they had promoted war by their delegates, and then urged Egan and Oytes to make it, he said: "You have called them fools (the Pi-Utes) to stay on the reservation and starve; and another thing, you have helped the Bannocks to fight the soldiers. After all that, it must be a beautiful sensation to cut a man or woman to pieces and then skin their heads and fasten them on a pole and dance around them as if you were happy!"

After these events I divided my command again in order to follow up the numerous trails of the hostiles, visit every hiding-place, and search the entire field. My object was to bring in the Indians as prisoners, and, if possible, allay the wild fears of the ranch people and settlers, who never felt sure of protection until they saw the troops.

I kept up this work for more than a month, sweeping southward across the John Day Valley and on to Harney Lake, and westward over all our campaigning ground, using at times as many as ten different columns.

When passing the Malheur agency for the second time I put Colonel M. P. Miller there to do what he could to bring in the Indian stragglers. He thoroughly probed the country, gathered many wanderers, kept the prisoners sent to him, and caught all who fell into his net. The old Indian woman whom Sarah and Mattie had cared for had come back to health and strength. Miller sent her out to hunt for frightened people, be they men, women or children, instructing her to show them where they could come for food, shelter, and permanent peace. Miller wrote to me afterwards:

"The pickets brought them in (those that the old woman had seen and informed) and they had a talk with me to the effect that their band desired to surrender. I told them that they could come in as prisoners of war." There came to him in all twenty-seven warriors, seventy-two women and children, with fifty horses and ponies and ten guns.

Colonel J. W. Forsyth, who in the subsequent operations commanded my right column, rendered me an account of his several days of marching: "It was up and down steep canyons, over the highest ridges of the mountains, and through a perfect network of fallen timber." He went there because the hostile Indians had led the way. He struck their rear guard in a deep ravine on the north fork of the John Day River. The ascent was so steep that in getting out of it several of the pack animals rolled into the stream and were lost.

The Indians kept a rear guard of about forty warriors. Forsyth's eight scouts were close upon their heels. One of them accidentally discharged his carbine and this set the Indians to firing. They killed our courier, Mr. Forman, and severely wounded one of our scouts. Forsyth instantly rushed his line forward up a precipitous hill, but not soon enough to get a fair chance at the foe, who had mounted and fled before the troops could reach the crest.

When I reached Boise again I found there twenty Indian prisoners that Lieutenant Guy Howard of the Twelfth Infantry, with a part of Captain Vivien's company, had succeeded in gathering up near Ladd's Canyon. In like manner other small detachments had found Indians in hiding and had brought them in until at last there were at Camp Harney over six hundred Indians under guard.

There were no more battles of any consequence and scarcely any organized resistance, excepting on the part of the Bannock contingent which had separated and fled from the Pi-Utes and other allies.

Major Sanford wrote, on July 18th: "I received information from Lieutenant Williams in command of our Nez Percé scouts (near Ladd's Canyon) that he had been fired upon by a party of white men, and that one of his Indians was mortally wounded." The other Nez Percé scouts were very much incensed at what they considered an outrage, and determined to return home. The white men claimed that they thought these scouts were Bannocks, but the Nez Percés insisted that they were dressed in their scouts' uniform, and were moving in a proper way. After that they distrusted the white men altogether. Before his death the wounded Indian scout sent for the white man who had shot him, took him by the hand, looked him in the face, told him that he forgave him, and besought the other scouts to do the same. His comrades gave him a simple Christian burial. One of their number prayed, another repeated some words from the Scriptures, and all joined in singing as they committed his body to earth. Could a white Christian have been nobler than that dying Nez Percé scout?

There was one band of mounted Indians that,

in spite of shelling and rifle shooting, started to cross the river. These were scattered, though a very few of them succeeded in reaching the other shore. This was the band that had murdered Mr. and Mrs. Perkins, and brought suspicion upon five hundred other Indians along the upper Columbia who had continued to be faithful to their promises.

Our campaign was not finished until I had returned to Umatilla and had a prolonged council with the different bodies of Indians, — Cayuses, Columbias, Walla Wallas, and Umatillas.

The results of the Umatilla council were to send several prominent Indians whose loyalty was suspected to safe forts, there to be kept for a time as hostages for the good behavior of the remainder.

When the councils were concluded Lieutenant Wood and myself took the first steamer down the Columbia. The lieutenant, worn out by fatigue, was soon fast asleep upon a side seat. I was sitting near him and half dreaming when a burly citizen approached and roughly accosted me. He was fairly well dressed, but had evidently been drinking. On seeing me he had doubtless boasted to his boon companions that he would show me how the white settlers felt toward me and the authorities who were over me. He began: "I hear that you have allowed those accursed Indians to surrender."

"Of course I have," I answered. "Whenever Indians give up and put out the white flag they are taken as prisoners of war."

He then said savagely: "I wouldn't have done it. Every last one of 'em should have been killed!"

"Then, sir," I replied, "you would have been

a murderer. It would be more than my commission is worth to do such a dastardly thing as to kill prisoners of war."

Showing great anger, he uttered more insulting language, and imputed unworthy motives to my officers and myself. The crowd seemed to be encouraging him to provoke a quarrel with me.

I then arose and said with all the decision of manner I could muster: "Sir, I do not know who you are, but I wish you to understand that I am a soldier who has never turned a corner to avoid a bullet; now what do you want?"

He instantly changed his tone and said, as if ashamed of himself: "Oh, nothing—come, take a drink."

The crowd was now on my side, and after hurrahing for me, I was left to join my aide-de-camp in his undisturbed repose.

Sarah Winnemucca, some time after the war, gave a succinct account of our transferring the Pi-Utes from Camp Harney, where we had collected most of them, to the Yakima agency some sixty miles away. She said: "No human being would do such a thing as that, send people across a fearful mountain in midwinter!" We could have kept them until spring, but our instructions were imperative to deliver them to Agent Wilbur at Fort Simcoe. The work was done by Captain William H. Winters of the First Cavalry. He made short marches, and succeeded in taking them through the rough country with his small escort of two troops of cavalry. Two adults, who were already ill, and three children perished on the journey.

Sarah says: "One afternoon Mattie and I were out to get five women who got away during the night; an officer was sent with us. We were riding very fast and my sister Mattie's horse jumped to one side and threw her off. The blood ran out of her mouth and I thought she would die right away, but, poor dear, she went on, for an ambulance was at our command." This injury finally caused her death.

On the Simcoe reservation, notwithstanding the great care of the venerable Indian agent, Mr. Wilbur, there was very bitter feeling between the newcomers and the occupants of the reservation, who were already far advanced in the ways of civilization. Sarah denounced not only the agent himself and other employees, but all the civilized Indians with whom the Pi-Utes had to do.

Later, upon Mr. Wilbur's request, I saw Sarah and gave her letters to Washington, which she could use after she had visited her father and all the friendly Pi-Utes who were then in Nevada. One remark in a letter which she bore is this: "Mr. Wilbur, the Yakima Indian agent, thinks Sarah is now a Christian and wishes me to aid her to prosecute her journey to Nevada, which I have gladly done. . . . Please do what you can to assist her to have a fair interview with Mr. Stickney of the Indian board and also with the Commissioner of Indian Affairs."

Friends of humanity may say, "The pictures you have given us are sad enough, and do they not show how cruel the whites have been to these Indians?" I answer: "Yes, if we take only the Indians' point of view." But surely our army officers were not cruel toward them. The Indians first believed one of their old Dreamers about the coming of the Messiah. Then the Pi-Utes took advantage of a grievance, viz.: the removal from them of a good agent and his wife and giving them another whom they claimed to be bad. I would have helped them to remedy that, if they had asked. They conspired with the Bannocks and renegades and appealed to arms, and believed for a time that they were strong enough, when combined, to defeat the white troops and clear their region of the soldiers and all the settlers. The outbreak was met promptly by the troops. The Indians were defeated in every battle; they broke into small parties, but were pursued relentlessly until a part were captured and the rest driven far beyond the field of operations. The prisoners were gathered together at Fort Harney and Vancouver Barracks and the whole case submitted to Washington for instructions.

It would have been a reward to misconduct to have given them back the reservation which they had robbed and deserted when they went to war. Any hardships that occurred were merely incidental to the circumstances. Camp Harney, in the midst of the mountains, could not easily be provisioned to keep the garrison through the winter, and it appeared necessary to the Indian bureau to have the Indians sent to a better place at once. Extraordinary expense was incurred for their protection and comfort. The extreme destitution of the women and children was due to the rigors of war,

—a war which every soldier would, if in his power, gladly have prevented. Had the Pi-Utes accepted the situation at Yakima, cultivated their lands, and built houses and fences, as the Simcoe Indians had done, they would have been prosperous and happy.

But it was too much of a transformation to effect in a single season. Many of the Simcoe Indians, as we have seen, live in good houses and are prosperous farmers; some of them are each worth several thousand dollars—fortunes accumulated by their own industry. They were indeed an object lesson to the Pi-Utes, but the Pi-Utes were not yet far enough along "the white man's road" to take advantage of their good fortune. They became homesick, and begged to go from a land of fertility to a comparatively barren waste in Nevada which had always been the hunting and fishing ground of their people. Their cry was heeded, like that of Joseph and the non-treaty Nez Percés, and so they returned to beat their tom-toms and dance and dream in their old haunts.

# CHAPTER XXXII.

## AMONG THE SHEEP-EATERS — CAMPAIGNING IN "THE LAND OF THE SEVEN DEVILS."

A Visionary Old Dreamer — Some Alarming Reports — Getting Ready to Take the Warpath — A Select Company of Indian Scouts and Sharpshooters — Campaigning in a Fearfully Rough Country — Pursuing a Band of Marauding Horse-thieves — Defeat of Our Troops — Five Days of Terrific Forced Marches — Stumbling Upon an Indian Ambuscade — Completely Surrounded by Indians — Setting Fire to the Grass and Timber — Heroic Efforts of the Troops to Extricate Themselves — A Bannock Spy Who Played Me False — Teaching Captive Indians — Escape of the Bannock Spy.

IN the early part of 1879 I was looking for the establishment of a new army post near the mouth of the Spokane River. While in camp on the opposite side of the river and in view of the San Poels, or Sheep-Eaters, I was visited by a delegation from that tribe, who were solicitous for entire and absolute independence of all white men and all Indians. The acting chief, a *tooat,* was lame and much given to visions. His dreams, when I was in the neighborhood, were extraordinary, but sensible, and I anticipated no great trouble from his people, who were temperate and industrious. The substance of this man's dreaming was the prayer of an aged Presbyterian divine who had visited the tribe when he was young. This prayer had remained in his memory and appeared to be leading him to good and high aspirations. At frequent intervals he would point to approaching serious troubles with the wild tribes in and around the fearfully rugged Salmon River country — often called "The Land of the Seven Devils" — and would urge immediate preparations to meet and resist the same.

I had not long been returned to Vancouver, my headquarters, before I received a dispatch stating that the Indian agent at Lemhi had reported a revolting murder of miners at a place called Oro Grande, on Loon Creek, about eighty-five miles northwest of Boisé. General McDowell, the division commander, directed me to send troops from Boisé as soon as the trail could be traveled, for the purpose of investigating this murder and other alarming reports coming from the rough Salmon River country. I was already advised of these troubles, and was convinced that hostile Indians of the previous year had united with the Sheep-Eaters on the Middle Fork of the Salmon River for the warpath. In addition to the troops from Boisé, I ordered another command from Camp Howard, near Mt. Idaho, to prepare to take the field as soon as it might be possible to cross the rugged mountains between the Snake River and the South and Middle Forks of the Salmon.

Anticipating trouble at various places, because of the reappearance of some of the hostile Nez Percés who escaped to British America after the Nez Percé campaign of 1877, and hostile demonstrations by Pi-Utes and Bannocks who had participated in the war of 1878, and wishing to keep well informed and strike effectively, I ordered Lieutenant Edward S. Farrow of the Twenty-first

GROUP OF KOOTENAI INDIANS AND THEIR CAMP.—IDAHO.

Infantry, fresh from West Point and full of activity, to enlist a company of Indian scouts and to form a detachment of picked men, selected for endurance and their skill in marksmanship. I placed these Indian scouts and sharpshooters under the independent command of Lieutenant Farrow, gave him private instructions, and sent him in the direction where the hostile Nez Percés had been reported. I then gave orders to the commanding officer at Boise to send a troop of cavalry, under command of Captain Bernard, to Challis, Idaho, with instructions to operate from that point, indicating that when the command sent from Camp Howard reached Bernard that he should command both columns. The same instructions, in substance, went to the commanding officer at Camp Howard, to operate toward Challis and unite with Bernard as soon as possible. These instructions were promptly carried into effect, the troops starting early in June; but great delay was occasioned owing to impassable trails, the fearfully rough country, and the deep snows through which the commands had to dig their way in order to reach the roaming ground of the Indians.

On July 6th Bernard dispatched me these words: "To enable us to get up the Middle Salmon a trail through timber and rocks had to be made all the way." This was done with the river, already a flood, constantly rising, so that crossing and recrossing the swift torrent became extremely slow and difficult. Bernard added: "The mountains closed in, forming such a canyon as to cause us to leave the river and try the mountains, which were covered with snow and very rocky. . . . Pack mules were carried down stream, having rolled down the mountains, causing the loss of many rations and other supplies."

Lieutenant Catley, leading the force from Camp Howard, reported from Warrens, a hamlet near the South Fork of the Salmon, that nothing could be done toward getting into the country where the Indians were supposed to be until later, when more of the snow was gone. The middle of June he had gone only seven miles from Warrens and was obliged to turn back because it was absolutely impossible to get through. It was not until the 11th of July that he succeeded in getting into the region of the Salmon River country and camped on the South Fork.

On the 15th of July Bernard reported from Cape Horn Valley that "The country was rougher than any of the United States, and to get at the Indians would be a work of great difficulty. Should they discover us before we do them, they can hide in the timbered Rocky Mountains for a long time, and go from point to point much faster than we can, even if we knew where to go." He added: "We have traveled over much country that no white man ever saw before; old guides and miners declared that we could not get through at all."

Lieutenant Farrow, with his command, crossed the Blue Mountains and moved with celerity to the Snake River, which he crossed at Brownlee's Ferry on July 11th. By the 16th of July he reported from Council Valley that he had found signs of Indians near Wood Creek. After two days' pursuit he dispersed these Indians, they seeking refuge on the Lapwai and Lemhi reservations. Lieutenant Farrow then gave his attention to an organized band of marauding horse thieves, whom he pursued to the highest peaks of the Seven Devil Mountains, where he dispersed them and captured a large lot of stock and supplies stolen from the government. Several notorious Indians, prominent in the campaigns of 1877 and 1878, were in company with these marauders, and these Lieutenant Farrow, after capture, impressed as guides and scouts. He then proceeded in search of the reported returning Nez Percés, having ascertained the then whereabouts of the commands of Bernard and Catley.

The three commanders slowly and cautiously forced their way through that impassable country like hunters in search of wildest game. On the 5th of August a message came to me from Bernard to the effect that he had just received a dispatch from Lieutenant Catley stating that the Indians had attacked and defeated his command on July 29th, and had captured his pack train and all supplies. The force of Indians was reported as well posted on Big Creek, a stream that flowed from the west and emptied into the Middle Fork of the Salmon.

About this time Lieutenant Farrow was advised by couriers of Catley's defeat. He at once caçhed his supplies and equipage, and, living off the country, made forced marches in the shortest line across mountains and canyons to Catley's relief. After five days of terrific forced marches Farrow camped with Catley's retreating command on the South Fork of the Salmon at Rains Crossing. Leaving a few of his footsore men and horses with Catley, Lieutenant Farrow crossed the South Fork of the Salmon at daybreak the next morning and hastened in the direction of Big Creek, the scene of Catley's disaster.

Catley accounted for his misfortune by saying that his command struck an ambuscade from which, after determining that it was impossible to do anything because the Indians were lodged in a point of rocks across the creek, where they had so fortified themselves that their exact location could not be discovered, he took the responsibility of ordering a prompt retreat some two miles up the creek to a point which he thought could be held defensively. Here he camped one night, and the next morning, putting his wounded men upon hand litters, he moved up a steep ridge which he believed would lead him into the mountains and back to the trail by which he had come. But here, unfortunately, he lost his way, and to make matters worse the Indians kept ahead of him, occupying rocky points on his right and left. Completely surrounded by Indians, he finally ordered the pack train unloaded and instructed his men to take such cover as they could find in the rocks and behind the cargo, and hold the position if possible should the Indians attempt to approach.

To increase his troubles the Indians set fire to the grass and timber. The base of the mountain seemed to be entirely on fire. The wind was high, and the terrible roaring of flames and dense clouds of smoke seemed to approach from every direction. The heroic efforts of his men in "counter-firing" prevented the singed and scorched command from immediate destruction. As soon as possible, after dark, the command moved slowly and quietly down the precipitous side of the mountain, having abandoned all public property and personal effects. His condition was such after the loss of his property, supplies, animals, equipage, and clothing, that he at once decided to return to Camp Howard.

The back movement of Lieutenant Catley was promptly arrested by Colonel Wheaton, from Fort Lapwai, as soon as the report of the defeat reached him. Captain Forse of the First Cavalry, with his company, was hurriedly sent out to reinforce Catley and turn him toward the Indians, and in support of Farrow, who was then advancing into the Sheep-Eater country. On August 24th I hurriedly sent dispatches to Bernard, stating that the Indians had been encouraged by Catley's defeat, that the trouble was extending, and urging every activity in promptly moving on the Indians. In answer I received a more hopeful dispatch from Bernard, saying that "Farrow (30 miles ahead of him) was pursuing the hostile Indians down the Middle Salmon canyon, had captured thirty-five horses, and had caused them to abandon all their luggage." Bernard, now joined by Forse, followed Farrow's trail down Big Creek to the Middle Fork of the Salmon and went into camp where Farrow was recuperating after his plunging pursuit down the Middle Salmon canyon. From this camp Bernard sent me a dispatch saying: "The country is so rough that animals cannot be got through at all. All our stock except a few of Captain Forse's horses and the animals captured by Farrow are exhausted. Most of our horses and mules have given out and have been shot."

It seemed so impossible to capture these flying Indians, who ran from peak to peak faster than the troops could follow, and, realizing the intense suffering of the troops engaged, I at last sent orders for Bernard, if in his judgment it was impossible to do more than had been done, to leave that fearful country and distribute his forces to the posts where they belonged. Bernard acted promptly on this order, and with his own command proceeded southward to Boise. Forse and Farrow went westward to the South Fork of the Salmon on the trail made by Catley in his retreat. Upon reaching the South Fork hostile Indians were seen near by, and several prospectors were attacked and killed, while numerous signal smokes indicated that the Indians were following Forse and Farrow and would doubtless attack all ranches south and west of Warrens after the troops had left that section of the country.

In view of this situation Lieutenant Farrow remained in camp on the South Fork of the Salmon to watch the Indians until all whites could get out of the neighboring country, while Captain Forse proceeded to his post at Fort Lapwai.

Lieutenant Farrow now abandoned most of his equipage and with a portion of his command advanced upon the Indians once more and finally attacked them in their stronghold on the Middle Fork of the Salmon. After numerous assaults, finally flanking the Indian position and destroying the Indian camp, he forced the entire band to surrender, and then by sixty-two days of marching through fearful snows over rugged mountains he reached the Columbia River with his captive tribe and delivered them to me at Vancouver Barracks as prisoners of war, thus enabling me to fully realize every hope I may have had as to the favorable outcome of this most hazardous expedition.

In my order of congratulation I stated that "the men in this expedition, one and all, deserve special mention for gallantry, energy, and perseverance, resulting in success."

As a reward for his services in this campaign, Lieutenant Farrow has a brevet commission signed by President Cleveland.

When Lieutenant Farrow brought his Indian prisoners to Fort Vancouver it was the headquarters of the Twenty-first Infantry, with six companies present for duty. Colonel Henry A. Morrow, who was a general by brevet and had been my comrade in the Civil War, was in command of the regiment, and the post captain, John A. Kress, who had been a lieutenant-colonel of volunteers on the staff of General Wadsworth, was in command of the Vancouver Arsenal. Upon arrival at the post these Sheep-Eater Indian prisoners were the objects of curious scrutiny. For the most part they were substantially the same as the Bannocks in manners and customs, but dressed in scanty attire of mountain sheep and other skins. The band was composed of Bannocks, Pi-Utes, Snakes, Nez Percés, and Cayuses. One of the Bannocks had been a spy for Buffalo Horn and Egan during the Indian campaign of 1878. When I was encamped at Sheep Ranch, actively engaged in the Bannock campaign, this Indian came to my headquarters and so won my regard and the confidence of those about me that I decided to send a message by him from that point some two hundred miles to Camp Harney. As he was more loyal to the other side he carried my dispatches straight to Chief Egan (the enemy) in Stein's Mountains instead of to Camp Harney. This Bannock spy was the only one of all the Indians in the Northwest that I had to do with directly who played me false.

It was not long before confidence and contentment reigned throughout the encampment. Sarah Winnemucca visited Fort Vancouver about this time, and as an interpreter rendered invaluable service in arriving at a better understanding of the Indian prisoners and their needs, and instituted a good school for the children and others and began teaching them English.

Major Kress was the superintendent of our Sunday-school, and Indians, old and young, were gathered into that. In this the ladies of the garrison became teachers, and, with Sarah, they had sewing classes and proper instructions in that line. General Morrow set the Indians to work, being delighted at the opportunity to relieve his soldiers from ordinary and extraordinary police duty. The Indians came out of the guard-house to whitewash the fences, make paths, build and improve roads, and to put the whole outer face of things in prime condition.

I often watched groups of these Indians while

they were at work. They never appeared to relax their energy and effort to do everything required of them, and to do it well. The spy, taking with him two other Indians, succeeded in making his escape, crossing the broad Columbia, and disappearing in the forests of Oregon. I did not blame him much for getting away as soon as possible, even after he had made his solemn promise to obey all regulations and to remain at Vancouver till properly released, because he was conscious all the while of having done those things in war which would subject him to the severest penalty, and as he knew that the white man could not really trust him he was not willing to trust General Morrow's word as to his own safety.

As a rule, when an Indian looked in my face and gave me his promise to do a certain thing, he was scrupulous to perform that promise. Some one asked me after my long experience among Indians if I did not find them treacherous. I answered: "No, not so much so as the Anglo-Saxon." I did not mean to say that they were not as outrageous as they possibly could be during the activities of what they called "war," but that after the war was over none of them ever entered into a deliberate plan to deceive and injure me and mine as many an educated white man has done.

## CHAPTER XXXIII.

AMONG THE SPOKANES — I AM WELCOMED BY CHIEF LOT — RELIGIOUS SERVICES AMONG INDIANS — INSTANCES OF INDIAN GRATITUDE.

The Spokanes — A Filibustering Indian — Chief Lot — Preparations for a Wedding — An Indian Bride — Listening to Indian Songs — Trying to Build "a Bona fide White Man's House" — A Queer Piece of Architecture — Religious Service With the Spokanes — Indian Confessions — Shedding Tears of Contrition — A Dissenting Old Indian Woman — "Sit Down, My Girl, Sit Down!" — Chief Lot's Confession — My Indian Escort — Preparations for Leaving the Department of the Columbia — Unexpected Appearance of Lot — His Journey of Five Hundred Miles to Bid Me Good-bye — "You Must Not Go!" — Instances of Indian Gratitude.

DURING the summer following our council at Fort Simcoe, I caused my aide-de-camp, Captain Wilkinson, in company with the Indian inspector, Colonel E. C. Watkins, to meet several kindred bands of Indians in a council to be held at Spokane Falls. The Colville Indians, the Upper Spokanes, the Okanagans, the Cœur-d'Alenes, and the Lower Spokanes were all represented. The agent at Colville nominally had these Indians in charge, but they were not all upon reservations.

The Spokanes under different chiefs were very much scattered. Those off from reservations were grouped, several of them under Chief Moses, and several others under Spokane Garry, who had achieved a great war record in his early life, but during the councils showed himself more of a lawyer than a fighter. At one time, in a council at which I was present, I thought that Garry could make the longest speech of any Indian I had ever listened to, and he knew how to filibuster like a congressman when he had a point to gain by continuous talking. Garry's main desire was to have a reservation set apart for himself and his followers. His own band did not exceed three hundred, but he hoped to increase his importance by having several bands collected and placed by the government under his leadership.

Spokane Garry was short in stature, dressed in citizens' clothing, and wore his hair cut very short for an Indian. He was shriveled, blear-eyed, and repulsive in appearance, but wiry and tough, and still able to endure great fatigue, though he must have been at least seventy years of age.

The results of the councils at Spokane Falls were quite satisfactory. All the renegades and Spokanes off from reservations secured from Colonel Watkins the promise of a new and ample reservation, with metes and bounds well defined, and in return for this promise they agreed to keep the peace during the threatened Indian troubles whose shadow was already upon us. Altogether there were between three thousand and four thousand Indians represented at these councils.

The year before I had gone from band to band and made some observations. When I first struck a portion of the Lower Spokanes they were in camp near a bridge that led over the Spokane River on the Colville wagon road. They were living in lodges built like those of the Flatheads and the Blackfeet, erected with good lodge-poles and covered with canvas and skins. I was welcomed by them, and on my approach to their camp their chief, by the name of Lot, came out to meet me at the head of a small company. Lot was a man of remarkable height; he spoke a little English, but preferred to use the "Chinook" in his intercourse with white men.

We pitched our camp close to the river and not far from the Indian lodges. These Indians had been taught by an old missionary whom they called "Father Eells," and were decidedly Presbyterian. That night a weary but faithful minister, with a halting gait, joined us at the bridge, having come some distance from Spokane Falls obedient to the call of the Indians. He was to officiate at a wedding. It appeared that a rough white man, Richards by name, had been living near the bridge and had traded extensively with the Indians and fraternized with them more than with white men. He had become attached to an Indian maiden who had consented to become his wife, and the minister was on hand to marry them. The ceremony was conducted after the simple form of the Presbyterian church and had nothing remarkable about it. The girl was very young and bashful, but she seemed happy to accept the white man. I wondered that she did not prefer one of the young Indians to that rough and uncouth specimen of the Anglo-Saxon race, whose appearance indicated that he was what is called in that country a "squaw-man."

After the wedding, which took place in the evening, the Indians returned to their lodges. Soon

Indian songs sung in Indian words to tunes that were familiar to me from childhood arose from every lodge and produced a strange effect upon us all. The singing was part of their evening worship and had nothing to do with the wedding.

After the Indian wars of 1877 and 1878 were over I accompanied two Presbyterian ministers to the home of a very ambitious Indian who had essayed to build something beyond the common lodge, namely, a *bona fide* white man's house. A few Indians had secured some land thickly covered with trees and on this Spokane William had erected his dwelling. The house measured, I should judge, about forty feet each way, and its plan was as nearly square as the Indian could lay it out. It had a roof, and a door in one corner, but there was not a window or a fireplace in it, and nothing between the ground and the rafters. But it was a beginning, and William was proud of it.

The day we were there the ministers held a religious service with the Indians. The Spokanes came in and filled William's house. They sat on the ground, all facing toward a table, while the ministers and guests occupied the few chairs that William possessed. Chief Lot was present, and sat upon the edge of the table. The singing was similar to that I had heard in the Spokane lodges on the evening of the wedding; the reading of the Scriptures and the sermon preached by one of the ministers were translated by a good interpreter.

After the regular service communion was partaken of. It was customary for those frontier ministers to require short talks and confessions from Indians who had departed from the faith, or been guilty of trangressions according to the Bible code which Father Eells had given them. One after another arose and confessed. One young Indian said that he had taken two horses from a white man, but that he had restored them, and he was very sorry for his conduct and would never again steal. Others, both men and women, confessed the specific sins which they had committed. They shed tears of contrition, all ending with promises to do their best in future. At last a very sharp-voiced Indian woman rose in the back part of the house and, talking with great rapidity, seemed to be indulging in crimination and fault-finding. I could not understand her, but as I was looking toward Lot I saw him rise slowly to his full height and then lift up his hand and wave it downward with considerable emphasis. The interpreter told me that Lot said: " Sit down, my girl, sit down! "

She dropped down, when he added: " We can confess our own sins; we have a right to do that, but we have no right to confess other people's sins."

When Chief Lot's turn came he owned that he had not always done what he ought to have done and had sometimes set a bad example to the people of his band, but he was sorry, and he purposed with all his soul to lead a good and Christian life hereafter.

On a later visit to the north I heard that Lot and his Indians were much troubled and persecuted by white settlers. They had gone to a portion of the country far above the Spokane River and high up among the hills, where they had found a fertile, well-watered plain. Lot had there between four thousand and five thousand acres of good land enclosed by a fence. Along the borders of this common territory Indian houses, barns, and lodges were located at intervals within this fence, and fair crops appeared near every building and lodge. They were living upon and cultivating part of the public land, but they had no reservation and no visible right to remain there.

Lot heard of my coming and just at night came out some ten or twelve miles to meet me, accompanied by twenty Indians. They were greatly delighted that I had come. We encamped near a stream of water in the woods. In that bivouac—it was more of a bivouac than a camp, for we had no tent—I did not feel the same sense of danger that I did among the Apaches, the non-treaty Nez Percés, or among the Pi-Utes, when at my first visit they sang their wild songs. Lot and his people, though very little advanced in our customs, were nevertheless Christian Indians. They were trying to square their conduct by a good code of morals.

On looking over the land that Lot had selected I tried to persuade him to have his Indians take up the land in severalty, as the settlers do after public surveys have been made, but he said to me: "I cannot do it. Only a few of us would know how, and we have no money to pay what the land office demands. A few might learn to do that kind of farming, but most of our Indians would perish if they tried to get a living on farms of their own. They cannot do it. Set apart a tract big enough for us all and we can cultivate it together, and I will see that the old and infirm and the children are fed and taken care of."

I protected Lot as well as I could until 1880, when the President and General Sherman made a visit to Oregon. Then I had the papers made out for setting apart the tract which Chief Lot had selected and was then cultivating. General Sherman joined me heartily in recommending the reserve, and signed his name to the paper, and President Hayes gladly added his strong approval. Many greedy white men, who believed that Indians had no rights which a white man ought to respect, were much chagrined at this action, but, fortunately, they could not overturn it, so that Lot and his people were made happy in spite of the continued and bitter opposition of their white neighbors.

When I was about to leave the Department of the Columbia for the East and had gone on board the San Francisco steamer lying at the dock in Portland, and had entered my room for the night to get a good sleep and be ready for a very early start the next morning, my door was suddenly darkened by a tall human form. I turned and saw that it was an Indian dressed in citizen's clothing, but with a blanket over his head and shoulders. As soon as he spoke I recognized Lot. He had come all the way from his reservation above the Spokane to Wallula on horseback and thence down the river by steamers, and had arrived in Portland just in time to see me before my departure. It deeply touched me to learn that an Indian would travel over five hundred miles in the way I have described to bid me good-bye before my final farewell to the Pacific Coast. I instinctively thought that my going had troubled the veteran chief, and that he probably had some special message for me. He began by reciting some of the things that I had done. He spoke of our meeting at different times, and of my giving him a reservation and having it confirmed by the approval of General Sherman and the President.

"Now," said Lot, "after all this you go away?"

"Yes," I said, "I must go. The President has ordered me to go East, and I must obey his orders as your men obey yours."

"But," he entreated, "you must not go; you cannot go! You are the Indians' friend. If you stay everything will go on right, but if you go the white men around me will get my land and there will be trouble. You must not go!"

The old man's voice was tender and his eyes were full of tears as he pleaded with me in better broken English than I thought he could command. His fears were quieted before we separated. Probably before he came to me he was convinced that I would obey my orders and go to my new department, but he could not refrain from expressing his gratitude and confidence, and his strong desire for me to remain.

This was the third incident in which an Indian had shown strong emotion and good will on parting with me. Cochise had embraced me twice and spoken very gently and expressed a wish for me to stay; Moses had taken me by the hand and looked in my face and said that he would come to me whenever I should call him, but Lot had traveled over five hundred miles to see me, and had shown all the tenderness and affection of a brother when he bade me good-bye. These are recollections which show a oneness in the love and sympathy which is a common heritage of God's children of every race, and give me special satisfaction.

# CHAPTER XXXIV.

## PERSONAL EXPERIENCES AMONG THE CROWS — A TRIBE OF WARRIORS AND THIEVES — SECRET HELPERS OF OUR FOES.

The Crow Reservation — An Ingenious Plot — Meeting a Delegation of Mounted Crows — Fraternizing with Our Indian Scouts — A Crow Escort — A Tribe of Thieves — Finding Bodies of White Men — Marriage Customs of the Crows — Their Dress and Personal Appearance — Religious Belief — Looking Forward to a Coming Messiah — Settlers' Opinion of the Crows — "Thieves, Marauders, and Murderers" — Justly Entitled to Their Reputation — Bad Feeling Between the Sioux and Crows — A Nomadic Tribe — Full of War and Revenge — Incidents of Life Among the Crows — A Reign of Terror — Driving Them from Their Reservation.

IN my account of the Nez Percé war I described how our columns followed the Nez Percés through the Yellowstone Park and then, turning gradually northward, went from Wyoming into Montana in a northeasterly direction. As we descended from Hart Mountain we touched the Crow reservation. The Crow Indians were the secret helpers of our foes. Some of them succeeded in turning General Sturgis away from his camping ground and leading him and his command some forty miles out of the way of Joseph's advance just at the right time.

Undoubtedly this ingenious plot was carried out by Joseph's scouts, but the Crows very kindly gave the scouts the information that enabled them to guide the hostiles through a safe pass that they might without material interruption continue their eastern march toward the British territory, where Sitting Bull was at that time. As soon as I arrived in the neighborhood of the Crows a mounted delegation of them, with bright faces, came straight to me from the Indian agent with profuse offers of hospitality. They were, however, a little overfriendly, and I suspected at the time that their duplicity had misled Sturgis.

It was surprising to see how quickly they would pick up a stray horse, and how ready they were at the first opportunity after detection to return anything that belonged to our camps. Like the Flatheads, as soon as they came near us they fraternized with our Indian scouts,—the Bannocks under Buffalo Horn, and the few Nez Percés who were with us. A group of them, not very well dressed, nor as fine appearing as the Flatheads, but always well mounted, kept along beside our marching column for two or three days, going as far as Sturgis' battle-field near the Musselshell. From us and from the Indians who were fleeing from us the Crows managed to gather much booty, such as cast-off clothing and blankets, pack mules that had strayed away loaded with provisions, and numerous animals temporarily lame or otherwise broken down with the hardships of a long journey. These they gathered up and took back to their lodges, and with so much adroitness that no harm seemed to be intended and no complaint was made against them. Really the Crows gloried in thefts, — to snatch a pony without detection was for a Crow a highly praiseworthy act.

An officer who was serving at that time with the

cavalry told me that not one of the messengers and scouts that Sturgis sent out to get news of the coming Nez Percés ever returned. We found the bodies of a few white men after we descended from Hart Mountain, but whether they were slain by the Nez Percés or the Crows we could not determine.

The Mountain Crow Indians were noted among surrounding tribes for their shrewdness and activity. Having now become half-civilized they show the change in their dress, wearing partly the white man's and partly the Indian costume. They have, however, always preferred the tepee to the dwellings provided for them through the Indian bureau.

It is said that when any Plains Indian wishes to marry he agrees to give the father a certain number of ponies in return for the possession or promise of his daughter. But the marriage ceremony had no binding force among the Crows, for if at any time the husband became weary of his wife he could return her to her parents, and she was free to marry again. Some of these Indians have more than one wife.

Like the Apaches, Crow parents were over-indulgent to their children. They were under no restraint, and when the boys were old enough to ride and use the bow they were very wild, yet happy together in their varied sports. The Crows trusted in the Good Spirit, and regarded any evil or disaster as a punishment to chasten them. When relief came the Good Spirit had brought it, and they were comforted. In this faith they differed from most wild Indians, who imputed all evils to the Bad Spirit, whom, by various ways, they endeavored to appease.

The religious faith of the Crows did not differ much from that of the non-treaty Nez Percés. Like them they held tenaciously to the idea of a coming Messiah, who was to restore the hunting grounds and privileges of their fathers.

Among our frontier settlers the reputation of the Crows was bad. They were denounced as thieves, marauders, and murderers. Such they undoubtedly were, and such they taught their children to be; still they managed to get along with white men without open war. We saw many evidences in the neighborhood of their domain of old conflicts with other Indian tribes, and were told by men who had long resided among them that their lodge-poles had been dropped in great quantities on all "the old trails" while they were running away from the Blackfeet, with whom they were constantly at war.

The Crows were natural herders. They liked to own live stock, and seemed to take a lively pleasure in herding cattle and horses. They gradually gained the appliances of civilization, and a large number of them are now employed every year by government agents in hauling supplies. Many are farmers and succeed fairly well when the seasons are favorable.

In noticing the *totems* of Sioux warriors I have often observed that about the first act depicted was the killing and scalping of a Crow Indian. Sometimes the record of distinguished prowess included the slaying of Crow women and the seizing of their ponies. Sitting Bull in his younger days, while he was laying the foundation of his fame as a warrior, put great stress upon his killing of Crows, taking their scalps and their property. These curious records show that the Sioux and Crows were deadly enemies, and were perpetually at war with each other.

Their code of honor was substantially the same. The Crows did not believe in robbing each other, but took great delight in killing and robbing their enemies. Were not the white settlers their enemies? How could they have our code of morals except through Christianization and civilization?

At the time I crossed their reservation their limits extended from the north line of Wyoming to the Yellowstone and the one hundred and seventh meridian. They were then known as the River and the Mountain Crows. The former had long been especially nomadic, and roamed north of the Missouri with little regard to metes and bounds. They had constantly fallen in with white men who, through the use of whisky, drove good trades with them. The government agent, however; had succeeded in getting some twelve hundred of them to join the Mountain Crows, then about three thousand strong, and to remain at least during the cold months within reasonable distance of his agency buildings.

# CHAPTER XXXV.

## LIFE AMONG THE FLATHEADS — THEIR PECULIARITIES AND CUSTOMS — OUR INDIAN RESERVATION METHODS.

**Plea of Chief Carlos — On the Lolo Trail — Friendly Emissaries and Good Spies — A Diplomatic Tribe — My Two Flathead Messengers — How They Were Dressed — Method of Flattening the Head — Efforts to Have the Practice Discontinued — A Tribal Peculiarity — How the Flatheads Lived — Their Homes in the Bitter Root Valley — Generally Friendly to the Whites — Old Indian Trails — A Drunken and Terror-inspiring Indian — Settlers' Dread of Indian War — Work Preferable to Starvation — Effect of Confining Indians on Reservations — Education of Indian Children — Eagerness to Adopt the White Man's Ways.**

"ON the 2d of March, 1889, an act of Congress proposed a fresh negotiation with the Carlos band (the Flatheads) with a view to their acceptance of the local warrants, or the assent to the sale of the land thus allotted for their benefit, and their own removal to the reservation already occupied by a majority of their people."* During the negotiation Chief Carlos forcibly emphasized the just claims of his people—claims existing from time immemorial—and he especially pleaded his own action during the Nez Percé war substantially as follows:

"It is admitted by the whites that, with a band of less than one hundred of my men, we saved the white families of the valley from extermination. This worthy act we did before Howard and Gibbon could concentrate a sufficient force to meet Joseph

---

* Extract from United States Census Report, 1890.

and Looking-Glass in the field." This brief statement, however, is misleading, but doubtless it appeared true at the time to the inhabitants of Bitter Root Valley and vicinity, and to the Indians.

Two Flatheads, as fine-looking Indians as I ever saw, met my column while we were following the Lolo Trail before we came to the Montana border, and represented that they and all their people were peaceably inclined toward us. The tribe they represented, however, did not interfere in any way with the wild Nez Percés, except to negotiate between them and the white people living in that country. They professed and practiced neutrality. They did, however, give the hostile Indians all the information they needed to escape from us when Gibbon was hemming them in near Fort Missoula. They also carried information to the Indians that my command was about to strike the Nez Percés while they were clustered around Gibbon's camp at the Big Hole, gradually picking off and killing or wounding his soldiers one by one. Indeed, in my opinion, they furnished friendly emissaries to the white people and at the same time were good spies for the hostile Nez Percés, and managed adroitly to keep peace with us all. Such neutrality passes current among Christian nations, if not too minutely investigated.

My two Flathead messengers were men above the ordinary size, very neat in their attire, and quite showy. They had on low-crowned hats with stiff brims, one wearing in his hat a dark plume, and the other something that looked like an eagle's wing. Both wore buckskin breeches and skin jackets, the latter ornamented with painting, fringes, and beadwork; they had also blankets of Navajo make, variegated in stripes of different colors.

There was nothing in these two Indians nor in the numerous individuals of the band then occupying portions of Bitter Root Valley which made noticeable the distinctive feature which gave rise to their name. The method of flattening the head is still persisted in to some extent notwithstanding the strong efforts of Christian missionaries to have the practice discontinued. The infant is placed on its back on a wide piece of bark or slab of wood. A shorter piece is fastened to the end of this in such a way as to press down gently but continually upon the forehead of the child. As the bones yield to the pressure the thongs are drawn tighter, and the skull, being soft and pliable, gradually assumes the desired formation and never regains its normal shape. In some cases the flattening has been carried to the extent of a gross deformity. What is remarkable is that the intellect seems not to have been at all impaired, even though the apparent shape of the head has become that of an idiot. Of course this was a tribal peculiarity and was considered not only a mark of distinction but, in spite of our taste, of increased beauty.

The Flatheads made their homes in the Bitter Root Valley. There were other bands, however, associated with the Flatheads proper on the Jocko reservation just above the town of Missoula who were often described in connection with the Flatheads who lived near the government agency. They were doubtless kindred bands; they had the same root language, but were far from being the same in energy, enterprise, and thrift.

While the buffalo lasted and the Flatheads could go upon winter hunts, they supplemented what they could raise in the valley during the short season of that northern country, and were comparatively wealthy. As General Gibbon's troops, and mine following them, moved rapidly from the end of the Lolo Trail through the Bitter Root Valley and on to Gibbon's battle-field at the Big Hole, some of the Flatheads kept in or near our camp all the way and showed every sign of friendly feeling. The white people in that region were vexed because we did not stop the pursuit of Joseph and his warriors altogether, declaring that peace would be quickly established if General Howard would cease operations. The whites also gave liberal supplies to the fleeing Indians, so that at that time their Indian protectors, the Flatheads, surely seemed more friendly to us and to the government than were the Anglo-Saxon settlers of western Montana.

The Nez Percés often joined the Flatheads in their long winter excursions into the buffalo country, and were uniformly on friendly terms. With them they constantly intermarried. They helped to make the "old trails," which for hundreds of miles coursed along in several parallel lines from valley to valley, ridge to ridge, and mountain side to mountain side, at that time the only discernible routes from Idaho to Dakota. These trails were distinctly marked and more quickly seen by traders and Indians than the old national roadway from

Montana to Oregon. They were called the Nez Percé buffalo trails, and must have existed when the *voyageurs* of Canada were planting the old forts—Hall and Walla Walla—and when the first Flatheads came all the way from the region of the Bitter Root to St. Louis to find the Book which had made the white men wise and prosperous.

About the time I first met the Flatheads it was said of them that all the Indians of the Jocko reservation had ever been friendly to the whites. Still, complaints were continually made that horses were stolen by them, that they set fire to the grass and woods in many places, sometimes on purpose that new and tender grass might spring up and young brushwood might grow, and sometimes through sheer carelessness. It was said in a report (1875) that only one white person had ever been killed on the Flathead reservation, and that the murder was committed by a Pen d'Oreille and not by a Flathead. He was quickly surrendered, tried, and executed.

Another accusation was that many of them drank liquor, and that, though he might not rob or murder, a Flathead when intoxicated was utterly wild, and in his drunken frenzy frightened the settlers in the hamlets where he resorted. A squaw-man, a cowboy, or a "sport" is bad enough when intoxicated, but nothing is so terror-inspiring as a drunken Indian! It is the same old story everywhere from generation to generation.

A year before our Nez Percé war reports were current that an outbreak on the part of some strange Indians who came every year over the mountains had long been feared by the citizens. The strangers came from Oregon and Idaho, equipped for the annual hunt of buffalo and other game, and large numbers of the Flatheads had been accustomed to join them as they crossed the Bitter Root Valley. The governor and all other white people knew how peaceably the Flatheads had always conducted themselves, but were in great dread lest they should enter into combination with the non-treaty Nez Percés, Spokanes, Cœur d'Alênes, and others, and so cause a general disturbance of the peace. The settlers had a perpetual dread of savage war.

It was upon such representations as these that the post of Missoula was finally established and maintained. The object of the post was to furnish soldiers to prevent all roaming by bands of Indians in that vicinity.

Agent Medary has recorded this remarkable statement: "An Indian will naturally work rather than starve, and if confined within the limits of his proper country he would have to turn his attention to some industrial pursuit." This is very much like the Spanish general Weyler's policy in Cuba. He established small reservations near the cities, called stations of concentration; he placed soldiers with arms in their hands close by to prevent non-combatants—old men, women, and children—from going outside of the prescribed limits, and held them there to starve and die.

The reservation process for the Flatheads was not, of course, so bad, because there was a possibility of their getting a living within the limits assigned. But it seems never to have occurred to many of our wise men that these people who had been accustomed for generations to get their living by hunting the buffalo, killing game, and selling peltries, could not immediately be transformed into gardeners and farmers.

For the feeding of cattle and the herding of horses, and the pasturing of large flocks of sheep, immense tracts of the rolling prairies of the West have been needed and taken by white men, and they have not hesitated to use freely the public domain. It would be a hardship which our white frontiersmen could not bear to shut them up together upon a ranch, however fertile, and keep them there by military force in order to convert them from shepherds and herders into successful farmers. They would in time doubtless come to it by some such pressure, especially if attended with a reasonable degree of starvation. Such inhumanity is plain when whites and not Indians are concerned.

I notice, in one treaty with the Flatheads, that Arlee, their chief, in many talks with our Indian inspectors, referred to the Garfield agreement (1872). He claimed that six hundred bushels of wheat, guaranteed to be delivered to his people the first year after their removal to the reservation, had never been provided. By referring to the instrument it may be seen that the superintendent of Indian affairs for Montana was to furnish the six hundred bushels of wheat in question. He did not do it. I wonder if this also was a starvation policy to benefit the Indians by withholding from them seed and sustenance, so as further to drive them into habits of industry!

I feel more strongly than ever that our reservation method is not the best in dealing with Indians who have always been self-supporting, and that a starvation process is wicked and foolish, and must end in failure.

The Jocko reservation furnishes another object lesson. It is in the education of children. An agent says: "The education of girls alone might be a greater benefit if it were not certain that they would finally marry ignorant Indians and soon lapse into semi-barbarism. . . . If boys alone were instructed they would make better use of their acquirements; if they should marry uneducated girls they would take pride in imparting their knowledge to them."

These statements suggest the thought: how very neglectful of duty is our government in not providing that all the children shall be educated. Education, and not the squalor, degradation, and utter demoralization that go with a starvation policy, is the only relief in sight for these superb Flathead Indians, who are really eager to learn the white man's ways. The treaty Nez Percés, whom they most resemble, are considerably in advance of them, but the slavery of a reservation constantly checks and represses them.

If years ago the Flatheads could have had the privileges that the white men of Idaho enjoy,—the privileges of land ownership, self-government, and education, which are the common privileges of citizenship,—they would now be abreast of the most advanced Indians in the Indian Territory. For years they were allowed to elect their head chief, who was to help the agent. They did it well and counted it a great privilege, but even this small help toward self-government was taken from them. The reservation system is a system under which the Indian people can never make much progress. It is a system plainly for the benefit of white men, —settlers and Indian employees.

How hard it is for our lawmakers to shake off prejudice and break up the unhappy complications of years, and establish a government for the Indians that will assure to them the same rights, privileges, and responsibilities that other people have! Here is a work for some patriotic and far-seeing young statesman to inaugurate.

## CHAPTER XXXVI.

### LIFE AND EXPERIENCES AMONG THE WARLIKE SIOUX — SOME DANGEROUS CHARACTERS.

My New Field of Duty — The Fierce and Warlike Sioux — Some of Their Influential Chiefs — Interviewing the Brulés — Indian Police — Fine Physical Specimens of Indians — The Wife of Lone Wolf — Honoring My Arrival at the Rosebud Agency — Attending the Omaha Dance — A Characteristic Indian Performance — Getting Ready for the Sun Dance — The Country Inhabited by the Sioux — In the Bad Lands — How the Sioux were Fed and Clothed — Their Delight in War and Pillage — The Mischief-making Dreamers — Dangerous Character of Sitting Bull — Raising Up False Messiahs — Frenzied Indian Dancers.

I HAD been six years in the great Department of the Northwest when President Hayes, after his visit, decided to transfer me to the East. Just at that time there was quite a ferment at West Point, occasioned by a colored cadet named Whittaker, who claimed to have been badly maltreated and wounded by some of his fellow cadets, many of whom insisted that the wounds were inflicted by his own hands. The President seemed to think that I was the one to settle such a complicated case, and this feeling doubtless hastened my orders.

I arrived at the Military Academy in the winter of 1880 and 1881, and was retained there almost two years. Late in the fall of 1882, being relieved from West Point when it ceased to be a department, I was assigned to the Department of the Platte, which at that time included Iowa, Nebraska, Wyoming, Utah, and part of Idaho, with headquarters at Omaha. This brought me in contact with the Indian tribes east of the Rocky Mountains and north of Kansas, and also with Indians who did not live or have their hunting-grounds in the Platte country, but who frequently passed back and forth over that part of our domain.

The Sioux were the first to receive my special attention. I had two forts near them, one at Niobrara near the Rosebud agency, the other, Fort Robinson, being near the Pine Ridge agency. The Indians that were gathered at Fort Niobrara and upon the reservation were mostly Brulé Sioux. Crow Dog and Short Bull were their principal chiefs. Upon the Pine Ridge reservation—extensive enough in acres if not rich in fertility—were gathered the Ogalala Sioux. Red Cloud, Short Bull, Spotted Tail, and Crazy Horse were among the chiefs who exerted great influence at that time.

Taking with me the commanding officer of Fort Niobrara, and Lieutenant Charles G. Treat, an aide-de-camp, with a few civilian friends, I went to the headquarters of Agent Wright to interview the Brulés. There was no special trouble amongst them at that time, but the agent, who had only just assumed his duties, was evidently a little uncertain how to deal with his charge. I found that the same old struggle between Indian customs and the white man's ways was still rife. Their Indian police was not yet efficient. The agent had not succeeded in enlisting Indians of good repute in the tribe, and Indian opposition was so strong that he found it somewhat difficult to enforce his authority.

At a later day, both at this agency and at Pine

Ridge, some full-blooded Indians expressed a willingness to join the police force for pay. After that the agent had something besides his own will to strengthen his rule among them. Probably,—under the reservation system—there never was a better or more conservative method than the organization and use of Indian police, for the chief of police, when well selected, was soon recognized as the strongest chief in the tribe.

The Brulés were the finest physical specimens of Indians that I had yet seen. Their chiefs usually wore their hair long, parted in the middle, and falling upon their shoulders. They were not so particular in their dress as the Flatheads or the Nez Percés. The chief's rank was indicated by one or more feathers standing erect in his hair, a breast-plate of porcupine quills, and sometimes a fur or skin jacket ornamented in various ways. Ordinarily all these Indians wore trousers, but their feet were shod with moccasins instead of shoes; a showy blanket to throw on and off at will completed the outfit.

The wife of Lone Wolf wore her hair quite neatly arranged, with small braids on each side of her head, while several ornaments dangled from the back part of her ears. She wore a jacket or shirt made of buckskin ornamented with rows of small shells. On her arm she carried a handsome blanket, and around her neck were two or three strings of beads.

The Indians desired to honor the occasion of my arrival at the Rosebud, so they obtained from Agent Wright permission to come to the agency and give a dance on a beautiful plateau near the agent's quarters. It was midsummer, so we could all sit round out-of-doors among the non-dancing Indians and look on. The dance, which they said was the dance of peace, was by them called the "Omaha Dance," and was performed altogether by the males. Most of the Indians who took part were naked, except for the breech-cloth, and various ornaments, made of feathers, wings of birds, or evergreen branches, worn upon their heads or hanging around their necks. The dancers were fantastically painted from head to foot.

We could not trace anything very distinctive in the dance, nor very well interpret what it meant. They used the same odd steps characteristic of nearly all Indian dances. The men, when together, retained sufficient space for individual movement. A man would take two steps first with one foot and then with the other, then putting his hands together he would bend down and look on the ground as if eagerly searching for something, all the time keeping step with the beat of the tom-toms. The antics of one Indian were not always like those of another. One would indicate the chase and represent a deer, antelope, or buffalo, and others would represent wild geese, turkeys, or ducks.

After most of the dancers had ceased their performance, one—sometimes two or three—would jump up and dance for a long time, going through with all kinds of movements and gyrations, and looking down, and up, and off. Mingled with the sound of the tom-tom was the incessant chanting of the lookers-on, who sat with their heads thrown

WARRIORS CHARGING AROUND THE SUN POLE.—A SCENE AT THE GREAT SUN DANCE.

back. The chant was participated in to some extent by the dancers, but they confined themselves mostly to punctuating it with whoops and yells, which made the dance, though intended to symbolize peace, almost as startling as that which portended war.

The next day, hearing that the Indians were assembling for a large summer encampment, and in fact that a camp of several thousand Indians, mostly Sioux, was already located and many lodges erected, a company of us proceeded to the grounds. On reaching them we found that the Indians were busy making preparations for a great sun dance, which was to take place the following day. Our interpreter explained how the dance was to be performed, and showed me the level piece of ground in the midst of the encampment which had been set apart for it.

The detail of the dance, which I did not care to see, was sufficiently described by an Indian chief through the interpreter. The chief said he was opposed to the sun dance, but his Indians would be filled with grief if it should be stopped.

I had already heard much about the sun dance and had done all in my power to discourage the Indians from the self-inflicted tortures incident to it, but I had not yet used the troops to prevent it. Such an act on my part would have done no good at that time, but might have provoked another Indian uprising; indeed, the Sioux were a people free from fear, and, being ever ready for war, were not easily mastered by force.

The Sioux occupied that portion of the United

States lying between the Mississippi River and the Rocky Mountains north of the fortieth parallel of latitude. Their lands were drained by the great Missouri River and its many tributaries. Their reserved lands, early set apart for them, have gradually been made smaller and smaller until upwards of thirty thousand Sioux inhabit a tract of country called "The Sioux Reservation," which contains about thirty-five thousand square miles of territory. Much of this is grass-covered rolling prairie, with timber along the creeks and rivers. The soil is alluvial and through it the streams have cut deep ravines, and the country is everywhere much broken. In some places are apparently underlying deposits of coal; such portions are called the Bad Lands, being exceedingly rough and incapable of producing much vegetation. The reservation now occupied by the Sioux is what remains of that allotted to them by treaty nearly forty years ago. Whenever the reservation has been reduced the United States has been the purchaser of the portion surrendered.

As soon as the buffalo was extinct and game of all kinds scarce, it became necessary to furnish the Indians with clothing and food, and to assist and encourage them in everything that would contribute to their self-support. The emergency, in fact, came too suddenly for the Indians to begin the new life with much hope of success, so that the feeding and clothing was done by collecting the Sioux in groups at several points within their reservation. Each camp was placed under the care of a civil agent, who was charged not only with feeding the Indians, but also with their instruction in the peaceful arts. There are now five Sioux agencies, or groups, from one to two hundred miles from each other, viz.: Standing Rock, Cheyenne River, Brulé, Rosebud, and Pine Ridge. I found at these agencies two distinct classes of Indians, the progressive and those who have long resisted progress, i. e., the reactionary.

The progressive Indians were willing to till the land, live quietly and honestly, and were more or less Christianized. The reactionaries were at all times subject to excitement, and delighted in war and pillage. From time to time they made raids against other Indians, with now and then a hostile expedition against white settlers.

Over this turbulent element there arose in every camp the spirit-leader, sometimes called a "Dreamer," and among the Indians farther west a "*tooat*." Sitting Bull, an Indian of large capacity and great energy, rose to power by becoming a chief and a Dreamer. He was at last allowed by the Indians to exercise supreme command, as was shown in the bloody massacre of General Custer and his command during the summer of 1876. The Messiah craze, to which I have several times alluded, and which all the Dreamers believed in, was taken advantage of by Sitting Bull and men like him to divide the Indians and excite them to fanatical enthusiasm, and his adherents were ever ready to carry out his evil machinations. Sitting Bull's death did not pacify the wilder Sioux. It only increased the terror of the timid and infuriated those who had already been intoxicated by the weird ghost dance. He was a dangerous character, and his death was really a benefit to all the Sioux, and much more so to the white settlers of South Dakota and Nebraska.

White people are sometimes led into extreme enthusiasm and behold a Messiah coming in *propria persona,* and they have at times done extravagant things at which the worldly-wise have jeered and laughed. Some satanic agencies delight in raising up false Messiahs and false Christs, so that good and well-disposed people are deceived.

The Pi-Ute Indian who started the wild theory of the coming of the Messiah who should restore Indian supremacy, walked a thousand miles to carry it from tribe to tribe. He encouraged the wild ghost dance that grew fiercer and more frenzied under his teaching. One might as well have asked the untamed lion not to roar, or the tigress robbed of her young not to spring upon the robber, as to ask the wild Sioux to keep the peace after their old dances and new ghost dances had stirred them up and roused all the fierceness of their untamed nature.

# CHAPTER XXXVII.

## THE MESSIAH CRAZE AMONG THE SIOUX — INDIAN DREAMERS AND THE GHOST DANCE — FRONTIER TRAGEDIES.

The Messiah Craze — The Real Message and How it Originated — Urged to Wild Frenzy by the Dreamers — "We Will Always be Indians" — White Men's Broken Promises — Bad Influence of Land Boomers and Speculators — "Indians are Coming!" — How Indian Wars Were Often Started — Causes of the Great Sioux Outbreak — Big Foot's Band of Warriors — The Battle of Wounded Knee Creek — Indiscriminate Slaughter of Indians — Death of Lieutenant Casey — The Horrors of Indian War — Another Side of the Story — Murder of Few Tails — Sad Journey of a Wounded Indian Woman.

A PERSONAL witness speaking of the "Messiah craze" said: "The delusion has taken possession of the wilder portion of the Indians. The leaders have invigorated old heathen ideas with snatches of Christian truth, and managed to excite an amount of enthusiasm which is amazing. They teach that the Son of God will presently appear as the avenger of the wild Indians; the earth will shiver and a great wave of new earth will overspread the face of the world and bury all the whites and Indians who imitate their ways, while the real Indians will find themselves on the surface of the new earth, basking in the light. The old Indian customs will all be restored in primitive vigor and glory, and the buffalo, antelope, and deer will return."

The turmoil and bloodshed that followed what was called the Messiah craze among the Sioux created the idea that the Indian who first promulgated the doctrine and styled himself a "prophet,"—commonly called by other Indians the Messiah,—taught that the Indians were to rise from the dead, and that living Indians were to help them put to death all white men, after which the Indian hunting grounds were to be restored to them in their primal condition; but the actual message from the prophet, as it came to the Comanche, Wichita, and Arapaho agencies, was in effect: "You must do right. Do no harm to any one. Do right always."

Wovoka was a Pi-Ute, living in Nevada about forty miles from Walker Lake. Some years ago he was stricken with a severe fever, which was followed at intervals by trances. While he was ill there was an eclipse of the sun, whereupon he declared that "when the sun died" he fell asleep in the daytime and was taken up to heaven.

Out of his disordered imagination, caused, no doubt, by his sickness, and the effects upon him and his people of the eclipse, were derived his alleged revelations. When we read the full text of his message, which he said the Lord wanted him to deliver to the Indians, we find nothing which should have harmful or injurious consequences.

The free rendering of the message sent by him to other Indians (given in Powell's 14th Annual Report) shows the nature and extent of what Wovoka (or Jack Wilson) the prophet desired to communicate. Here is all of it:

"When you get home you must make a dance to continue five days. Dance four successive nights, and the last night keep up the dance until the morning of the fifth day, when

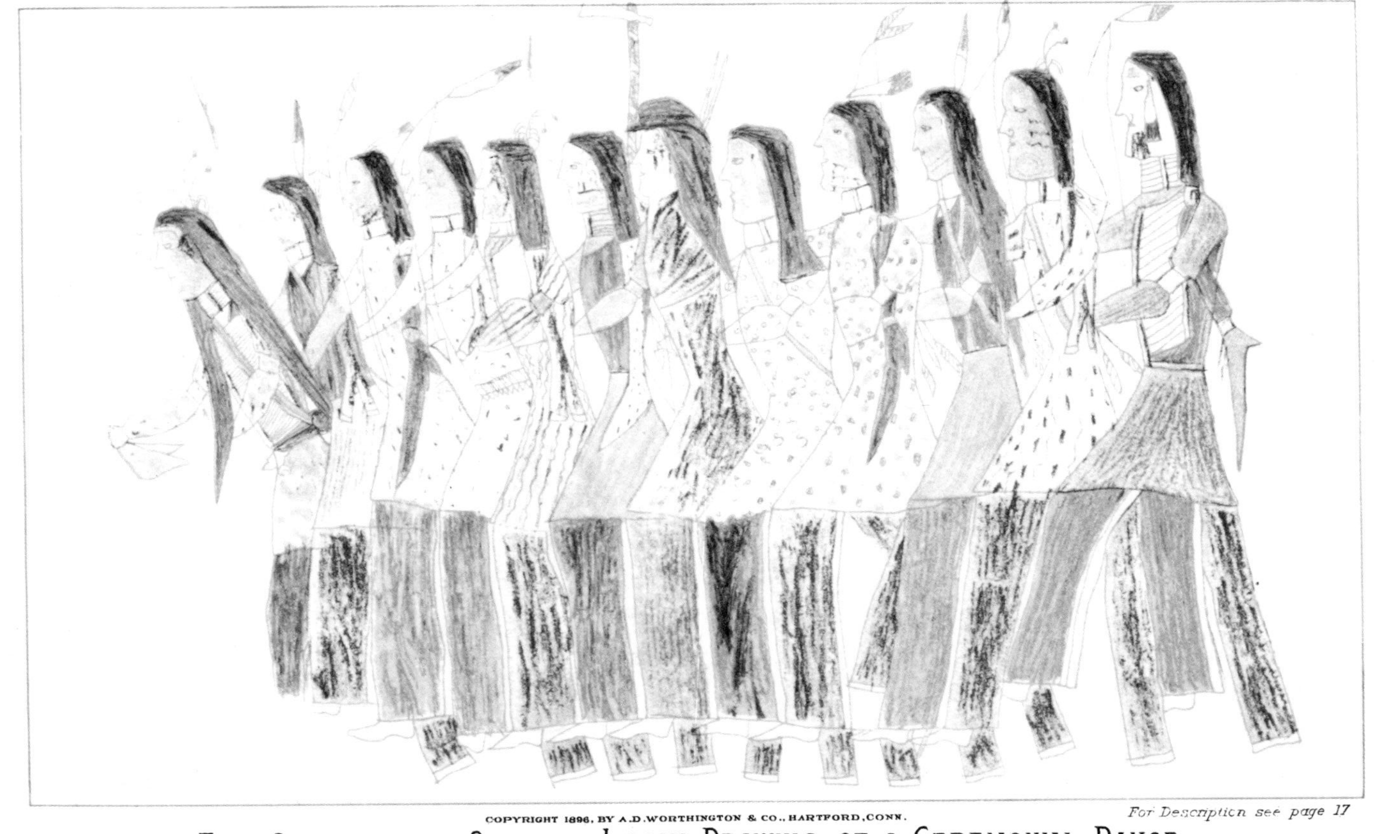



For Description see page 17

FAC-SIMILE OF AN ORIGINAL INDIAN DRAWING OF A CEREMONIAL DANCE.

Shows facial decoration Drawn with colored crayons and pencils by Big Back, a Cheyenne.

EXACT REPRODUCTION OF THE ORIGINAL IN DRAWING AND COLORING.

all must bathe in the river and then disperse to their homes. You must all do in the same way.

"I, Jack Wilson, love you all, and my heart is full of gladness for the gifts you have brought me. When you get home I shall give you a good cloud (rain), which will make you feel good. I give you a good spirit and give you all good paint. I want you to come again in three months, some from each tribe there (the Indian Territory).

"There will be a good deal of snow this year and some rain. In the fall there will be such a rain as I have never given you before.

"Grandfather (a universal title of reverence among Indians and here meaning the Messiah) says, when your friends die you must not cry. You must not hurt anybody or do harm to any one. You must not fight. Do right always. It will give you satisfaction in life. This young man has a good father and mother. (Possibly this refers to Casper Edison, the young Arapaho who wrote down the message of Wovoka for the delegation.)

"Do not tell the white people about this. Jesus is now upon the earth. He appears like a cloud. The dead are all alive again. I do not know when they will be here, maybe this fall or in the spring. When the time comes there will be no more sickness and every one will be young again.

"Do not refuse to work for the whites and do not make any trouble with them until you leave them. When the earth shakes (at the coming of the new world) do not be afraid. It will not hurt you.

"I want you to dance every six weeks. Make a feast at the dance and have food that everybody may eat. Then bathe in the water. That is all. You will receive good words again from me some time. Do not tell lies."

The ghost dance and the ghost shirt were not instituted by Wovoka. There is nothing in the above to warrant any wicked conduct. On the contrary, if this teaching had been even partly followed, I believe it would have led to better behavior among all the uncivilized tribes of the Indian Territory.

But behold the dancing picture! A lot of dancing, excited Indians, each dressed in a calico shirt, called "the mysterious shirt," cut very short like the army jacket, the Dreamers preaching while the Indians are singing and shouting, "The buffalo are coming! the buffalo are coming!" Then seizing each others' hands they go round and round in dizzy circles, becoming wilder and more frenzied until one after another of the dancers falls down unconscious. The medicine men declare these prostrate Indians dead, and announce that they are making a visit to the Great Spirit world, where they will meet the Son of God and all true Indians who have gone before. When these "dead" Indians are restored to life they naturally have wonderful stories to tell of their strange visions.

The good bishop of Dakota said that he looked upon this movement as the efforts of heathenism grown desperate in the attempt to recover its vigor and be reinstated. Many of the missionaries foretold that such a struggle among Indians would some time come. I was once in council with some wild Indians who believed in and practiced spiritism. They beat their tom-toms continuously around every sick man, woman or child, and listened to the voice of their medicine men. They questioned me very closely and said: "Will you give us schools, churches, farms, houses, and implements for all kinds of work, if we will do as you tell us?"

"Yes," I answered, "the government that I

represent will do all of that, and teach you to live as white men do."

"Now, General Howard," was the answer, "we tell you plainly that those are the very things we do not want. We want the earth to be as it is,—nothing should break up the surface of the earth. We will not have schools, nor churches, nor farms, nor white men's houses, nor their ways of living! We will always be Indians!" This was, indeed, the fundamental spirit that actuated every wild Indian in whose soul slumbered the fire of Indian manhood—a manhood after their ideas.

Of course, if the United States maintains the reservation system, there always will be secondary causes, as in the Sioux outbreak. For example: promises not speedily fulfilled, or, worse still, never fulfilled at all. For years the Sioux waited for the fulfillment of promises made by general officers, by United States commissioners, and government agents. After a pledge or promise of money it has always taken a long time to get the necessary appropriation through both Houses of Congress. No officer or agent can transfer his feelings of sympathy to our legislators. Often for years and years solemn pledges made to Indian tribes,—I state it with sorrow,—have remained unfulfilled.

The consent of the Sioux to the breaking up of their reservation was not unanimous on their part. The dissenters very soon found an opportunity to revenge themselves. Minorities among white men are at times dissatisfied and occasionally turbulent. A Sioux minority was sure to exceed the fervor of white men. When a citizen has a claim against the government he prosecutes it with patience and waits sometimes for many sessions of Congress for a decision and an appropriation. The reactionary Sioux could not be made to comprehend the reasons for such long periods of waiting. They interpreted them as resulting from forked tongues and bad hearts. For example, after the war of 1876, led by Sitting Bull, when certain Sioux were disarmed and deprived of their ponies, all who were not hostile were promised payment for their losses. That payment has never yet been made.

Another secondary cause came from ambitious white men living near the Sioux. A land boom ends disastrously and white men are "land poor." They try to mend their fortunes by encouraging the incoming of troops which, of course, is followed by the purchase of supplies and the circulation of more money. But these crafty speculators are easily thrown into a panic; they are afraid of a few drunken Indians who may be found at a brothel or saloon; their fears magnify the situation: "Indians are near! Indians are insolent! Indians are dancing! Indians are coming! they will wipe us out!" Governors, congressmen, and editors are appealed to. "Troops, troops, more troops!" they cry. The governor sends the militia or volunteers, and the government is obliged to bring up at least a few companies of regulars. During such a time money flows in and trade is quickened. Frontiersmen of the roughest kind, who have nothing to lose and everything to gain by such disturbances, get for a time congenial employment, and the means,

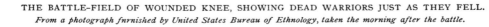

THE BATTLE-FIELD OF WOUNDED KNEE, SHOWING DEAD WARRIORS JUST AS THEY FELL.

*From a photograph fnrnished by United States Bureau of Ethnology, taken the morning after the battle.*

too often, for a renewal of their dissipated modes of living.

But some one asks: "Does this make war?" Yes, it does. The rumors are enough. Poor ranchmen far and near become terrified at the reports and rush with their families to the nearest settlement. The Indians also have heard these rumors, ten times exaggerated, so that the wild become wilder, and Indian women and children are blinded by the common terror. Ambitious young braves have a special inspiration and go off in small parties to steal cattle and horses, and murder whites indiscriminately. They return with their booty and display the scalps, followed by a scalp dance, and they become at once the lions of their tribe. Again and again peace councils have been overridden and savage war brought upon us, with all its sickening outrage and horror, by just such wickedness and folly; the mustard seed becomes a great tree. This was the case in the great Sioux outbreak.

Indian agents deserve some attention and kindly consideration. They have had hard and trying positions. They must have unusual ability and character to control a storm at such times. Doubtless some are not suited to their work, and some are not wise governors, but I have found among them true and very competent men. No one man, however, can quench the fire of a blazing house after it has passed beyond his control.

In my judgment, under the excitement of the Messiah craze and the ghost dances the agents at the five great centers of the Sioux nation would have been more than human to have maintained peace without adequate help from the army.

Nor should the army be blamed for the frightful conflicts that occurred in the Sioux war. In this, as in every Indian war, the troops, except in small garrisons, were used as a last resort. The killing of Sitting Bull, and the bloody combats that followed, the rushing of the worst Indians to the famous Bad Lands, the urgent calls from neighboring villages and hamlets for arms and soldiers, the killing here and there of white men, then of one or two Indians—these stories came over the wires like successive waves of the ocean. This time more quickly than usual the troops, abundantly equipped, were called, and promptly transported to different points all around and upon the great reservation, occupied the agencies, and gradually drew nearer to the hostile camps.

At the very last the Seventh Cavalry, attempting to disarm Big Foot's band near Wounded Knee Creek, was suddenly, through the treachery of a single Indian and the fear and fierce hostility of others, brought into deadly conflict. Twenty-five of our soldiers were quickly slain and thirty-eight wounded. At least one hundred and fifty Indians perished, including women and children, and many others were maimed for life. Their bodies, frozen stiff from exposure to a Dakota blizzard, were buried a few days later in one long trench. In this battle Captain Wallace fell in death and several other officers received severe wounds. The worthy priest, Father Crafts, who had hastened from New York to use his known in-

THE BATTLE-FIELD OF WOUNDED KNEE AFTER THE BLIZZARD, THREE DAYS AFTER THE FIGHT, SHOWING INDIAN WOMEN AND CHILDREN JUST AS THEY FELL.

*From a photograph furnished by the United States Bureau of Ethnology.*

fluence with the Indians in the hope of restoring peace, fell mortally wounded. A little later, Lieutenant E. W. Casey, a most worthy and promising army officer, who had been with me instructing cadets but a few years before at the Military Academy was shot and killed while reconnoitering in front of a band of hostiles, by Plenty Horses, a Brulé Indian. Lieutenant Casey had distinguished himself in the command of Indian scouts, and given them instruction and discipline, and he firmly believed that he was beloved by them all.

Such is only a hint of the sad condition of affairs during the Sioux war, but the army went steadily on as usual to accomplish its work. The extensive field of operations was diminished little by little, while every inducement was offered, finally with success, to all friendly Indians to escape to the protection of the troops, and to all the hostiles, regardless of what they had done, to make a timely surrender.

The horrors of this Indian war, like all such, were terrible and revolting. The conflict was an unusual one and occurred contrary to all predictions.

We cannot fail to admire the courage and endurance displayed by our regular soldiers in these arduous campaigns. They constantly endured the rigors of the keenest cold, the thermometer often ranging thirty degrees below zero. They will always, as at Wounded Knee, give a dreadful reception to such enemies if they should renew the bloody contest, but there should always be enough of them to make success and victory so sure that every hostile Indian may recognize the fact, and realize the utter folly of beginning a conflict.

But there is sometimes another side to the story of these outbreaks besides the one that generally appears to us before and after an Indian war. Here is an example: A party of Ogalala Sioux, consisting of Chief Few Tails, a peaceable and quiet old Indian, his wife, far advanced in years, and another brave named One Feather, with his wife and two children,—one being a girl thirteen years old and another a babe,—had been out hunting in the Black Hills, and had a regular pass from the Indian agent. They were returning from a successful hunt, and camped for the night at the mouth of a creek.

Early in the morning they set out for Pine Ridge, but had proceeded only a few hundred yards when some concealed white men fired upon them. These white men, who were well known, had sent one of their number into the Indian camp as a messenger the evening before, so that they knew who the parties were, and had not the shadow of an excuse for their infamous conduct. Few Tails was slain at the first shot and the ponies attached to his wagon were killed. As his wife leaped to the ground she was twice wounded, but not fatally. One Feather, being considerably behind the chief, seeing what had happened, turned his wagon in another direction, telling his wife, who had just been shot, to drive for her life and try to save the children. He himself jumped upon a pony and skillfully stood off the murderers until his family had gone some distance.

As the wounded woman passed a settler's house more shots were fired at her, but fortunately she was not hit, and her husband speedily coming up placed himself between her and the new danger. One Feather kept on until his wagon ponies were exhausted; then, putting his two children upon one of his spare ponies and his crippled wife upon another, he continued the retreat rapidly enough to distance his pursuers, finally succeeding in bringing in his family to the cover of the troops at the agency. The old wife of the chief was unconscious for some time, but after regaining her senses the next morning she went to a settler's house only to be driven away. With great difficulty she pursued her lonely journey to the Bad Lands, and from there succeeded, after many weary days and nights, in reaching a military camp.

She said at the close of this terrible journey: "I had no blanket and my feet were swollen and I was ready to die. After I got to the tent a doctor came in, a soldier doctor, because he had straps on his shoulders, and washed me and treated me well."

It is said of Young-Man-Afraid-of-his-Horses, a prominent Sioux chief, that he objected to the surrender of the slayers of Lieutenant Casey and a herder by the name of Miller in these words: "No, I will not surrender them; if you will bring to me the white men who killed Few Tails I will deliver to you the Indians who killed the white soldier and the herder."

At one time, when Red Cloud was in his prime, he was a great leader among the Sioux, but during our last struggle with them, though he sympathized with the Dreamers and felt indignant at the non-fulfillment of promises on the part of our government agents, he stood aloof from the conflict and did not join in active operations against the troops. I saw him not long before this outbreak. He was considerably wrinkled with age, but had still a great abundance of black hair, parted in the middle and hanging down over his shoulders. He was dressed completely in citizens' clothing, including a shirt-front, collar, and necktie. His wife was with him. Her long hair fell in braids below her waist, and shell ornaments were pendent from her ears. Around her neck she wore what appeared to be a broad band made of porcupine quills. Her face was that of a woman in middle life, keenly observant, thoughtful in expression, and not unpleasant to look upon. Her husband's face when at rest was more forbidding, but indicated a strong character.

The Cheyenne and Sioux scouts, who had been carefully selected, had a remarkable history during this conflict. They were so true to what they had promised and so well led by their chief that everybody was pleased with them, and certainly no loyalty could be more thoroughly tried than was theirs under those circumstances. It is true that Lieutenant Casey, who had trusted the scouts, was killed, but it was by a Brulé Indian who belonged to the hostiles. The scouts, who were much affected by his death, were greatly attached to him and were ever ready to obey his slightest behest.

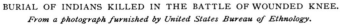

BURIAL OF INDIANS KILLED IN THE BATTLE OF WOUNDED KNEE.

*From a photograph furnished by United States Bureau of Ethnology.*

# CHAPTER XXXVIII.

## IN THE COUNTRY OF THE CHEYENNES — MASSACRE OF GENERAL CUSTER AND HIS COMMAND — A FRONTIER TRAGEDY.

The Fierce and Warlike Cheyennes — Chief Black Kettle — Brutal Massacre of Southern Cheyennes by White Troops — Retaliating on White Settlers — The Notorious Chief Sitting Bull — Dull Knife, the Cheyenne Chief — The Cheyennes and Sioux Join Forces — Annihilation of General Custer and His Command — A Tragedy that Shocked the Civilized World — General Terry's Account of the Battle — A Desperate and Bloody Fight — Horny Horse's Story of the Battle — Narrative of Chief Red Horse — Chief High Wolfe and His Necklace of Human Fingers — Arrival of General Terry's Relief Column — Appearance of Custer's Battlefield — Mutilating the Dead Bodies of Soldiers — Burial of the Dead.

THE great tribe of Cheyennes has for many years been divided into two bodies known as the Northern and the Southern Cheyennes. There is but little difference between them.

When we first knew them they were living in villages on the Cheyenne River. In early contests with the Sioux they were gradually pushed farther west, but were always found somewhere on the southern branches of the Yellowstone. The country immediately east of the Black Hills was the favorite location from which they started on their hunting expeditions.

The first treaty between the United States and the Cheyennes was made in 1825 near Fort Benton, at the mouth of the Teton River. The Cheyennes were then at peace with the Sioux, with whom they were so often allied, but they were constantly quarreling with the Pawnees and other distant tribes of Kansas and Nebraska, which shows how far from home they roamed. At that time their numbers altogether were recorded as three thousand two hundred and fifty.

The Cheyennes were, as a rule, friendly to all white settlers as late as 1862, and yet they made constant raids across their valleys far to the southward. After that time difficulties gradually sprang up between them and various mining prospectors, which finally culminated in open hostility and in fighting United States troops. During the Civil War the Southern Cheyennes were continually on the warpath and we had many battles with them. Finally peace was declared, but it was abruptly terminated by the indiscretion of Colonel Chivington of the First Colorado Cavalry, who, either believing or feigning to believe that the Southern Cheyennes were still on the warpath, came, in November, 1864, upon one of their villages located on what was known as Sand Creek in the southeastern part of Colorado.

The head of the village was Black Kettle, who, in accordance with instructions given by army officers during a recent peace council, was flying the United States flag above his lodge. Furthermore the bravest of the Cheyennes, thinking there was some mistake on the part of Chivington and his troops, confidently pointed to the flag as a sign of their loyalty and their desire for peace, but no attention was paid to them or their entreaty. Without a shadow of excuse the Colorado cavalry fired straight at them and into the Indian village, killing armed Indians, old men, women, and little children indiscriminately. The white volunteers furthermore treated their dead bodies with barbarity that no savages could have surpassed. They even carried off their scalps as evidence of their own infamous brutality.

The few that escaped from this slaughter carried the dreadful tidings to all the Southern Cheyennes and those Indians who were allied with them, and a horrible massacre followed of all settlers within their reach. The war that followed between the Southern Cheyennes and our troops continued with more or less virulence until 1867, when General Hancock checked it by burning the village of "the Dog soldiers,"— a band of young Cheyenne Indians who had some pretence to military organization and who committed frequent murderous raids and depredations accompanied by unusual ferocity. This blow was not severe enough, however, to wholly discourage them, and they soon continued the war and pushed it with more persistency than ever. General Custer followed them up as far as the borders of Colorado and defeated them in battle, killing Black Kettle and thirty-seven of his warriors.

Finally, in 1868, the Southern Cheyennes and their allies, the Arapahoes, were thoroughly beaten in southern Kansas by United States troops, and a large number of them were captured and sent to Camp Supply in the Indian Territory. Some stray villages of Cheyennes, however, remained ugly and defiant, and endeavored to preserve their independence and their roving habits. Finally, in

March, 1875, the remnants of the Southern Cheyennes, tired of constant warfare, came in and surrendered at Fort Sill, and, with the exception of a single outbreak, have since lived upon their present reservation in Oklahoma.

The Northern Cheyennes were even more fierce and warlike than the Southern branch. They lived in villages in the country north of the Black Hills. In 1876 they joined Sitting Bull and the Sioux, who were just then unusually hostile to the whites and to the government, and with them took a prominent part in the Custer massacre on the Little Big Horn River in July of that year.

Sitting Bull was a great medicine man and a regular Sioux chief who had early imbibed the religious ideas of the Dreamers which, as we have seen, was so nearly universal in its hold upon the minds and hearts of the different tribes that it may be called the principal tenet of their faith.

Mrs. Custer says: "The most powerful chief of the different bands was known by the title of Sitting Bull." She places him among those who from their youth entertained implacable hatred to the whites and stood out for the Indians' original habits of life. Individual Indians, who for one cause or another wished to leave a reservation, hastened to cast their lot with Sitting Bull or Crazy Horse of the Sioux or Dull Knife of the Cheyennes. At the beginning of his career Sitting Bull had but few lodges and not more than a hundred warriors, but before 1876 his village had become a large one; and Crazy Horse, with whom he now united, had at the start three times as many warriors as Sitting Bull. After Dull Knife and his Cheyennes had joined them, together with innumerable warriors from all the Sioux agencies, there were two or three thousand fighting Indians combined in the hostile camps, and Sitting Bull became the war chief of them all.

He was very reluctant to attend any council where white men were present. Mrs. Custer describes him as "a heavily built Indian, with a large massive head, and, strange to say, brown hair, unlike most Indians. He was heavily marked with smallpox." Sitting Bull's career as portrayed by himself in some Indian drawings shows him first as a young brave without special dress or insignia; another represents him in the act of killing a Crow Indian on a horse and securing his scalp. In each one of another series of sketches he is shown in the act of taking the life of Indians or of whites; in one he has captured herds of ponies; fifty-five drawings were boastful representations of robbery, murder, and theft. In writing of the noted chief Mrs. Custer records other characteristics of his. She said that he was an Indian of unusual powers of mind, and a warrior whose talent amounted to genius, while his stubborn heroism in defense of the last of his race was undeniable. Cruel he undoubtedly was, but that was from the instincts of his race; a general of the first natural order he must have been to have defied the United States as he did for more than ten years. That he was able to do this so long was owing to his skillful use of two advantages—a central position surrounded by the Bad Lands and the quarter of a circle of agencies from which he drew supplies and allies for every campaign.

I have a good picture of Sitting Bull as he appeared after the surrender at Fort Buford in the spring of 1877.

When this picture was taken he was forty years of age, but the deep and heavy wrinkles in his forbidding face gave the impression that he was nearer sixty. His features indicate strong character, power to plan, to act, and to persevere until what he undertook to do should be accomplished. There is no sign of tenderness or mercy in his countenance.

There are so many accounts of the Custer massacre, and Mrs. Custer's history is so thoroughly complete and good, that I need not attempt more than the briefest account of it, and this for the purpose of showing something of the part the Cheyennes took in that disastrous battle, and of giving the Indians' version of it, for not one of Custer's command survived to tell the story. This can be briefly done by extracts from General Terry's published story, which he wrote from the field the 27th of June, 1876:

"It is my painful duty to report that day before yesterday, the 25th inst., a great disaster overtook General Custer and the troops under his command. At twelve o'clock on the 22d he started with his whole regiment, and a strong detachment of scouts and guards, from the mouth of the Rosebud. Proceeding up that river about twenty miles he struck a very heavy Indian trail, which had previously been discovered, and pursuing found that it led, as was supposed, to the Little Big Horn River. Here he discovered a village (of Sioux and Cheyennes) of almost unexampled extent, and at once attacked it with that portion of his force which was immediately at hand. Major Reno, with three companies, A, G, and M, of the regiment, were sent into the valley of the stream at the point where the trail struck it. General Custer, with five companies, C, E, F, I, and L, attempted to enter it about three miles lower down. Reno forded the river, charged down its left bank, and dismounted and fought on foot until finally, completely overwhelmed by numbers, he was compelled to mount, recross the river, and seek a refuge on the high bluffs which overlook its right bank.

"Just as he recrossed Captain Benteen, who, with three companies, D, H, and K, was some two miles to the left of Reno when the action commenced, but who had been ordered by General Custer to return, came to the river, and rightly concluded that it would be useless for his force to attempt to renew the fight in the valley; he joined Reno on the bluffs. Captain McDougal, with his company, B, was at first at some distance in the rear with a train of pack-mules. He also came to Reno soon. This united force was nearly surrounded by Indians, many of whom, armed with rifles, occupied positions which commanded the ground held by the cavalry,—ground from which there was no escape. Rifle pits were dug and the fight was maintained, though with heavy loss, from about half past two o'clock of the 25th till six o'clock of the 26th, when the Indians withdrew from the valley, taking with them their village.*

"His (Custer's) trail (made by his horses) from the point where Reno crossed the stream passes along and in rear of the crest of the bluffs on the right bank for three miles, then it comes down to the bank of the river, but at once diverges from it as if he had unsuccessfully attempted to cross, then turns upon itself, almost completes a circle and closes. It is marked by the remains of his officers and men, the bodies of his horses, some of them dropped along the path, others heaped where halts appeared to have been made. There is abundant evidence that a gallant resistance was offered by the troops, but they were beset on all sides by overpowering numbers."

General Terry states the entire loss in that engagement as two hundred and fifty killed, and with Reno fifty-one men were wounded. Major Reno and Captain Benteen estimated the number of Indians engaged as not less than two thousand five hundred.

Captain John J. Bourke in his work "On the Border with Crook" relates some incidents as told by Indians who were in the fight. Horny Horse said: "Some lodges came out from Standing Rock agency and told us the troops were coming. The troops charged on the camp (village) before we knew they were there. The lodges were strung out about as far as from here to the Red Cloud agency slaughter-house (about two and a half miles). I was in the council-house with a lot of the

* General Terry knew at that time no details of the massacre, because not one of those who accompanied General Custer were living.

old men when we heard shots fired from up the river. The troops first charged from up the river. We came out of the council-house and ran to our lodges.

"All the young bucks got on their horses and charged the troops. All the old bucks and squaws ran the other way. We ran the troops back. Then there was another party of troops on the other side of the river. One half of the Indians pursued the first body of troops (Reno's), the other half went after the other body (Custer's). I didn't see exactly all the fight, but by noon all of one party (Custer's) were killed and the others driven back into a bad place. We took no prisoners. I did not go out to see the bodies, because there were two young bucks of my band killed in the fight and we had to look after them.

"We made the other party of soldiers (Reno's) cross the creek and run back to where they had their pack-train. The reason we didn't kill all this party (Reno's) was because while we were fighting his party we heard that more soldiers were coming up the river, so we had to pack up and leave. We left some good young men killed in that fight. We had a great many killed in the fight, and some others died of their wounds. I know that there were between fifty and sixty Indians killed in the fight. After the fight we went to Wolf Mountain, near the head of Goose Creek. Then we followed Rosebud down and then went over to Blue Stone Creek."

Dr. Charles E. McChesney, acting assistant surgeon United States army, communicated to the

Bureau of Ethnology at Washington a unique Indian account, both in carefully noted gesture-signs and in pictographs, of the battle of the Little Big Horn. These drawings were made and the account which accompanied them was given by Red Horse, a Sioux chief, and a prominent actor in the battle. His narrative, closely translated into simple English, is herewith given. The drawings were made on rough manilla paper, some of them with colored pencils. Some of these drawings are presented in this volume, not only as specimens of Indian art, but as a contribution from the Indian standpoint to our knowledge of Custer's last fight. Here is the story of Red Horse:

"Five springs ago, I, with many Sioux Indians, took down and packed up our tipis (tepees) and moved from Cheyenne River to the Rosebud River, where we camped a few days; then took down and packed up our lodges and moved to the Little Big Horn River and pitched our lodges with the large camp of Sioux.

"The Sioux were camped on the Little Big Horn River as follows: The lodges of the Uncpapas were pitched highest up the river under a bluff. The Santee lodges were pitched next. The Ogalalas' lodges were pitched next. The Brulé lodges were pitched next. The Minneconjoux lodges were pitched next. The Sans-Arcs lodges were pitched next. The Blackfeet lodges were pitched next. The Cheyenne lodges were pitched next. A few Arikara Indians were among the Sioux (being without lodges of their own). Two-Kettles (a tribe of Sioux), among the other Sioux (without lodges).

FACSIMILE OF AN INDIAN DRAWING BY RED HORSE, A SIOUX, SHOWING GENERAL CUSTER'S TROOPS CHARGING AN INDIAN CAMP IN THE BATTLE OF THE LITTLE BIG HORN.

*Reproduced from the original drawing by permission of United States Bureau of Ethnology.*

"I was a Sioux chief in the council lodge. My lodge was pitched in the center of the camp. The day of the attack I and four women were a short distance from the camp digging wild turnips. Suddenly one of the women attracted my attention to a cloud of dust rising a short distance from camp. I soon saw that the soldiers were charging the camp. To the camp I and the women ran. When I arrived a person told me to hurry to the council lodge. The soldiers charged so quickly we could not talk (council). We came out of the council lodge and talked in all directions. The Sioux mount horses, take guns, and go fight the soldiers. Women and children mount horses and go (meaning to get out of the way).

"Among the soldiers was an officer who rode a horse with four white feet. The Sioux have for a long time fought many brave men of different people, but the Sioux say this officer was the bravest man they had ever fought. I don't know whether this was General Custer or not. Many of the Sioux men that I hear talking tell me it was. I saw this officer in the fight many times, but did not see his body. It has been told me that he was killed by a Santee Indian, who took his horse. This officer wore a large-brimmed hat and a deerskin coat. This officer saved the lives of many soldiers by turning his horse and covering the retreat. Sioux say this officer was the bravest man they ever fought. I saw two officers looking alike, both having long yellowish hair.

"Before the attack the Sioux were camped on the Rosebud River. Sioux moved down a river running into the Little Big Horn River, crossed the Little Big Horn River, and camped on its west bank.

"This day (day of attack) a Sioux man started to go to Red Cloud agency, but when he had gone a short distance from camp he saw a cloud of dust rising and turned back and said he thought a herd of buffalo was coming near the village.

"The day was hot. In a short time the soldiers charged the camp. (This was Major Reno's battalion of the Seventh Cavalry.) The soldiers came on the trail made by the Sioux camp in moving, and crossed the Little Big Horn River above where the Sioux crossed, and attacked the lodges of the Uncpapas, farthest up the river. The women and children ran down the Little Big Horn River a short distance into a ravine. The soldiers set fire to the lodges. All the Sioux now charged the soldiers and drove them in confusion across the Little Big Horn River, which was very rapid, and several soldiers were drowned in it. On a hill the soldiers stopped and the Sioux surrounded them. A Sioux man came and said that a different party of soldiers had all the women and children prisoners. Like a whirlwind the word went around, and the Sioux all heard it and left the soldiers on the hill, and went quickly to save the women and children.

"From the hill that the soldiers were on to the place where the different soldiers (by this term Red Horse always means the battalion immediately commanded by General Custer, his mode of distinction being that they were a different body

FACSIMILE OF AN INDIAN DRAWING BY RED HORSE, A SIOUX, SHOWING THE SIOUX FIGHTING CUSTER'S BATTALION IN THE BATTLE OF THE LITTLE BIG HORN.

Red Horse was present at the battle. In his drawing he shows dead soldiers in the foreground with limbs and heads cut off. and the bodies otherwise mutilated. Bugles, hats, and flags are scattered around, some of the wounded cavalrymen are shown falling from their horses. Wounds are generally indicated by spots from which blood is flowing. One cavalryman is shot in the mouth with an arrow. The drawing will repay careful study.

*Reproduced from the original drawing by permission of United States Bureau of Ethnology.*

from that first encountered) were seen was level ground with the exception of a creek. Sioux thought the soldiers on the hill (i. e., Reno's battalion) would charge them in rear, but when they did not the Sioux thought the soldiers on the hill were out of cartridges. As soon as we had killed all the different soldiers the Sioux all went back to kill the soldiers on the hill. All the Sioux watched around the hill until a Sioux man came and said many walking soldiers were coming near. The coming of the walking soldiers was the saving of the soldiers on the hill. Sioux cannot fight the walking soldiers (infantry), being afraid of them, so the Sioux left.

"The soldiers charged the Sioux camp about noon. The soldiers were divided, one party charging right into the camp. After driving these soldiers across the river the Sioux charged the different soldiers (i. e., Custer's) below, and drove them in confusion; these soldiers became foolish, many throwing away their guns and raising their hands, saying: 'Sioux, pity us; take us prisoners.' The Sioux did not take a single soldier prisoner, but killed all of them; none were left alive for even a few minutes. These different soldiers discharged their guns but little. I took a gun and two belts off two dead soldiers; out of one belt two cartridges were gone, out of the other five.

"The Sioux took the guns and cartridges off the dead soldiers and went to the hill on which the soldiers were, surrounded, and fought them with the guns and cartridges of the dead soldiers. Had the soldiers not divided I think they would have killed many Sioux. The different soldiers (i. e., Custer's battalion) that the Sioux killed made five brave stands. Once the Sioux charged right in the midst of the different soldiers and scattered them all, fighting among the soldiers hand to hand.

"One band of soldiers was in the rear of the Sioux. When this band of soldiers charged the Sioux fell back, and the Sioux and the soldiers stood facing each other. Then all the Sioux became brave and charged the soldiers. The Sioux went but a short distance before they separated and surrounded the soldiers. I could see the officers riding in front of the soldiers and hear them shouting. Now the Sioux had many killed. The soldiers killed 136 and wounded 160 Sioux. The Sioux killed all these different soldiers in the ravine.

"The soldiers charged the Sioux camp farthest up the river. A short time after the different soldiers charged the village below. While the different soldiers and Sioux were fighting together the Sioux chief said: 'Sioux men, go watch the soldiers on the hill and prevent their joining the different soldiers.' The Sioux men took the clothing off the dead and dressed themselves in it. Among the soldiers were white men who were not soldiers. The Sioux dressed in the soldiers' and white men's clothing fought the soldiers on the hill.

"The banks of the Little Big Horn River were high, and the Sioux killed many of the soldiers while crossing. The soldiers on the hill dug up the ground (i. e., made earthworks), and the soldiers and Sioux fought at long range, sometimes the

Sioux charging close up. The fight continued at long range until a Sioux man saw the walking soldiers coming. When the walking soldiers came near the Sioux became afraid and ran away."

In this terrible engagement a large number of Cheyennes under Chief Dull Knife participated. He was seconded by Little Wolf and Standing Elk, two of his bravest warriors, and by High Wolf, who was a medicine man and a Dreamer. Of High Wolf Captain Bourke said: "He had been proud to wear as his pet decoration a necklace of human fingers, which he knew had fallen into my possession." Of this necklace I shall have more to say in another chapter.

On the morning after the battle the Indians resumed fighting and continued until late that day, when, on learning of the approach of General Terry's command, they hastily started for the Canadian frontier.

General Terry arrived too late to save Custer. But he brought relief to Major Reno and his troops, who had become separated at some distance from Custer, and was prevented by a great number of warriors from joining him. Reno was hemmed in by Indians, and but for the timely arrival of General Terry's command his troops would certainly have shared Custer's fate. Of the arrival of General Terry Captain Godfrey, who was with Reno, and whose account of what happened was published in the *Century* magazine, says:

"About 9.30 A. M. a cloud of dust was observed several miles down the river. The assembly was sounded, the horses were placed in a protected situation, and camp kettles and canteens were filled with water. An hour of suspense followed, but from the slow advance we concluded that they were our own troops. 'But whose command is it?' We looked in vain for a gray-horse troop; it could not be Custer; it must then be Crook, for if it was Terry, Custer would be with him. Cheer after cheer was given for Crook. A white man, Harris, I think, soon came up with a note from General Terry, addressed to General Custer, dated June 26th, stating that two of our Crow scouts had given information that our column had been whipped and nearly all had been killed; that he did not believe their story, but was coming with medical assistance. The scout said that he could not get to our lines the night before, as the Indians were on the alert. Very soon after this Lieutenant Bradley, Seventh Infantry, came into our lines and asked where I was. Greeting most cordially my old friend, I immediately asked, 'Where is Custer?' He replied, 'I don't know, but I suppose he was killed, as we counted one hundred and ninety-seven dead bodies. I don't suppose any escaped.' We were simply dumbfounded. This was the first intimation we had of his fate. It was hard to realize; it did seem impossible.

"General Terry and staff and officers of General Gibbon's column soon after approached, and their coming was greeted with prolonged hearty cheers. The grave countenance of the general awed the men to silence. The officers assembled to meet their guests. There was scarcely a dry eye, hardly a word was spoken, but quivering of lips

THE KNOLL ON THE BATTLE-FIELD OF THE LITTLE BIG HORN WHERE GENERAL CUSTER AND HIS MEN FELL AND WERE BURIED.

The cross marks the spot where General Custer fell. Gravestones mark the places where some of his soldiers fell around him. General Custer's monument is at the top of the knoll. One hundred and ninety-two soldiers killed in this battle are buried on this spot.

SOLDIERS' CEMETERY ON CUSTER'S BATTLE-FIELD.

The remains of one hundred and six soldiers massacred by Indians at Fort Phil Kearney were removed to Custer's battle-field and buried on this spot. The white spots in the distance mark places where some of Custer's men fell at the battle of the Little Big Horn.

and hearty grasping of hands gave token of thankfulness for the relief and grief for the misfortune. . . .

"On the morning of the 28th we left our intrenchments to bury the dead of Custer's command. The morning was bright, and from the high bluffs we had a clear view of Custer's battle-field. We saw a large number of objects that looked like white boulders scattered over the field. Glasses were brought into requisition, and it was announced that these objects were the dead bodies. Captain Weir exclaimed, 'Oh, how white they look!'

"All the bodies, except a few, were stripped of their clothing. According to my recollection nearly all were scalped or mutilated, but there was one notable exception, that of General Custer, whose face and expression were natural; he had been shot in the temple and in the left side. Many faces had a pained, almost terrified expression. It is said that Rain-in-the-Face, a Sioux warrior, has gloried that he had cut out and had eaten the heart and liver of one of the officers. Other bodies were mutilated in a disgusting manner. The bodies of Dr. Lord and Lieutenants Porter, Harrington, and Sturgis were not found, at least not recognized. The clothing of Porter and Sturgis was found in the village, and showed that they had been killed. We buried, according to my memoranda, two hundred and twelve bodies."

## CHAPTER XXXIX.

### GENERAL MACKENZIE'S FIGHT WITH THE NORTHERN CHEYENNES — A NIGHT ATTACK ON AN INDIAN CAMP — INDIAN BRAVERY — A STORY OF TERRIBLE SUFFERING.

"The Bravest Tribe of Indians on this Continent" — Crazy Horse and His Band of Sioux — Dull Knife and His Fierce Cheyennes — Indian Scouts and Allies — Searching for Camps of Hostile Indians — Sitting Bear and His White Flag — MacKenzie's Search for the Cheyenne Village — Campaigning with the Thermometer Thirty Degrees Below Zero — Night Attack on the Unsuspecting Cheyennes — Death of Lieutenant McKinney — Examples of Reckless Bravery — Setting Fire to the Indian Village — Relics of the Custer Massacre — Unparalleled Sufferings of the Indians — Women and Children Frozen to Death — End of a Bitter War.

THE Northern Cheyennes have been called "the bravest tribe of Indians on this continent," but they were completely crushed by General Ranald S. MacKenzie in a fierce fight in the foothills of the Big Horn Mountains, when Dull Knife lost his power and his desire ever to fight the whites again.

I knew MacKenzie when he was a cadet at West Point. He was in a class that I taught which entered the Military Academy in 1858 and finished its course in 1862. During the Civil War he displayed an ability, dash, and courage, especially in the cavalry service, which constantly brought him into notice, and while his health continued there was no more reliable commander for a district or an active campaign.

During the winter of 1876 General Crook was commanding the Department of the Platte. As a consequence of the Custer massacre, and the fights which the troops were constantly engaged in with the Indians in Crook's and Terry's geographical departments, the spirit of the hostiles had not been broken, but had grown even more confident and determined. For the winter season the Indians had, as usual, separated into villages and pitched their lodges in some sheltered ravines among the foothills of the Big Horn Mountains. Crazy Horse had a large body of Sioux somewhere on the tributaries of the Big Horn, while Dull Knife had a smaller village of Northern Cheyennes.

General Crook, who had more experience in Indian warfare than any of our general officers, thought it would be wise to strike the Indians in a winter campaign, where our troops would have the advantage of being better prepared for moving and for resisting the terrific cold of Wyoming and Montana.

General Crook fixed upon Fort Fetterman, famous in our annals for Indian battles of the past, as the place for gathering his troops. Here he assembled eleven companies of cavalry under MacKenzie and eleven of infantry and four of artillery under Colonel Richard I. Dodge.

General Crook was especially successful in securing Indian allies, who were always more effective than whites as scouts, and very often acted no small part in battle. He drew for this campaign large quotas from the friendly Sioux, Cheyennes, Pawnees, Arapahoes, and Shoshones, with a few

Bannocks and Nez Percés. These he had at the start. A little later the Crows added a considerable contingent, which joined his expedition about ninety miles ahead, near old Fort Reno. The strength of his command was then, all told, about nineteen hundred men,—fifteen hundred white troops and four hundred Indian scouts. The scouts were not a single body by themselves, but were divided into detachments, and over each detachment was placed an army officer who had the confidence of the Indians and considerable knowledge of the country. These Indian scouts were picked men and could not be excelled by any of the hostiles in bravery, energy, or endurance.

General Crook was to use wagons as far as he could conveniently take them, but beyond that he depended upon his pack train. The pack trains, so essential beyond wagon transportation, were in charge of a competent and experienced man, and in men, material, mules, and discipline were as complete as any company of the expedition.

I seem to see the column as it drew out from Fetterman, where, as the historian says: "The scene was certainly most picturesque and full of animation; everything moved like clockwork. Each man, horse, wagon, and mule was in proper place." A reasonably comfortable march, considering the extreme cold, was made, averaging about twenty-five miles a day. The Indian scouts were kept out many miles to the right and left and front. Nothing escaped their observation. When they met prospectors, white horse thieves, or Indians, they promptly galloped in and reported.

General Crook thought at this time that the principal hostile Sioux village, under Crazy Horse, was on the Rosebud toward the Big Horn Mountains, and a search was begun for it. As they were marching along Sitting Bear, a friendly Cheyenne scout, appeared carrying a white flag. He had just come from the Red Cloud agency and was on his way to try to secure a surrender from Crazy Horse before a battle should be brought on. He brought important information; it was to the effect that there was a large Cheyenne village somewhere near the sources of the fork on which they were moving, and not far away. It was situated in a deep and well-sheltered ravine, but was only to be seen on close approach. The Cheyennes were in ignorance that their camp had been discovered.

Crook's objective was Crazy Horse, but on receiving this information he instantly changed his plans. The exact location of the Cheyennes was not known to the scouts, but they immediately proceeded cautiously up Crazy Woman's Fork. MacKenzie was detached with his cavalry and a part of the scouts to find the Cheyenne village, while Crook kept with him the remainder of the command. On the 23d of November MacKenzie marched in the direction of the Cheyenne camp. His Indian allies soon were far ahead, and preceding all by eight or ten miles, was a very small detachment of Indian scouts, selected with special reference to their knowledge of this section of country, their coolness, good judgment and experience in war.

The cold was becoming more and more intense; often at night the thermometer ranged as low as thirty degrees below zero. After their first bivouac the cavalry, as they struggled along, had great difficulty in passing deep-cut ravines, dry enough at the time, but filled with rushing water in the springtime. The banks were then steep and frozen solid, so that they had to be cut through in order to get down to the bottom and ascend the other side. While MacKenzie was doing this and keeping his command well closed up, the advance scouts came rushing back with news that the much sought Cheyenne village was very near. Two of the scouts, Red Shirt and another Indian, remained at the front, hiding among the crags that overlooked the village.

MacKenzie did not hasten. He waited till the moon would give him sufficient light to work his way up the ravine of Willow Creek to the village. Bourke, who was present, says: "All night we groped our way, floundering, slipping, struggling over smooth knolls of glassy surface, making the slowest kind of progress but still advancing. Not a word was spoken above a whisper. Not a match was lighted, and the soldier's faithful friend—his pipe—was not allowed outside the saddle bag."

At last a halt was called. The Indian scouts and all the cavalry were formed and ready for the word. MacKenzie left no time for anxious suspense. The Cheyennes were not asleep. The sound of their tom-toms and the shouts of dancers could be distinctly heard. They were indulging in a grand war dance in honor of a victory over a party of Shoshones.

The word "gallop" was given and the cavalry

rushed forward in a terrific charge up the ravine, which opened wider as it came to the lodges strewn for some two or three hundred yards along the creek. The hostile Cheyennes had barely time enough before the cavalry was actually upon them to run off their old men, women, and children, with whatever clothes they had on, to shelter among the steep crags and behind protecting rocks and trees, while some of the warriors, hastily grasping their rifles and ammunition, ran to the nearest cover.

The shouting of white men and the yelling of Indian scouts made a fearful din, but the hostiles quickly crept into positions of such great strength as to check MacKenzie's advance. Seeing a strong defensive bed of rocks and crags held by the hostiles, MacKenzie ordered Lieutenant John A. McKinney to carry it with his company. McKinney made a gallant charge, but his horse was wounded and he was slain, and several of his men were killed or wounded. Other officers of his regiment brought their companies to his assistance, while the Indian scouts gradually worked up and occupied a higher peak. From there they delivered a descending fire upon the Cheyennes' position and it was soon taken. Other scouts, under good leadership, had gathered nearly all the herd of horses belonging to the Cheyennes.

It was evident that MacKenzie had won his battle, but the Cheyennes would not surrender. One of the friendly scouts succeeded in reaching and talking with Dull Knife, the principal chief of the hostile Cheyennes, who asserted that he had lost three of his children in the battle and that he himself would like to give up, but that Little Wolf, Old Bear, Grey Head, Roman Nose, and other leading Indians would not consent. To the friendly Cheyennes some of the hostiles cried out: "Go home, you have no business here. We can whip the white soldiers alone, but can't fight you too!" They stated also that they were sure of getting help from Crazy Horse.

The reckless bravery displayed by some of the Cheyennes, even after the contest was hopeless, is remarkable. One brave, wearing the war bonnet of a chief and carrying a buffalo hide shield, rode out defiantly into the open. He was fired at from every direction by the troops, but none of the bullets reached him. He laughed at his Indian foes and derided them, when a lieutenant, taking steady aim, hit him, and he fell dying from his horse.

In the midst of the tumult that followed the fall of this bold warrior a young brave, a friend of the fallen, mounted on a swift pony, rushed from the midst of the hostile Cheyennes; he also carried a shield of buffalo hide, and one that proved to be of extraordinary hardness. This fearless young brave directed his horse toward his fallen friend. The air was full of hissing bullets. Faster and faster horse and rider went, and both seemed to have a charmed life, for nothing touched him or his steed. Dismounting he lifted the body of his friend and threw it across the pony in front of the pommel, then remounting moved slowly back to where his comrades were defending the rocks and crags. When he had almost reached the safety of a ravine several bullets pierced him

PLENTY HORSES. LITTLE CHIEF STARVING ELK.

NOTED CHEYENNE INDIANS IN THEIR WILD STATE.

*From photographs furnished by United States Bureau of Ethnology from negatives made many years ago on government expeditions.*

through and through, and he, too, dropped from his horse dead.

General MacKenzie now believed it the wisest policy to utterly wipe out the Cheyenne village. Two troops of cavalry were assigned to this work and it took them the entire night to destroy the Indian camp, with plenty of fuel gathered and at hand to aid the burning. There were two hundred lodges, some being covered with large buffalo skins to make them comfortable during the bitter cold of winter. There was plenty of ammunition, an immense supply of buffalo meat, and other provisions, fur robes and peltries of every description, together with hammers, knives, spades, shovels, picks, axes, and innumerable utensils.

What arrested the special attention of the officers were the hundreds of articles that had been captured in the Custer massacre. Among them were personal articles of value, with the names of the slain officers upon them; and letters were found that had been written by some of Custer's men just before the massacre and were ready for mailing.

The large number of valuable fur robes, beautifully ornamented, and the great amount of Indian furniture destroyed on that night shows that the Cheyennes had already accumulated considerable wealth, together with much that belonged to civilization. With the exception of a few articles stolen by some of the Indian scouts, everything was consumed.

MacKenzie's losses were one commissioned officer and six enlisted men killed and twenty-six wounded. After a few weeks it was ascertained, from the Indians' own testimony after they had surrendered, that they had forty killed, but the number of wounded they were never willing to give. They stated also that eleven infants were afterwards frozen to death while being carried in the arms of their destitute and starving mothers. Many women, unprovided with clothing, perished from the cold. It was stated further that some ponies were killed in order to preserve the old and feeble from dying, by inserting their feet within their warm bodies.

Colonel R. I. Dodge vividly describes the horrors of that flight. He says: "Unfortunately, the preceding night had been intensely cold, not less than twenty degrees below zero. Indians when in camp, and unsuspicious of danger, habitually sleep naked. The Cheyennes were so, and, aroused as they were, had no time to clothe themselves; some few had seized a blanket or robe in their flight, but the large majority had no covering whatever. Human nature could not stand it, and notwithstanding their favorable tactical position, they were compelled to get back into the main canyon, and retreat to a position where they could build fires and procure food. Collecting what was left of their herds of ponies, they fled during the night. . . . The sufferings of these Indians during the three months succeeding the battle can never be known. Numbers perished, principally women and children. With no food but the flesh of their ponies, no covering but the green hides of the same faithful animals, the survivors made their way across the Big Horn Mountains, and after a long and terrible march presented themselves to Crazy Horse, then encamped on Mizpah Creek.

"At no time previous had the Cheyennes been otherwise than welcome visitors to the Sioux, but here was a band of near fifteen hundred people, absolutely impoverished, in want of tepees, clothing, food, everything. The warriors still possessed their gallant spirit, and burned for an opportunity for revenge upon their white enemies, but their arms were in poor condition, their ammunition expended. It was too great a tax on the Sioux chieftain, and he received the newcomers so coldly and with so scant a charity that they soon left his inhospitable camp.

"They had received a blow far worse than a bloody defeat, and from which they knew it would take years to recover. Their women were suffering, their children dying, Crazy Horse, their last hope, had failed them. Struggle as they might their fate was too hard for them, and in 1877 they came in and surrendered."

Perhaps Crazy Horse could not give Dull Knife and his destitute Cheyennes the aid and shelter they sought, and preserve his own village, which had to be kept in readiness for an attack that might be made at any time.

Spotted Tail, who while he lived was the leading Sioux chief, had early made up his mind that it was folly to contend further against the government. Doubtless he influenced Crazy Horse to yield, for he went to see him and proved to him that there was no help to be expected from the scattered Sioux, because Terry and Crook had so stationed their troops that the Indians could not get away in any large numbers from the reservations, and that more and more Indian scouts were enlisted every day, showing themselves on the side of the government. Crazy Horse decided in the early spring to come in and surrender himself and all his people to the Pine Ridge reservation. But Dull Knife and Little Wolf had led the way and had already surrendered all that remained of their Cheyennes after MacKenzie's fight, but they showed their bitterness toward Crazy Horse and the Sioux by asking only one condition: that if Crazy Horse remained hostile they might help the troops to conquer him and destroy his village.

This surrender occurred near Fort Robinson, Nebraska, where the Northern Cheyennes were first placed under surveillance, but they were finally sent to the Indian Territory and placed on a reservation at Fort Reno (the new fort). The remnants of the tribe numbered at that time about one thousand souls. They were, however, so bitterly dissatisfied with their new home that the government consented to remove them again to the north; they were first escorted to the Pine Ridge agency, and in 1891 a new reserve and agency was given them in Montana, just east of the Crows, called "The Tongue River Agency."

But all this was not accomplished without a struggle. Dull Knife, Wild Hawk, and Little Wolf, with other chiefs, had started back to their old hunting grounds. The army was obliged to follow them, and desultory fighting was resumed.

Many men, women, and children among the settlers were killed by the Indians, and we lost several soldiers in the skirmishes and small battles that took place. The hostiles were at last captured in Nebraska, in October, 1878, and after being kept some time under guard were returned to the Indian Territory. The move to Montana then followed. It is declared in the reports that in the raids between 1878 and 1881 more than five hundred Cheyennes perished. Only a small remnant of them at last found a resting place on Tongue River near the Crow reservation.

The history of this fierce and remarkable tribe, if given in detail, would show how terrific and persistent was the struggle of the Indians of the Plains to maintain their supremacy and independence. They waged a long and bitter war against all influences to make them submit to and participate in civilization.

# CHAPTER XL.

## SQUAW MEN — HOME LIFE OF WHITE MEN WHO HAVE MARRIED INDIAN WOMEN — INCIDENTS.

White Men Who Marry Indian Women — Results of Intermarrying with Indians — Effect of Such Marriages upon Indian Women — An Indian Wife's Efforts to Please Her White Husband — The Squaw Man's Loss of Self-respect — A Shipload of Marriageable White Teachers — Story of an ex-Governor Who Married an Indian Woman — A Cultured Frenchman and His Indian Wife — A Squaw Man's Children — Proud of Their Indian Blood — Indian Half-Breeds — Story of a Government Official Who Married an Indian Woman — Keeping an Indian Wife's Existence Secret — A Bride's Dissipation — Living the Life of a Squaw Man.

AN old friend has often remarked to me that the Bible story of the children of Israel and their heathen neighbors always reminded him of Indian customs. The converse is more nearly true, namely, that the customs of our Indian tribes and their relations to their rough white neighbors often remind us of the ancient Israelites and the people who dwelt in their vicinity.

In the tribe of Dan, for example, Sampson, a giant in strength, seems to have been set apart for the punishment of wicked Philistines who were uncomfortable neighbors to the Danites. On one occasion Sampson went down to Timnath and saw a Philistine woman who delighted his eyes, so he said to his father: "Get her for me, for she pleaseth me well." Sampson married her, and the result of uniting Hebrew and heathen was a most unhappy life for both. By threats of burning her and her father's house, the heathen enemies of Israel succeeded in making her betray her husband, and through this treachery a terrific war was brought on. The story is familiar to all.

A like experience, as thoroughly true, has often repeated itself among scores of our Indian tribes. On our frontiers the white man, whether Spaniard, Mexican, Frenchman, Englishman, or American, who married an Indian woman was called a "squaw man," and in not a few instances the squaw man suffered betrayal, like Sampson of old. Then followed relentless Indian wars, accompanied with outrage, burnings, and slaughter; but as far as my observation goes the results have not been uniformly bad.

Naturally, a civilized white man is lowered in many respects by marrying an uncivilized Indian woman; still, many an Indian woman married to a white man has borne him worthy children.

I have seldom visited a tribe of Indians without finding at least one white man married to an Indian woman. Frequently the wife learned from him to live in a house, and to do, often in a rough way, it is true, such work as white women did in the home of his youth. Her marriage to a white man elevated her to a higher plane of living than that of the tepee or the lodge; she learned to dress fairly well, and in most cases showed herself to be a true friend and companion to her husband, but too often the man himself descended to a much lower level than that in which he was reared in his early home. His personal cleanliness suffered; his clothing became shabby, and his self-respect degraded. In such a pair the man soon lost his dignity and showed indifference to his former habits and life, while the woman usually showed even more pride than the wife of an Indian chief. Still, she could not compete with her white sisters in the essentials of a prosperous and well-ordered home life.

Many years ago a young man who had come from the East settled upon a farm near Fort Stevens, Oregon. That was before an ex-governor of what was then Washington Territory sent a ship load of marriageable white teachers around Cape Horn, when white women in that territory were few and far between. Under the circumstances he did the best he could. He himself married a woman of a neighboring Indian tribe. He carried on a good trade with the garrison at the fort, was enterprising, and often obtained fat contracts, which enabled him to accumulate a comfortable fortune.

His Indian wife was a good woman, hard-working, and faithful. Her love for him caused her to learn all she could, and to study to make his home more and more acceptable as the years went on, but she was very careful to keep apart from white women. She became the mother of good children, who learned, as they grew to manhood and womanhood, to dress better than their mother, and to gather much useful knowledge, social and practical, from other American youth. The eldest son succeeded his father in an honest and profitable business, and the daughters all married well. In this family the results of a mixed marriage were good, but who can tell of the heartburnings of the father and mother during the period of their children's development?

In eastern Oregon a few years ago lived a family that I knew very well. The husband was a tall, dark-eyed Frenchman. At one time, and in fact for many years, he was a trusted employee of the government. He had three beautiful daughters by his Indian wife. In grace of figure and movement, in elegance of attire, and in the varied accomplishments of gifted women few could surpass them. The wife and mother, however, at the time I visited them, always kept in the kitchen. She was really the servant of the household. She did not speak French, knew but little English, and shrank from every social attention. Though she advanced far beyond the women of her tribe, she never for one moment forgot that she was an Indian, so that even in this successful instance of white and Indian intermarriage it was next to impossible for that polished French gentleman to rise in the estimation of his white neighbors above the commonly recognized condition of a "squaw man."

The old *voyageurs,* French emigrants to the far West from Canada, who served the northwestern fur companies and traveled largely through the wilds of Oregon, were encouraged to settle in fertile valleys, whose small rivers and creeks contributed to swell the waters of the great Columbia. They naturally married Indian women. It was the policy of the Hudson Bay Company in particular to favor such marriages. In my travels through the Department of the Columbia I was constantly meeting young half-breeds, descendants of those enterprising French *voyageurs*, who were the first white men to appear in the vast region of the Northwest. They were not the equals of the best business people on the Pacific Coast, though some of them were on the front line of progress. Yet they were at all times a kind, hospitable, steady, industrious, self-supporting people. Their sires or their grandsires had taken Indian women for wives, and many of their descendants in Oregon, Washington, and Idaho are today proud of their Indian blood.

I have already spoken of my first visit to the Spokane country and of a wedding which occurred near the Spokane bridge. At that bridge was a white man who exemplified the poorer class of squaw men. He took the meager toll of passers-by and lived in a wretched apology of a house. The Indian lodges were far preferable to his home, particularly in cleanliness and order. He had a poor, hopeless-looking Indian wife, and numerous half-wild children, who gazed from under their shaggy locks with timid curiosity upon strangers, and ran instantly to cover upon our approach. This family appeared to me, at first thought, to be beneath the level of the best of the uncivilized Indians, yet before this twentieth century began the country had become settled, Spokane Falls had become a city, and schools had been established so near that bridge that all the little ones of this Indian household had for some years the opportunity of being educated with white children, and some of them have grown up to be enterprising young men and women and prosperous citizens of the State of Washington.

Again referring to the people of Israel, we have seen in the Bible that a certain Levite married a woman of Bethlehem, and that, notwithstanding that she was his wife and he himself is distinctly named in the records as her husband, our translation calls her his concubine. Several similar intermarriages have taken place between whites and Indians on what was once called our frontier. For example: an old and distinguished government official, whose name should I repeat it would be recognized anywhere in this country, was married to an Indian woman. The pair had a little girl born to them, but for some reason the father left his Indian wife, probably giving her a divorce after the Indian fashion. He then married a lady of his own people, and since then he and his wife have brought up a large and beautiful family. The squaw wife, after the husband had separated from her, went back to her tribe, taking the child with her.

On one of my trips to Puget Sound I visited the schools of Father Chirouse and there learned that this child had been for some years attending the school, and was then about fourteen years of age. Already an enterprising young Frenchman had set his eyes upon the beautiful girl and an announcement of their approaching marriage had just been made. I managed to be at Tulalip at that time and was present at the wedding. It seemed a pity that a girl should be married so young, but Father Chirouse said that it was a good thing for young people to marry early; that it was the very beginning of right living and proper training. The little half-breed, with a fair bit of education, started in as a housekeeper in a neat cottage, while her enterprising husband maintained the family by log-work at a neighboring mill. Before our Father above the mother of that half-breed girl was doubtless, like the concubine of the ancient Levite, a *bona fide* wife. Men, however, who rise so high in the world as her husband did were never called squaw men, and often in later years the fact of the Indian wife's existence was carefully suppressed.

The son of a leading citizen, in the wild days of his youth, thought it would be an amusing surprise to his friends, and certainly gratifying to himself, to marry an Indian girl. The maiden he selected was bright and handsome, and, under the care of some Sisters of the Catholic faith, had received a fair education in the common branches of Spanish and English. She spoke English with facility, and with a pretty accent. Having seen only the rough camp life of frontiersmen, scarcely ever having been in contact with white women except with the Sisters of Charity, she was flattered and delighted with her prospects, and looked forward full of eager anticipation to performing all the social functions expected of a young white man's wife.

After marriage, like some other wild young men, he drank freely of whisky, his favorite beverage, and unlike white grooms generally he frequently induced his Indian bride to drink with him. Whisky never agreed with Indian blood, and it made the young woman at times wild and unmanageable. After a time the pair visited the nearest great city and soon overturned all the staid customs of society. It took much ready money and all of its influence to keep these young people out of the clutches of the law.

For a while our young friend lived the life of a veritable squaw man, and doubtless might have been adopted into the tribe and become a chief, and led thousands of Indians in their subsequent wars against white men. But his hopes were nipped in the bud; his parents and influential friends interposed and forced him to send the young woman back to her tribe. He, too, gave the Indian wife a *quasi*, Indian divorce, and afterward married a white lady and raised a family. His first bride, after that one reckless frolic into which her husband led her, never ceased to maintain a high degree of self-respect, and managed to live and work in good homes of white people. Those circumstances made this a mésalliance, yet in my judgment the first marriage was the valid one, and the Indian woman whom, as well as her husband, I knew for years, was far superior to him.

A very able gentleman from an eastern city fell into evil ways and was attacked by a terrible disease which badly disfigured his face. A deep sense of shame came over him, and in profound melancholy he abandoned civilized life and began to wander among our Indian tribes. I first saw him in the Sierra Nevada Mountains of Arizona.

He was then attached to a small band of Indians who had a sensible, good-hearted, half-civilized chief. He married, as the chief told me, into his royal family and had a goodly number of boys and girls, who lived as the Indians lived.

The tribe was nomadic; they had no tepees or lodges, always slept under the boughs of trees, planted fertile spots in the springtime with both corn and potatoes, and watched their herds of ponies. They were always with the wildest Indians when on the warpath. Our poor friend, though a man of culture, lived for many years with the Indians as an Indian and was but little more. He was, however, at times a sort of chief-of-staff and gave good advice. He preferred peace to war and he brought all his influence to bear in that direction. Still, his sympathy for the Indians was so great that he fearlessly took their part in all their quarrels with their white neighbors, and somehow managed very often to settle their difficulties amicably, and to prevent the frequent outrages and bloodshed that marked the line of the frontier.

When at last the wild tribe to which he belonged was forced to take up land and be confined on a permanent reserve this squaw man secured a hundred and sixty acres, three times repeated, which were assigned to his wife and children. At last a good house was built in one corner and near it a large barn. Oats, barley, corn, and hops grew upon his well-chosen acres. Fences were built, trees planted, and orchards enclosed. Artesian wells were sunk, and the water was sufficient to irrigate the land that was under cultivation. Here was a type, that I knew well, of squaw men often met in Arizona, New Mexico, and elsewhere. In loving Indian women well enough to expatriate themselves these squaw men husbands nevertheless managed to obtain reasonable compensation.

I do not like the expression "squaw man," for if we define the term as we ought it should mean only the husband of an Indian woman. As a matter of fact such marriages have touched some of the highest in the land, directly and indirectly, including judges of the United States courts, members of Congress, generals in the army, officers of the general staff, prominent merchants, and hundreds of citizens of the best standing in the community where they lived.

Two things are often asserted and commonly believed where Indian and civilized society come in contact. One is that the man who marries an Indian girl has degraded himself, and the other is that the issue of such a marriage is uniformly bad; that is, that half-breeds are bright and shrewd enough, but deficient in moral character. As a general statement this is far from true.

I know that nearly all of our interpreters and many of our guides were squaw men or half-breeds, and that their moral character was not always of the best. Yet I must say that they compared favorably with our own citizens who had white wives and growing families, who clustered around the numerous Indian reservations and were evidently there for what they could make.

# CHAPTER XLI.

## CHARACTERISTICS OF AMERICAN INDIANS — THE SIGN LANGUAGE — THE SCALP AND OTHER CEREMONIAL DANCES — A NECKLACE OF HUMAN FINGERS.

The Sign Language — Its Origin — How Indians of Different Tribes Converse with Each Other — Curious Method of Communication — Ceremonial Dances — The Scalp Dance — A Secret Performance — Elaborate Preparations for the Dance — Wands with Dangling Scalps — A Weird Performance — Frenzied Condition of the Dancers — Nervous Excitement of Spectators — Medicine Bags and Totems — A Necklace of Human Fingers — Captain Bourke's Story of its Capture — A Buckskin Bag filled with the Right Hands of Papooses — Curious Contents of an Indian Medicine Bag — Gruesome Ornaments made of Human Bones.

I AM often asked, "Can you speak the Indian language?" My answer is that I would have to speak more than two hundred languages to speak the Indian tongue of each tribe. Few realize how great was the number of these tribes, and how marked the differences were between them. There is, however, a language common to nearly all Indians, known as "the sign language." It is made by the hands, the fingers, the arms, and, in fact, by motions of the whole body, and enables Indians of tribes speaking different languages, to hold intercourse with each other. Old frontiersmen who have long mingled with various Indian tribes are nearly always experts in the sign language.

It was among the Plains Indians that gesture-

Friend or Foe?—"Standing off" Indians.

A Powwow with the Cheyennes in the Sign Language.

COMMUNICATION BY SIGNS.

speech arrived at such perfection that it might properly be called a language, for the reason that these tribes used it not only in intercourse with people whose oral language they neither spoke nor understood, but for everyday intercourse among themselves. In their own camps and families this method of communicating ideas was used so constantly that it became a natural and instinctive habit. Col. Richard I. Dodge, whose experience among the Plains Indians was perhaps greater than that of any other army officer, in his book entitled "Our Wild Indians," published when he was a colonel and aide-de-camp to General Sherman, suggests the origin of the sign language. He says:

"All the Plains tribes depended almost entirely on the buffalo for everything. That animal, in his migrations (going north in the spring, and south in the fall and winter), was exceedingly erratic, his visits to any particular section of country depending on his own food supply, and the condition of the grass. One year, the country of a tribe of Indians might be overrun by herds whose numbers were simply incalculable; the next year, the same territory might be visited by scarcely a single animal.

"If the buffalo did not come to the Indian, the Indian must go to the buffalo, at whatever hazard. Runners were sent out, the location of the buffalo discovered, and long journeys were made by tribes and bands into countries to which they had no claim.

"The same necessity possibly actuating many

bands and tribes, the country in the vicinity of the buffalo became dangerous ground. The tribe or band in whose territory they were, regarded the buffalo as their own property, an evidence of the favor of God. They resented the intrusion of other bands and hunting parties, not only as killing and driving off their property, but as interfering with their 'medicine,' the medicine chief taking care that all should understand that his influence with God brought the buffalo. Each year, the country occupied by the buffalo became a vast battle-ground, the proper owners attacking the interlopers at every favorable opportunity.

"But hunting parties met other hunting parties of tribes not hostile. To distinguish between the hostile and the friendly, and to communicate with, and possibly make common cause with the latter, some means of intercourse must be had. Not being able to speak or understand each other's language, communication was had by signs.

"We may suppose that at first only signs most natural and expressive were used. By-and-by other signs were introduced, always conventional, but becoming more and more arbitrary, until there resulted a means of communication almost as perfect as if each understood and spoke the oral language of the other.

"The Plains Indians themselves believed that the sign language was invented by the Kiowas, who, holding an intermediate position between the Comanches, Tonkaways, Lipans, and other inhabitants of the vast plains of Texas, and the Pawnees, Sioux, Blackfeet, and other Northern tribes, were the general go-betweens; trading with all, or making peace or war, with, or for, any or all. It is certain that the Kiowas were more universally proficient in this language than any other Plains tribe. It is also certain that the tribes farthest away from them, and with whom they had least intercourse, used it with least facility."

Ceremonial dancing in various forms was a prominent feature in Indian life. Those tribes that were expert horsemen were generally shambling and awkward in walking or running on foot, the natural result of their being almost constantly on horseback from childhood to old age. Indian dances did not require much agility on the part of the performers. The body was kept stiff and the legs were moved forward and back, and up and down. It appeared to me as I watched the dances of Indians that every dancer cultivated rigid action of the muscles, even when bending over or looking skyward.

As to the scalp dance, I doubt if many white men ever witnessed the whole performance. Colonel Dodge in his book gives a good description of that ceremony. He says:

"The day after the return to the home encampment of a successful war party, by which scalps had been taken, a ceremony was performed by the warriors who took them, no other person whatever being permitted to be present.

"I have been a spectator at a distance, but all to be seen was a number of Indians, sitting on the ground in a close circle. During this ceremony, the scalps were trimmed, cleared of all fleshy matter, and the skin cured by some process. Each scalp was then stretched by thongs inside of a hoop of wood a little larger than itself, and the hair was carefully combed and greased. Each warrior then attached his scalp or scalps, in their hoops, to a peeled willow wand, from eight to ten feet long.

"This ceremony was called 'counting the coups,' and was 'Big Medicine,' that is, very important in a religious point of view. It was preparatory to the scalp dance.

"When it had been satisfactorily completed, all the warriors marched gravely one behind the other, back to camp, each bearing his wand with its burden of dangling scalps in his hand. The wands were planted in a circle in the center of the camp.

"By this time, the whole population of the village was crowded around this center of interest. The warriors who took the scalps were now joined by those who had taken part in the fight, or who belonged to the party which did the fighting, and thus won for themselves the right to participate in the dance.

"All assembled in a circle around and facing the circle of wands. At a signal, all the warriors joined hands, and commenced the monotonous song and dance, turning slowly about the scalps. As the dance progressed, the warriors soon loosed hands, and varied the song by whoops and yells, and the dance by bounds, gestures and brandishing of weapons, working themselves up to a condition of excitement bordering on frenzy.

"The eyes of the spectators were strained upon scalps and dancers as each slayer in turn sprang from the circle, and bounding to his wand, vaunted in extravagant terms his own prowess, and acted over again the taking of the scalps.

"When the fortunate takers of scalps had all exhausted themselves in self-laudation, others of the dancers sprang by turns into the circle, each explaining by what unfortunate interference of the 'Bad God,' he was prevented on this occasion from taking a scalp, and recounted in glowing language his successful prowess on some previous occasion, or what he proposed to do at the next opportunity. This was continued until each dancer had full opportunity to show how brave and great a warrior he was. Dancers and spectators grew wild with excitement, and by the time the dance was over, the whole population was little short of insane.

"This nervous intoxication was a special delight of the Indians, and when they felt like indulging in it, and there were no fresh scalps, they brought out some old ones, and went through with the same performance, the same scalps in 'piping times of peace' being made to do duty over and over again.

"I have been told that, wild as the dancers appeared to be, each knew perfectly well what he was doing, having previously in some solitude gone over his speech and acted his part time and again.

"I was once spectator at a scalp dance which was a special and exceptional occasion, for not only had a goodly number of scalps been taken, but two prisoners — a woman of about forty, and boy of twelve years of age — were to grace the ceremony. The peeled wands bearing the hoops and stretched scalps had been planted in a circle in the ground. The prisoners were brought by the warriors who had captured them, from the lodge in which they were confined, and forced to take their places in the circle, their hands being held by the warriors on each side of them. The woman-prisoner accepted the situation, and in looks and actions appeared to take as enjoyable an interest in the dance as any of the proper performers. Not so the boy; with eyes downcast, without a voluntary motion of foot or body, he was dragged around the circle, taking only such walking-steps as were necessary to avoid being pulled down. All the turmoil and excitement failed to produce on him the slightest effect. Not once in the dance of more than an hour did he lift his eyes to the scalps, to which were directed all the eyes and attention of his captors, nor did he evince the slightest interest in any of the proceedings.

"I could not but admire the proud determination of one so young to resist all the efforts of a crowd of enemies to force him into even a semblance of rejoicing over the scalps of his people, possibly of his own father."

Medicine bags and totems were common among the medicine-men. The necklace of human fingers, a facsimile illustration of which is inserted in this volume, belonged to the principal medicine-man of the Cheyennes, from whom it was taken in Gen. MacKenzie's battle with them, which I have already mentioned. It is described as follows by the late Captain John G. Bourke, United States Army:

"Among the bitterest losses of valuable property suffered by the defeated Cheyennes on this occasion were the two necklaces of human fingers which came into my possession, together with the small buckskin bag filled with the right hands of papooses belonging to the tribe of their deadly enemies, the Shoshones. These were found in the village by one of our scouts — Baptiste Pourrier, who, with Mr. Frank Gruard, was holding an important and responsible position in connection with the care of the great body of Indian scouts already spoken of. From these two gentlemen I afterwards obtained all the information that is here to be found regarding the Cheyenne necklace.

"The second necklace, consisting of four fingers, was buried, as General Crook did not wish to have kept more than one specimen, and that only for scientific purposes. Accordingly, the necklace here depicted was sent first to the United States Military Academy at West Point, N. Y., and later to the National Museum at Washington, where it was believed it could better fulfill its mission of educating students in a knowledge of the manners and customs of our aborigines.

"The buckskin bag, with the papooses' hands, was claimed by the Shoshone scouts, who danced and wailed all night, and then burned the fearful evidence of the loss sustained by their people.

"The necklace is made of a round collar of buckskin, incrusted with the small blue and white beads purchased from the traders, these being arranged in alternate spaces of an inch or more in length. There are also attached numbers of the perforated wampum shell beads of native manufacture. Pendant from this collar are five medicine arrows, the exact nature of which, it was, of course, impossible to determine from the owner himself. Both Frank and Baptiste agreed that an arrow might become "medicine" either from having been shot into the person of the owner himself or into the body of an enemy, or even from having been picked up under peculiar circumstances. The owner, High Wolf or Tall Wolf, admitted as much after he had surrendered at the Red Cloud Agency and had made every effort to obtain the return of his medicine, which was this necklace.

"The four medicine bags to be seen in the picture are worthy of attention. They were carefully examined under a powerful glass by Dr. H. C. Yarrow, United States Army, in the city of Washington, and pronounced to be human scrota. The first of these contained a vegetable powder, somewhat decomposed, having a resemblance to hoddentin; the second was filled with killikinnick; the third with small garnet-colored seeds like the chia in use among the Apaches, and the fourth with a yellow, clayey-white vegetable matter not identified. The fifth, also, remained unidentified.

"Besides the above, there are artificial teeth, resembling those of the fossil animals abundant in the Bad Lands of South Dakota, but cut out of soft stone.

"The fingers — eight altogether — are the left-hand middle fingers of Indians of hostile tribes, killed by High Wolf. I obtained the list and could insert it here were it worth while to do so. The fingers have not been left in the natural state, but have been subjected to very careful and elaborate

(1) NECKLACE OF HUMAN FINGERS, ARROW HEADS AND TEETH, ATTACHED TO A BEADED BUCKSKIN COLLAR.

(2) NECKLACE MADE OF THE FIRST JOINTS OF HUMAN FINGERS.

*For Description see page 17.*

PHOTOGRAPHED AND PAINTED FROM THE ORIGINAL OBJECTS EXPRESSLY FOR THIS WORK.

antiseptic treatment in order thoroughly to desiccate them. They were split longitudinally on the inner side, and after the bone had been extracted, the surface of the skin, both inside and out, received a treatment with a wash or paint of ocherous earth, the same as is used for the face. I was told that the bones were not replaced, but that sticks were inserted to maintain the fingers in proper shape.

"Of the reason for making use of such a trophy or relic, there is not much to be said; even the savages know little and say less. From the best information that I have been able to gather, it would seem to be based partly upon a vainglorious desire to display the proofs of personal prowess, and partly upon the vague and ill-defined, but deeply-rooted, belief in the talismanic or 'medicinal' potency possessed by all parts of the human body, especially after death. It was such a belief that impelled the Mandan, Aztecs, and others of the American tribes to preserve the skulls of their dead as well as (among the Aztecs) those of the victims sacrificed in honor of their gods.

"The use of necklaces of human fingers or of human teeth is to be found in many parts of the world, and besides the fingers themselves, we find the whole arm, or in other cases only the nails. The Cheyennes did not always restrict themselves to fingers; they generally made use of the whole hand, or the arm of the slaughtered enemy. In a colored picture drawn and painted by one of themselves I have a representation of a scalp dance, in which the squaws may be seen dressed in their best, carrying the arms of enemies elevated on high poles and lances. There is no doubt in my mind that this custom of the Cheyennes of cutting off the arm or hand gave rise to their name in the sign language of the 'Slashers,' or 'Wrist Cutters,' much as the corresponding tribal peculiarity of the Dakotas occasioned their name of the 'Coupe Gorge' or 'Throat Cutters.'

"The necklace of human fingers is found among other tribes. A necklace of four human fingers was seen by the members of the Lewis and Clarke expedition among the Shoshones at the headwaters of the Columbia. Early in the spring of 1858, Henry Youle Hind refers to the allies of the Ojibwa on Red River as having 'two fingers severed from the hands of the unfortunate Sioux.'

"The necklace of human fingers is not a particle more horrible than the ornaments of human bones to be seen in the cemetery of the Capuchins in Rome at the present day. I have personally known of two or three cases where American Indians cut their enemies limb from limb. The idea upon which the practice is based seems to be the analogue of the old English custom of sentencing a criminal to be 'hanged, drawn, and quartered.'"

# CHAPTER XLII.

## CHARACTERISTICS OF AMERICAN INDIANS, CONTINUED—THEIR STOLIDITY, SECRETIVENESS, AND HUMOR—INDIAN SPIES—CURIOUS STORY TOLD BY A KIOWA.

How Indians Conceal their Real Feelings and Intentions—Thievery as a Profession—Attempt of Satanta, a Kiowa Chief, to Kill General Sherman—His Narrow Escape from Death—Satanta's Fate—The Instinct of Revenge—Expertness of Indian Spies—Surpassing the Feats of White Men—Indian Sense of Humor—Laughing at the Queer Looks and Ways of White Men—Making Merry over Whiskers—Bald Heads Versus "Forked Tongues"—Story of the Giant Sinti and the Prairie Dogs—A Good Specimen of Indian Fiction—Boisterous Hilarity of Indians—The Spirit of Gambling—Barbarous Cruelty When Intoxicated.

MEN of limited experience, particularly those who have suffered from Indian depredations, stoutly declare that all Indians were stolid, secretive, and treacherous. It is true that most of them assumed a demeanor intended to conceal their real feelings and intentions when they came into the presence of white men whom they did not know, or into association with Indians who were strangers to them. But when well acquainted with each other and confidence was once established, all stolidity disappeared. Some Indians, like the Comanches, were taught from childhood to be secretive; and they practiced thievery all their lives; but this habit was exercised, as a rule, toward their recognized enemies. I cannot recall any case within my personal experience where Indians robbed their friends, or manifested toward them any greater secretiveness than we white men do to each other in ordinary business life.

I have seen several instances of treachery of Indian to Indian, and of Indians to white men, like that shown by the Modocs about the time General Canby was killed, but these instances, those referred to included, always occurred in what the Indians considered a state of war. According to our ideas of peace and war, the Indians would be condemned; we often thought that certain Indians were at peace when they were actually preparing for a hostile foray, or were in the frenzy of a warlike outbreak.

In 1874, just before the wild flight of the Kiowas to the Plains, when several army officers were at Fort Sill to have a talk with them, Satanta, a Kiowa chief, stood, rifle in hand, in the midst of a group of his people. The commander of the army, General W. T. Sherman, was present. Suddenly in a fit of rage at something that was said Satanta sprang to his feet, aimed his rifle at General Sherman's head and fired, but another Indian who was friendly struck the rifle just in time to save the General's life. Some time previous to this, Satanta had been imprisoned for leading a raid against a wagon train of supplies in Texas, in which all the men in charge of the wagons were slain and the mules and goods carried off. To keep the Kiowas from an outbreak he was released on parole. He was again imprisoned after attempting to kill General Sherman. This time, feeling that there was no hope of release, he sprang from a high window of the jail in which he was confined and ended his own life.

They have had before them, permeating their thoughts, their talk, and their actions, actual causes of war. For example, if a white man killed an Indian, and had taken his corn or tobacco, or had appropriated to his own uses the valley where he had cultivated small patches of land, to the Indian mind the cause of war was very plain, and to him it already existed.

Before an outbreak revenge had long been meditated and settled on; it was a sacred principle. The Indian who did not seek revenge was despised by the men and women of his tribe. This disposition, as a principle, has not altogether disappeared among white men. In our mountain country it is still recognized as the necessary function of the head of the family as against another and rival family. Christianity has not yet succeeded in fully eradicating this terrible cause of feuds among some of our bravest people. Of course there are some qualities that Christianity has not yet removed from the human heart. Generally, however, white men know the right whether they do it or not; but the savage has conscientiously adhered to the principle of merciless revenge.

In my experience I found Indian spies to be experts in their profession and frequently their performance was phenomenal; they always equaled and often surpassed the best feats of white men. In the midst of war, an Indian spy would come into the presence of a hostile commander with a plausible story and a look of innocence, which made him, to all intents and purposes, a safe visitor. He would gather all the information he wanted and easily make off without arousing suspicion, carrying the much-needed information to his friends. The Indian spy was generally as handsome, stalwart, intelligent, and shrewd as any man that could be selected for a dangerous mission. Indeed, he rose to the character and conduct of our most famous scouts in civilized warfare. He was honored during and after the war as our spies and scouts never have been. We use our scouts to get for us all needed information, and when their work is completed we treat them with contempt.

It is commonly believed that the Indians have no sense of humor. This is far from true of the numerous tribes with which I have had to do. Of course there were different ways of manifesting humor. The Nez Percés laughed among themselves at the queer looks and ways of white visitors. They made merry over the white man's odd whiskers, and compared his forehead to the peculiar front of some bird, or pig, or sheep. A bald head was full of suggestions to them. It seemed to mean deception, untruthfulness, or signified what they called a "forked tongue." These conclusions were derived from their experience with bald-headed men whom they had met in council, and whose promises were never fulfilled. They laughed heartily, as children do, at small accidents which occurred in their games and sports. I noticed everywhere among the Nez Percés a *badinage* as frequent, as hearty, and as amusing as that among college students or frisky lads at play.

A prominent character in the humorous stories of the Kiowas was Sinti, whom they described as a long-legged giant with an insatiable appetite, and an incurable liar and trickster. As a sample of the imaginative productions of the Kiowas, and of their strong sense of humor, I give one of their stories, as told by Mr. James Mooney, who for many years lived among them, with facsimile illustrations drawn by an aboriginal Kiowa artist, loaned by Mr. Mooney to illustrate this story:

### THE STORY OF SINTI, THE PRAIRIE DOGS, AND THE LAME COYOTE.

"'One day Sinti was out walking, with his club over his shoulder, looking for something to eat. He was very hungry, for he had tricked the animals so often that most of them now managed to keep a good distance away from him. At last he came to a prairie dog town. The dogs were not much afraid of him because they were so little, hardly a mouthful apiece, that Sinti had never thought it worth while to bother with them. So he called them and said:

"'Doggies, nephews,'—Sinti called everybody nephew—'wouldn't you like to learn a new dance?'

"'Yes,' said all the little dogs, 'that would be nice.'

"'All right, then. I'll sing the song and show you how to dance, and then you stand around me in a circle and shut your eyes and sing the song after me, and stamp your feet the same way.'

"So the prairie dogs formed a circle around Sinti, all standing on their hind legs, and Sinti began to sing the song, keeping time with his big club like a rattle, as he stamped with his feet upon the ground:

"'Doggies, doggies, whisk your tails,
Whisk your tails, whisk your tails,
Just the way I say.'

"It was a very pretty song, but the big club frightened the prairie dogs and they were almost

THE GIANT SINTI FOOLING THE PRAIRIE DOGS.
"Doggies, doggies, whisk your tails just the way I say."
(*Facsimile of an original drawing made by a Kiowa.*)

ready to run, so Sinti said, 'Don't be frightened, nephews; that's just the way the dance goes. Now shut your eyes and sing with me.'

"So they all shut their eyes and he began again:

"'Doggies, doggies, whisk your tails,'—

but every time he stamped his foot he brought his club down on the head of a prairie dog. They were all singing so loud that they couldn't hear the squeak, and as they had their eyes shut they didn't know what Sinti was doing, until one little dog began to think that the dance was lasting a long time, so he peeped out of one eye, and there he saw all the rest of his friends stretched out dead on the ground with their paws up. He made one big jump to get away and ran for his hole, with Sinti after him. But the little dog got there first and was safe, and so there are still prairie dogs in the world.

"Sinti looked into the hole and said to himself, 'That little dog would have had very sweet marrow, but I guess I can make a meal from the others.' So he walked back to where the dogs were lying and gathered a lot of wood to roast them in their skins, Kiowa fashion.

"While he was turning them over the fire, up came a lame coyote, with one paw held up from the ground, and altogether looking very poor and hungry, and asked Sinti to please give him something to eat.

"'Get out!' said Sinti, 'run and get your own meat.'

"'I can't,' said the coyote. 'I've broken my leg and I can't run fast enough.'

"'Very well, then,' said Sinti, with a sneer, 'we'll race for it. We'll run to that hill over yonder, go around it and run back, and the one who gets here first takes the meat.'

"'But I'm lame,' said the coyote, 'and you have such long legs.'

"'O, well,' said Sinti, 'I'll tie stones on my ankles and then we'll be even.'

"So Sinti tied two big stones on each ankle, and away he started, with poor coyote limping painfully behind as well as he could. Sinti quickly reached the hill, although the stones *were* very

THE LAME COYOTE FOOLING THE GIANT SINTI.
(*Facsimile of an original drawing made by a Kiowa.*)

heavy, went round it and started back on a walk because there was no need to hurry and the stones bothered him. At last the coyote reached the hill. Sinti had sat down to rest awhile, and looked around to see how the coyote was getting on, and here he was coming on at a gallop.

"The coyote wasn't lame at all!

"The next moment the coyote passed him, running as if after a jack-rabbit. Sinti untied the stones from his ankles as quickly as he could. But it was too late now. The coyote got there first, and when Sinti arrived there was nothing left but the bones."

The wild Apaches talked freely about matters pertaining to the human body as nobody would ven-

INDIAN AND WHITE SCALPS, SCALPING KNIVES, SHEATHS, BOW, BOW-CASE AND QUIVER, ARROWS, ETC.

*For Description see page 18*

PHOTOGRAPHED AND PAINTED FROM THE ORIGINAL OBJECTS EXPRESSLY FOR THIS WORK.

ture to do in polite society, but to them there appeared to be no sense of vulgarity. Some Indians were low and indecent in their talk, but this did not come so much from their own ways and customs as from the suggestions of degraded white men who had settled among them and taught them such things. They were only trying to please their teachers. As far as I can judge, profane expressions and curses were invariably learned from white men.

Many times I have seen Apache chiefs laugh at sudden surprises until they could hardly breathe; I have seen them roll on the ground and bend themselves double in the excess of their merriment. But after all, Indians were not so full of boisterous hilarity at all times and upon all sorts of occasions as Africans. Strong drink developed this disposition among the Indians, and in the beginning of their intoxication they seemed greatly to enjoy a good time, using *tizwin, mescal,* or corn soaked and fermented when the white man's liquor could not be obtained. Under the influence of these drinks, they delighted in gambling and dancing; yet this hilarity was soon followed by the terrible savagery that strong drink always awakened in them. A drunken white man is hard to manage, but a drunken Indian, with few exceptions, was beyond control. Nothing appeared to give him greater satisfaction than acts of barbarous cruelty to men and animals. All who have had any experience with Indians will admit that strong liquor never agreed with them.

Fun was everywhere observable among Indian

children who were healthful and free to act. Indian parents were seldom cruel to their children. They loved them and humored them, often beyond reason, yet they fiercely demanded such obedience from them as was necessary to keep a child quiet, or to make a child do what he was reluctant to undertake. Parents laughed heartily at the odd ways and unexpected pranks of their children. Wherever I succeeded in getting the good-will of the children I was sure to have the women on my side for anything that I desired to accomplish in the interest of the government or of the Indians.

# CHAPTER XLIII.

CHARACTERISTICS OF AMERICAN INDIANS, CONTINUED—ORATORS AND ORATORY—EXPERT HORSEMANSHIP—SURPRISES AND AMBUSCADES—FUTURE OF OUR INDIANS.

An Indian Council Attended by the President of the United States—Characteristic Indian Oratory—Indian Gestures—Peculiarities of their Speeches—Indian Horses and Horsemanship—Method of Breaking and Training Colts—Severe Cruelty to Animals—"Bucking" Ponies—A Lesson Learned from the Indians—Indian and White Riders Compared—Organizing an Attack on a Wagon Train—Averting a Threatened Disaster—Curious Way of "Trying to Please Me"—Looking Back to Early Days—Retrospection—Looking Forward to the Future with Hope and Confidence.

OUR Indians are without exception natural orators. President Hayes and General Sherman, with several officers and ladies, visited the Puyallup Reservation during the President's tour in Oregon and Washington Territory in 1880. The principal chief of the Puyallup tribe and several heads of bands took their turn during a formal council to make their wants known to the great Father of the Republic. Surely no Indians ever had a better opportunity. When the council was over the President said to me, "What remarkable oratory! There is no hesitation. Their gestures are always natural and graceful, and not one of them has failed to make a good speech. Of course I judge them by the translations. Their figures of speech are choice and well carried out.

Indeed, they seemed to have been born orators." In the scores of councils which I attended I always noticed the excellence of their speeches. Their metaphors were often strong and always pointed. An Apache chief, observing a flinty stone which I had placed on the mesa, said: "As long as this stone shall endure so long let there peace between us."

Again, when the prospects of a lasting peace between the Indians and the white men were brightest, the same chief said: "Hereafter the deep canyons shall be filled up and the crooked trails shall be made straight for the white man and the Indian."

The famous Cochise translated the Spirit's words thus: "Hereafter the Indian and the white man shall eat bread together." The oratory of the medicine men everywhere was more remarkable and more influential than even their weird ceremonials. Through this they controlled, combined, and directed movements of vast extent and consequence in all the Indian wars and massacres.

The Plains Indians whom I met always had horses, either Indian ponies or those which were a cross between the Indian pony and the American horse. They showed great skill in breaking and training them. But seldom did I find an Indian boy or grown man of these tribes who was kind to his horse. The severest cruelty was exercised in breaking the horse to the bridle and the saddle. An Indian did not spend much time in the operation. He would lasso a wild one, thrown him down and bind him, never letting him up till he believed the animal's spirit had been sufficiently toned down to allow him to mount and ride. Sometimes he would tie the animal's head to the limb of a tree, stretching his neck into a painful position, and keep him so during an entire night. By morning the horse was glad enough to submit to anything, be it saddle, or bridle, or an Indian on his back. The *bona fide* bronco, after a few days, was very likely to attempt to take his revenge by resorting to the well known trick of "bucking." He would rear again and again; he would kick, round up his back and run, often in a circle, as soon as the saddle touched him. For this outbreak the Indian subjected him to new and severer discipline, which was repeated at every attempt of the animal to assert his independence. The Indian would mercilessly beat him and tie him up again and again until the beast was completely subjugated.

The Nez Percés, Flatheads, Cayuses, Spokanes, and Colville Indians were much kinder to their animals than the Plains Indians. They used the same methods, however, in breaking their colts; but afterwards they did not, when they could avoid it, put packs or saddles upon backs that were galled and raw from rough usage. They divided the overworked and lame ponies into separate droves. When moving from place to place they herded and grazed them with much care, even in a trying campaign. Many a good horse so treated was in a few days restored to full vigor. I learned from the Indians to husband the strength of my own horses in a similar way. We could not do this of course until we had secured animals enough for extra mounts. Chief Joseph, the leader of the Nez Percés, had a large surplus of ponies from the start, so that his riders could change horses every day, while each of my pursuing cavalrymen was at first allowed but one horse. I soon, however, found it necessary to increase my supply, which I did from the half-breed horses I found while marching through Idaho, Montana, and the Dakotas.

The Comanches led every other tribe in horsemanship. They had the swiftest mounts in their races, and outstripped American riders with American horses every time they had a trial. Our young officers on the Plains during intervals of peace were fond of trying the speed of their horses with the war chiefs and principal men of the Comanches, and I have no incident on record in which these Indians, when putting forward their best ponies, did not win the race.

The Comanches were like the Kurds of Eastern Turkey. A band of Comanches, say a hundred strong, beholding afar off the dust of a wagon train with its escort and a guard of our cavalry, would manage noiselessly to get into some ravine where they could easily and suddenly descend upon the train. They would do this so quickly and conceal themselves so effectually that not even a suspicion of their presence was aroused until a body of them, without apparent order, charged like a whirlwind upon the escort and train. They would shoot as they charged, terrifying and stampeding horses, mules, or oxen, and putting everything into hopeless confusion with such speed that none but an officer of experience was able to withstand them. If

AN INDIAN HORSE RACE.—THE FINISH.

the officer rallied his cavalry upon a knoll near by and was ready for a counter-charge, the Indians cut the terrified animals loose and drove them off at full speed. If forced to abandon them the Comanches would disappear as quickly as they came, always bearing away their wounded.

I once watched a band of such Indians making preparation for a charge upon a mule train which had a small guard. My influence in this instance over the chief prevented the disaster that was plainly in sight. In an incredibly short space of time the Indians painted their faces and concealed themselves in a convenient ravine just behind a line of foothills. They then mounted and placed themselves in no particular order, the chief being near the center and the Indians on his right and left and rear, but so that every man had sufficient room to turn his horse in any direction. Every man was armed, some with carbines; the chief had a rifle which he had taken from a white man, and some had only bows and arrows. They sprang forward in a trot, then a gallop, and then a fast run, but in some way the chief was able to stop them by a signal doubtless agreed upon beforehand. They came within a quarter of a mile of the train and must have startled the escort and drivers beyond expression at their wild approach, but they turned and bore off to the right; when the chief joined me he smiled and said it would have been good sport, but that he was at peace now, and he wanted to please me.

My earliest knowledge of Indians greatly prejudiced me against them. My grandfather, a man of the olden time when Indians were very troublesome, had nothing good to say of them. His experience in fights with them was not to their advantage. Their war-paint, their depredations, their knives, tomahawks, bows and arrows, and wild life were the themes of common conversation. In his day their conversion, instruction, and up-building were very little considered. The general purpose of our people was then, as it has been all along, to conquer them in battle, drive them out, or exterminate them, in order that savagery might give place to civilization.

A few men believed, and I came in time to join them, that a portion of them might be civilized and made respectable citizens; but that was not the general conviction of the white man at the beginning of the nineteenth century.

Osceola and his followers had a special grievance. They wished to preserve their habitations and they fought hard against being sent off beyond the Mississippi. Osceola was brave, wary, revengeful, and able, but in time he and his followers were obliged to give way before the white men. Whites began the Seminole war. General Sherman used to say that they began every war. This one they commenced by publicly whipping five Indians. All of the Indian outrages, including Dade's massacre, followed that shame which no Indian would bear.

Wild Cat's dissipation was brought on by soldiers and whisky dealers. Through them the Florida Indians were corrupted, and after a time were always at war. White men killed them on sight, and the Indians naturally retaliated, burnt houses, and killed everything that had life, especially human beings. If they spared the live stock of the country it was to carry it off for their own use. In fear of them, treaties were made with a view to move them westward. Surely our action, legislative and executive, was usually hostile—never really friendly. Indians were feared and they were hated.

In my own time Billy Bowlegs led a remnant of the Seminoles to war, they having risen up to dispute the treaty; they raided the settlements, as the Indians before them had done; they waylaid the stage lines; now and then they killed a settler; after that our army was brought in to crush them. Volunteers and regulars made it almost impossible for Indians to live. The volunteers were especially unscrupulous and unsparing of human life. From my observations then and there, the war that raged in 1856 and 1857 was dreadful. This encounter ended in our superior force getting the advantage and enforcing its demands. All other Indian wars began, continued, and ended in the same way.

It does not seem to be difficult to teach Indian boys and girls of every tribe our code of morals, and they appear to be as conscientious as other children in the observance of Christian precepts. The most pronounced success in moral and Christian teaching is where the children are separated from the degrading influences of their rough life. I have noticed, however, that the educated young Indian is always troubled about the condition of his own tribe or people, and greatly desires their amelioration. One of them said to me at Carlisle, "Why cannot my people be more independent? Why can they not take care of themselves? Why is it necessary to throw meat to them as to dogs? Surely the best way is for all the children somehow to learn and practice self-support."

I need not prolong this chapter further. It is my hope and belief that a remnant of the American Indians will be saved, perhaps not in any tribal way, but in communities and villages such as I have referred to in the preceding pages. It is a slow process to get entirely rid of the old savagery and all that goes with it, and the development is not rapid even among the best; but it is going on, and there are today hundreds of communities where Indians are living in comparative comfort, and their children are looking forward with hope and confidence to a reasonable prosperity. May the time never come when Christian people shall forget to help those who are lowly and slower than themselves to attain unto the blessings of a civilized and Christian life.

THE END.